OPEN BORDERS
TO A REVOLUTION

CULTURE, POLITICS, AND MIGRATION

EDITED BY
Jaime Marroquín Arredondo, Adela Pineda Franco,
and Magdalena Mieri

A SMITHSONIAN CONTRIBUTION TO KNOWLEDGE

Smithsonian Institution
Scholarly Press

Washington, D.C.
2013

Published by SMITHSONIAN INSTITUTION SCHOLARLY PRESS
P.O. Box 37012, MRC 957
Washington, D.C. 20013-7012
www.scholarlypress.si.edu

Front cover image: Mexican revolution, 1913–1914: stream of refugees walking and riding, Library of Congress Prints and Photographs, reproduction number LC-USZ62-49069, Call number LOT 9563-16.

Library of Congress Cataloging-in-Publication Data

Open borders to a revolution : culture, politics, and migration / edited by Jaime Marroquín Arredondo, Adela Pineda Franco, and Magdalena Mieri.
    p. cm.
  Includes bibliographical references and index.
  ISBN 978-1-935623-12-0 (alk. paper)
  1. Mexico—History—Revolution, 1910–1920—Influence. 2. United States—Civilization—Mexican influences. 3. Popular culture—United States—Mexican influences. 4. Mexican-American Border Region—Civilization. 5. Mexico—Relations—United States. 6. United States—Relations—Mexico. I. Marroquín Arredondo, Jaime, 1971– II. Pineda Franco, Adela. III. Mieri, Magdalena.
  F1234.O58 2013
  327.72073—dc23

2012036212

ISBN: 978-1-935623-12-0

Printed in the United States of America

CONTENTS

ACKNOWLEDGMENTS

The editors owe a great debt to numerous people. First of all, they thank the contributors of this volume for their willingness to participate in this collective enterprise with scholarly work of the highest order. We are particularly indebted to Gilbert M. Joseph, who crystallized the critical objectives of this book with great insights into the Mexican Revolution in his Foreword. We also extend our gratitude to Ginger Strader, Director of the Smithsonian Institution Scholarly Press, for her assistance and care as the book moved into production. Our special thanks to Barbara Appell Tenenbaum from the Library of Congress and Alejandra de la Paz from the Mexican Cultural Institute in Washington, D. C.

We are grateful to Sergio Waisman, Chair of the Romance Languages Department at George Washington University, and Eduardo Diaz, director of the Smithsonian Latino Center, for their support throughout the project. Special thanks to Christopher Maurer, Professor of Spanish literature at Boston University, for his careful reading and insightful comments to the introduction and to the chapter "Hollywood Villa and the Vicissitudes of Cross-Cultural Encounters." We also thank Boris Corredor, for his ideas to develop the cover of this book and for his comments on "Hollywood Villa and the Vicissitudes of Cross-Cultural Encounters." Many thanks to Eduardo de la Vega Alfaro for sharing his expertise on Mexican film with Adela Pineda Franco; Barbara Hall at the Academy of Motion Picture Arts and Sciences, and Albert Palacios at the Harry Ransom Center in Austin Texas for providing invaluable research information and assistance regarding the production of the film *Viva Villa!*; Don Lee for granting permission to reproduce James Wong Howe's original sketches on Mexican themes; and Santiago Corredor-Vergara for his original drawing of Wallace Beery as Pancho Villa. We also express our gratitude to Alia Wong, Adela Pineda Franco's UROP research assistant at Boston University, who conducted invaluable archival research; Cindy Medina, Jaime Marroquín's student at George Washington University, who assisted in the editing and formatting processes; Susana Plotts, student at the International School of Boston who read and edited several chapters, and Steve Velasquez and Amy Bartow-Melia for their support and encouragement. David Villarreal, Caitlin Donnelly, and Nicholas Wagner, interns at the Smithsonian Latino Center, assisted in facilitating communications with the authors of this volume.

This book stems from "Creating an Archetype: The Influence of the Mexican. Revolution in the United States," a large-scale symposium that took place at the National Museum of American History in September 2010. Many thanks to those institutions that sponsored this event and opened the possibility to develop this book: the National Museum of American History, George Washington University, University of Maryland, College Park, Boston University, and the Mexican Institute of Culture in Washington, D.C.

Finally, the biggest gratitude goes to our beloved family members: Clyde, Rodolfo, Fabian, Juan, Blas, Teresa, Jaime, Alejandra, Susi, Santi, Boris, Susana, and Carlos (in memoriam) for their love and support.

INTRODUCTION

Adela Pineda Franco, Magdalena Mieri, and Jaime Marroquín Arredondo

Open Borders to a Revolution is a collective enterprise studying the immediate and long-lasting effects of the Mexican Revolution in the United States in such spheres as diplomacy, politics, and intellectual thought. The seed of this book was planted in 2010, which marked both the bicentennial of Latin America's independence from Spain and the centennial of the Mexican Revolution, an anniversary with significant relevance for American history, one that the National Museum of American History deemed appropriate to commemorate by critically analyzing the relationship between Mexico and the United States at the time of this Revolution.

Under the initiative of Magdalena Mieri, Director of the Program in Latino History and Culture at the Smithsonian Latino Center, the Museum partnered with several institutions including the Library of Congress, the University of Maryland, George Washington University, Boston University, and the Mexican Cultural Institute and organized a series of cultural events, among them an academic symposium whose program was envisioned and developed by the editors of the present volume. Under the title "Creating an Archetype: The Influence of the Mexican Revolution in the United States," the symposium gathered nine scholars who engaged in conversation and debate on several aspects of U.S.-Mexico relations, including the Mexican-American experience. Performance artist Guillermo Gómez Peña delivered a keynote address and an epilogue, bringing to the symposium his urgent reflection on the current condition of this bilateral relation. The present volume consolidates the results of those intellectual exchanges, adding new voices, and providing a wide-ranging exploration of the topic.

Many of this volume's chapters explore the role of high art, popular culture, and the mass media in the shaping of the Revolution's imaginary, addressing the question of why it became so significant for Americans during certain historic periods, and how, for diverse political and economic reasons, it was reconfigured by Mexicans living in the United States. The book covers a span of one hundred years without following a chronological order. Some chapters focus on the heated years of the armed conflict, while others reenact these years through an exploration of several sites of memory, surveying specific periods in American and Mexican history.

Despite their different disciplinary approaches, the collaborators in this volume highlight the importance of culture not only as an intellectual endeavor but also as an important symbolic dimension of politics and as the lived experience of the everyday. This volume also questions the conventional binary logic through which U.S.-Mexico relations have been approached (north/south, self/other, center/borders). Recent studies have shown that Mexican nationalism cannot merely be regarded as a monolithic construct derived from the policies of the one-party State born out of the Revolution and that the U.S. presence in Mexico as a one-directional imperialistic power is also an unsatisfactory framework. The U.S. perception of Mexico comprises a constellation of economic, political, and cultural actors within contested fields. By challenging a clear-cut "American" imaginary of the "Mexican" Revolution and foregrounding the experiences of borderland subjects, several essays in this volume provide models for a new conception of U.S.-Mexico history. These essays unveil the transnationality and cross-nationality of nationhood and challenge the widely accepted imagined boundaries of modern Mexican identity. At the same time, they remind the reader that the U.S.-Mexico border was a key historical scenario where some of the Revolution's major political, economic, social, and military developments took place.

For all of these reasons, the volume stresses the theoretical dimension of "borders" as a privileged locus of enunciation from which to unfold a critique of pristine national signs. It also demonstrates that such theorizing does not obliterate current power and economic relations on the border, a site of governance, vigilance, and exploitation. On the contrary, border thinking unveils the contradictions involved in American discourse, which is still based on an unsustainable binary logic (the civilized "American" self against the "Mexican" other). For the authors in this volume, the inquiry into the dialectics of the power relations that shape the conflicted history between the United States and Mexico remains very significant.

The notion of borders, which recalls the nineteenth-century concept of frontier, the line indicating the unyielding advance of civilization over barbarism, produced a rich imaginary of geographic boundaries as well as clear-cut distinctions between those considered civilized and barbarian. The imaginary of the "American West" is full of such metaphors, and it has often fictionalized the U.S.-Mexico divide as a paradigmatic frontier. But, aside from the specificity of territorial frontiers, the notion of "borders" also involves social and cultural experiences. The essays in this volume consider the political aspects of territorial border control, the shifting realities of borders, and the imaginaries through which they have been experienced. All the essays in this collection explore the enormous, living intersections that continue to unite and confront these two nations.

This volume is organized in two sections. The first one, "Traveling Borders," investigates the transnational impulse behind historical processes, cultural enterprises, and political debates that remind us of the Mexican Revolution's relevance in the United States. The essays in this section stress the dynamics of movement and exchange across the two countries, rather than the fixity of national origins. The second section, "Living Borders," focuses on social, cultural, and political experiences that take place on the fringes of nationhood.

Nurtured by border studies and postcolonial scholarship, this section privileges the perspectives of "hybrid" subjects and challenges the binary logic of national identities.

Implicitly or explicitly, both sections of this book question narrow nationalist approaches to the historiography of U.S.-Mexico relations. Nevertheless, while the first section keeps the nation as a focal point and follows a transnational approach to the study of interstate relations and cultural transfer, the second establishes a more pronounced break with the national paradigm, highlighting the advantage of the ambivalent stance of "in-betweeness." An important concern within the theoretical range of Border Studies has been the relative autonomy of borderland cultures. However, the endorsement of a total autonomy of an "in-between" subject would obscure the ways in which national paradigms remain influential in both sides of the Río Grande. Consequently, far from suggesting a triumphalist emancipation of an "in-between" identity ascribed *a priori*, the editors consider border thinking as a vantage point that enables a radical critique of U.S.-Mexico dialectics. Any attempt to atomize the national paradigms that have configured the history of U.S.-Mexico relations demands internal coherence and, in the case of the present volume, notable for the variety of its subject matter and points of view, an awareness of the interrelatedness of its chapters and of their connection with wide-ranging questions of historical development.

The first section comprises general as well as specific case studies on Mexico's revolutionary legacy in the United States, particularly during the progressive era and the depression years. John Britton and Helen Delpar explore complex interactions across the spheres of culture, politics, and economics, expanding their findings in previous books, particularly in *Revolution and Ideology* (1995) and the *Enormous Vogue of Things Mexican* (1995). Britton assesses the role of a group of Mexico-based leftist American intellectuals as transnational actors who mediated the impact of Mexican postrevolutionary constitutional reforms on U.S. economic interests and foreign policy. Previous scholars have described the early role of such "transnational intellectuals" as lobbyists for the Mexican state in the United States, shaping American public opinion on Mexico or as counselors of Mexican politicians on American matters.[1] However, by presenting this sphere of transnational agency as a contested field of competing interests, Britton displays the problematic relationship between intellectuality, economic interests, and state politics in both sides of the Río Grande. The author highlights the, at times, strenuous relationship that many of these intellectuals had with American (and also Mexican) governments regarding American property rights in Mexico and arrives at a Bourdieuian conclusion: the functioning of this intellectual formation was relatively autonomous from state power. He also points to the experiential relationship that these intellectuals had with Mexico City, implicitly recalling the notion of "structure of feeling" (Raymond Williams) as a set of shared perceptions and values shaping their affective lives within the specific social and cultural environment of postrevolutionary Mexico.

Several chapters in this section develop the dynamics between the "structure of feeling" of these American expatriates and the paradigmatic ideology of Mexican nationalism, which, according to Roger Bartra, was most effective in securing a connection between mythology and politics by means of emotion. To what extent did the utopian and telluric view of "Mexicanness" (endorsed by Mexican nationalism) enrich American artistic and intellectual trajectories and nurture a better understanding between the two countries? The chapters by Helen Delpar; Mary Kay Vaughan and Ted Cohen; Adela Pineda Franco; Jaime Marroquín; and Rick López attempt to answer this question with varied, sometimes opposing perspectives.

In a bilateral study addressing the influence of Mexico in the United States and the presence of the United States in Mexico during the first half of the twentieth century, Helen Delpar considers that Mexican art was positively received in the United States precisely because of nationalism; it was interpreted as a plastic expression of the Revolution and as a great synthesis of tradition and modernity. Such positive assessment diffused the political tensions between the two countries at crucial moments in history. Likewise through their study of the artistic and musical trajectories of Miguel Covarrubias and Carlos Chávez in the United States, Mary Kay Vaughan and Ted Cohen arrive at a comparable conclusion. For Vaughan and Cohen these Mexican artists epitomize the positive agency of nationalism; first, they incorporated vernacular (Indian and African) expressions into the cosmopolitan avant-garde language of the time; second, they influenced the emergence of an "ethnicized" African American art in the United States. Concomitant to this argument are Delpar's final comments on African American painters Charles White and John Wilson, who transformed the techniques and themes of Mexican art in favor of their own political and aesthetic causes.

Rick López also presents a constructive relationship between Mexican nationalism and the personal story of one of the most outspoken emissaries of Mexico's cultural renaissance in the United States during the twenties and thirties: Anita Brenner. López recasts the master narrative of nationalism as a pluralistic enterprise by endorsing ethnicity as a prime category of identity. According to López, Anita Brenner's awareness of her Jewish identity and her emancipatory *Indigenista* Mexican project were intertwined events. The conflation of a collective narrative (nationalism) and a personal story (identity) is also the subject matter of Jaime Marroquín, who approaches the twenties and thirties vogue of Mexico through the work of American writer Katherine Anne Porter. By analyzing two of Porter's Mexican-based short stories, *María Concepción* and *Flowering Judas*, Marroquín Arredondo discusses the author's alienation with America's urban-industrial society and her consequent search for authenticity and wholeness in Mexico. Unlike López, Marroquín Arredondo sees disenchantment instead of celebration regarding the possible conflation between a personal artistic project and Mexico's nationalist imaginary. Porter provides one of the earliest and most radical critiques of the political and cultural realities of postrevolutionary Mexico. Marroquín Arredondo claims that Porter goes as far as questioning the Hegelian faith that informs modern political liberalism: the impossible dream of a society ruled by reason and Christian-like ethics.

The connections between nationalism and artistic endeavor cannot be fully addressed without looking at power relations and economic interests between the two countries. American expatriates were attracted to the non-Western, anticapitalist, *Indigenista* imaginary endorsed by Mexican nationalism exactly at the time of this imaginary's internationalization, commodification and political sanitation. Despite her optimistic point of view, Delpar also refers to certain instances in which the correlation between American commercial recognition and the political neutralization of Mexican art was present.

Hollywood, the epitome of mass media culture, is the ideal site to explore power relations and economic interests behind the symbolic capital of the Mexican Revolution in a transnational arena. By documenting the making and reception of *Viva Villa!* (1934), Adela Pineda Franco argues that the film's two-sided representation of Villa (epic hero and clownish villain) was the result of two converging interests: Hollywood's calculated attempts to reach a wider audience in the United States, and Mexico's postrevolutionary official culture promoting the political neutralization of Villa's subversive memory. Despite the rhetoric of anti-Americanism and "non-Westerness" endorsed by Mexican nationalism during the thirties, Mexican state politics and American economic interests found common ground in this cinematic portrayal of the Revolution. Pineda Franco's documentation of the film's divergent reception in Mexico and the United States tests the limits of nationalism as a possible cultural and political bridge between the two countries.

The authors in the second section address similar concerns regarding the emancipatory possibilities of nationalism, but they do so through a decentered account of U.S.-Mexico relations, inscribing a "third" subject to the dialectical equation. Yolanda Padilla critiques nationalism by confronting Mexico's literary canon (the "Novel of the Mexican Revolution") with a set of narratives produced by Mexican American writers. This confrontation leads her to interpret Mexican American literary discourse as disruptive of Mexico's ideology of national unity.

In her discussion of Luis Valdez' theatrical production in the United States, Alma Martínez takes a similar Mexican American standpoint and gives account of an alternative culture of the Mexican Revolution. While Padilla resorts to a confrontational approach, Martínez privileges artistic strategies of what we may term cannibalization. In his play *The Shrunken Head of Pancho Villa*, Valdez subversively reappropriated postrevolutionary nationalism, devouring Mexican nationalist symbols, like Villa's severed head, and transforming them in the process, in order to invigorate and politicize Chicano culture. Martínez's essay shows how the much debated master narrative of Mexican nationalism is, at all times, open to political and artistic contestation.

Oswaldo Zavala invokes the "specter" of Pancho Villa with similar political overtones in his discussion of recent historical interpretations of the battle of Ciudad Juárez (1911). According to these interpretations, the battle evidenced Villa's notorious act of insurrection against Francisco I. Madero's compromising politics. Zavala rethinks this event as a radical subaltern break from the hegemonic tactics of the Revolution's liberal and lettered factions. It is worth noting that, according to historian John Womack, Jr., in American mainstream media culture Villa has been more attractive than Zapata because of Villa's individualist appeal as a "Cowboy at war."[2] In a quite different scenario, the territory of migrant workers along the border of Ciudad Juárez and El Paso, Zavala invokes Villa as a postnational Derridean specter in the service of an unsettling reality of violence and misery, which, according to Zavala, constantly dismantles the epic narrative of the 1910 Revolution.

Although concepts such as liminality and marginality provide a flexible ground for methodological and analytical innovation, these categories can easily lose critical effectiveness and lead to a depoliticized perspective. This is an implicit argument in David Dorado Romo's reconstruction of the historical memory of the Mexican Revolution in El Paso,

Texas. As a sort of unconventional archeologist, Dorado Romo uncovers the temporal layers of the built environment in El Paso, Texas, in order to provide an alternative view of the city's revolutionary past. In doing so, he highlights not the marginality but the centrality of this border city as a key scenario of some of the Revolution's major developments. Cautious in his treatment of borders as "fluid" liminal spaces, the author also recalls the geopolitics that mark the El Paso-Juarez divide as a concrete geographical boundary legitimized by power and economic relations.

Questions related to inverted political uses of the Mexican Revolution's imaginary are present in Elaine Peña's study of what she terms the "American" ethos of a patriotic organization founded in Baltimore in the nineteenth century and housed in Laredo, Texas. The Improved Order of Red Men (IORM) was involved with arm trafficking during the war, and several of its members were also associated with key counterrevolutionary figures like General Bernardo Reyes. Consequently, with respect to the ideological uses of the Revolution's symbolic capital, the IORM differs radically from that other American formation of intellectual expatriates based in Mexico City during the twenties and thirties, discussed in the first section of this volume.

A concise interview with historian John Womack, Jr., brings the first section to a close, while performing artist Guillermo Gómez-Peña ends the second section with a fiery open letter addressed to a fictional drug cartel boss. As rhetorical genres, the interview and the letter do not conform to academic and scholarly conventions. These genres connect to the ephemeral circumstances in which they were produced or performed and bring a sense of immediacy to the discussion. Despite their radical differences, Womack's and Gómez Peña's contributions serve the overarching purpose of this book.

Womack shares his thoughts on the changes in historical practice in the field of the Mexican Revolution, hints at the role of the nation and nationalism as organizing principles behind this historiography, and, without dwelling on methodology and epistemology, contrasts Mexican and American historical discourse. The uninitiated reader of Mexican affairs may want to supplement these tightly condensed ideas with other accounts, such as Alan Knight's brief discussion of the scholarly generations comprising Mexico's revolutionary historiography up until the eighties or Arthur Schmidt's more recent critique of Mexican revisionist history since 1940.[3] Likewise, Womack's acute interpretation of Elia Kazan's film *Viva Zapata!* (1952) goes hand in hand with readings, such as those of Peter Biskind and Paul J. Vanderwood that highlight the movie's manipulation of the Revolution for idiosyncratic or Cold War political purposes.[4] Finally, his profound distrust of "public" (historical or media) memory in the recovery of Zapatismo as the political consciousness of today's destitute heirs of Emiliano Zapata leads to a stark appraisal of our postnational condition, that wasteland invoked with particular outrage by Guillermo Gómez Peña.

In his poignant letter to a hypothetical Mexican crime cartel boss, Gómez-Peña also raises questions regarding the legacy of the Mexican Revolution in today's unsettling, violent audiovisual culture—globalized and yet fragmented. The overwhelming reality of the drug war permeates the U.S.-Mexico divide and affects the lives of Mexicans and Americans alike. Gómez-Peña's letter leaves us wondering if there is a place left for the memory of this frozen Revolution.

NOTES

1. A useful article on the subject is Jesus Velasco, "Reading Mexico, Understanding the United States: American Transnational Intellectuals in the 1920s and 1990s." *Journal of American History* 86, no. 2 (September 1999), 6641–67.

2. See the interview in this volume.

3. Alan Knight, "Interpreting the Mexican Revolution," *Texas Papers on Mexico* (Mexican Center, Institute of Latin American Studies, University of Texas at Austin, pap. no. 88-02), 26 pp.; Arthur Schmidt, "Making It Real Compared to What? Reconceptualizing Mexican History Since 1940." In *Fragments of a Golden Age: The Politics of Culture in Mexico, 1940-2000*, ed. Gilbert Joseph, Anne Rubenstein, and Eric Zolov (Durham, N. C.: Duke University Press, 2001), 23–68.

4. Paul J. Vanderwood, "American Cold War Warrior. Viva Zapata! (1952)." In *American History/ American Film. Interpreting the Hollywood Image*, ed. John E. O'Connor, and Martin A. Jackson (New York: Ungar, 1979), and Peter Biskind "Ripping Off Zapata Revolution Hollywood Style," *Cineaste* 7, no. 2 (Fall 1976), 11–15.

SECTION I

TRAVELING BORDERS

CHAPTER ONE

INTERVIEW WITH JOHN WOMACK, JR.

Adela Pineda Franco and Jaime Marroquín Arredondo

Professor John Womack, Jr. has published one of the most influential books about the Zapatista movement in Morelos: *Zapata and the Mexican Revolution* (1968). He has also published, *Rebellion in Chiapas: An Historical Reader* (1999) and "Doing Labor History: Feelings, Work, Material Power" at the *Journal of the Historical Society* (2005). Additionally, he serves on the board of directors for FFIPP-USA (Faculty for Israeli-Palestinian Peace-USA). This interview was conducted on November 21, 2010.

PINEDA FRANCO AND MARROQUÍN ARREDONDO: In your opinion, what are the main contributions of American historiography to the study of the Mexican Revolution?

WOMACK: They began very early, with Frank Tannenbaum, Ernest Gruening, and others in the 1920s who got into the subject more for political than for intellectual reasons, as young, educated participants in U.S. campaigns to prevent U.S. military intervention in Mexico. None of them was a professional historian, but they all did some interesting and useful historical work. I believe no professional historian went far into the subject until after World War II, and then only a few tried it. The main figures were Charles Cumberland (Ph.D. at Texas, 1949), Stanley Ross (Ph.D. at Columbia, 1951), and Robert Quirk (Ph.D. at Harvard, 1951). Most influential of them into the 1970s was Ross, a student of Tannenbaum's and his intellectual heir on the subject. Teaching at Texas, Ross had many students who learned Tannenbaum's benign view of the Revolution as a popular, social revolution, the Mexican people acting at large, on their own, without any special ideas or intellectuals telling them what to do, and running from 1910 to completion or establishment (during the U.S. New Deal) under Cárdenas. This view originally, in Tannenbaum, implied a kind of veiled anarchism, in its populist form then (and still) very appealing to U.S. Americans; later, during the Cold War, in Ross, it meant an almost explicit anticommunism, then very satisfying in the U.S. academy. It was, moreover, the view most Mexican intellectuals also took, after 1945 the PRIista view of the Revolution. After 1968, things changed. Because of the Cuban Revolution, there were many more U.S. young people studying Latin America, wanting courses, justifying the employment of professors in these areas, which justified more young people going to grad school to learn to teach them; and because of '68 in Mexico, the ones who concentrated on Mexico had to deal at least skeptically with the established Institutional Revolution. More and more, if only to finish their dissertations on time, young U.S. historians of the Revolution turned from the national story to provincial stories, monographs on what happened locally, in one local place or another, 1910–1920. Few tried to put it altogether in a new national story. Probably, the most influential work in the United States was that of the late, lamented Friedrich Katz, already an accomplished historian when he came here, the great expert on imperialism in Mexico, who became the great expert on the revolution in Chihuahua and Pancho Villa. He did more than anyone else to keep clear that sooner or later a new national story would be necessary.

PINEDA FRANCO AND MARROQUÍN ARREDONDO: Are there any substantial ideological or methodological differences between Mexican and American historiography or is it more a question of generational differences regarding both?

WOMACK: Mexican historiography has had two heavy currents, one ideologically conscious, to try to make historically materialist sense of the Revolution, the other hopefully unideological, to try to do historically social science on it. Most prominent and influential in the first current would be Adolfo Gilly; in the second, probably Lorenzo Meyer and Héctor Aguilar. In the USA, it has been different. It has almost all been one big mainstream, a very U.S. American kind of populist social science, in the 1970s and '80s, and then in the '90s a very U.S. American kind of hermeneutics. I don't think there's a big generational difference among Mexican historians of the Revolution; the difference remains more a matter of purpose, between historians trying to understand the Revolution for purposes of public justice now and historians trying to understand it as a fact in the past, quite separate from any private worries they might have about public justice now. In the USA, I think there has been a difference, between the historical concerns of the '70s and '80s and the historical concerns of the '90s and '00s, but it's not altogether generational, since plenty historians of the '70s and '80s changed their concerns in the '90s and '00s, same guys, different strokes—though, of course, the new generation of the '90s and '00s has mostly adopted these new strokes.

PINEDA FRANCO AND MARROQUÍN ARREDONDO: According to film critics, one of the most cited movies on the Mexican Revolution is *Viva Zapata* by Elia Kazan. Is there any reason why this movie became so influential from the historical point of view? What is your opinion of this movie?

WOMACK: Two reasons: (1) There aren't many movies about the Mexican Revolution. (2) Any movie starring Brando is famous with critics. My opinion of the movie is basically the opinion I had 40+ years ago: It's good about some things, the sense of a little country town in Mexico, the bonds, modesty, reticence, honor of people there then, all of which I think came from Steinbeck's love of country neighborhoods and small towns and the sweet "idiocy of rural life." It's not only wrong in fact, but bad, artificial, in bad faith, false in affect about other things, everything telescoped for simple, quick delivery, nothing complicated, Z's pitiful illiteracy, his social climbing (=social elevation via marriage), his blessed ignorance, the wicked intellectual, all U.S. American populist, kibbutznik, anticommunist, Cold War mythology.

PINEDA FRANCO AND MARROQUÍN ARREDONDO: Does it have to do more with American politics and culture than with the Mexican Revolution and Zapata?

WOMACK: Yes, as explained just above. Steinbeck and Kazan were U.S. Americans in culture (different tribes, but all in the same culture) and both dealing with their sense of the world during the early years of the Cold War, McCarthyism, New York, Hollywood, Washington, and why people would pay to go see their movie. The movie has very little to do with the historical Zapata or what actually happened in Mexico between 1910 and 1920.

PINEDA FRANCO AND MARROQUÍN ARREDONDO: Why would American audiences be interested in such a movie?

WOMACK: It is an artful, maybe still effective appeal to U.S. American conceptions of who poor Latin Americans were, or are. They are looking at U.S. projections of poverty and injustice in Mexico, maybe feeling vicariously aggrieved, anyway indignant, angry at treacherous guys with ideas, relearning not to trust thinking about their problems, relieved there is no political analysis for them to understand, and so on. It's a classic U.S. American tale.

PINEDA FRANCO AND MARROQUÍN ARREDONDO: What is the relevance of Zapata and of the Zapatistas' historical memory for today's Mexico?

WOMACK: Deep and not easy to see or explain: In Mexico, for complicated, still largely unexamined historical reasons, the exploited classes cannot count on politicians or intellectuals for guidance to overthrow the systems of exploitation, centered in New York, proliferated into several centers in Mexico, concentrated, of course, in Mexico City. Like the people in Morelos, 1900–1911, the exploited have to figure it out for themselves, not trusting the politicians they know whatever they howl, whatever they promise. But they can and do learn about the real world as they fight it, and they can learn to evaluate ideas, to judge which ideas they use in their struggles for justice, to become themselves in this sense intellectuals, to judge the world they fight, and to act more intelligently against it. But the historical memory, which is now again, despite what historians may have written, just the official and the public memory, or to be more precise, the publishers' memory, the media's memory, is a trap for them. They have to discover the true relevance of the Ejército Libertador del Sur [Liberation Army of the South] all over for themselves, because politicians and publishers cannot help but tell them lies.

PINEDA FRANCO AND MARROQUÍN ARREDONDO: Does this historical memory have any relevance for the U.S.?

WOMACK: Only insofar as the political and the mediatic lies make it harder for the exploited in Mexico to understand what is happening to them, where the trouble is coming from, and what to do about it—all of which is relevant to U.S. finance, beneficial to it.

CHAPTER TWO

FROM ANTAGONISM TO ACCORD
The Controversy over the Mexican Revolution in the Political Culture of the United States

John A. Britton

Contemporary events in the Mexican Revolution were the subject of extensive discussion and frequent controversy in the United States for thirty years. The tumultuous decade after the fall of Porfirio Díaz saw two U.S. military interventions and several diplomatic crises involving Washington and Mexico City, but even the restoration of more stable conditions during the presidency of Álvaro Obregón (1920–1924) did not bring an end to heated discussions of Mexican affairs north of the border. For example, in May of 1922, Secretary of State Charles Evans Hughes and editor of *The Nation*, Ernest Gruening, engaged in an acrimonious exchange. Gruening's journal of political commentary accused Hughes of heavy-handed interference in Mexico's internal affairs, and Hughes' State Department responded with charges of reportorial falsehoods—"a batch of lies"—and termed an article in the *Nation* a "most atrocious thing."[1] The basis for this disagreement will be explored in more detail later in this essay, but the intensity of the language indicates the depth of feeling in the United States about the Mexican Revolution both in government and in the print media.

The acrimony between Hughes and Gruening was typical of the heated exchanges that often involved presidents, secretaries of state, senators, ambassadors, and business executives on one side and editors, reporters, academics, and novelists on the other. The debates came to public attention mainly in journals and magazines such as the *Nation, The New Republic*, and even *Reader's Digest* and also books published by commercial as well as academic presses. This controversy had a twist, however. For a relatively brief span of about five years in the 1930s, U.S. government officials in the administration of President Franklin D. Roosevelt and several leftist commentators found grounds for agreement, thereby temporarily creating a tenuous accord on events in Mexico.

Previous publications on the impact of the Revolution in the United States have concentrated on diplomacy, the border, U.S. interventions, ideology, and art.[2] This essay has a different focal point: the cultural framework in which political leaders, policy makers, journalists, and academics attempted to explain the Mexican Revolution in order to justify their positions to the U.S. public. In particular, this essay will examine the writings of a fluid and informal but influential community of revolutionary sympathizers in this debate. This community emerged in Mexico City in the early 1920s. It consisted of a wide variety of individuals: journalists such as Gruening, Carleton Beals, Herbert Croly, and Anita Brenner, academics such as Frank Tannenbaum, social activists such as Hubert Herring, and political agitators (Communists) Bertram and Ella Wolfe. Ideology played a role, but it was the revolutionary culture of Mexico City that was crucial for this group more than a formalized set of ideas. These people frequented the city's restaurants, theaters, art galleries, bars, and dance halls; strolled the margins of the Zócalo and the streets of Colonia Roma; and often attended gatherings that featured lively discussions of politics, social theory, and international relations. In a sense, this community of U.S. visitors to Mexico City and their Mexican colleagues stretched the boundaries of U.S. political culture to include the internal workings of the Mexican Revolution as a part of a national debate in the United States.[3]

The term political culture in this essay refers to the mix of values, ideas, policies, and laws that form the basis of the discussion of political issues. This approach follows the conceptual frameworks employed by Walter Hixson, Robert David Johnson, Gil Joseph, Emily Rosenberg, and Thomas O'Brien, among others in their studies of U.S. relations with other nations.[4] Political culture is a broad term, and it is helpful here to add that this essay will refine its focus to concentrate on the status of private property and its legal protections under Mexico's Constitution of 1917. This community of observers/commentators from the United States used concepts regarding the role of the nation-state in the regulation of the use of and, ultimately, the extension of public control over private property. These concepts were embedded in Article 27 of the Constitution of 1917 and subsequent laws enacted to implement its provisions.[5] Article 27 clashed with well-established legal practices and cultural values in the United States. These traditions bestowed advantages on the holders of private property under the political and legal system of the United States. The Supreme Court of the United States had conferred on corporations a status that amounted to the legal equivalent of persons under the Fourteenth Amendment. This standing in the courts resulted in protections for the industrial plant and natural resources owned by these corporations.[6] At the same time, business leaders projected an image of responsible property stewardship, technological innovation, the promise of business profits, and national prosperity.[7] The special position of property ownership persisted through the Progressive Era of the early twentieth century and into the 1920s. Challenges to this system fared poorly. Cooperative movements were confined to the periphery of politics and culture. The Socialist Party peaked in the election of 1912 and declined thereafter.[8]

The privileged status of property ownership and corporate institutions in the United States had an impact on U.S. foreign policy. Republican Secretaries of State Hughes and Frank Kellogg, Presidents Warren G. Harding and Calvin Coolidge, Senator Albert Fall, and oil company executives Edward L. Doheny and William F. Buckley wanted U.S. intervention or the threat of intervention to push the Mexican government to abandon the enforcement of Article 27.[9] Defenders of the Revolution such as Gruening adopted the Mexican point of view and thereby injected into the discussion in the United States the notion that within the broad parameters of free enterprise capitalism (which Mexico had not abandoned),[10] there was a place along the left side of the ideological spectrum in which private ownership had to defer to the larger public good as determined by the nation-state.

THE EMERGENCE OF THE PROPERTY ISSUE

The Mexican Revolution was a broadly based, violent uprising that included peasants, workers, lawyers, military officers, intellectuals, and aspiring politicians, among others who were caught up in events that veered out of control for a decade after the 1910 overthrow of Porfirio Díaz. In this chaotic span, the United States engaged in large-scale military interventions in 1914 and 1916, and both Wilsons (Ambassador Henry Lane and President Woodrow) used manipulation and intimidation to play their intrusive roles in Mexico's internal politics. Francisco Madero's election to the presidency in 1911 had seemed to indicate that Mexico was on the path to political stability and moderate reform, but his brutal assassination in 1913 threw the nation into bitter civil strife. General Victoriano Huerta's harsh regime encountered popular uprisings led by Emiliano Zapata in the south and Pancho Villa in the north, but it was the Coahuilan political boss Venustiano Carranza who managed to assemble a coalition that eventually marched into Mexico City and in October 1915 gained the formal diplomatic recognition of the Wilson administration. Recognition did not mean supportive cooperation, however. President Wilson's complaints, blandishments, and the 1916 intervention did little for Mexico's stability.[11]

Discussions of Mexican affairs in the United States often concentrated on justifications for the interventions. Prominent reporters who ventured into Mexico emphasized political instability and violent conflict. Jack London, Richard Harding Davis, and James Creelman presented the military occupation of Veracruz as the appropriate policy.[12] Radical journalist John Reed followed Pancho Villa's exploits but seldom penetrated beyond the excitement of the battlefield and the aura of Villa's personality.[13] The lingering influence of these reporters tended to obscure a crucial event: the writing of the Constitution of 1917. The authors of this document intended to give the Revolution and the Mexican national government a sense of direction that would gain the support of rebel leaders such as Villa and Zapata. In particular, Article 27 revised the status of private property by giving the government control over subsurface resources including petroleum (a return to Spanish colonial law that had been abandoned in the 1880s) and also by establishing a legal basis for the breakup of the hacienda system and the redistribution of agricultural properties to landless peasants.[14]

The implications of Article 27 for oil companies and landowners had a large impact on the discussion of Mexican affairs in the United States. Accounts of revolutionary uprisings and violence tended to reinforce the assertions of Senator Albert Fall of New Mexico whose investigation in 1919 set an agenda to justify another military intervention—this time to protect corporate investments in oil fields along the Gulf of Mexico. Mexico's legal provisions for compensation to former owners did not win the confidence of anxious U.S. corporate executives. The recently formed Association of Foreign Oil Producers in Mexico mounted a publicity campaign in major U.S. newspapers and in the U.S. Congress. This organization and the Fall Committee hearings dominated the flow of information in the newspaper press. Fall worked with oilmen Edward L. Doheny and William F. Buckley to publicize their point of view: Article 27 should not apply to petroleum properties. Doheny, Buckley, and Fall saw the status of foreign-held petroleum lands in Mexico as outside the domain of Mexico's new laws and similar to the position of privately owned resources in the United States. This perspective drew from concepts deeply rooted in U.S. political and legal traditions.[15]

The hearings chaired by Senator Fall found rebuttal from a small number of reporters and activists who had visited Mexico. Samuel Guy Inman was a Protestant minister and missionary who had written a book, *Intervention in Mexico*, in which he argued that the outcome of the Mexican Revolution would be a reformed society and economy. This conclusion led to Inman's opposition to another U.S. intervention. Invited to testify before the Fall Committee, Inman was surprised by the open hostility: "the predominant impression was that one was appearing before an Oil Committee rather than a Committee of the United States Senate. I could detect no desire to get any information that I might possess about Mexico . . .but simply an effort to disprove all that I had ever said on the subject."[16] Inman was one of a handful of writers who attempted to explain the movements for land reform and labor organization in Mexico. Perhaps the first such exponent of this point of view, Alexander McKelway used the pseudonym "McGregor" to cover his identity as an advocate for child labor legislation in the early years of the Wilson administration.[17] Muckraker Lincoln Steffins and leftist reporter John Kenneth Turner wrote about the Revolution's potential to restructure Mexico's economy and society.[18] Leander de Bekker authored perhaps the most direct attack against the oil companies, the Fall Committee, and the Wilson administration in his 1919 book with the accusatory title *The Plot Against Mexico*.[19]

Both de Bekker and Inman criticized the Fall Committee, and both expressed their dismay at the overwhelming publicity/propaganda advantage of the oil companies. For support, Inman cited the assessment of James D. McDonald, the chairman of the League of Free Nations Association, a group set up to counter the petroleum interests. McDonald saw the defense of Mexico's right to implement Article 27 as important but nearly impossible: "It is a discouraging task because the forces against us have not merely unlimited resources to draw upon, but can and are capitalizing (on) the powerful forces of nationalism, prejudice, and ignorance."[20] The power of these forces became evident when Inman's book, *Intervention in Mexico*, was removed from bookstores soon after his appearance before the Fall Committee. The publisher, the Association Press, refused to reissue the book in spite of Inman's protests. Inman and many of his associates were convinced that the oil companies were responsible for this suppression. Eventually, the free market of ideas trumped the apparent capitalist censorship when George Doran republished *Intervention* in 1920, but the strength of the petroleum interests in politics and publishing was evident.[21] Cándido Aguilar, a Mexican diplomat who served as his nation's special ambassador to the United States and Europe reached similar conclusions. Aguilar considered the attitudes of U.S. corporate leaders and the negative predisposition toward Mexico in the U.S. press and public opinion as the two most powerful influences in the push for intervention.[22]

CONFRONTATION

Senator Albert Fall and the oilmen had the advantage in 1919, but the 1920s witnessed a confrontation in the print media of the United States in which the two sides seemed better matched. The exchange between Gruening and Hughes began with the publication of an article entitled "Mexico: The Price of Recognition" in the May 16, 1922, issue of the *Nation*. The author, Henry Alsberg, wrote with the full backing of Gruening an extensive condemnation of the Harding-Hughes State Department's policy toward the Obregón government. Washington refused to extend formal recognition of the new Mexican government, which made Obregón's job very difficult because the U.S.-imposed isolation made it nearly impossible for Mexico to obtain foreign government loans and private investments. Because the British and French followed the U.S. lead, the isolation was even more extensive. According to the *Nation's* article, Obregón was willing to compromise by excluding from the application of Article 27 the properties on which positive acts—such as drilling for oil—had taken place before 1917. Hughes and Harding were determined to follow the Republican Party's pro-business agenda and would not accept this compromise. Nonrecognition continued, and the Mexican government's limited fiscal resources handicapped its efforts to pursue an extensive social and economic agenda. Reporter Alsberg and editor Gruening leveled serious charges against Secretary Hughes: "Our (U.S.) State Department appears to be putting into effect a private and unofficial imperialism of its own in (Mexico and the rest of) Latin America." Furthermore, the State Department under Hughes "has sent a series of notes to the Mexican government which, if acceded to, would have deprived Mexico of her standing as an independent nation." The *Nation* claimed that the price Mexico would have to pay would reduce that country "to the status of a protectorate."[23]

Hughes responded to Gruening and Alsberg in no uncertain terms. A diplomat of high standing because of his accomplishments at the Washington Conference of 1921–1922 in limiting the worldwide naval arms race, Hughes denied that his policies interfered with Mexico's internal politics.[24] Hughes did state, however, that his intention—even obligation—was to protect the property rights of U.S. citizens who had acquired assets in Mexico. The State Department "had asked (for the) protection of the valid titles of American citizens which had been acquired in accordance with Mexican Laws . . ."[25]

Gruening promptly issued his rejoinder—a protest against "Mr. Hughes' repeated frank assertion of (the) right and intention to interfere in the property regime in Mexico." The Hughes approach to Mexico was not diplomacy according to Gruening. Instead, "This so-called protection of American property is sheer bullying and a shameful chapter in American history."[26] Gruening took this issue and the Mexican Revolution so seriously that in December of 1922 he, his wife, and two young sons left their New York home to take up residence in Mexico City, where he began an extensive investigation into Mexico and its history that resulted in several periodical articles and a lengthy tome entitled *Mexico and Its Heritage*. Enthusiastic about his research and gregarious in nature, Gruening quickly established contacts in Mexico to facilitate his work. He interviewed President Obregón and got to know Minister of Education José Vasconcelos and other government officials.[27]

One of his most helpful contacts was freelance journalist Carleton Beals. Arriving in Mexico in 1918, Beals worked as an English language teacher in Mexico City for a while and by 1923 had also traveled into provincial cities and rural areas. He and Gruening agreed on many issues regarding the Mexican situation and especially in their opposition to U.S. policy toward Obregón. Beals identified the large U.S. oil companies as the source of much of the pressure to intimidate the Obregón government. In his 1923 book, *Mexico: An Interpretation*, Beals accused the oil companies of conducting an anti-Mexican propaganda campaign in the United States press.[28] Beals shared with Gruening a disdain for the Hughes-Harding policy: "We (the United States) have demanded that the president of Mexico should be a criminal bound not by the laws of Mexico, but by the wishes of American politicians in Washington whose shifting demands will in turn be shaped by the winds of political exigency and financial intrigue. Such is the noble spectacle of the diplomacy of the American democracy in relations to a sovereign people which is attempting to emerge from feudalism and save its racial and social integrity."[29]

The Mexico City–Washington tensions diminished temporarily with the Bucareli agreement in the summer of 1923. The U.S. State Department accepted Mexico's commitment to abandon retroactive enforcement of Article 27 against owners who had made "positive acts" to develop petroleum and other resources. The Obregón government received formal recognition, and Washington gave up its demand for a formal treaty protecting U.S.-owned private property in Mexico.[30] However, Obregón's successor in the presidency, Plutarco Elías Calles, reasserted Mexican nationalism with the threat to enforce strictly the legal restrictions on foreign-held property. Article 27 and the U.S. conception of the inviolability of private property again clashed. Recently elected President Calvin Coolidge and his Secretary of State Frank Kellogg objected strenuously to Mexico's new policy.[31]

The dispute about property rights in Mexico was again center stage in the United States, and Beals and Gruening increasingly buttressed their arguments with information about Mexico's domestic policies. Their initial defense of Mexico was largely an anti-imperialist argument that focused on Mexican sovereignty, but by the mid-1920s both Gruening and Beals shifted their attention to the Mexican government's push for social and economic reform. Article 27 set the legal foundation for the redistribution of property, which was essential to the breakup of the haciendas to benefit the landless peasants. The same constitutional provision gave the government authority to regulate the international oil companies, a potential benefit for Mexican workers and their unions. They saw these efforts to deal with the nation's social and economic problems as essential parts of the Revolution, and they found support in the research and writing of Frank Tannenbaum. After several years of activism in New York City's radical politics, Tannenbaum visited Mexico briefly in 1922 and returned for longer periods throughout the next two decades. He worked first as a journalist, then as a graduate student at the Brookings Institution, and, after 1935, as a faculty member at Columbia University.[32] He knew both Beals and Gruening by the mid-1920s. Tannenbaum's first publication on Mexico was entitled "The Miracle School" in the *Century* magazine and dealt with an innovative urban education project in Mexico City. He followed that publication by editing an issue of the *Survey* on Mexico, including articles by Beals, Diego Rivera, and Manuel Gamio. Tannenbaum agreed with Beals and Gruening that government programs in urban and rural education, land reform, and labor legislation furnished evidence that Mexico was engaged in a large and challenging effort to uplift peasants and workers.[33] Tannenbaum's academic work specialized in land reform or the breakup of the hacienda system and the redistribution of its landed wealth among peasant farmers.[34] This program, like the government policy toward the oil companies, constituted a threat to those U.S. citizens who owned property in Mexico. The idea that the nation-state could redistribute private property, as part of a program of social and economic reform was not acceptable in the dominant political culture of the United States.

These three writers were prolific in their coverage of events in Mexico during the middle and late 1920s. Gruening was editor of the *Nation* for much of this period, and that journal published thirty articles on Mexico.[35] Guest editor Tannenbaum assembled eleven contributions for *The Survey's* May 1, 1924 issue.[36] Beals placed over thirty pieces on Mexico in a variety of journals.[37] Each one published a book on Mexican affairs. Beals was the first with his *Mexico: An Interpretation* released by B.W. Huebsch of New York in 1923. Gruening's 728-page volume, *Mexico and its Heritage*, benefitted from a handsome format and solid promotion by the Century publishing house in 1928. Tannenbaum's *Mexican Agrarian Revolution* was an academic publication from the Brookings Institution in 1929. While the three did not always agree on Mexican issues,[38] they did share a consensus on the positive potential of the Revolution for the improvement of a large portion of the nation's population. Peasants stood to gain from the redistribution of productive agricultural land. Industrial workers benefitted from the organizational efforts of labor unions and their tools of political pressure, negotiation with management, and strikes. The government sought to enhance the nation's economic development by the regulation of foreign corporations within Mexico.[39]

While Gruening, Beals, and Tannenbaum were formulating their conclusions on trends in Mexico, Secretary of State Kellogg with the approval of President Coolidge issued a threatening challenge to President Calles. Kellogg rejected Calles' reassertion of the Mexican government's authority over the nation's petroleum resources. According to Kellogg's June 12, 1925, statement, Calles and Mexico were "on trial before the world," and it seemed that the Coolidge administration would serve as the court and render the verdict. In addition, officials in Washington were concerned about Mexico's activities in Central America, where, according to some diplomatic reports, Mexican agents were fomenting revolution perhaps in league with Bolsheviks. Kellogg and Coolidge issued warnings about the spread of revolutionary movements along the isthmus that could ultimately undercut the institutions of private property and place the stability of the region in jeopardy. There is evidence that Kellogg may have deliberately overstated his allegations, and the memory of the interventions of 1914 and 1916 and later threats of intervention gave weight to the possibility that U.S. troops might again invade the Mexican coastline or cross the Rio Grande.[40]

The public controversy over Mexican-U.S. relations reached a crisis stage in late 1926 and early 1927. Rumors circulated about plans for a U.S. invasion of Mexico, and the State Department's alarm about Mexican and/or Soviet aid to the Sandino movement in Nicaragua seemed to connect these two crises. Given their sympathy for the Mexican Revolution and its commitment to social and economic reform, Beals and Tannenbaum responded to the threats emanating from Washington. The front-page headline in the *Nation* of January 26, 1927, offered a succinct comment: "No War with Mexico." An editorial headline was equally blunt: "No, Mr. Coolidge—No!" The editorial claimed that Kellogg's policy was based on shallow, emotion-laden reasoning.[41] Beals contributed an article to the same issue that accused the Coolidge-Kellogg policy of attempting to undermine Calles in order to weaken and perhaps destroy his government.[42]

Tannenbaum added his protests against "the now famous Kellogg note with its poorly veiled welcome" to the overthrow of Calles. In the pages of the scholarly *Annals of the American Academy*, Tannenbaum argued that "a new Mexico" had emerged in the Revolution characterized by declines in militarism and the strength of the hacendados and the rise of labor unions, the agrarian movement, and respect for Indian culture. The Coolidge-Kellogg threat of armed intervention served to make the work of the Mexican government more difficult and the status of the nation's political institutions uncertain. Nevertheless, Calles had the support of peasant farmers because of the government's plans for the redistribution of land and also had the loyalty of the working class through the expansion of organized labor.[43] In Tannenbaum's view both of these movements were crucial to Mexico's stability, but they also placed U.S. property investments and business interests in jeopardy. Kellogg and Coolidge, much like Hughes and Harding, felt obligated to construct their policies on the protection of the interests of U.S. citizens who owned property in Mexico.[44]

Beals continued his defense of the Mexican revolution with three articles in Herbert Croly's *New Republic*. This situation attracted the attention of Croly, a prestigious figure in journalism and one of the founder of the *New Republic* in 1914, Croly decided to visit Mexico in early 1927 and sought out Beals for advice while in the nation's capital.[45] Croly's conclusions were close to those of Beals and Tannenbaum. Kellogg and Coolidge pursued "a clumsy and bungling" diplomacy. According to Croly "the main purpose of the present actions is to drive home to the Calles government the supremacy of the United States in the western hemisphere." The primary motive of Kellogg, the architect of this policy, was to block the enforcement of Mexico's "domestic land and oil laws' to protect U.S. private interests.[46] In a signed article, Croly stressed the divergences between Mexico and the United States: "the radical differences in national tradition, make-up, and psychology which have been brought about their sharply contrasted histories." Croly concluded that the Calles administration or any government in Mexico had to regulate and restrict U.S. capital in order to complete the commitments arising from the Revolution.[47]

Walter Lippmann also criticized the Kellogg-Coolidge policy. One of the most respected press commentators of the twentieth century, Lippmann had worked with Croly in the establishment of the *New Republic* and then moved on to author several books and write a widely read column in the *New York World*.[48] While he was not an enemy of capitalism, Lippmann opposed Kellogg's transparent advocacy on behalf of the oil companies. Lippmann was blunt: "there is a very real danger in setting up as unqualified dogma the theory that American investments in Latin America are in fact extra-territorial, and that the State Department may on its own authority exercise the powers of the Supreme Court under the Fourteenth Amendment over all the governments of this hemisphere."[49]

The heated debate between the Coolidge-Kellogg administration and the liberal-leftist print media reached a climax in December 1926 and January 1927. The pointed commentary of the revolutionary sympathizers had, according to historian Robert Freeman Smith, "struck a very sensitive nerve in U.S. officialdom." Coolidge, irritated and exasperated by the steady barrage of criticism against his policies in Mexico and Central America, called on the press to provide the U.S. public with coverage that presented his administration in a favorable light.[50] Evidently, the reportage of Beals and Tannenbaum and the commentary of Croly and Lippmann disturbed the White House and the State Department. Coolidge's complaint further diminished his credibility. Lippmann replied to the President in terms that, in effect, constituted a defense of the revolutionary sympathizers and the First Amendment: "There is a name for the kind of press Mr. Coolidge seems to desire. It is called a reptile press. This is a press which takes its inspiration from government officials and from great business interests. It prints what those in power wish to have printed. It suppresses what they wish to have suppressed . . . It takes what is handed to it and it does what it is told."[51]

Lippmann's eloquent protest on behalf of press freedom marked a turning point. Ambassador James Sheffield's hard-line position in Mexico City reflected the Kellogg-Coolidge approach, so the appointment of Dwight W. Morrow, a friend of Walter Lippmann, to replace Sheffield in September 1927, represented a shift in U.S. policy. Although his reputation as a Wall Street banker preceded him, Morrow was actually a conciliator. He worked diligently to find a compromise with the Calles government.[52] Morrow also took the exceptional step of cultivating friendly relationships with Beals and Gruening. Morrow knew Croly well and persuaded his editor/friend to open a channel of communications with Beals through a trusted lawyer, George Rublee.[53] This effort bore fruit. Rublee saw Beals frequently in Mexico City, and Beals eventually enjoyed dinner with the Morrows at the U.S. embassy.[54] Morrow also met with Gruening to explain his new direction in policy.[55] By the end of 1928 the tensions in Mexican-U.S. relations abated, and the new U.S. ambassador had established a cordial relationship with members of the community of revolutionary sympathizers who wrote for the U.S. press from Mexico.[56]

THE COMMUNITY: BOLSHEVIKS, BOHEMIANS, AND REVOLUTIONARY SYMPATHIZERS

In spite of their different approaches to diplomacy, both Morrow and Sheffield shared a broad skepticism about the pro-Revolutionary writers in Mexico City.[57] Sheffield's views were more extreme. In a letter to Morrow, Sheffield claimed that these writers "played a sinister part" in the effort to foil U.S. policy. He wrote to Secretary Kellogg in 1926 that the Mexican government paid "as agents magazine writers, newspaper correspondents, clergymen, social uplifters, and many radical sympathizers" to generate anti-interventionist propaganda in the United States.[58] Sheffield and his embassy staff accused their media critics of dual duplicity—of ties with Bolsheviks and also the Mexican government.[59] To what extent were these suspicions correct? There is sufficient documentation to evaluate these charges.

The Mexican government in the 1920s, like most governments, did employ practitioners of public relations and propaganda from the United States and other countries to gain favorable press coverage. This practice, often called public diplomacy, had been used by many governments since the nineteenth century. Administrations in Mexico City in the

1880s and 1890s under Porfirio Díaz used public diplomacy, and the government in later years did make payments to journalists such as Emile Dillon and Robert Hammond Murray and labor activist/propagandist Roberto Haberman. Archival records contain evidence of these arrangements, but the evidence is weak to nonexistent for Gruening, Beals, and Tannenbaum. Instead, there is evidence to the contrary. For example, William Randolph Hearst's newspapers published allegations that Gruening was in the pay of the Mexican government. Gruening denied the charges, took Hearst to court, and won his case. Hearst retracted the accusations and paid Gruening a cash settlement.[60]

The issue of Bolshevik influence in Mexico was more complicated. The controversy about policy toward Mexico provoked several investigations in the United States. As early as 1918–1919, U.S. State Department officials, the *New York Times*, and independent writer William Gates all reported that Bolsheviks were active in Mexico.[61] The Justice Department's Bureau of Investigation—later the Federal Bureau of Investigation—uncovered documents that alleged a large Bolshevik presence in Mexico. The Bureau's head, J. Edgar Hoover, saw to it that these documents reached the state Department in 1921. Secretary of State Hughes was aware of the documents but exercised caution and did not use them in official justifications for withholding recognition of the Obregón government. His caution proved fortuitous because the documents were fakes—the concoctions of Jacob Nosovitsky, an enterprising ex-Bolshevik who counted on the gullibility of lower level U.S. officials.[62]

The official restraint of Secretary Hughes diminished in the Kellogg-Coolidge years. Secretary Kellogg sought information that would incriminate Mexico, and Ambassador Sheffield reported to Washington that Communism had taken root there. Sheffield summarized his conclusions of those associated with Gruening, Beals, and Tannenbaum: "Some of this group were communistic in ideals and anti-American in practice, but they were able to get their views published in many magazines and newspapers in the United States."[63] State Department officials reinforced these views with documents that circulated between Mexico City and Washington. Joseph Grew observed that Beals frequently associated with the staff of the Soviet embassy in Mexico City and "was also in charge of Bolshevik propaganda in Mexico."[64] Sheffield accumulated reports on Tannenbaum and met with him at least once. From these and other impressions, the Ambassador surmised that Tannenbaum was a left-wing extremist in league with the Communists. State Department records insisted that Gruening was "a radical and professional propagandist" who worked closely with Beals and Tannenbaum.[65] Sheffield and Grew saw these three as misguided propagandists who pushed an anti-United States, pro-Communist, pro-Mexican point of view in their publications. The appearance of Nosovitsky's "documents" in a pamphlet published in the United States 1924 and Kellogg's report to the Senate Foreign Relations Committee entitled *Bolshevik Aims and Policies in Mexico and Central America* in 1927 added a hypothetical, highly imaginative context in which Communism and the Mexican revolution seemed intertwined.[66]

While Kellogg and Sheffield were engaged in the spread of fundamentally flawed information on this trio of writers, active Communist organizers and their recruits were present in Mexico City, but their numbers were small and their influence limited. In the years before Bertram and Ella Wolfe arrived in Mexico City, Carleton Beals recalled, perhaps in jest, that party membership had dropped to six or seven, a census that sometimes included a calico cat.[67] The Wolfes, both in their twenties, were enthusiastic proselytizers who had some success in their first few months in Mexico City but soon discovered the limits of what they could do. Bert complained of the lack of interest in Moscow for his work in Mexico. He and Ella knew Gruening, Beals, and Tannenbaum, but there is no evidence any one of the trio helped the Wolfes in their work.[68] Bert was also concerned that the party in Mexico was made up largely of artists who did not have connections with working class people.[69] There were numerous frustrations. Bert even urged Diego Rivera to resign from the party: "The best thing you can do for the movement is paint. As a sympathizer you are more valuable than any member. As a member who forgets what day it is . . . you are constantly being threatened with expulsion for missing meetings."[70] The Wolfes had some success with Tina Modotti, a young artistic photographer, who read Communist publications and worked diligently for the Anti-Imperialist League of the Americas and Red Aid (the communist version of Red Cross).[71]

The Wolfes' Communist Party building in Mexico came to an end on June 29, 1925, when two Mexican law enforcement officers chased Bert on foot a few blocks from the Zócalo and placed him in custody. The government then expelled him to the United States. Ella soon followed.[72] This episode was indicative of the deterioration of relations between Mexico and the Soviet Union. Calles' Minister of Industry, Commerce, and Labor, Luis Morones, was hostile to the Communists' criticisms of his labor policies. That rivalry and other tensions led to the formal break of relations between Mexico City and Moscow in 1930.[73]

The end of the Wolfes' endeavor symbolized the failure of Communism in Mexico in the 1920s and also indicated that the Kellogg-Sheffield concerns about Bolshevism in Mexico were far off the mark. The State Department and its informants had identified a community of revolutionary sympathizers, however, which leaves the question: What contributed to this group's sense of unity? State Department officials failed to grasp that these print media commentators, their associates among norteamericano artists and novelists, and their Mexican colleagues formed a spontaneous, largely Bohemian community that flourished for nearly a decade in the restaurants, bars, art salons, and apartment buildings of central Mexico City. Communism and government subsidies were not their main inspirations; rather, it was Mexico's own revolutionary ambience. In a sense this community of writers used their publications to make this Mexico City environment a part of the political culture of the United States.

Gruening, Beals, and Tannenbaum developed a shared appreciation of the Revolution, and they also established a personal rapport that continued for several years despite some jealousy and discord. Beals was the first to publish a book on Mexico, and he received complimentary letters from his colleagues. Gruening praised *Mexico: An Interpretation*: "What a perfectly bully book you have written" and expressed concern his own projected volume because Beals had set "such a high standard."[74] Tannenbaum wrote Beals from "drab" New York in early 1924 to express his longing for Mexico City and the revolutionary atmosphere "with loaded pistols at the dinner table carried by mild-looking poets."[75] There was a sharing of editorial information among the three. Tannenbaum helped Beals place manuscripts for articles with New York publishers and included a Beals essay in the especially edited issue of *The Survey* in 1924.[76]

Gruening came to rely on a precocious young woman for research assistance and editorial advice. Anita Brenner was born in Aguascalientes, Mexico, in 1905 and grew up during the tumultuous period of the revolution. Her family moved from her birthplace to Texas to improve their chances for survival. Bilingual and gifted with an inquisitive mind, Brenner quickly won the confidence of Gruening, who hired her to do research for what became a multiyear project: the writing of *Mexico and Its Heritage*.[77] Gruening introduced her to visitors from the United States. Anita soon became an important interlocutor between the gringos and Mexican intellectuals and artists. She had an attractive, outgoing sociability that combined with her growing intellectual depth to make her a central figure in the community. She occasionally poked fun at Tannenbaum because of his overly serious scholarly manner but, ultimately, applauded his work: " . . . everybody smile indulgently at Frank. But his blundering, romantic, naïve way of getting his theories (born of shrewd analysis) into practice . . . (is praiseworthy). I admire him very much."[78] She also admired Gruening and Beals, although she detected a materialistic, aggressive streak in Gruening that sometimes troubled her.[79]

Brenner was one of several young women who found in Mexico City in the 1920s this convivial, open community that gave them the opportunity to express themselves intellectually. Employed by the hard-driving Gruening, Brenner found the time to produce a mature study of Mexico's art and culture in *Idols Behind Altars* in 1929 at the age of twenty-five.[80] Ella Wolfe went beyond her recruitment efforts for the Communist Party to express respect for Brenner's multitasking.[81] Tina Modotti, by contrast, became a willing convert to Communism, assisting Ella Wolfe in efforts to expand party membership.[82] All three of these women knew Frances Toor, a norteamericana who became a dedicated student of Mexico's native American peoples. She edited *Mexican Folkways*, a magazine that collected information on native traditions and also their contemporary status. Although Ella Wolfe admired her as "completely devoted to the common folk,"[83] and Beals frequently consulted her,[84] Brenner considered her less than reliable probably because of a disagreement over the publication of one of Brenner's early essays.[85]

Carleton Beals was a frequent choice as guide for visitors to Mexico City from the United States—especially editors and writers on a quick trip south of the border. While in Mexico City during the crisis of early 1927, *New Republic* editor Herbert Croly relied on Beals to show him around the city as well as to explain some nuances of Mexican politics.[86] Novelist John Dos Passos also turned to Beals on his 1925 sojourn in Mexico City.[87] Katherine Anne Porter expressed her affinity for the revolutionary ambience of the city in a letter to Beals and attended some of the social gatherings frequented by revolutionary sympathizers.[88]

Congregationalist minister Hubert Herring became one of the U.S. citizens most deeply involved in Mexican affairs. Inspired by a vision of improved relations between the two countries through seminars made up of ministers, teachers, and other cultural leaders from the United States, Herring made Mexico City his workshop. His letter of May 18, 1926, to Beals expressed his thanks for the journalist's help on the first seminar. Herring continued to rely on Beals, Tannenbaum, and others in the community to form the programs for his seminars.[89] One late arrival who became a participant was philosopher/social critic Waldo Frank, who brought his own conceptual framework by which he measured the Mexican Revolution. Frank was a member of the Herring seminar in 1929 and also conversed with Brenner and Beals about Mexican affairs.[90] Frank was one of several observers from the United States who acquired a lasting interest in the government's social and economic programs that continued through the 1920s and into the 1930s. Sociologist Eyler Simpson came to Mexico in 1927 to begin an extensive study of land reform. Hubert Herring introduced Simpson to Beals. Soon Simpson turned to Brenner and Tannenbaum as well as Beals to serve as guides for firsthand observations in Oaxaca and other rural states. Beals enjoyed his travels with Simpson, whose serious scholarly demeanor and penchant for rigid schedules often encountered light-hearted belittlement from the flexible, spontaneous journalist.[91]

The publications, letters, and memoirs of the revolutionary sympathizers also contain a portrait of the Mexico City environment in which they worked and, in a sense, also played. They came together in the city center, the area east of Paseo de la Reforma with the Alameda, Sanborn's, and the Zócalo as focal points. This part of the city was a mix of restaurants, hotels, bars, apartment buildings, government offices, the scattered edifices of the National University, and private businesses. In her commentary, Susannah Glusker captured the informal ambience: "The community was small . . . They socialized regularly and, thanks to the manageable size of Mexico City at that time, bumped into one another on the street, at Sanborn's, or at the movies." Many enjoyed popular street entertainment such as las carpas, the mobile tent theaters that featured burlesque comedy and political satire.[92] Brenner and Beals frequented restaurants such as the Lady Baltimore, the Café Lido, and the Hollywood, and wrote approvingly of hotels with popular eating facilities such as the Regis, the Ritz, and the Genève. Beals had a penchant for the Salón Azteca, a center of conviviality he termed a "beer hall."[93] Edward Weston, a noted artistic photographer and the companion of Tina Modotti, described the dancing at the Salón Azteca as an "unrestricted exhibition of individual expression, desires, passions, lusts, mostly crude unvarnished lusts."[94]

Modotti organized another type of exhibition—Weston's photographic show in the Aztec Land, "a Madero Avenue tourist shop and tea salon."[95] Modotti and Weston paired with Beals and Frances Toor to attend a musical at the Teatro Lírico followed by a late night party at a nearby residence.[96] Tina Modotti occupied an apartment on Abraham González where her neighbor was the elusive German writer B. Traven.[97] Modotti, Weston, Traven, and Beals found their apartments convenient for socializing and entertainment but often noisy with the streets invaded by legions of automobiles.[98] The socializing sometimes had a more formal air especially in the dinner parties hosted by Ernest and Dorothy Gruening at their rented house in Colonia Roma. Brenner's journals contain her reflections on the social chatter, political discussions, and philosophical musings that indicated these occasions had a cultural component that rivaled and perhaps surpassed Herring's seminars.[99] The parties hosted by Modotti and Weston (usually on Friday nights) were livelier with risqué humor, song, and dance but still had cultural and political dimensions. Weston recorded in his *Daybooks* that on one such event seven nationalities were represented: French,

Spanish, German, Italian, and Hindu in addition to Mexican and North American. Bertram and Ella Wolfe attended this 1924 gathering. Weston's strongest impression was of Bert's "waggish humor"—hardly expected of a proselytizer for Marx, Lenin, and Stalin. Most probably Herring, a Protestant minister, and Tannenbaum, a dedicated and somewhat reserved scholar, would not have been comfortable in some of these festivities, but they associated regularly with the celebrants on other occasions in discussing and writing about the Revolution.[100]

At most of these parties the visitors form the United States explored their concerns about the Revolution by mingling with several Mexicans. These government officials, writers, and artists also often joined the norteamericanos for lunch or dinner. Many of the U.S. visitors spoke at least passable Spanish, and most of their Mexican colleagues were fluent in English. Their informal meetings, therefore, resulted in an open, mutually enjoyable cultural exchange. In terms of this study, the "balance of trade" or the flow of information tended to favor the U.S. visitors who translated these interpersonal exchanges into insights for their articles, essays, and books that gave them, at least for a few years, an importance in the print media and political discussions in the United States. The Mexicans who consorted with these visitors were too numerous for a complete cataloging here. This short list will omit some who deserve full attention. Obviously, Diego Rivera, Frida Kahlo, José Clemente Orozco, and David Alvaro Siqueiros were prominent.[101] However, Anita Brenner, a Mexican by birth, had a large presence in the norteamericano community and blossomed as an intellectual and writer in her own right in the U.S. print media in the 1930s.[102] Other individuals who were vital contributors were government officials Jesús Silva Herzog, finance expert Eduardo Villaseñor, educator Moisés Sáenz,[103] feminist Concha Michel, feminist and Communist Elena Torres, artists Nahui Olin and Gerardo Murillo (known as Dr. Atl).[104] On a more formal level, Gruening, Beals, Tannenbaum, and Herring interviewed high ranking leaders including Presidents Álvaro Obregón and Plutarco Elías Calles, and Ministers of Education José Vasconcelos and José Manuel Puig Casauranc.[105]

This community, in spite of its vitality, was only temporary. The strains of disagreements, personality clashes, and jealousies began to take their toll by the early 1930s. Gruening, Beals, and Tannenbaum drifted apart. Gruening shifted into politics and government service in the New Deal.[106] Beals enjoyed some success as a freelance journalist and eventually settled in Connecticut.[107] Tannenbaum found a position at Columbia University in New York by 1936.[108] The three came to disagree on several issues—especially Tannenbaum and Gruening—over questions raised by Article 27.[109] There were also traumatic events that did severe damage to the community. The assassination of Julio Antonio Mella, a Cuban radical, on the corner of Abraham González and Morelos streets on January 10, 1930, was a shock to his companion and lover, Tina Modotti, who in the confusion following his death, was wrongfully accused of complicity in a plot to commit this political murder. The clumsy investigation and adverse publicity were painful for her and many in the community.[110] Another blow came with the arrest and brief incarceration of Beals in February 1930 by Mexican military police. The reason for the arrest remains unclear, but Beals suspected that his article in the *New Republic* that criticized the Mexican government's crackdown on the Communist Party led to an overzealous reaction.[111]

The false accusations against Modotti, Beals' arrest, and the general dispersal of the community, coupled with the conservative turn in government policy after the 1928 assassination of Obregón, weakened the enthusiasm among the revolutionary sympathizers. Although the community itself lost it cohesiveness, some individuals continued their efforts to explain Mexican affairs through the print media in the United States well into the 1930s. In this sense the influence of the community survived these difficult times. For many of these North Americans, their experience in Mexico City in the 1920s was an education, and as graduates of the Bohemian, free-thinking community/university, they carried its ideas into the next decade.

ACCORD

Several of the original revolutionary sympathizers continued to write about Mexico. Tannenbaum, from his vantage point at Columbia University, and Beals, ensconced on the Connecticut coast, both visited Mexico to update their understanding of the current scene. Herring relished the peripatetic work of organizing his seminars. Gruening moved on to other interests, but his protégé, Anita Brenner emerged as one of the main commentators on Mexico. Her career path included three years at Columbia University, where she earned a doctorate in anthropology in 1930, an even more impressive accomplishment because she did not have an undergraduate degree.[112] Late arrivals Eyler Simpson and Waldo Frank also became important contributors to U.S. publications. Bertram Wolfe, one of the first to depart, returned in the mid-1930s to continue his work for the Communist Party. In addition, there were new North American commentators: left-wing reporters Nathaniel and Sylvia Weyl and ballerina-turned-cultural observer Verna Carleton Millan. These late arrivals and new additions had missed much of the camaraderie of the 1920s, but they built on the insights of their predecessors.

The "old hands" and the new observers shared a renewed enthusiasm for Mexican affairs with the rise of Lázaro Cárdenas in national politics. A youthful president-elect in 1934, Cárdenas outmaneuvered and then expelled former president Plutarco Elías Calles, who was associated with the drift to the right in the early 1930s.[113] Cárdenas combined an idealistic view of the purposes of the revolution with a tenacious determination to carry out the specifics of several government programs. Land reform was a priority. The Cárdenas government oversaw the redistribution of forty-nine million acres of rural land taken from large estates including those owned by U.S. citizens. Much of this land was placed under the aegis of peasant villagers often as community farms known as ejidos. According to historian Frederick Pike, "Cárdenas initiated the greatest program of land redistribution in the Spanish New World since the time of the conquest."[114] The new president also gave organized labor a high priority by encouraging the expansion of unions and supporting them during strikes.[115] The culmination of these leftist policies came with the dramatic expropriation of foreign-owned petroleum properties on March 18, 1938, after a lengthy dispute between Mexican workers and the international oil firms.[116]

Land reform carried both historical and immediate meanings. For Tannenbaum, Beals, Herring, and Brenner the breakup of the old haciendas was a large step in remodeling the unbalanced social structure that had handicapped Mexico for generations. As Herring put it, land reform was central to the struggle by which "Mexico fights her colonial past." The establishment of the ejidos and the creation of their credit and transportation facilities were at the top of the agenda in Mexico City. Through these projects, Herring concluded, the Mexican people felt "that Lázaro Cárdenas fulfills the promise of Emiliano Zapata."[117] Tannenbaum also saw Cárdenas as the catalyst for the transformation of rural Mexico. The Columbia University historian reached a wide audience in the United States with his article "Mexico's Man of the People" originally published in *The Survey Graphic* and republished in condensed form in the mass circulation *Readers' Digest*. Tannenbaum praised Cárdenas for his commitment to the ordinary citizens of Mexico: "in the past few years . . . Cárdenas has slowly been giving the mass of people faith in their government. As he says 'How can we ever become a great nation unless we treat the people with justice?'" Land reform was essential in that quest.[118]

Carleton Beals and Eyler Simpson agreed that land reform was a necessity. Beals had accompanied Simpson on some of his research trips into rural Mexico.[119] The journalist gave the sociologist high praise in his 1937 book, *America South*, however, by directing his readers to the massive 849 page volume that contained Simpson's finding from his eight years of diligent work. Simpson thanked both Beals and Tannenbaum for their help, and after a detailed examination of the complexities of land reform, Simpson cast aside academic nuances to issue a clarion call for the creation of village-based socialization of much of the farm land in Mexico.[120] In these passages, Simpson expressed some of the leftist idealism that had been so prominent in the community of revolutionary sympathizers in the 1920s.

Land reform was a long-term project that affected millions of acres and hundreds of thousands of people including property owners in the United States, but the oil expropriation of 1938 was an event that, to the U.S. public, seemed sudden, unexpected, and, therefore, dramatic. It pitted a populist-nationalist government against the bête noirs of capitalism: the multinational oil companies led by Standard Oil of the United States and Royal Dutch Shell of Great Britain. Not all observers were caught by surprise, however. Herring saw a parallel between the assertiveness of the nation-state in land reform and in its petroleum policy. In June 1937 he pointed out that the Cárdenas government had created the "General Administration of National Petroleum" to oversee all state-owned oil reserves and "all foreign-held leases as they expire." Herring concluded that the step "seemingly marks the beginning of a program of oil nationalization." He also noted that Cárdenas had more room to act because, unlike Republicans Coolidge and Kellogg, the Democratic Roosevelt administration "no longer contemplates armed intervention" to protect the property of U.S. corporations.[121]

Cárdenas announced the nationalization of the Standard and Royal Dutch Shell properties late in the day of Friday, March 18 by means of radio. Five days later he made a second public statement about the nationalization to a cheering crowd of about 200,000 gathered in the Zócalo. One revolutionary sympathizer from the United States provided an eyewitness account. Verna Carleton Millan, a talented writer and a trained ballerina from Boston had come to Mexico City as the wife of a young Mexican doctor. Millan established her reportorial credentials as the author of evocative prose in her 1938 book, *Mexico Reborn*—especially in her description of this celebration: "There was a moment of absolute madness when Cárdenas' voice swept the multitude. I doubt if anyone heard a word he said." According to Millan this emotional outburst marked a revolutionary change: "An entire nation, accustomed for centuries to the perpetual humiliation of the under dog, reared it head proudly for the first time. . . . No more humble pie, no more kowtowing to arrogant foreign officials."[122]

Millan was one of several writers who came to the defense of the Cárdenas administration. Hubert Herring's account, unlike Millan's celebratory version, recognized the complexities that faced Mexico. Unlike the controversies of 1919 and 1925–1927, the events of 1938 involved the actual appropriation of millions of dollars of foreign-held private property by the Mexican government. The United States and Great Britain, after the initial shock, began to press the question of compensation for the oil companies. Herring elaborated on some of the problems in these negotiations and came to the conclusion that the Roosevelt administration grasped the political as well as the economic importance of the expropriation. Ultimately, the egalitarian goals of the overall Cárdenas reform program gave the nationalization legitimacy.[123] These pro-Cardenas writers had a broad reach in the U.S. print media. Herring wrote for the *Nation* and *Scholastic* in addition to *Harper's*. Beals contributed to *Current History*. Waldo Frank placed articles in the *Nation* and *Foreign Affairs*, and Samuel Guy Inman wrote for *The Survey Graphic*. Nathaniel and Sylvia Weyl gave extensive coverage to the expropriation in the *American Mercury* and their Oxford University Press book, *The Reconquest of Mexico*, and Anita Brenner reached the readers of the *New York Times*.[124]

The response of the Roosevelt administration to the expropriation and its defenders offered a sharp contrast to the Harding-Hughes and Coolidge-Kellogg-Sheffield reactions to the radical policy statements in the 1920s. The hard-line opposition to the threats to U.S.-owned property gave way to a willingness to negotiate. Roosevelt himself accepted this approach that was consistently advocated by the U.S. ambassador to Mexico, Josephus Daniels. There was opposition to negotiation led by Secretary of State Cordell Hull, an advocate of a form of Wilsonian internationalism not far removed from the Coolidge-Kellogg directives of the previous decade. But Daniels and Roosevelt made the policy, and they also welcomed the commentary and the company of those who defended the revolution. This is not to say that the State Department followed the advice of these commentators, but it is worth noting that these politicians and diplomats were in agreement with the leftist media commentators. Several of these commentators were on cordial and even friendly terms with Daniels and his advisors, Lawrence Duggan and Pierre Boal. Herring, Beals, Tannenbaum, Frank, and Inman praised Daniels but tended to be distant from and critical of Hull.[125]

The sense of accord in the U.S. print media was more circumscribed than the contemporary outpouring of articles and books might suggest. Anita Brenner had the misfortune to discover its boundaries. By 1938 she was a reputable writer with publications on art history and criticism, travel, politics, and civil strife including the Spanish Civil War. In that year she contracted with *Fortune* magazine to write an unsigned piece on Mexico. Obviously, the oil nationalization was to be the central theme. Her research included an interview with President Cárdenas. The editors of *Fortune* took great liberties with her manuscript, however, perhaps because it was to be published anonymously. Brenner's intent to present the Cárdenas perspective disappeared. Instead, as Susannah Glusker described it: "the article published was a derogatory, paternalistic presentation of Mexico, its history, and economic development in the light of the recent oil expropriation."[126] Ambassador Daniels read both the original and what appeared in the pages of *Fortune* and was dismayed. An experienced newspaper editor of the *Raleigh News and Observer*, he surmised "she will not recognize her own baby."[127] Brenner wrote a letter of apology to Cárdenas in which she explained the wrenching twists of *Fortune's* editorial process. She did not relent, however, in her determination to present the Mexican perspective to the U.S. public. Her contributions to the *New York Sunday Times Magazine* and *Harper's* and her book *The Wind That Swept Mexico* accomplished that purpose.[128] Even these publications did not satisfy her old friend from Mexico City of the 1920s, Katherine Anne Porter, who in a complimentary review of the book insisted that Brenner could have carried her condemnation of the oil companies further.[129]

Brenner's frustrations with *Fortune* represented one aspect of the criticism directed against the revolutionary sympathizers and the Cárdenas administration in the U.S. print media. Much of this commentary came from conservative writers and editors who disagreed profoundly with the notion that the Mexican government had the right to take control of privately owned property. The *New York Times* was prominent in its advocacy of this argument. Reporters Frank Kluckhohn and J. H. Carmichael emphasized the oil company evaluations of their property to make the case that full compensation from the Mexican government was highly unlikely if not impossible.[130] Kluckhohn also stressed Mexican oil sales to Germany and the growing fascist influence in Mexico.[131] His book dwelt on similar themes.[132] Raymond Moley, a former New Dealer who had turned against Roosevelt, led *Newsweek* in its coverage of the expropriation. *Newsweek* claimed that Mexico was at the vanguard of a left-wing offensive against private investments throughout Latin America.[133] The most extensive press campaign against the expropriation had the financial support of the oil companies. The *Atlantic Monthly* sacrificed journalistic ethics to publish a special issue that endorsed the oil company perspective.[134] Also in the pay of the petroleum companies, Burt McConnell assembled a collection of newspaper editorials that defended Standard Oil and Royal Dutch Shell.[135]

There was also an attack from the far left. Bertram Wolfe returned to Mexico to resume his recruitment work for the Communist Party and in 1937 produced an ideological diatribe against the Cárdenas government that was the mirror image, in many ways, of the rightist attacks engineered by the oil companies. Wolfe described Cárdenas as a dictator who ran his government "primarily in the interest of native capital, as the junior partner of American (U.S.) capital." The Mexico City administration was adept at propagandistic claims for democracy and reform, but, according to Wolfe, it was as corrupt and self-serving as previous regimes. Wolfe criticized the quiescence and "immaturity" of the Mexican working class and the peasantry.[136]

For several extended periods during 1938 and 1939 the Mexican oil expropriation was arguably one of the most prominent issues in U.S. politics. These discussions often expanded to include other related questions. Newspapers, newsmagazines, and publishing houses turned out a large and steady stream of publications not only on the nationalizations of oil and land but also on political and social movements in Mexico. Diplomats, cabinet officials, and congressmen debated these topics.[137] At this critical time, Hadley Cantril conducted a public opinion poll that asked the pertinent question: "Should the United States use force to protect American property if Mexico or any other Latin American nation seized it?" The results revealed a divided public. Thirty-nine percent favored armed intervention, and the same number opposed it. Only twenty-two percent expressed no opinion or remained neutral.[138] The property issue, dramatized by the nationalization of 1938, brought the Revolution into the mainstream of U.S. public opinion. The revolutionary sympathizers had attempted to counter the largely negative image of the Mexican Revolution in the U.S. print media, and it is not unreasonable to view the thirty-nine percent opposition to intervention as a result, at least in part, of their success. Certainly, the debate in the late 1930s offered a contrast to the slanted coverage of Mexico in the Fall Committee hearings of 1919.

CONCLUSIONS

The Mexican government, the oil companies, and the Roosevelt administration engaged in negotiations that eventually brought a settlement in 1941. U.S. and British property owners received only a fraction of their original demands. Mexico agreed to pay the U.S. and British oil companies $30,000,000 considerably below the $250,000,000 to $400,000,000 demanded by industry representatives in 1938.[139] The compensation to U.S. owners of agricultural properties amounted to $22,000,000 as contrasted to the $136,000,000 in claims. Roosevelt's Good Neighbor Policy and the need for hemispheric cooperation during World War II had priority over lengthy property evaluation disputes.[140] Meanwhile the moderate Manuel Avila Camacho succeeded Cárdenas in the presidency, and the Revolution adopted an institutional character.[141] The heyday of Mexico's radical programs and the contemporary commentary they elicited from sympathetic U.S. observers had passed into history.

What was the contribution of these revolutionary sympathizers to the political culture of the United States? One obvious conclusion emerges: They extended the political culture north of the border to include heated discussions of the limits to the rights of property ownership. They justified these limits through concerns about social and political equity—concerns that often conflicted with the interests of owners, managers, and stockholders. Inman's dismay at the dominant presence of oil company interests in the Fall Committee hearings and Gruening's confrontation with Hughes on the status of foreign-owned petroleum properties under the constitution of 1917 indicated a fundamental disagreement with long-standing assumptions embedded in the polity of the United States. Gruening, Beals and Tannenbaum's defense of the policies based on Article 27 against the Coolidge-Kellogg administration spearheaded a shift in print media opinion in the United States in support of large-scale socioeconomic reform. The eminent Walter Lippmann defended the revolutionary sympathizers in his 1927 editorial against President Coolidge's awkward efforts to intimidate his critics.

The experiences of the revolutionary sympathizers in Mexico of the 1920s directed them toward a critique of private property and the free enterprise system that anticipated some of the ideas that underpinned the New Deal of the 1930s. Herring, Beals, Tannenbaum, and

Brenner continued this critique in the decade of the Great Depression and found reinforcement in the writing of Simpson, Frank, Millan, and the Weyls. They used this ideological opening to justify Mexican land reform, labor legislation, and expropriation of the oil properties. The Roosevelt administration, spurred by Ambassador Daniels, accepted the nationalization and fraternized with the revolutionary sympathizers. These debates again became issues in U.S. politics—in effect the injection of Mexico's revolutionary struggles into the mainstream of U.S. political culture or at least an important current in that mainstream. The old assertions of dominance via armed intervention, threats of intervention, and withholding recognition to encourage internal opposition faced rebuttals in discussions of the role of national sovereignty to protect Mexican domestic initiatives. Through the writing of these sympathetic commentators, U.S. political culture came to encompass discussions of social and economic justice from the point of view of a developing nation caught up in a large-scale and lengthy revolution. This leftist critique of the sanctity of private property and the advocacy of socioeconomic reform resonated with the cultural values associated with the New Deal.[142]

Finally, there should be some emphasis on the physical location and cultural environment from which this commentary emanated. Mexico City, sometimes slighted in historical discussions of the Revolution, was the place where these observers congregated.[143] The city's restaurants, theaters, galleries, bars, libraries, apartment buildings, and street corners possessed a unique, stimulating ambience in which these writers interacted with each other and Mexican intellectuals, politicians, and artists. In this partly Bohemian environment, revolutionary sympathizers rejected traditional values in favor of innovation and experimentation in politics and socioeconomic change. Energized by the camaraderie of this vibrant urban environment, these writers left a legacy in the print media of the United States that remains a valuable word portrait of the Mexican Revolution.

NOTES

1. Ernest Gruening, ed., "Ten Questions for the Secretary of State," *Nation* 114 (May 10, 1922), 614–15; Charles Evans Hughes, "To the Editor of the Nation," *Nation* 114 (May 10, 1922), 614–15; and "Plan Commission to Study Mexican Issue," *New York Times*, May 9, 1922, 1.

2. On diplomacy, see Robert Freeman Smith, *The United States and Revolutionary Nationalism in Mexico, 1916–1932* (Chicago: University of Chicago Press, 1972); Mark Gilderhus, *Diplomacy and Revolution: U.S.–Mexican Relations under Wilson and Carranza* (Tucson: University of Arizona Press, 1977); Linda B. Hall, *Oil, Banks, and Politics: The United States and Postrevolutionary Mexico, 1917–1924* (Austin: University of Texas Press, 1995); Friedrich Schuler, *Mexico between Hitler and Roosevelt: Mexican Foreign Relations in the Age of Lázaro Cárdenas, 1934–1940* (Albuquerque: University of New Mexico Press, 1998); and Josefina Zoraida Vázquez and Lorenzo Meyer, *The United States and Mexico* (Chicago: University of Chicago Press, 1985). On the border and intervention, see Charles Harris and Louis Sadler, *The Texas Rangers and the Mexican Revolution* (Albuquerque: University of New Mexico Press, 2004); Linda Hall and Don Coerver, *Revolution on the Border: The United States and Mexico, 1910–1920* (Albuquerque: University of New Mexico Press, 1988); and John S. D. Eisenhower, *Intervention! The United States and the Mexican Revolution, 1913–1917* (New York: Norton, 1993). On ideology, see Eugenia Meyer, *Conciencia histórica norteamericana y la Revolución de 1910* (Mexico City: Instituto Nacional de Antropología e Historia, 1970) and John A. Britton, *Revolution and Ideology: The Image of the Mexican Revolution in the United States* (Lexington: University of Kentucky Press,

1995). For art, see Helen Delpar, *The Enormous Vogue of Things Mexican: Cultural Relations between the United States and Mexico, 1920–1933* (Tuscaloosa: University of Alabama Press, 1992).

3. This essay concentrates on those writers who were in Mexico for months or even years or who frequently traveled to Mexico and wrote on Mexican affairs from their own personal observations. For the wide range of U.S. citizens in Mexico during the Revolution—especially those involved in business—see John M. Hart, *Empire and Revolution: The Americans in Mexico since the Civil War* (Berkeley: University of California Press, 2002), 269–399. For Mexico City in this period, see Anita Brenner, *Your Mexican Holiday* (New York: Putnam, 1932), pp. 42–81, 304–17; T. Philip Terry, *Terry's Guide to Mexico* (Boston: Houghton Mifflin, 1933), 233–341; Carleton Beals, *Mexican Maze* (Philadelphia: Lippincott, 1931), 151–63, 248–58; and Patrice Elizabeth Olsen, "Revolution in the City Streets: Changing Nomenclature, Changing Form, and the Revision of Public Memory," in *The Eagle and the Virgin: Nation and Cultural Revolution in Mexico, 1920–1940*, ed. Mary Kay Vaughan and Stephen K. Lewis (Durham, N.C.: Duke University Press, 2006), 119–34,

4. Walter Hixson, *The Myth of American Diplomacy: National Identity and U.S. Foreign Policy* (New Haven: Yale University Press, 2008); Robert David Johnson, ed., *On Cultural Ground: Essays in International History* (Chicago: Import Publishers, 1994); Emily Rosenberg, *Financial Missionaries to the World: The Politics and Culture of Dollar Diplomacy, 1900–1930* (Durham: Duke University Press, 2003); Gil Joseph, "Close Encounters: Toward a Cultural History of U.S.–Latin American Relations," in *Close Encounters of Empire: Writing the Cultural History of U.S.–Latin American Relations*, ed. Gil Joseph, Catherine LeograND, and Ricardo Salvatore (Durham, N.C.: Duke University Press, 1998), 3–46; Thomas O'Brien, *The Century of U.S. Capitalism in Latin America* (Albuquerque: University of New Mexico Press, 1999), and Michael Hunt, *Ideology and U.S. Foreign Policy* (New Haven; Yale University Press, 1987).

5. Berta Ulloa, *Historia de la Revolución Mexicana, 1914–1917: La Constitución de 1917* (Mexico City: El Colegio de México, 1983) and E. V. Neimeyer, *Revolution at Querétaro: The Mexican Constitutional Convention of 1916–1917* (Austin: University of Texas Press, 1974).

6. Jack Beatty, *Age of Betrayal: The Triumph of Money in America, 1865–1900* (New York: Vintage, 2008); Jackson Lears, *Rebirth of a Nation: The Making of Modern America, 1877–1920* (New York: Harper, 2009), 51–91, 276–326; Alan Trachtenbeg, *The Incorporation of America: Culture and Society in the Gilded Age* (New York: Hill and Wang, 1982); Tom Bethell, *The Noblest Triumph: Property and Prosperity through the Ages* (New York: St. Martins, 1999); and Alan Dawley, *Struggles for Justice: Social Responsibility and the Liberal State* (Cambridge, Mass.: Belknap Press of Harvard University Press, 1991).

7. Thomas P. Hughes, *American Genesis: A Century of Invention and Technological Enthusiasm* (New York: Viking, 1989); Charles Morris, *The Tycoons: How Andrew Carnegie, John D. Rockefeller, Jay Gould, and J.P. Morgan Invented the American Supereconomy* (New York: Holt, 2005); and Jill Jonnes, *Empires of Light: Edison, Tesla, Westinghouse, and the Race to Electrify the World* (New York: Random House, 2003).

8. Rebecca Edwards, *New Spirits: Americans in the Gilded Age, 1865–1905* (New York: Oxford University Press, 2006), 201–53; Nick Salvatore, *Eugene V. Debs: Citizen and Socialist* (Urbana: University of Illinois Press, 1982). On the election of 1912, see Lewis Gould, *Four Hats in the Ring: The 1912 Election and the Birth of Modern American Politics* (Lawrence: University of Kansas Press, 2008), and James Chace, *Wilson, Roosevelt, Taft, and Debs—The Election That Changed the Country* (New York: Simon and Schuster, 2004).

9. Jonathan Brown, *Oil and Revolution in Mexico* (Berkeley: University of California Press, 1993); Myrna Santiago, *The Ecology of Oil: Environment, Labor, and the Mexican Revolution, 1900–1938* (Cambridge, UK: Cambridge University Press, 2006); and Lorenzo Meyer, *Mexico and the United States in the Oil Controversy, 1917–1942* (Austin: University of Texas Press, 1977).

10. Thomas O'Brien, *The Revolutionary Mission; American Enterprise in Latin America, 1900–1945* (Cambridge, UK: Cambridge University Press, 1996), 251–311; Julio Moreno, *Yankee Don't Go Home:*

Mexican Nationalism, American Business Culture, and the Shaping of Modern Mexico, 1920–1950 (Chapel Hill: University of North Carolina Press, 2003); and Lorenzo Meyer, Rafael Segovia, and Alejandra Lajous, *Historia de la Revolución Mexicana, 1928–1934: Los Inicios de la Institucionalización* (Mexico City: El Colegio de México, 1977), 189–249.

11. Gilderhus, *Diplomacy and Revolution*, and Alan Knight, *The Mexican Revolution*, Volume 2, *Counter-revolution and Reconstruction* (Lincoln: University of Nebraska Press, 1986), 171–527.

12. Britton, *Revolution and Ideology*, 27–30. For more depth on the discussion of Mexican affairs in Washington in this period, see Darden Asbury Pyron, "Mexico as an Issue in American Politics, 1911–1916" (PhD diss., University of Virginia, 1975).

13. John Reed, *Insurgent Mexico* (New York: Simon and Schuster, 1969) and Robert Rosenstone, *Romantic Revolutionary: A Biography of John Reed* (New York: Vintage, 1981). An excellent study among many of value on Pancho Villa is Fredrich Katz, *The Life and Times of Pancho Villa* (Stanford, Calif.: Stanford University Press, 1998).

14. Brown, *Oil and Revolution*, 224–306, Ulloa, *Constitución* 452–92, and L. Meyer, *Oil Controversy*, 42–73.

15. Dan La Botz, *Edward L. Doheny: Petroleum, Power, and Politics in the United States and Mexico* (Westport, Conn.: Praeger, 1991), 19–58; Brown, *Oil and Revolution*, 212–52; Hall, *Oil, Banks, and Politics*, 36–59; Smith, *Revolutionary Nationalism*, 150–89; Gilderhus, *Diplomacy and Revolution*, 87–105; and U.S. Congress, Senate, Committee on Foreign Affairs, *Investigation of Mexican Affairs*. 66th Congress (Washington: U.S. Government Printing Office, 1919).

16. Samuel Guy Inman, "Memorandum in Reference to Mexican Investigation," September 20, 1919, Inman Papers, Manuscripts Division, U.S. Library of Congress, Washington, D.C. and Inman, *Intervention in Mexico* (New York: George Doran, 1920).

17. McGregor (Alexander McKelway), "Revolution and Concessions," *Harper's* 58 (December 6, 1913), 7–8 and "Eating Its Children," *Harper's* 59 (December 19, 1913), 596. See also Britton, *Revolution and Ideology*, 34–35.

18. Britton, *Revolution and Ideology*, 35–40.

19. Leander de Bekker, *The Plot against Mexico* (New York: Knopf, 1919).

20. Quoted in Inman, "Memorandum "(undated but written in 1919), 2, Inman Papers.

21. Inman to Harris, February 24, 1920, Inman Papers, Kenneth Flint Woods, "Samuel Guy Inman: His Role in Inter-American Cooperation," (PhD diss., American University, 1962), 49–81 and Inman, *Intervention in Mexico*.

22. Hall, *Oil, Banks, and Politics*, 22–23.

23. Henry Alsberg, "Mexico: The Price of Recognition," *Nation* 114 (May 10, 1922), 561–62; Gruening, ed., "Ten Questions"; and Hughes, "To the Editor," *Nation* 614–15.

24. On the Harding-Hughes policies, see Linda Hall, *Oil, Banks, and Politics* and Kenneth Grieb, *The Latin American Policy of Warren G. Harding* (Fort Worth; TCU Press, 1976), 129–55.

25. Gruening, ed., "Ten Questions," and Hughes, "To the Editor," 614–15.

26. Gruening, ed., "Ten Questions," 614–15.

27. Robert David Johnson, *Ernest Gruening and the American Dissenting Tradition* (Cambridge, Mass.: Harvard University Press, 1998), 44–67; Gruening to Carleton Beals, November 16, 1923 and March 22, 1924, Carleton Beals Papers, Mugar Memorial Library, Boston University.

28. Beals, *Mexico: An Interpretation* (New York: Huebsch, 1923), 245.

29. Ibid., 280.

30. Martha S. Neuman, *El Reconicimiento de Alvaro Obregón: Opinión Americana y propaganda Mexicana, 1921–1923* (Mexico City: UNAM, 1983) Hall, *Oil, Banks, and Politics,* 84–154.

31. Jurgen Buchenau, *Plutarco Elías Calles and the Mexican Revolution* (Lanham, MD: Rowman and Littlefield, 2007), 111–42.

32. Helen Delpar, "Frank Tannenbaum: The Making of a Latin Americanist," *The Americas* 45 (October 1988), 153–71, and Charles Hale, "Frank Tannenbaum and the Mexican Revolution," *Hispanic American Historical Review* 75 (May 1995), 251–46.

33. Tannenbaum, "The Miracle School" *Century* 106 (August 1923), 499–506 and *The Survey* 52 (May 1, 1924).

34. Tannenbaum, *The Mexican Agrarian Revolution* (Washington, D.C.: Brookings Institution, 1930) and *Peace by Revolution* (New York: Columbia University Press, 1933).

35. For the *Nation's* articles on Mexico, see *The Readers' Guide to Periodical Literature, 1922–1924*, v. VI. 1922–1924 (New York: H.W. Wilson Co., 1925), 1074–1076 and vol. VII, *1925–1928*, 1583–86.

36. *Survey,* 52 (May 1, 1924)

37. For an analysis of these articles, see Britton, *Carleton Beals: A Radical Journalist in Latin America* (Albuquerque: University of New Mexico Press, 1986), 30–67.

38. Tannenbaum's review of Gruening's "Mexico and Its Heritage," *New Republic* 57 (December 12, 1928), 108–109.

39. These generalizations are derived from the three books and the articles mentioned in footnotes 23 and, 25–38 above.

40. James J. Horn, "Diplomacy by Ultimatum: Ambassador Sheffield and Mexican–American Relations, 1924–1927" (Dissertation, SUNY Buffalo, 1969), and Buchenau, *Calles,* 111–142.

41. *Nation* 124 (January 26, 1927).

42. Beals, "Mexico's Bloodless Victory," *Nation* 124 (January 26, 1927): 85–86.

43. Tannenbaum, "Mexican Internal Politics and American Diplomacy," *Annals of the American Academy* 132 (July 1927), 172–75.

44. Christopher McMullen, "Calles and the Diplomacy of Revolution: Mexican–American Relations, 1924–1928" (Dissertation, American University, 1980), 30–150; Horn, "Diplomacy by Ultimatum," and Smith, *Revolutionary Nationalism,* 229–44.

45. Croly to Beals, not dated (January 1927), February 8, 1927, March 18, 1927, March 30, 1927, April 7, 1927, May 12, 1927, June 2, 1927, October 20, 1927, November 7, 1927 December 12, 1927, Beals to Croly, January 31, 1927, June 22, 1927, September 27, 1927, December 23, 1927, all in Beals Papers.

46. (Croly), "The Way Out of the Mexican Muddle," *New Republic* 29 (January 19, 1927), 234–235.

47. Croly, "Mexico and the United States," *New Republic* 50 (March 30, 1927), 162.

48. Ronald Steel, *Walter Lippmann and the American Century* (Boston: Little, Brown, 1980), 58–234.

49. Lippmann, "Vested Rights and Nationalism in Latin America," *Foreign Affairs* 5 (April 1927), 361.

50. Smith, *Revolutionary Nationalism,* 240 and "Calles Promises Oil Issue Justice; Move for Solution," *New York Times,* January 1, 1927, 1.

51. Steel, *Lippmann,* 239.

52. Buchenau, *Calles*, 111–42; Steel, *Lippmann*, 239–44; and Richard Melzer, "Dwight Morrow's Role in the Mexican Revolution: Good Neighbor or Meddling Yankee?" (Dissertation, University of New Mexico, 1979), 158–274.

53. Croly to Beals, November 7, 1927 (2 letters), December 12, 1927, Rublee to Beals, November 21, 1927, and Beals to Morrow, December 31, 1927, all in Beals Papers.

54. Elizabeth Morrow to Beals, Monday (December 1927), Beals Papers and Beals, *Glass Houses*, 266–82, 308–18.

55. Johnson, *Gruening*, 78–79.

56. Morrow to Rublee, February 2, 1928 and Rublee to Morrow, February 13, 1928, Dwight Morrow Papers, Amherst College, Amherst, Massachusetts.

57. Morrow to Rublee, February 2, 1928 and Rublee to Morrow, February 13, 1928, Morrow Papers.

58. Sheffield to Morrow, November 17, 1927 and August 1, 1929, Morrow Papers, and Sheffield to Kellogg, July 1, 1926, Sheffield Papers, Sterling Memorial Library, Yale University, New Haven, Connecticut.

59. Sheffield to Morrow, August 1, 1929 and Sheffield "Mexico" (unpublished manuscript on his ambassadorship), Sheffield Papers.

60. Ernest Gruening, *Many Battles* (New York: Liveright, 1974), 131–34; Johnson, *Gruening*, 62–63; and Britton, "In Defense of Revolution: American Journalists in Mexico, 1920–1929," *Journalism History* 54 (Winter 1978–79), 127–30, 136. For studies on Mexican government propaganda during the period of the Revolution, see Pablo Yankelevich, "En la Retaguardia de la Revolución Mexicana: Propanganda y Propagandistas Mexicanos en América Latina, 1914–1920," *Mexican Studies/Estudios Mexicanos* 15 (Winter 1999), 35–71; Michael Smith, "Carrancista Propanganda and the Print Media in the United States: An Overview of Institutions," *The Americas* 52 (October 1995), 155–74; and the same author's "Gringo Propangandist: George F. Weeks and the Mexican Revolution," *Journalism History* 29 (Spring 2003), 2–11. For examples of archival sources on the Obregón government's public relations and propaganda in the United States, see Manuel Vargas to Álvaro Obregón, February 15 and April 7, 1921, Adolfo de la Huerta to Robert Hammond Murray and Byron Butcher, April 28, 1921, Murray and Butcher to Obregón, May 22, 1921, and July 11, 1921, all in Archivo General de la Nación, Ramo Obregón-Calles (hereinafter AGN-OC) 242-A1-D. On the Calles administration, see Aaron Sáenz to Fernando Torreblanca, June 24, 1925, AGN-OC 121-R-G-9 and Manuel Téllez to Soledad González (Calles' secretary) December 1, 1925, AGN-OC 104-A-36. For historical studies, see John A. Britton, "Propaganda, Property, and the Image of Stability: The Mexican Government in the U.S. Print Media, 1921–1929." *SECOLAS Annals* XIX (March, 1988), 5–28 and Buchenau, *Calles*, 101–102, 132–35. Mexican government officials like their counterparts in other nations in the modern era used interviews, planned tours, and other special arrangements to create favorable impressions with visiting journalists and academics. These "techniques of hospitality" usually did not involve financial rewards but relied on persuasion and manipulation. The journalists and academics in this study were the subjects of such influences, but they also enjoyed the opportunity for spontaneous, unsupervised travel in Mexico. See Britton, "Political Pilgrimage and the Mexican Revolution," *SECOLAS Annals*, XXVI (March, 1995), 67–76 and Paul Hollander, *Political Pilgrims: Travels of Western Intellectuals to the Soviet Union, China, and Cuba* (New York: Harper, 1983).

61. Spenser, *Triangle*, 18–19; William Gates, "The Four Governments of Mexico," *The World's Work*, 37 (April 1919), 654–65.

62. Spenser, *Triangle*, 28–31.

63. Sheffield, "Mexico," Sheffield Papers.

64. Grew to Alexander Weddell, October 9, 1925, Records of the United States Department of State (hereinafter D.S.) 812.20211/39, National Archives, Washington, D.C.

65. U.S. Department of State, Division of Mexican Affairs, "Memorandum," February 15, 1926, D.S. 711.12/695.

66. For more extensive treatments of the workings of the U.S. Embassy in Mexico City and the U.S. State Department, see Horn, "Diplomacy by Ultimatum," 63–95 and Spenser, *Triangle*, 79–92.

67. Beals, *Glass Houses: Ten Years of Freelancing* (Philadelphia: Lippincott, 1938), 50–53.

68. Bert to Ella Wolfe, July 13, 1924, Bertram Wolfe Papers, Box 16, Folder 24, Hoover Institution, Palo Alto, California.

69. Bertram Wolfe to Charles Shipman, January 21, 1966, Bertram Wolfe Papers, Box 13, Folder 66.

70. Bertram Wolfe, *A Life in Two Centuries* (New York: Stein and Day, 1981), 305.

71. Author's Interview with Ella Wolfe, July 24, 1984 and Patricia Albers, *Shadows, Fire, Snow: The Life of Tina Modotti* (New York: Clarkson N. Potter, 1999), 144–147. See also Margaret Hooks, *Tina Modotti: Photographer and Revolutionary* (London: Pandora, 1993).

72. Wolfe, *A Life*, 355–72.

73. Spenser, *Triangle*, 95–190.

74. Gruening to Beals, November 16, 1923, December 3, 1923, and January 22, 1924, Beals Papers.

75. Tannenbaum to Beals, December 18, 1923, Beals Papers

76. Beals to Tannenbaum, December 9, 1923, May 31, 1924, July 25, 1928; Tannenbaum to Beals, July 5, 1928, Tannenbaum Papers, Butler Library, Columbia University, New York; Johnson, *Gruening*, 49–50; and *The Survey*, 52 (May 1, 1924).

77. Susannah Glusker, *Anita Brenner: A Mind of Her Own* (Austin: University of Texas Press, 1998), 11–43.

78. Anita Brenner Journals, February 12, 1926, and November 21, 1925, Anita Brenner Papers, Harry Ransom Humanities Research Center, University of Texas at Austin.

79. Brenner Journals, March 12, 1927, April 12, 1927, April 24, 1927, and March 5, 1928.

80. Anita Brenner, *Idols Behind Altars* (Boston: Beacon, 1970 republication of 1929 edition), 80.

81. Ella Wolfe to author, July 27, 1984, author's papers.

82. Albers, *Shadows*, 145–147 and Ella Wolfe to author, July 27, 1984.

83. Ella Wolfe to author, July 27, 1984.

84. Beals interview with author, June–July, 1973.

85. Brenner Journals, February 27, 1927, Brenner Papers and Glusker, *Brenner*, 7072.

86. Croly to Beals, no date (January 1927), February 8, 1927, March 18, 1927, March 30, 1927, April 7, 1927, May 12, 1927, June 2, 1927, October 20, 1927, November 7, 1927 December 12, 1927, Beals to Croly, January 31, 1927, June 22, 1927, September 27, 1927, December 23, 1927, all in Beals Papers.

87. John Dos Passos to Beals, December 13, 1925, Beals Papers.

88. Katherine Ann Porter to Beals, January 16, 1926, Beals Papers.

89. Herring to Beals, May 18, 1926, February 25, 1927, June 9, 1927, August 21, 1927, January 2, 1928, November 30, 1930, and January 26, 1931, all in Beals Papers; Herring to Tannenbaum, October 27, 1928 and "Program" for "The Seminar in Mexico" July 13–August 3, 1929, both in Tannenbaum Papers; and Helen Delpar, *Vogue*, 47–50.

90. Frank to Beals, September 2, 1930, Beals Papers, Glusker, *Brenner,* 127, 158–59, and "The Seminar in Mexico: A Co-operative Study of Mexican Life and Culture, Mexico City, July 13–August 3, 1929" in Frank Tannenbaum Papers.

91. Herring to Beals, June 9, 1927, Beals Papers, Henry Allen Moe to Brenner, December 23, 1930, Brenner Collection, and Beals, *House in Mexico* (New York: Hastings House, 1958), 120–27.

92. Glusker, *Brenner,* 46. For the history of Mexico City in this era, see John Leer, *Workers, Neighbors, and Citizens: The Revolution in Mexico City* (Lincoln: University of Nebraska Press, 1997); Enrique Krauze, Jean Meyer, and Cayetano Reyes, *Historia de la Revolución Mexicana, 1924–1928: La Reconstrucción Económica* (Mexico City: El Colegio de México, 1977), 273–87; Olsen, "Revolution in the City Streets," 119–34, Terry, *Terry's Guide,* 233–341, and Brenner, *Mexican Holiday,* pp. 42–93, 287–317. For commentary on las carpas, see Beals, *Mexican Maze,* 248–58.

93. Brenner, *Your Mexican Holiday* (New York: Putnam's, 1932), 312–13, and Beals, *Glass Houses,* 184–86, 360.

94. Edward Weston, *Daybooks of Edward Weston,* Vol. I., ed. Nancy Newhall. (Millertown, N.Y.: Aperture, 1973). 80.

95. Albers, *Shadows,* 120–21.

96. Weston, *Daybooks,* I, 132.

97. Albers, *Shadows,* 166

98. Weston, *Daybooks,* 75–76.

99. Brenner Journals, February 16, 1927 and March 12, 1927.

100. Weston, *Daybooks,* I., 58–60. On Bohemian communities see Jerrold Siegel, *Bohemian Paris: Culture, Politics, and the Boundaries of Bourgeois Life, 1830–1930* (Baltimore: Johns Hopkins University Press, 1999); Albert Parry, *Garretts and Pretenders: A History of Bohemianism in America* (New York: Dover, 1960); and Christine Stansell, *American Moderns: Bohemian New York and the Creation of a New Century* (New York: Holt, 2000).

101. Hayden Herrera, *Frida: A Biography of Frida Kahlo* (New York: Harper & Row, 1983), and Martha Zamora, *Frida Kahlo: The Brush of Anguish* (San Francisco: Chronicle Books, 1990).

102. Glusker, *Brenner,* especially chapters 5–17.

103. Beals, *Glass Houses,* 243, 366.

104. Glusker, *Brennner,* 57–73.

105. Britton, "In Defense of Revolution," 125–126 and *Revolution,* 50–66.

106. Johnson, *Gruening,* 68–186.

107. Britton, *Beals,* 123–34.

108. Delpar, "Tannenbaum," and Hale, "Tannenbaum and the Mexican Revolution."

109. Tannenbaum's review of Gruening's *Mexico and Its Heritage* in "Viva Mexico" *New Republic* 57 (December 12, 1928), 108–109, and Gruening's response *New Republic* 57 (December 26, 1928), 166–67. Beals criticized Tannenbaum's positive assessment of the Mexican situation in a review of *Peace by Revolution.* See *Nation* 138 (January 10, 1934), 50–51.

110. Albers, *Shadows,* 189–236, *El Universal,* January 11, 13, 14, 15, 20, 1929; Mildred Constantine, *Tina Modotti: A Fragile Life* (New York: Paddington, 1975), 141–45; Beals interview with author, August 13, 1975

111. Britton, *Beals,* 94–99.

112. Glusker, *Brenner*, 112–20.

113. Buchenau, *Calles*, 143–72.

114. Frederick Pike, *FDR's Good Neighbor Policy: Sixty Years of Generally Gentle Chaos* (Austin: University of Texas Press, 1995), 187. For thorough examinations of the impact on U.S.-owned properties, see John J. Dwyer, *The Agrarian Dispute: The Expropriation of American-Owned Land in Postrevolutionary Mexico* (Durham: Duke University Press, 2008), and Luis González, *Historia de la Revolución Mexicana, 1934–1940: Los Días del Presidente* Cárdenas (Mexico City: El Colegio de México, 1981), 201–13.

115. Lorenzo Meyer, *Oil Controversy*, 149–72, and the same author's *Los Grupos de Presión Extranjero y el México Revolucionario* (Mexico City: Secretaria de Relaciones Exteriores, 1973); Schuler, *Mexico*, 63–89; Myrna Santiago, *The Ecology of Oil*, 205–348; and Joe Ashby, *Organized Labor and the Mexican Revolution* (Chapel Hill: University of North Carolina Press, 1977).

116. Schuler, *Mexico*, 91–112, González, *Los Días del Presidente* Cárdenas, 172–92, and Lorenzo Meyer, *Los Grupos*, 69–93.

117. Hubert Herring, "The Unconquerable Mexican," *Harper's* 175 (June 1937), 46–56. Quotes from pp. 48 and 51.

118. Tannenbaum, "Mexico's Man of the People," *Survey Graphic* 26 (August 1937) and *Reader's Digest* 31 (October 1937), 43–44. Quote from p. 44. In spite of his respect for Cárdenas, Tannenbaum did not write in support of the oil expropriation. For a discussion of this aspect of Tannenbaum's understanding of the Mexican Revolution, see Britton, *Revolution and Ideology*, 159–63.

119. Beals, *America South* (Philadelphia: Lippincott, 1937), 380–81.

120. Eyler Simpson, *The Ejido: Mexico's Way Out* (Chapel Hill: University of North Carolina Press, 1937), See especially pp. 482–509.

121. Herring, "Unconquerable Mexican," 52. Herring later gave more emphasis to international politics, the fascist threat, and post-nationalization negotiations between Mexico City and Washington. See his "Cárdenas of Mexico," *Harper's* 177 (October 1938), 489–502.

122. Verna Carleton Millan, *Mexico Reborn* (Boston: Houghton Mifflin, 1938), 198–99. For the Mexican public response to the expropriation, see John A. Britton "Redefining Intervention: Mexico's Contribution to Anti-Americanism," in *Anti-Americanism in Latin America and the Caribbean*, ed. Alan McPherson (New York: Bergahan Books, 2006), 37–60, and Alan Knight, *U.S.–Mexican Relations, 1910–1940: An Interpretation* (San Diego: Center for U.S.–Mexican Studies, University of California, San Diego, 1987).

123. Herring, "Cárdenas," 489–502.

124. Herring, "Mexico Claims Its Own," *Nation* 145 (April 16, 1938), 440–42, and "Mexico Walks the Tight Rope," *Scholastic* 36 (April 22, 1940), 8–9. Among the many defenders of the expropriation, see Samuel Guy Inman, "Mexico in Transition," *Survey Graphic* 30 (February 1941), 79–82; Beals, "Mexican Challenge," *Current History* 48 (April 1938), 28–30; Brenner, "Mexico Shatters the Mold of Centuries," *New York Times Magazine* August 28, 1938, 5, 19; Waldo Frank, "Mexico Today: The Heart of the Revolution," *Nation* 149 (August 5, 1939), 140–44; "Cárdenas of Mexico," *Foreign Affairs*, 18 (October 1939), 91–101; and Nathaniel and Sylvia Weyl, *The Reconquest of Mexico* (New York: Oxford University Press, 1939), 279–374; and "Mexico under Cárdenas," *American Mercury* 50 (July 1940), 349–53. Although Tannenbaum was a strong advocate for Mexico's land reform and the expropriation of foreign-owned agricultural properties, he did not support the oil expropriations. See Britton, *Revolution and Ideology*, 158–70.

125. Pike, *FDR's Good Neighbor Policy*, 185–96; Britton, *Revolution and Ideology*, 128–34; E. David Cronon, *Josephus Daniels in Mexico* (Madison: University of Wisconsin Press, 1960), 203–29; Schuler,

Mexico, 113–151. For contacts of Beals and Herring with Daniels, see Daniels to Beals, August 28, 1934, January 5, 1939, and January 29, 1935, and Beals to Daniels, February 17, 1935 and February 27, 1938, all in Beals Papers.

126. Glusker, *Brenner*, 203–6. Quote on p. 205.

127. Cronon, *Daniels*, 211.

128. Glusker, *Brenner*, 205–8 and Brenner to Cárdenas, November 8, 1938, Fondo Lázaro Cárdenas, 432.2/253.8 Archivo General de la Nación (AGN), Mexico City..

129. Glusker, *Brenner*, 208.

130. *New York Times* (all in 1938) March 20, 1, March 27, III., 1, April 13, III., 1, April 17, 1938, II., 1, May 1, II.,7, May 14, 1, May 15, II., 1, June 12, III., 1, and June 19, III., 1.

131. *New York Times*, August 15, 1938, 1.

132. Frank Kluckhohn, *The Mexican Challenge* (New York: Doubleday, Doran, 1939). The Cárdenas administration expelled Kluckhohn in December 1938 because of his report that falsely claimed the government had paid Italian land owners for expropriations but rejected U.S. demands for compensation. Newspaper coverage in the United States generally was critical of the expropriation and supported the oil companies. See Hugh Joseph Morgan, "The United States Press Coverage of Mexico during the Presidency of Lázaro Cárdenas, 1934–1940," (PhD diss., Southern Illinois University, 1985), 556–59.

133. *Newsweek* (all 1938) March 28, 20, April 4, 11, April 18, 22, July 4, 13, July 18, 4, August 15, 19. See also Morgan, "United States Press," 420–555 for the U.S. press response to the expropriation.

134. *The Atlantic Presents: Trouble below the Border* (July 1938). *The Nation* exposed the role of Standard Oil of New Jersey in financing this issue of the magazine. See Morgan, "United States Press," 532–42.

135. Burt McConnell, *Mexico at the Bar of Public Opinion* (New York: Mail and Express Publishing Company, 1939).

136. Bertram Wolfe and Diego Rivera, *Portrait of Mexico* (New York: Covici Friede, 1937), 196–211. Wolfe wrote the text and Rivera did the illustrations.

137. Morgan, "United States Press, "and Cronon, *Josephus Daniels*, 185–271. Cárdenas monitored the U.S. press from several sources. Ambassador Francisco Castilla Najera to Raúl Castellanos (Cárdenas staff), October 31, 1938 and November 4, 1938, and Ramón Beteta (Cárdenas staff) to Raul Castellanos, May 2, 1938 in Fondo Lázaro Cárdenas 432.2/253-8, AGN. The Departmento Autónomo de Prensa y Publicidad (DAPP) sent regular reports to President Cárdenas on the U.S. press. See DAPP Reports in Fondo Lázaro Cárdenas 432.2/253-8, AGN. Frank Tannenbaum also sent comments to Cárdenas on the U.S. press. See Tannenbaum to Cárdenas, Fondo Lázaro Cárdenas 135.1/3 AGN and Tannenbaum to Cárdenas April 20, 1938, and Tannenbaum to Beteta, May 25, 1938, both in Tannenbaum Papers.

138. Hadley Cantril, *Public Opinion, 1935–1946* (Princeton, N.J.: Princeton University Press, 1951), 549.

139. Gellman, *Good Neighbor Diplomacy*, 54–55 and Vázquez and Meyer, *United States and Mexico*, 145–57.

140. Dwyer, *Agrarian Dispute*, 159–65.

141. Schuler, *Mexico*, 173–207, and Luis Medina, *Historia de la Revolución Mexicana, 1940–1952: Del Cardenismo al Avilacamachismo* (Mexico City: El Colegio de México, 1978). For a contemporary account, see Betty Kirk, *Covering the Mexican Front: The Battle of Europe vs. America* (Norman: University of Oklahoma Press, 1941).

142. Among the many studies of New Deal culture, see Dawley, *Struggle for Justice*, 334–417, Pike, *Good Neighbor Policy*, 2–176, Jason Scott Smith, *Building New Deal Liberalism: The Political Economy of Public Works* (Cambridge, UK: Cambridge University Press, 2006); Adam Cohn, *Nothing to Fear: FDR's Inner Circle and the Hundred Days that Created Modern America* (New York: Penguin, 2009); William Brock, *Welfare Democracy and the New Deal* (Cambridge, UK: Cambridge University Press, 1988); Nick Taylor, *American Made: The Enduring Legacy of the WPA* (New York: Bantam, 2009); and Kirsten Downey, *The Woman Behind the New Deal: The Life and Legacy of Frances Perkins, Social Security, Unemployment Insurance, and the Minimum Wage*, (New York: Anchor, 2010); Richard Pells, *Radical Visions and American Dreams; Culture and Social Thought in the Depression Years* (New York: Harper & Row, 1973), and Robert McElvaine, *The Great Depression* (New York: Times Books, 1984).

143. More recent studies that emphasize the role of Mexico City in the Revolution include Leer, *Workers, Neighbors, and Citizens*, Krauze, Meyer, and Reyes, *La Reconstrucción económica*, 273–87, Olsen, "Revolution in the City Streets," 119–34,

BIBLIOGRAPHY

Albers, Patricia. *Shadows, Fire, Snow: The Life of Tina Modotti.* New York: Clarkson N. Potter, 1999.

Alsberg, Henry. "Mexico: The Price of Recognition." *Nation*, 114 (May 10, 1922): 561–562.

Anita Brenner Papers, Harry Ransom Humanities Research Center, University of Texas at Austin.

Archivo General de la Nación, Mexico City, Mexico.

Ashby, Joe. *Organized Labor and the Mexican Revolution.* Chapel Hill: University of North Carolina Press, 1977.

The Atlantic Monthly. *The Atlantic Presents: Trouble below the Border* (July 1938) special issue.

Beals, Carleton. *America South.* Philadelphia: Lippincott, 1937.

———. *Glass Houses: Ten Years of Freelancing.* Philadelphia: Lippincott, 1938.

———. *House in Mexico.* New York: Hastings House, 1958.

———. "Mexican Challenge." *Current History*, 48 (April 1938): 28–30.

———. *Mexican Maze.* Philadelphia: Lippincott, 1931.

———. *Mexico: An Interpretation.* New York: Huebesch, 1923.

———. "Mexico's Bloodless Victory." *Nation*, 124 (January 26, 1927): 85–86.

Bertram Wolfe Papers, Hoover Institution, Palo Alto, California.

Bethell, Tom. *The Noblest Triumph: Property and Prosperity through the Ages.* New York: St. Martins, 1999.

Beatty, Jack. *Age of Betrayal: The Triumph of Money in America, 1865–1900.* New York: Vintage, 2008.

Brenner, Anita. *Idols behind Altars.* Boston: Beacon, 1970 (republication of 1929 edition).

———. "Mexico Shatters the Mold of Centuries." *New York Times Magazine.* pp. 5, 19, August 28, 1938.

———. *Your Mexican Holiday.* New York: Putnam, 1932.

Britton, John A. *Carleton Beals: A Radical Journalist in Latin America.* Albuquerque: University of New Mexico Press, 1986.

———. "In Defense of Revolution: American Journalists in Mexico, 1920–1929." *Journalism History*, 54 (Winter 1978–79): 127–130, 136.

———. "Political Pilgrimage and the Mexican Revolution," *SECOLAS Annals*, XXVI (March 1995): 67–76.

———. "Propaganda, Property, and the Image of Stability: The Mexican Government in the U.S. Print Media, 1921–1929." *SECOLAS Annals* XIX (March 1988): 5–28.

———. "Redefining Intervention: Mexico's Contribution to Anti-Americanism." In *Anti-Americanism in Latin America and the Caribbean.* ed. Alan McPherson, pp. 37–60. New York: Bergahan Books, 2006.

———. *Revolution and Ideology: The Image of the Mexican Revolution in the United States.* Lexington: University of Kentucky Press, 1995.

Brock, William. *Welfare Democracy and the New Deal.* Cambridge, UK: Cambridge University Press, 1988.

Brown, Jonathan. *Oil and Revolution in Mexico.* Berkeley: University of California Press, 1993.

Buchenau, Jurgen. *Plutarco Elías Calles and the Mexican Revolution.* Lanham, Md.: Rowman and Littlefield, 2007.

Cantril, Hadley. *Public Opinion, 1935–1946.* Princeton, N.J.: Princeton University Press, 1951.

Carleton Beals Papers, Mugar Memorial Library, Boston University, Boston Massachusetts.

Carmical, J. H. "Britain May Take Firmer Stand on Oil." *New York Times.* May 15, 1938: 1, 8

———. "Little Faith Put in Mexican I O U," *New York Times,* April 3, 1938: III, 1, 6.

———. "Mexican Seizure of Oil Detailed," *New York Times,* April 17, 1938: III, 1, 5.

———. "Mexican Oil Blurs Wide Trade Vistas," *New York Times,* June 19, 1938: III, 1, 4.

———. "Mexico's Oil Move Hits U.S. Policies," *New York Times,* March 27, 1938: III, 1, 5.

———. "Oil Dispute Delay Weakening Mexico," *New York Times,* June 12, 1938: III, 1, 7.

———. "Oil Impasse Hits at Mexican Labor," *New York Times,* May 1, 1938: III, 1, 8.

Chace, James. *Wilson, Roosevelt, Taft, and Debs—The Election That Changed the Country.* New York: Simon and Schuster, 2004.

Cohn, Adam. *Nothing to Fear: FDR's Inner Circle and the Hundred Days that Created Modern America.* New York: Penguin, 2009.

Constantine, Mildred. *Tina Modotti: A Fragile Life.* New York: Paddington, 1975.

Croly, Herbert. "Mexico and the United States." *New Republic,* 50 (March 30, 1927): 162.

———. "The Way Out of the Mexican Muddle." *New Republic,* 29 (January 19, 1927): 234–235.

Cronon, E. David. *Josephus Daniels in Mexico.* Madison: University of Wisconsin Press, 1960.

Dawley, Alan. *Struggles for Justice: Social Responsibility and the Liberal State.* Cambridge, Mass.: Belknap Press of Harvard University Press, 1991.

de Bekker, Leander. *The Plot against Mexico.* New York: Knopf, 1919.

Delpar, Helen. *The Enormous Vogue of Things Mexican: Cultural Relations between the United States and Mexico, 1920–1935.* Tuscaloosa: University of Alabama Press, 1992.

———. "Frank Tannenbaum: The Making of a Latin Americanist." *The Americas,* 45 (October 1988): 153–171.

Downey, Kirsten. *The Woman behind the New Deal: The Life and Legacy of Frances Perkins, Social Security, Unemployment Insurance, and the Minimum Wage.* New York: Anchor, 2010.

Dwight Morrow Papers, Amherst College Archives and Special Collections, Amherst, Massachusetts.

Dwyer, John J. *The Agrarian Dispute: The Expropriation of American-Owned Land in Postrevolutionary Mexico.* Durham, N.C.: Duke University Press, 2008.

Edwards, Rebecca. *New Spirits: Americans in the Gilded Age, 1865–1905.* New York: Oxford University Press, 2006.

Eisenhower, John S. D. *Intervention! The United States and the Mexican Revolution, 1913–1917.* New York: Norton, 1993.

Fondo Lázaro Cárdenas. Archivo General de la Nación, Mexico City, Mexico.

Frank Tannenbaum Papers, Butler Library, Columbia University, New York, N.Y.

Frank, Waldo. "Cárdenas of Mexico." *Foreign Affairs,* 18 (October 1939): 91–101.

———. "Mexico Today: The Heart of the Revolution." *Nation,* 149 (August 5, 1939): 140–144.

Gates, William. "The Four Governments of Mexico." *The World's Work,* 37 (April 1919): 654–665.

Gilderhus, Mark. *Diplomacy and Revolution: U.S.-Mexican Relations under Wilson and Carranza.* Tucson: University of Arizona Press, 1977.

Glusker, Susannah. *Anita Brenner: A Mind of Her Own.* Austin: University of Texas Press, 1998.

González, Luis. *Historia de la Revolución Mexicana, 1934–1940: Los Días del Presidente* Cárdenas. [History of the Mexican Revolution, 1934–1940: The Days of President Cárdenas] Mexico City: El Colegio de México, 1981.

Gould, Lewis. *Four Hats in the Ring: The 1912 Election and the Birth of Modern American Politics.* Lawrence: University of Kansas Press, 2008.

Grieb, Kenneth. *The Latin American Policy of Warren G. Harding*. Fort Worth, Tex.: TCU Press, 1976.

Gruening, Ernest. *Many Battles*. New York: Liveright, 1974.

———. "Ten Questions for the Secretary of State." *Nation*, 114 (May 10, 1922): 614–615.

Hale, Charles. "Frank Tannenbaum and the Mexican Revolution." *Hispanic American Historical Review*, 75 (May 1995): 251–246.

Hall, Linda B. *Oil, Banks, and Politics: The United States and Postrevolutionary Mexico, 1917–1924*. Austin: University of Texas Press, 1995.

Hall, Linda B. and Don Coerver. *Revolution on the Border: The United States and Mexico, 1910–1920*. Albuquerque: University of New Mexico Press, 1988.

Harris, Charles and Louis Sadler. *The Texas Rangers and the Mexican Revolution*. Albuquerque: University of New Mexico Press, 2004.

Hart, John M. *Empire and Revolution: The Americans in Mexico since the Civil War*. Berkeley: University of California Press, 2002.

Herrera, Hayden. *Frida: A Biography of Frida Kahlo*. New York: Harper & Row, 1983

Herring, Hubert. "Cárdenas of Mexico." *Harper's*, 177 (October 1938): 489–502.

———. "Mexico Claims Its Own." *Nation*, 145 (April 16, 1938): 440–442.

———. "Mexico Walks the Tight Rope." *Scholastic*, 36 (April 22, 1940): 8–9.

———. "The Unconquerable Mexican." *Harper's*, 175 (June 1937), 46–56.

Hixson, Walter. *The Myth of American Diplomacy: National Identity and U.S. Foreign Policy*. New Haven, Conn.: Yale University Press, 2008.

Hollander, Paul. *Political Pilgrims: Travels of Western Intellectuals to the Soviet Union, China, and Cuba*. New York: Harper, 1983.

Hooks, Margaret. *Tina Modotti: Photographer and Revolutionary*. London: Pandora, 1993.

Horn, James J. "Diplomacy by Ultimatum: Ambassador Sheffield and Mexican-American Relations, 1924–1927." PhD diss., SUNY Buffalo, 1969.

Hughes, Charles Evans, "To the Editor of the Nation." *Nation*, 114 (May 10, 1922): 614–615.

Hughes, Thomas P. *American Genesis: A Century of Invention and Technological Enthusiasm*. New York: Viking, 1989.

Hunt, Michael. *Ideology and U.S. Foreign Policy*. New Haven, Conn.: Yale University Press, 1987.

Inman, Samuel Guy. *Intervention in Mexico*. New York: George Doran, 1920.

———. "Mexico in Transition." *Survey Graphic*, 30 (February 1941): 79–82.

James Sheffield Papers, Sterling Memorial Library, Yale University, New Haven, Connecticut.

Johnson, Robert David. *Ernest Gruening and the American Dissenting Tradition*. Cambridge, Mass.: Harvard University Press, 1998.

Johnson, Robert David, ed. *On Cultural Ground: Essays in International History*. Chicago, Ill.: Import Publishers, 1994.

Jonnes, Jill. *Empires of Light: Edison, Tesla, Westinghouse, and the Race to Electrify the World*. New York: Random House, 2003.

Joseph, Gil. "Close Encounters: Toward a Cultural History of U.S.-Latin American Relations." In *Close Encounters of Empire: Writing the Cultural History of U.S.-Latin American Relations*. Gil Joseph, Catherine Leogrand, and Ricardo Salvatore, eds, pp. 3–46. Durham, N.C.: Duke University Press, 1998.

Katz, Fredrich. *The Life and Times of Pancho Villa*. Stanford, Calif.: Stanford University Press, 1998.

Kirk, Betty. *Covering the Mexican Front: The Battle of Europe vs. America*. Norman: University of Oklahoma Press, 1941.

Kluckhohn, Frank. *The Mexican Challenge*. New York: Doubleday, Doran & Company, Inc., 1939.

———. "Mexico Breaks Off Relations with Britain in Oil Dispute." *New York Times*, May 14, 1938: 1.

———. "Mines under Fire of Mexican Unions." *New York Times*, March 20, 1938: 31.

Knight, Alan. *The Mexican Revolution*. 2 vols. Lincoln: University of Nebraska Press, 1986.

———. *U.S.-Mexican Relations, 1910–1940: An Interpretation*. La Jolla: Center for U.S.-Mexican Studies, University of California, San Diego, 1987.

Krauze, Enrique, Jean Meyer, and Cayetano Reyes. *Historia de la Revolución Mexicana, 1924–1928: La reconstrucción económica.* [History of the Mexican Revolution, 1924–1928: Economic Reconstruction.] Mexico City: El Colegio de México, 1977.

La Botz, Dan. *Edward L. Doheny: Petroleum, Power, and Politics in the United States and Mexico.* Westport, Conn.: Praeger, 1991.

Lears, Jackson. *Rebirth of a Nation: The Making of Modern America, 1877–1920.* New York: Harper, 2009.

Leer, John. *Workers, Neighbors, and Citizens: The Revolution in Mexico City.* Lincoln: University of Nebraska Press, 1997.

Lippmann, Walter. "Vested Rights and Nationalism in Latin America." *Foreign Affairs,* 5 (April 1927): 361.

Manuscripts Division, U.S. Library of Congress, Washington, DC.

McConnell, Burt. *Mexico at the Bar of Public Opinion.* New York: Mail and Express Publishing Company, 1939.

McElvaine, Robert. *The Great Depression.* New York: Times Books, 1984.

McGregor, Alexander McKelway. "Revolution and Concessions." *Harper's,* 58 (December 6, 1913): 7–8.

———. "Eating Its Children." *Harper's,* 59 (December 19, 1913): 596.

McMullen, Christopher. "Calles and the Diplomacy of Revolution: Mexican-American Relations, 1924–1928." PhD diss., American University, Washington, DC, 1980.

Medina, Luis. *Historia de la Revolución Mexicana, 1940–1952: Del Cardenismo al Avilacamachismo.* [History of the Mexican Revolution, 1940–1952: From Cardenismo to Avilacamachismo.] Mexico City: El Colegio de México, 1978.

Melzer, Richard. "Dwight Morrow's Role in the Mexican Revolution: Good Neighbor or Meddling Yankee?" PhD diss., University of New Mexico, Albuquerque, 1979.

Meyer. Eugenia. *Conciencia Histórica Norteamericana y la Revolución de 1910.* [North American Historical Consciousness and the Revolution of 1910.] Mexico City: Instituto Nacional de Antropología e Historia, 1970.

Meyer, Lorenzo. *Mexico and the United States in the Oil Controversy, 1917–1942.* Austin: University of Texas Press, 1977.

———. *Los Grupos de Presión Extranjero y el México Revolucionario.* [Foreign Lobbyists and Revolutionary Mexico.] Mexico City: Secretaría de Relaciones Exteriores, 1973.

Meyer, Lorenzo, Rafael Segovia, and Alejandra Lajous. *Historia de la Revolución Mexicana, 1928–1934: Los Inicios de la Institucionalización.* [History of the Mexican Revolution, 1928–1934: The Beginnings of the Institutionalization.] Mexico City: El Colegio de México, 1977.

Millan, Verna Carleton. *Mexico Reborn.* Boston: Houghton Mifflin, 1938.

Moreno, Julio. *Yankee Don't Go Home: Mexican Nationalism, American Business Culture, and the Shaping of Modern Mexico, 1920–1950.* Chapel Hill: University of North Carolina Press, 2003.

Morgan, Hugh Joseph. "The United States Press Coverage of Mexico during the Presidency of Lázaro Cárdenas, 1934–1940." PhD diss., Southern Illinois University, Carbondale, 1985.

Morris, Charles. *The Tycoons: How Andrew Carnegie, John D. Rockefeller, Jay Gould, and J. P. Morgan Invented the American Supereconomy.* New York: Holt, 2005.

National Archives of the United States, Washington, DC.

Neimeyer, E. V. *Revolution at Querétaro: The Mexican Constitutional Convention of 1916–1917.* Austin: University of Texas Press, 1974.

Neuman, Martha S. *El Reconocimiento de Alvaro Obregón: Opinión Americana y Propaganda Mexicana, 1921–1923.* [Recognition of Alvaro Obregon: American Opinion and Mexican Propaganda, 1921–1923.] Mexico City: Universidad Nacional Autónoma de México, 1983.

O'Brien, Thomas. *The Century of U.S. Capitalism in Latin America.* Albuquerque: University of New Mexico Press, 1999.

———. *The Revolutionary Mission: American Enterprise in Latin America, 1900–1945.* Cambridge, UK: Cambridge University Press, 1996.

Olsen, Patrice Elizabeth. "Revolution in the City Streets: Changing Nomenclature, Changing Form, and the Revision of Public Memory." In *The Eagle and the Virgin: Nation and Cultural Revolution in Mexico, 1920–1940.* Mary Kay Vaughan and Stephen K. Lewis, eds., pp. 119–134. Durham, N.C.: Duke University Press, 2006.

Parry, Albert. *Garretts and Pretenders: A History of Bohemianism in America.* New York: Dover, 1960.

Pells, Richard. *Radical Visions and American Dreams: Culture and Social Thought in the Depression Years.* New York: Harper & Row, 1973.

Pike, Frederick. *FDR's Good Neighbor Policy: Sixty Years of Generally Gentle Chaos.* Austin: University of Texas Press, 1995.

Pyron, Darden Asbury. "Mexico as an Issue in American Politics, 1911–1916." PhD diss., University of Virginia, Charlottesville, 1975.

Ramo Obregón-Calles, Archivo General de la Nación, Mexico City, Mexico.

The Readers' Guide to Periodical Literature, 1922–1924. vol. VI, pp. 1074–1076. New York: H.W. Wilson Co., 1925.

The Readers' Guide to Periodical Literature, 1925–1928. vol. VII, pp. 1583–1586. New York: H.W. Wilson Co., 1928.

Records of the United States Department of State, Washington, DC.

Reed, John. *Insurgent Mexico.* New York: Simon and Schuster, 1969.

Rosenberg, Emily. *Financial Missionaries to the World: The Politics and Culture of Dollar Diplomacy, 1900–1930.* Durham, N.C.: Duke University Press, 2003.

Rosenstone, Robert. *Romantic Revolutionary: A Biography of John Reed.* New York: Vintage, 1981.

Salvatore, Nick. *Eugene V. Debs: Citizen and Socialist.* Urbana: University of Illinois Press, 1982.

Samuel Guy Inman Papers, Manuscripts Division, Library of Congress.

Santiago, Myrna. *The Ecology of Oil: Environment, Labor, and the Mexican Revolution, 1900–1938.* Cambridge, UK: Cambridge University Press, 2006.

Schuler, Friedrich. *Mexico between Hitler and Roosevelt: Mexican Foreign Relations in the Age of Lázaro Cárdenas, 1934–1940.* Albuquerque: University of New Mexico Press, 1998.

Siegel, Jerrold. *Bohemian Paris: Culture, Politics, and the Boundaries of Bourgeois Life, 1830–1930.* Baltimore: Johns Hopkins University Press, 1999.

Simpson, Eyler. *The Ejido: Mexico's Way Out.* Chapel Hill: University of North Carolina Press, 1937.

Smith, Jason Scott. *Building New Deal Liberalism: The Political Economy of Public Works.* Cambridge, UK: Cambridge University Press, 2006

Smith, Michael. "Carrancista Propanganda and the Print Media in the United States: An Overview of Institutions." *The Americas,* 52 (October 1995): 155–174.

———. "Gringo Propangandist: George F. Weeks and the Mexican Revolution." *Journalism History,* 29 (Spring 2003): 2–11.

Smith, Robert Freeman. *The United States and Revolutionary Nationalism in Mexico, 1916–1932.* Chicago: University of Chicago Press, 1972.

Spenser, Daniela. *The Impossible Triangle: Mexico, Soviet Russia, and the United States in the 1920s.* Durham, N.C.: Duke University Press, 1999.

Stansell, Christine. *American Moderns: Bohemian New York and the Creation of a New Century.* New York: Holt, 2000.

Steel, Ronald. *Walter Lippmann and the American Century.* Boston: Little, Brown, 1980.

Tannenbaum, Frank. The *Mexican Agrarian Revolution.* Washington, DC: Brookings Institution, 1930.

———. "Mexican Internal Politics and American Diplomacy." *Annals of the American Academy,* 132 (July 1927): 172–175.

———. "Mexico's Man of the People." *Survey Graphic,* 26 (August 1937): 425–427.

————. "Mexico's Man of the People." *Reader's Digest,* 31 (October 1937), 43–44.

————. "The Miracle School," *Century,* 106 (August 1923): 499–506.

————. *Peace by Revolution.* New York: Columbia University Press, 1933.

————. "Viva Mexico." *New Republic,* 57 (December 12, 1928): 108–109.

Taylor, Nick. *American Made: The Enduring Legacy of the WPA.* New York: Bantam, 2009.

Terry, T. Philip. *Terry's Guide to Mexico.* Boston: Houghton Mifflin, 1933.

Trachtenbeg, Alan. *The Incorporation of America: Culture and Society in the Gilded Age.* New York: Hill and Wang, 1982.

Ulloa, Berta. *Historia de la revolución mexicana, 1914–1917: La Constitución de 1917.* [History of the Mexican Revolution, 1914–1917: The 1917 Constitution.] Mexico City: El Colegio de México, 1983.

U.S. Congress, Senate, Committee on Foreign Affairs, *Investigation of Mexican Affairs.* 66th Congress. Washington: U.S. Government Printing Office, 1919.

Vázquez, Josefina Zoraida, and Lorenzo Meyer. *The United States and Mexico.* Chicago: University of Chicago Press, 1985.

Weston, Edward. *Daybooks of Edward Weston.* ed. Nancy Newhall. 2 vols. Millertown, N.Y.: Aperture, 1973.

Weyl, Nathaniel and Sylvia. "Mexico under Cárdenas." *American Mercury,* 50 (July 1940): 349–353.

————. *The Reconquest of Mexico.* New York: Oxford University Press, 1939.

Wolfe, Bertram. *A Life in Two Centuries.* New York: Stein and Day, 1981.

Wolfe, Bertram and Diego Rivera. *Portrait of Mexico.* New York: Covici Friede, 1937.

Woods, Kenneth Flint. "Samuel Guy Inman: His Role in Inter-American Cooperation." PhD diss., American University, Washington, DC, 1962.

Yankelevich, Pablo. "En la Retaguardia de la Revolución Mexicana: Propanganda y Propagandistas Mexicanos en América Latina, 1914–1920. [In Defense of the Mexican Revolution: Mexican Propaganda and Propagandists in Latin America, 1914–1920.]" *Mexican Studies/Estudios Mexicanos,* 15 (Winter 1999): 35–71.

Zamora, Martha. *Frida Kahlo: The Brush of Anguish.* San Francisco: Chronicle Books, 1990.

CHAPTER THREE

MEXICO'S REVOLUTIONARY ART AND
THE UNITED STATES, 1920–1940

A Friendly Invasion

Helen Delpar

Perhaps the earliest reference to an "invasion" of the United States by Mexican art appeared in an unsigned article in *Current Opinion* in March 1924.[1] The author's characterization of what was as yet a minor trend was undoubtedly premature but nonetheless prescient. Over the next fifteen years, Mexican art in all its formal and temporal manifestations would indeed be part of a powerful invasion that was welcomed by the artistic community in the United States. The strongest interest was in the production of murals, easel paintings, and lithographs of the so-called "big three"—Diego Rivera (1886–1957), José Clemente Orozco (1883–1949), and David Alfaro Siqueiros (1896–1974)—whose sometimes controversial work was shaped by the forces unleashed by the recent Revolution. Meanwhile, government officials from both countries encouraged the invasion, seeing in it a means of defusing the economic and political tensions that frequently strained relations between them after 1920 and of showing that Mexico was more than a land of banditry and violence as the stereotype would have it. To be sure, some would argue that these officials, as well as American curators and critics and the artists themselves, perhaps unwittingly contributed to an image of Mexico that was incomplete and incongruent with current realities. At the same time, many American artists, whether they traveled to Mexico themselves or viewed the work of Mexican artists in the United States, received inspiration from Mexican themes and styles. The Mexican example also contributed to a surge in publicly funded muralism during the 1930s. In short, the art invasion was arguably one of the most important influences of the Mexican Revolution on the United States.

The invasion culminated in the show called *Twenty Centuries of Mexican Art* at New York City's Museum of Modern Art (MoMA) in 1940. The largest and most comprehensive exhibition of Mexican art in the United States to date, it was cosponsored by the administration of Lázaro Cárdenas (1934–1940) at a time of heightened tension because of Mexico's recent expropriation of its foreign-owned oil industry. During the 1940s the influence of Mexican art in the United States subsided as new aesthetic approaches gained adherents in both countries. Even so, Mexican art continued to fascinate many Americans.

Americans had had opportunities to see Mexican art in the United States before the 1920s. In 1893, Mexico was the only Spanish-American country represented in the Fine Arts Building at the World's Columbian Exhibition in Chicago, where paintings and sculpture by José María Velasco and others were exhibited.[2] In addition, numerous buildings at the fair displayed pre-Columbian artifacts from Mexico, though these were not considered art objects at the time, being valued for their archaeological and ethnological significance.

It was a Mexican expatriate, Marius de Zayas, noted for his caricatures and commitment to modern art, who was the first to exhibit pre-Columbian pieces in his New York galleries from 1915 to 1921, alongside works by contemporary artists such as Picasso and Rivera, who was included as an artist of the Cubist school.[3] Similarly, the pre-Columbian masks and other items were seen as exemplars of primitive art rather than specifically Mexican in origin. Art works with Mexican themes by Crawford O'Gorman, an Anglo-Irish painter resident in Mexico, and Adolfo Best Maugard were exhibited in 1919 to critical praise but aroused relatively little interest.[4]

It was only in the mid-1920s that the cultural, political, and economic context in both Mexico and the United States was propitious for an outflow of art and artists from the former to the latter. By 1920 the violence of the previous decade had ebbed in Mexico, and the return of relative political stability permitted the revival of already vibrant and varied artistic endeavors disrupted by the Revolution. Moreover, the nationalism it had encouraged was reflected in artists' heightened appreciation for indigenous traditions and folk art. The fact that Rivera, Siqueiros, and other artists had gained first-hand exposure to European art trends enabled them to produce work that was undoubtedly modern as well as Mexican.

However, perhaps the major element in Mexico's artistic renaissance was the willingness of officials to allow painters to decorate the walls of public buildings with sometimes inflammatory interpretations of the recent conflict and of national culture. The beginning of the mural movement is usually associated with the tenure of philosopher José Vasconcelos (1921–1924) as Secretary of Public Education during the administration of Álvaro Obregón (1920–1924). Rivera and Siqueiros, both of whom had recently returned from Europe, were invited to paint the walls of the National Preparatory School, along with Orozco and other artists, among them Jean Charlot, a Frenchman of part-Mexican ancestry who created Mexico's first modern fresco, which showed the massacre of Indians during the Spanish conquest. From 1923 to 1929, Rivera was sporadically engaged in painting the walls of the new Public Education building. There, on 239 fresco panels he depicted the Revolution as well as Mexicans at work and at religious and political festivals; one set of panels illustrates *corridos*, or popular songs, of the revolutionary period. Although the murals painted at these and other sites created controversy in Mexico, and some were even defaced, admirers there and in the United States praised them for their emphasis on Mexican themes, their revival of fresco techniques, and their accessibility to the public. Indeed, Mexico's murals seemed to be realizing "the ideal goal of art," as a leftist manifesto signed by Rivera, Orozco, and Siqueiros in 1923 asserted: "an art for all, an art of education and of struggle."[5]

Mexico's new priorities in art production and appreciation began to coincide with those of the United States in the 1920s. With the apparent collapse of Europe as a result of World War I and the emergence of U.S. economic hegemony, nationalism became a significant element in art and other aspects of American culture. While modernism had gained acceptance, no dominant style or school prevailed in art. According to Francis O'Connor, the Mexicans "filled a cultural and ideological vacuum."[6] At the same time, the artistic community in the United States expanded during the 1920s as the number of artists, sculptors, and teachers of art rose by 62 percent during the decade while the total population increased by only16 percent. Sixty art museums were founded during the decade, including the MoMA in 1929.[7]

Even before the 1920s the search for authentically American sources of inspiration led some architects and designers in the United States to look to the pre-Columbian civilizations of Mexico, especially the Maya. The initial impetus probably came from the 1893 exposition, where casts of Mayan buildings in Yucatan were erected on the fair grounds and garnered much attention, and from the Washington headquarters of the Pan American Union (1908), where pre-Columbian decorative elements were prominent in the building's exterior and interior. Mayan influence can also be discerned in several Frank Lloyd Wright buildings of this period, such as the Barnsdall House in Los Angeles (1918–1921).[8]

During the 1920s, stirred by archaeological finds in Yucatan, architects such as Robert B. Stacy-Judd and Alfred C. Bossom, both of whom were English, argued that Mayan architecture was a more fitting source of inspiration for the United States than European models. Stacy-Judd's Aztec Hotel (1925) in Monrovia, California, has been described, despite its name, as "uniquely Mayan in its façade ornamentation and interior," while a contemporary writer called it "the only building in the United States that is 100% American."[9] Bossom believed that Mayan architectural principles could be adapted for the construction of modern skyscrapers: "Mayan architecture shows a complete understanding of the handling of great masses of material, and at the same time it employed carving with reserve and simplicity. It can be made a basis for our new types."[10] Bossom used indigenous motifs in his own home and in the Magnolia Petroleum Building in Dallas. Mayan style was also used for motion picture theaters in Los Angeles, Denver, and other cities.[11]

American and Mexican interests also converged in the new appreciation in both countries for the folk art of their respective peoples. Seen as an exemplar of cultural authenticity, American folk art, also called popular or applied art, began to be exhibited in the United States in the mid-1920s, with a major show at MoMA in 1932. During these years, individuals such as Abby Aldrich Rockefeller, wife of John D. Rockefeller, Jr., began to collect American folk art as well.[12]

A similar trend was evident in Mexico, where after the Revolution, artists and intellectuals began to collect the products of native craftsmen. In his autobiography, historian Daniel Cosío Villegas recalled the enthusiasm for folk art as part of the "nationalist explosion" that occurred after 1920, when every home had examples of popular crafts—a gourd from Olinalá or a pot from Oaxaca. Indeed, Rick A. López has argued that, starting in the 1920s, members of Mexico's intelligentsia consciously used the country's folk art to forge a distinctive national identity.[13]

In 1921, three artists—Dr. Atl (pseudonym of Gerardo Murillo), Jorge Enciso, and Roberto Montenegro—organized a large exhibition of folk art covering all periods of Mexican history for which Dr. Atl prepared a catalogue. Here he emphasized the extraordinary manual dexterity of Mexico's craftsmen as well as the aesthetic value of the diverse objects included in the show.[14]

The following year some objects from the exhibition were sent to the United States in an effort to stir friendly feelings toward Mexico at a time when there were no formal diplomatic relations between the two countries. For reasons that remain unclear the exhibition was seen only in Los Angeles, where it was well received by both critics and the public. Katherine Anne Porter, who had been living in Mexico, wrote an English language catalogue for the show. In it she articulated several themes that would be prominent in the discourse about Mexican folk art. For example, that it had been disdained in the nineteenth century and that despite the inroads of modernity, the Indian would retain his attachment to his village and his culture.[15]

Mexican folk art stirred great enthusiasm among Americans, both those living in Mexico and those who had an opportunity to view it in the United States. Frances Toor, for example, saw the 1921 exhibit while visiting Mexico City, and it was a factor in her decision to stay: "I wanted to know more of the country in which humble people could make such beautiful things." In 1925 she founded the government-subsidized magazine *Mexican Folkways* to disseminate information about native culture.

During his service in Mexico (1927–1930), U.S. Ambassador Dwight W. Morrow and his wife, Elizabeth Cutter Morrow, decorated Casa Mañana, their weekend retreat in Cuernavaca, with folk art. In the United States, Abby Aldrich Rockefeller also became a collector, as did her son Nelson.[16] As will be seen later, Mexican folk art was exhibited in New York on several occasions, usually in conjunction with contemporary painting, the implication being that the latter was in some ways a product of the former.

Mexican art of all kinds was promoted in the United States by a variety of individuals. The earliest was José Juan Tablada, a Mexican poet and intellectual resident in New York who was employed by the Mexican government as a kind of cultural ambassador. Starting in the mid-1920s, he published articles in leading art magazines extolling the new trends in Mexican painting. In "Mexican Painting of Today," which appeared in *International Studio* in 1923, he reviewed the work of Rivera and others and concluded that Mexican art was "at the dawn of a brilliant revival."[17]

Among the first American experts to see Mexico's artistic revival firsthand was Walter Pach, an artist and critic who was invited to lecture at the Summer School of the National University in Mexico City in 1922. There he met Orozco, Rivera, and other artists, witnessed the painting of the first murals, and described his very positive reactions in an article in *México Moderno*.[18] Later he recalled how impressed he had been by the revolutionary zeal he had found: "I doubt that latter-day Russia can show the spirit of new life I saw in Mexico, and I know that the land of the Soviets has no such idea of art."[19] Pach also arranged for Mexico to be represented in the Independents' 1923 show in New York. The Mexicans received mixed notices, but Pach continued his support of Mexican art in his writings and aided individual artists when they came to the United States.[20]

Anita Brenner displayed an even stronger commitment to Mexican art. Born in Mexico of European immigrant parents, she moved with her family to the United States during the Revolution but returned in 1923 at the age of eighteen and immediately immersed herself in the cultural ferment of the era. She began publishing articles on Mexican art and artists, starting with "A Mexican Renascence" in *The Arts* in September 1925. Here, speaking of a short-lived leftist Syndicate of Technical Workers, Artists and Sculptors to which Rivera and other artists belonged, she stated themes that would become a major part of the discourse regarding Mexico's artistic production: "Mexican theme, Mexican conception, Mexican subject, vitalized by passionately Mexican spirit—these have resulted in an art that surely is indigenous if any ever was." She also linked the current trends in art with the Revolution: "A political and social revolution did away with the rich man of Díaz's day. The peasant cry for land, liberty and schools joined a new outlook upon Mexico. . . . The reversal of values found its corresponding plastic expression."[21] Brenner developed these themes in *Idols Behind Altars* (1929), a history of Mexican art, which has been called "a compelling factor in attracting foreign artists to Mexico."[22]

During the second half of the 1920s, New Yorkers had numerous opportunities to view the work of Mexican artists. Rivera, Orozco, and others were represented in an exhibit at the Art Center in January–February 1928. The show was to have been accompanied by an exhibition of folk art specially purchased in Mexico for the occasion, but because of turmoil there, it was delayed until March.

The Art Center shows are worthy of note because they were conceived with the clear intent of using art to improve relations between the United States and Mexico. Seeking funds for the folk art show from the General Education Board, a Rockefeller philanthropy, Alon Bement, director of the Center, explained that he was making the request in the belief that cultural relations were the "true basis of understanding between nations." He also thought that a folk art exhibit might be a source of inspiration for design in the United States. Bement's request received a favorable response, with a grant of $5,000 for the purchase of the folk art.[23]

The Art Center had already turned down an offer by the administration of Plutarco Elías Calles (1924–1928) to finance the show, because the Center wanted "the native craftsmen [to] understand this movement to be an American recognition of Mexican crafts." The Mexican government, however, seeking to improve its image in the United States, did sponsor the exhibition of modern art. The juxtaposition of folk art with the modern paintings angered Orozco, who was living in New York at the time. He complained, "our works have merely served as propaganda placards for a commercial private business of foreigners!"[24]

Folk art and modern art were literally juxtaposed in the highly successful "Mexican Arts" exhibit at New York City's Metropolitan Museum of Art in the fall of 1930. Dwight W. Morrow is credited with conceiving the show, which was funded by the Carnegie Corporation of New York and sponsored by the American Federation of Arts. The Mexican government also gave its support.[25]

The chief organizer of the exhibit was René d'Harnoncourt, an Austrian count who had arrived in Mexico in 1926 and had quickly fallen in with individuals such as Roberto Montenegro, who cultivated folk art. Perhaps for this reason, the exhibit emphasized what he called the applied arts, which he said were "the truest form of self-expression of the Mexican people." The fine arts section included colonial "primitives" and portraits, *retablos*, or votive pictures, and contemporary paintings by twenty-five artists, Rivera and Orozco among them. According to d'Harnoncourt, it was only the work produced after 1910 that was authentically national. "The roots of the modern painter go deep into the simple life of the Mexican people, and the tradition of his work is genuinely Mexican, dating from the picture writing and frescoes of the pre-Conquest Indian ... down to the turbulent present."[26] In a review the critic Royal Cortissoz made explicit the link between the applied arts and modern painting: "even Rivera, so just in line, so sure in touch, so clearly the accomplished craftsman, holds us chiefly by his alliance with that native well-spring of energy which we have identified in the anonymous potters."[27]

The show, and especially the applied arts exhibited, was a success with both the critics and the public not only in New York but also in the thirteen other cities to which it traveled. It had been conceived as an exercise in cultural diplomacy, intended to alter negative stereotypes about Mexico, and there were many assertions that this indeed had been the result. An editorial in the *New York Times* declared:

> Particularly through the lurid years since 1910, dotted as they have been with revolution after revolution in the republic across the Rio Grande, we in this country have been handicapped in our effort to get at Mexico's motivating purposes. Much distrust has been bred on both sides. . . . Mexico seems so alien, so remote. Yet when we are privileged, as now, to seek her national point of view, in terms of art that has been so wisely and comprehensively chosen, barriers tend to go down and there grows a neighborly impulse toward reciprocity.[28]

According to Anna Indych-López, however, the exhibition's emphasis on crafts merely replaced the negative image with an equally superficial image of the country as "primitive, rural, and picturesque."[29]

By the late 1920s the Mexican invasion brought not only the exhibition of art but also the physical presence of the artists in the United States. Orozco, Rivera, and Siqueiros were among the many who crossed the border, each for his own reasons, but often in the hope of accessing a market for art that was larger and more affluent than Mexico's.

Facing bleak prospects for mural commissions in Mexico and unhappy about political conditions there, Orozco traveled to New York in December 1927. Articles by Tablada and Brenner had prepared the way, the former dubbing him "the Mexican Goya," and the latter "a Mexican rebel."[30] Brenner, who had come to New York to attend graduate school, performed an additional service for Orozco by bringing with her a series of black-and-white drawings he had recently done called *Horrores de la Revolución*, and by introducing him to Alma Reed, a journalist well known in Mexico, who quickly took charge of his career.

Although he initially received a stipend from the Mexican government, Orozco hoped that his New York stay would yield a financial return. The *Horrores* series found little favor, as the drawings were deemed overly gruesome and illustrative rather than artistic. Orozco proceeded to make lithographs of some of the drawings in the series, renamed *Mexico in*

Revolution, but omitting the more violent scenes. The lithographs proved successful, but the series was "sanitized, cleansed of the horrific details of civil struggle in order to make its commercial debut in the United States a commercial success."[31]

During the next year, Orozco sold not only his lithographs but also his first oil painting, *Coney Island—Side Show*, to Francis Biddle, future attorney general of the United States. Meanwhile, through his association with Alma Reed, he became acquainted with individuals prominent in society and the art world, and in 1930 she opened a gallery, the Delphic Studios, where his work would be featured. In addition, he received commissions to paint murals: *Prometheus* at Pomona College in California (1930), *A Call for Revolution and Universal Brotherhood* at the New School for Social Research in New York (1930–1931), and *The Epic of American Civilization* at Dartmouth College in New Hampshire (1932–1934).

In contrast to Orozco, when Rivera arrived in San Francisco in November 1930, he was "preceded by his enormous popularity and critical acclaim."[32] His Mexican murals were the subject of admiring articles by Tablada and others, and his easel paintings and other works had been exhibited in New York, San Francisco, and other cities. In 1925 his painting *Flower Day (Día de Flores)* was shown at the First Pan American Exhibition at the Los Angeles Museum of Art and won the $1,500 first prize. In 1929 he became only the second foreign artist to receive the Fine Arts Medal of the American Institute of Architects. The institute made the award to honor Rivera's murals and their representation of Mexico's national character.[33]

In San Francisco, Rivera painted two murals, an allegory of California in the Luncheon Club of the Stock Exchange and *Making a Fresco* at the California School of Fine Arts, as well as a portable fresco in a private home.[34] In December 1931 he was accorded a retrospective at MoMA, only the second living artist to be so honored. The exhibition consisted of more than 150 works, including paintings in oil and encaustic and watercolors, as well as eight portable frescoes that Rivera painted specifically for the show. Three had U.S. themes. Two of them, *Electric Power* and *Pneumatic Drill*, illustrated modern technology, but the third, *Frozen Assets*, offered a grim interpretation of capitalism and unemployment in New York during the Great Depression. The other five frescoes showed scenes of Mexican history. Four of them were reworkings of his Mexican murals that, according to Indych-López, depoliticized the originals.[35] From the MoMA show, Rivera went on to execute a major mural commission at the Detroit Institute of Arts. There he ignored the ravages of the Depression in Detroit and painted scenes of modern science and industrial technology, though he claimed to have depicted the struggle of the worker, as he understood it.[36]

Rivera's far left political views had produced controversy at every stage of his work in the United States, but the furor reached a peak in the celebrated "Battle of Rockefeller Center." Invited to paint a large mural in the lobby of the new RCA building, Rivera selected as his theme *Man at the Crossroads* and began work in April 1933. As the mural progressed, it became clear that Rivera was offering a Communist interpretation of contemporary society and painting a figure that was unmistakably Lenin at the center of the mural. Nelson A. Rockefeller, who had been involved with the project from the start, asked Rivera to remove Lenin's visage, noting that it had not been included in Rivera's preliminary sketches. When Rivera refused Rockefeller's request, his commission was cancelled, and the mural was destroyed in February 1934.[37]

As a result of the Rockefeller Center controversy, Rivera lost a commission to paint a mural in the General Motors Building at the upcoming Century of Progress fair in Chicago. In 1940, however, Timothy Pfluger, an architect and early Rivera patron, invited him to return to San Francisco to paint movable frescoes at the site of the Golden Gate International Exposition. In what was called the Art-in-Action pavilion, where fairgoers could watch him at work, Rivera began a ten-panel mural on the theme of *Pan American Unity*. The mural, he said, represented "the union of the technical and industrial genius of North America and the artistic and creative genius of South America."[38] As it turned out, Rivera did not complete the mural until after the fair had closed, and it generated little comment or debate.

Siqueiros was a more orthodox Communist than Rivera and was more deeply involved in radical politics in Mexico. Like Orozco, he deplored the folkloric aspects of Rivera's work, which he believed ignored the poverty and oppression of the Mexican masses. Although Siqueiros sold paintings and lithographs to private collectors such as Abby Aldrich Rockefeller and George and Ira Gershwin, his primary goal was to create murals and other work that would depict the evils of capitalism and inspire the masses to revolution. He also was a proponent of the use of modern industrial technology in creating his work.

In 1932, Siqueiros was invited to teach a course on mural painting at the Chouinard School of Art in Los Angeles. At the school he created an exterior mural, *Workers' Meeting*, notable for his use of a spray gun to apply pigment to a coating of white, waterproof cement. During his seven months in Los Angeles, Siqueiros painted two other exterior murals: a somber *Portrait of Present-Day Mexico*, in the patio of the home of film director Dudley Murphy, and *Tropical America*, on a wall of the Plaza Art Center in the city's Hispanic district. The latter, an allegorical depiction of U.S. imperialism in Latin America, proved controversial and was quickly whitewashed.[39]

In 1934, Siqueiros traveled to New York, where the Delphic Studios held an exhibition of his work, including ten large paintings and photographs of his murals in Mexico City and Los Angeles. He also lectured on mural painting at the New School. Returning to New York in 1936, he launched the Experimental Workshop, a collective enterprise intended to "be a laboratory for experimentation in modern art techniques" and to "create art for the people."[40] With the help of workshop members, Siqueiros designed parade floats, posters, and banners that reflected its close association with the U.S. Communist party. Siqueiros also continued to adopt innovative technical methods such as the use of pyroxylin, an industrial enamel, in several easel paintings of the period.

As the reaction to *Man at the Crossroads* and *Tropical America* shows, the Mexican artists did not always receive positive assessments, with unfavorable criticism usually based on both aesthetic and political grounds. For example, one critic praised the work of Rivera and Orozco at the 1928 Art Center show, but concluded: "On the whole, these painters treat form too cavalierly, their color is factitiously somber, and the whole tone is deplorably heavy."[41] It was, of course, the murals that received the strongest criticism. The critic Thomas Craven, for example, praised Rivera's Mexican murals but opined in 1934 that his "American murals seldom rise above the level of prodigious competence." The problem was his lack of genuine American experience. Harvey Watts, who was unhappy about the Mexican "craze," declared with respect to Orozco's Dartmouth murals (Figure 1), which

Figure 1. "The Departure of Quetzalcoatl," Panel 7 from Orozco's *The Epic of American Civilization*, 1932–1934. Fresco in the Baker Library at Dartmouth College. Commissioned by the Trustees of Dartmouth College, Hanover, New Hampshire. Reproduced with permission.

depicted the Mesoamerican deity Quetzalcoatl, the martyred revolutionary Emiliano Zapata, and what might be considered unflattering scenes of "Anglo-American" civilization:

> That the Mexicans should develop their vernacular is all right, whether
> it be Spanish or Aztec, Toltec, or Mayan, or just plain Mexican, but that
> we should grovel in it and fill our museums and colleges and banks with
> the crude message of radicals and visionary patriots of an alien civilization
> seems too ridiculous to be possible, even though it is in permanency at
> Dartmouth.[42]

Others deplored the granting of mural commissions in the United States to foreigners. American artists should be preferred over "mediocre foreign artists," especially in times of economic distress.[43]

In the early 1930s, Rivera was the target of vitriolic attacks from Communists associated with the U.S. party. Having been expelled from the Mexican party in 1929 and suspected of Trotskyite leanings, Rivera was condemned as a counterrevolutionary who accepted commissions from American millionaires and from the Mexican government, perceived as reactionary by 1930. As a result, he now faced "corruption as a man and bankruptcy as an artist."[44]

Rivera, Orozco, and Siqueiros were but three of the many Mexican artists represented in *Twenty Centuries of Mexican Art*, which opened at MoMA on May 14, 1940, and ran for four months. The exhibit was more comprehensive than its 1930 predecessor in that it included pre-Columbian pieces and gave more attention to colonial art and less to folk art. Modeled on a show planned in Paris that was canceled because of the outbreak of World War II, the New York exhibit featured a large fresco painted at the site by Orozco in view of the public. Called *Dive Bomber and Tank*, the fresco was made of up six interchangeable panels and suggested the horrors of modern technological warfare.[45]

The MoMA exhibit was similar to its 1930 predecessor in its linkage of art and revolution. According to Miguel Covarrubias, the artist and caricaturist who was in charge of the modern art section:

> Thus the art of Mexico has reached a turbulent maturity, attained only after
> a dogged struggle against the bonds that held it fast to the decaying cul-
> tures of Europe. The artistic liberation of Mexican art runs closely parallel
> to the social and political liberation of the nation itself, and if the par-
> ticipation of the artists in this struggle had been less than whole-hearted,
> perhaps modern Mexican art would never have shown its present freshness
> and vigor.[46]

The exhibit also resembled the 1930 show in that it was clearly intended to foster "good will" between the United States and Mexico, which assumed half of the cost, the balance being covered by the museum. As the show was being planned, negotiations over the 1938 oil expropriation were at an impasse and Mexico was being vilified in the U.S. media. It was hoped that the show would foster a friendly climate conductive to settlement of the oil controversy, encourage U.S. tourism to Mexico, and generally improve relations between the two countries.

Whether the show in fact improved relations between the two governments cannot be proved. It did, however, generate favorable reviews that emphasized Mexico's artistic gifts. Emily Genauer, for example, wrote that everybody "who saw the exhibition left it with a most profound respect for Mexico, for her rich artistic tradition, for the brilliance of her civilization, when our own land was a wilderness, for the versatility, inventiveness and gaiety of her peasant art . . . It's the feeling American art lovers have long held for France and Italy."[47]

By the early 1930s, Mexico's artistic renaissance was inducing many American artists to cross the border to study firsthand the murals of the great painters and to seek inspiration for their own work in the people and culture of that country. Howard Cook, Marsden Hartley, and a few others received grants, such as Guggenheim Fellowships, that enabled them to spend varying amounts of time in Mexico. Cook, who won a Guggenheim, spent more than a year there and recalled: "This gave my work tremendous stimulus, allowing me freedom to develop new techniques, including my first fresco, as well as to attempt to realize a portrayal of the serenity and beauty of the lives of the common Mexican people."[48] Visiting artists usually spent time in Mexico City, sometimes observing or assisting a muralist as he worked, but then fanned out to reach rural areas, such as the Isthmus of Tehuantepec or Taxco in the state of Guerrero, which was rapidly becoming s favored destination for artists, intellectuals, and ordinary tourists. In fact, William Spratling, the silver entrepreneur partly responsible for Taxco's emergence, noted in 1932: "There are lots of artists here now. You bump into them whenever you turn a corner. Where so much art will go god knows."[49]

As James Oles has shown, American painters in Mexico tended to depict indigenous people in idealized rural or village settings from which conflict and violence were absent.[50] This emphasis can be attributed in part to contemporary American questioning of their machine-based society, especially as the Great Depression took hold, a theme in much contemporary writing, notably Stuart Chase's best-selling *Mexico: A Study of Two Americas* (1931), which contrasted "Middletown" (Muncie, Indiana) with the village of Tepoztlán, usually to the latter's advantage.[51] Accordingly, scenes of village markets and other typical settings were popular, depicting subjects such as Howard Cook's watercolor *Market, Oaxaca* (1933). In 1929, George Biddle, brother of Francis and a lawyer-turned-artist, painted a tranquil scene of *Vendors in the Marketplace*. Biddle, however, was one of the few to portray the violence that still afflicted Mexico in the late 1920s. His oil painting *Shot by Bandits* (1929), based on an incident he witnessed, shows a woman beside the body of a man while soldiers watch in the background.[52]

Although American artists frequently incorporated elements of nature into their scenes of indigenous life, they rarely painted pure landscapes. The main exception was Marsden Hartley, who admired the Mexican mural movement, "the only one that shows any signs of spiritual re-birth." His *Popócatepetl: Spirited Morning* (1932) and *Carnelian Country* (1932) are notable for their flat, abstracted shapes and riotous color.[53]

American artists in Mexico tended to avoid depicting urban life or characters. The latter do appear in the gently satirical lithographs and paintings by Caroline Durieux, who spent a decade in Mexico (1926–1936) with her businessman husband. Several of these show presumably affluent Mexicans at leisure, such as *Bathers (Acapulco)* (1932) and *Café Tupinambá* (1934).[54] A scene of urban, working-class Mexicans at leisure is *En la pulquería* (1924) by Pablo O'Higgins, who went to Mexico to work with Rivera and eventually became a permanent resident. Allusions to contemporary poverty were also rare, though in 1936 O'Higgins, who shared Rivera's far left political views, painted a woman asleep on a street in the working-class district of Tacubaya.[55]

O'Higgins was one of eight Americans who were given the opportunity to paint murals in Mexico during the 1930s.[56] The commissions varied in terms of the murals' sponsors and purpose and the location of the walls to be covered. In 1933, Marion Greenwood, the first woman to paint a Mexican mural, and Howard Cook were commissioned by the American owners of a hotel in Taxco to decorate its corridors. According to Oles, their murals, both in fresco—*Taxco Market* and *Taxco Fiesta*—contributed to the rise of Taxco as a tourist destination by projecting an idealized view of Mexican culture.[57]

Very different was the project undertaken by O'Higgins, Marion Greenwood, her older sister Grace, and others in the Abelardo L. Rodríguez Market in Mexico City. Completed in 1934, the market complex, built in part of the colonial-era Colegio de San Gregorio, included a theater and day care center as well as a market hall. In their murals, O'Higgins and the Greenwood sisters depicted the continuing social injustice faced by Mexico's peasants and workers despite the Revolution while capitalists profited and prepared for war. Another American on the project, Isamu Noguchi, created a mural nearly six feet high and seven feet long entitled *History of Mexico* that was a sculptural relief in colored cement on a brick wall. Despite the title, it did not specifically address Mexican issues but looked to the defeat of capitalism and the triumph of labor.[58]

Philip Guston, who, like Noguchi, would later be recognized as a major American artist, also painted a mural in Mexico. In 1934, he and Reuben Kadish, who had worked as an assistant to Siqueiros in Los Angeles, obtained a commission for a fresco in the Museo Michoacano in Morelia, where Grace Greenwood had already completed a small mural on the theme *Man and Machines*. The Guston-Kadish mural, *The Workers' Struggle for Liberty*, depicts evils represented by the Medieval Inquisition and the Modern Inquisition (the Ku Klux Klan, Nazism).[59]

Marion and Grace Greenwood, George Biddle, and Howard Cook were among the many American artists who were able to paint murals in the United States during the 1930s. A few American artists had long been interested in muralism but had usually found little support among architects and patrons. After 1930, conditions became more favorable for several reasons. The example of the Mexicans was probably the strongest. One of the earliest mural proponents, Thomas Hart Benton, was a great admirer of the Mexicans despite his aversion to the political views displayed in some of their murals. He later recalled:

> I had looked with much interest on the rise of the Mexican school during the mid-twenties. In spite of the Marxist dogmas, to the propagation of which so much of its work was directed, I saw in the Mexican effort a profound and much-needed redirection of art towards its ancient humanistic functions. The Mexican concern with publicly significant meanings and

with the pageant of Mexican national life corresponded perfectly with what I had in mind for art in the United States. I also looked with envy on the opportunities given Mexican painters for public mural work.[60]

In New York, Benton became friendly with Orozco and Alma Reed and painted a series of murals under the rubric *America Today* in the New School, while Orozco was painting his at the same institution.

The Mexican example was also a factor in the availability of federal funding for murals during the 1930s. In 1933, George Biddle, a Groton classmate of Franklin D. Roosevelt, wrote to the president in support of such funding:

> The Mexican artists have produced the greatest national school of mural painting since the Renaissance. Diego Rivera tells me that it was only possible because [President] Obregón allowed Mexican artists to work at plumber's wages in order to express on the walls of the government buildings the social ideals of the Mexican Revolution. The younger artists of America are conscious as they never have been of the social revolution that our country and civilization are going through; and they would be very eager to express their ideals in permanent art form if they were given the government's cooperation.[61]

Lobbying by Biddle and others resulted in the creation of three New Deal programs that sponsored murals in public buildings. Two, the short-lived Public Works Art Project (1933–1934) and the Federal Art Project of the Works Progress Administration (WPA, 1935–1943), were mainly relief programs to aid destitute artists; the third, the Treasury Department's Section of Painting and Sculpture (later the Section of Fine Arts, 1934–1943), selected its artists not on the basis of need but in juried competitions.[62]

Many of the artists who participated in these programs had come under the influence of the Mexican muralists, either by studying their work in Mexico or by exposure to their U.S. murals. At least five of the more than twenty artists who created murals for San Francisco's 288-foot Coit Tower in 1934 had traveled to Mexico: Ray Boynton, Ralph Stackpole, Maxine Albro, Victor Arnautoff, and Bernard Zakheim.[63] The tower, which offered almost 3,700 feet of wall space, was the site of "the largest collective project financed as part of the federal programs, not just in San Francisco but in the country." It was also, according to Francis O'Connor, "the only mural site in the country that displays so varied a range of walls painted in the style and spirit of Diego Rivera."[64] Some of the artists on the project painted scenes of leisure and entertainment, but other like Arnautoff and Zakheim were Communists whose work was denounced as red propaganda. Their murals, along with Boynton's and Stackpole's, not only revealed Rivera's influence in their design and content but also alluded to the recent uproar over the latter's Rockefeller Center mural. As a result, controversy swirled around the project, particularly because the city was gripped by labor unrest while the artists worked, and the opening of the tower had to be postponed.

Ben Shahn learned fresco techniques while working as an assistant to Rivera on the destroyed Rockefeller Center mural. He went on to paint several murals for New Deal programs, including thirteen frescoes depicting Americans at work in agriculture and industry for the central post office in the Bronx, New York, in 1938–1939. The inclusion of the figure of Walt Whitman and a line from one of his poems led to accusations that the mural promoted irreligion, whereupon Shahn substituted a verse from another Whitman poem.[65]

George Biddle encountered criticism of his preliminary studies for his 1936 mural on *Society Freed through Justice* in the Justice Department building (Figure 2), but in general murals by the Greenwood sisters, Philip Guston, Isamu Noguchi, and others avoided political or social commentary likely to produce controversy.[66] More typical if perhaps more imaginative than most was Lowell Houser's mural in the Ames, Iowa, post office (1938), which interprets maize cultivation by a pre-Columbian Maya and his twentieth-century American counterpart. On one side of the mural, Houser, who had spent three years as an artist-in-residence at the Carnegie Institution's archaeological project at Chichén Itzá in Yucatan, depicted the Mayan farmer in loincloth and sandals working his cornfield with a hoe while surrounded by the corn god and other deities. Directly opposite, the American farmer in overalls husks corn amid symbols of modern agriculture such as a microscope and ticker tape showing commodity prices. Between them is a large ear of feed corn.[67]

Among those for whom the social content of the Mexican murals was especially meaningful were African-American artists. Charles Alston, for example, who painted a two-part mural for the WPA, *Magic in Medicine* (1940), at the Harlem Hospital Medical Center in New York, had previously watched Rivera at work in Rockefeller Center. Charles White, who painted murals for the WPA in Chicago and depicted *The Contribution of the Negro to Democracy in America* (1943) at the Hampton Institute in Virginia, is said to have been influenced by all of the "big three." Hale Woodruff worked on several federal project murals in Atlanta before receiving a grant that enabled him to go to Mexico City in 1936. There he worked with Rivera, learning the essentials of fresco technique. Upon his return to the United States, he painted his best-known mural, a three-panel work on the Amistad Mutiny (1939), in the Savery Library of Talladega College in Alabama.[68]

After 1940 the critical and popular enthusiasm that had greeted Mexican art in the 1920s and 1930s in the United States began to recede. During World War II the American artistic community welcomed European art refugees, who were able to continue producing work in the modern avant-garde, such as Surrealism, for which many of them were already well known. They also influenced American artists, contributing to the rise of Abstract Expressionism, which became the dominant mode of the avant-garde in the immediate postwar era and was viewed as a New York–based American movement that signaled the displacement of Paris as the capital of the art world. The emphasis of these artists on personal expression contrasted sharply with the often politicized, didactic production of left-leaning Mexicans, such as Rivera and Siqueiros. Moreover, as the Cold War intensified, such works could hardly be viewed with even the limited approbation of earlier decades. Ironically, the painter most closely associated with Abstract Expressionism, Jackson Pollock, had been part of the Siqueiros Experimental Workshop in 1936. The experience is said to have given Pollock "a vivid glimpse of what was possible in scale, in materials, even in fundamental assumptions about the nature of art,"[69] but he would eschew politicized work like that created by Siqueiros.

Figure 2. George Biddle at work on his mural *Society Freed Through Justice* at the Department of Justice, 1936. Unidentified photographer. Archives of American Art, Smithsonian Institution.

In Mexico the "big three" continued to paint murals until their deaths, and George Biddle painted a fresco, *The Horrors of War* (1945), in the Supreme Court building in Mexico City, but there too new artistic currents began to surface as revolutionary momentum ebbed. The visit of André Breton, a founder of Surrealism, in 1938 stirred interest in that movement, as did a 1940 exhibition of modern European art, which Breton helped organize. During the war, Mexico received its share of art refugees, who also furthered local exposure to contemporary European trends. There had always been artists such as Rufino Tamayo who, while acknowledging their Mexican roots, rejected the nationalist emphasis of the muralists. Now they were joined by artists of a younger generation, such as José Luis Cuevas, who resented the still dominant Mexican school. In a well-known essay, Cuevas argued that their ascendancy stifled artistic freedom and kept Mexico isolated from artistic trends in other countries. "What I want to see in my country's art are broad highways leading out to the rest of the world," he wrote, "rather than narrow trails connecting one adobe village with another."[70]

One group for whom the Mexican school still had an appeal was made up of African-American artists, several of whom, repelled by racism and red-baiting at home, joined the exodus of other American leftists to Mexico in the late 1940s and 1950s. Among them were Charles White and his wife at that time Elizabeth Catlett, who were attracted not only by the muralists but also by the Taller de Gráfica Popular, established in 1937 by O'Higgins and others to produce prints directed toward the working class. White soon returned to the United States, but Catlett remained permanently in Mexico. While working with the Taller, she produced *The Negro Woman* (1946–1947), a series of linocuts, and with other Taller artists she also created the series *Against Discrimination in the United States* (1953–1954). John Wilson, another African-American artist, also worked with the Taller after arriving in Mexico in 1950. Strongly influenced by the recently deceased Orozco, he painted a fresco, *The Incident* (1952), that depicts a lynching by the Ku Klux Klan as a black family watches from inside a dwelling, the father holding a gun in his hand.[71]

As early as the 1960s, an era of political and social turmoil, the influence of Mexico's muralists was apparent in the street murals created by blacks in Chicago and by Mexican-Americans in the West.[72] By the mid-1980s it was clear that the Mexican School was experiencing a substantial revival, as seen in record prices paid for Rivera paintings in 1983 and 1984.[73] In 1986 a major retrospective of Rivera's work was mounted at the Detroit Institute of Arts to commemorate the centenary of the artist's birth. In March 1990, work got underway to restore Siqueiros's Los Angeles mural *Tropical America*, though the project remained incomplete two decades later. Meanwhile, his mural in the Dudley Murphy house had been moved, along with the building in which it was located, to the Santa Barbara Museum of Art.[74]

That Mexican art could again be the subject of a "blockbuster" exhibition was evident in the show "Mexico: Splendors of Thirty Centuries" that opened at the Metropolitan Museum of Art in October 1990 and later traveled to San Antonio and Los Angeles. Initially conceived by Mexican media tycoon Emilio Azcárraga Milmo and enjoying strong support from President Carlos Salinas de Gortari (1988–1994), the show consisted of more than 400 pieces and boasted a massive catalogue with an introduction by poet Octavio Paz, who coincidentally was awarded the Nobel Prize in literature as the exhibit was opening. The exhibition omitted a separate section for folk or applied art, a few specimens of which were included in the large sections devoted to pre-Columbian and viceregal art. Rivera, Orozco, and Siqueiros were well represented in the section on twentieth-century art, along with Frida Kahlo, whose newly iconic stature in the United States has been attributed to Hayden Herrera's 1983 biography.[75]

This exhibit, like its predecessors of 1930 and 1940, has been interpreted as an exercise in cultural diplomacy. Funding came not only from the Mexican and U.S. governments and U.S. foundations but also from Friends of the Arts of Mexico, of which Ascárraga Milmo was chairman. Because the show appeared when the proposed North American Free Trade Agreement was under discussion, it has been seen as a vehicle for assuaging contemporary fears about Mexican poverty and corruption and promoting an image of Mexico "as both a timeless civilization and a modern, forward-looking trading partner."[76] According to an anonymous critic in the *New York Times,* however, the show not only left the viewer "with a heightened sense of the length and breadth of Mexican civilization," but was also "one of the few blockbusters that can be said to transcend the diplomatic and economic considerations that underlie it."[77]

During the two decades after 1920 the artistic community in the United States had for the first time many opportunities to view and study Mexican art of all types and epochs, but especially that associated with the postrevolutionary "renaissance." Alejandro Ugalde has identified forty-eight solo exhibitions by Mexican artists in New York between 1924 and 1940. In addition, New York hosted twenty-five group exhibitions featuring Mexican art between 1923 and 1940.[78] New York as the center of the U.S. art world was naturally favored, but similar exhibitions also took place in Philadelphia, San Francisco, and other large cities. During this period, art created by Mexicans often found a permanent home in the United States after being purchased by individual collectors or museums. Those interested in the work of the "big three" might seek them out as they painted murals in the United States, conversing with them or even assisting them. Artists and critics also flocked to Mexico to view the murals firsthand and promoted muralism in the United States, a goal furthered by the federal art programs of the 1930s. If enthusiasm for Mexican art diminished after 1940, it by no means disappeared and was experiencing a resurgence by the 1980s.

The discourse of American critics and promoters of the Mexican art invasion uniformly stressed several themes: that the work of the "big three" and others represented a "renaissance," presumably after a period of decadence; that the forms and subject matter of this renaissance were rooted in the indigenous and popular culture of Mexico; and that it was the Revolution that had created the conditions that allowed the emergence of this art. To repeat the words of Anita Brenner: "A political and social revolution did away with the rich man of Díaz's day. . . . The reversal of values found its corresponding plastic expression."

Modern scholars question the extent to which the Revolution did in fact produce a reversal of values, and art historians are aware of nationalism and aesthetic renewal before 1910. However, the causal link between the Revolution and the "renaissance' seems as unquestioned today as it was in the 1920s and 1930s. As Dore Ashton asserted in her essay for the catalogue of the 1990 "Splendors" exhibition: "No account of the arts in Mexico during the first fifty years of the [twentieth] century can negate the significance of the great circumstantial paroxysm of the Revolution."[79]

Leftists and liberals within the U.S. artistic community and the intelligentsia as a whole were sympathetic toward the goals of the Revolution and were not overly concerned about the anti-American and anticapitalist elements that Mexican artists occasionally incorporated into their murals and paintings. More conservative artists could still admire the work of the Mexicans for its nationalist and popular elements, which they considered models for what might be done in U.S. art. Mexican artists, meanwhile, came to the United States where they could find financial returns in an art market that was larger than that of their homeland as well as validation from U.S. critics. Although some U.S. diplomats and businessmen with interests in Mexico deplored the Revolution and the policies it engendered, others, such as Ambassador Morrow, favored rapprochement, recognizing the essential moderation of the Mexican government. In this environment, as contemporaries realized, art appeared to be a means of smoothing the rough edges of the two countries' relationship with each other.

As Joseph S. Nye has observed, a country can use "soft power," which may arise from the attractiveness of its culture, to "punch above [its] weight" in international relations.[80] For their part, Mexican officials were quick to take advantage of opportunities to encourage representations of Mexico that belied stereotypes of the country as riddled with poverty, violence, and corruption. These efforts were generally successful given the political and economic forces that favored the peaceful resolution of U.S.-Mexican conflicts. In summary, the "invasion" of Mexican art profoundly affected the American art world and fostered harmonious relations between the two countries.

NOTES

1. "The Mexican Art Invasion," *Current Opinion*, 76 (March 1924), 305–307. For a short account of the "invasion," see Helen Delpar, *The Enormous Vogue of Things Mexican: Cultural Relations Between the United States and Mexico, 1920–1935* (Tuscaloosa: University of Alabama Press, 1992), 125–64. The most complete account is Alejandro Ugalde, "The Presence of Mexican Art in New York Between the World Wars: Cultural Exchange and Art Diplomacy" (PhD diss., Columbia University, 2003).

2. Hubert Howe Bancroft, *The Book of the Fair*, Vol. 2. (Chicago: Bancroft Company, 1893), 717.

3. *New York Times*, October 8, 1916, sec. 5, 17; *Art News* 15 (October 14, 1916), 3; Ugalde, "Mexican Art in New York," 101–04.

4. *New York Times*, April 20, 1919, sec. 3, 4; Peyton Boswell, "Exhibitions in the New York Galleries," *Arts & Decoration* 11 (May 1919): 35; *New York Times*, December 4, 1919, 16.

5. On the early murals, see Leonard Folgarait, *Mural Painting and Social Revolution in Mexico, 1920–1940: Art of the New Social Order* (Cambridge, UK: Cambridge University Press, 1998), 33–85. The quoted lines are on p. 51.

6. Francis O'Connor, "The Influence of Diego Rivera on the Art of the United States during the 1930s and After," in *Diego Rivera: A Retrospective* (New York: Founders Society Detroit Institute of Arts, with Norton, 1986), 159.

7. Frederick P. Keppel and R. L. Duffus, *The Arts in American Life* (New York: McGraw-Hill Book Company, 1933), 20, 66.

8. Marjorie Ingle, *The Mayan Revival Style: Art Deco Mayan Fantasy* (Albuquerque: University of New Mexico Press, 1989), 7, 13–19.

9. Ingle, *Mayan Revival*, 25.

10. *New York Times*, October 4, 1925, sec. 13, 22.

11. "Furnishing the Modern Apartment with Distinction," *Arts & Decoration* 20 (February 1924): 24–25. Donald E. Marquis, "Archeological Aspects of the Mayan Theatre of Los Angeles," *Art and Archaeology* 29 (March 1930), 98–111; Ingle, *Mayan Revival*, 41–50.

12. Holger Cahill, "Introduction," *American Folk Art: The Art of the Common Man in America, 1750–1900* (New York: Museum of Modern Art, 1932), 26–27; Beatrix T. Rumford, "Uncommon Art of the Common People: A Review of Trends in the Collecting and Exhibiting of American Folk Art," in *Perspectives on American Folk Art*, ed. Ian M. G. Quimby and Scott T. Swank (Winterthur, Del.: Henry Francis duPont Winterthur Museum, 1980), 13–53.

13. Daniel Cosío Villegas, *Memorias* (Mexico City: Editorial Joaquín Mortiz, 1976), 91–92; Rick A. Lopez, "Lo Más Mexicano de México: Popular Arts, Indians, and Urban Intellectuals in the Ethnicization of Postrevolutionary Culture, 1920–1972" (PhD diss., Yale University 2001).

14. Dr. Atl, *Las Artes Populares en México* (Mexico City: Librería "Cultura," 1921); Lopez, "Lo Más Mexicano de México," 92–118..

15. James Oles, "Exhibiting Mexican Folk Art, 1820–1930," in *Casa Mañana: The Morrow Collection of Mexican Popular Arts*, ed. Susan Danly (Albuquerque: University of New Mexico Press, 2002), 18–22; Katherine Anne Porter, *Outline of Mexican Arts and Crafts* (Los Angeles: Young & McCallister, 1922); *Los Angeles Times*, November 11, 1922, sec. II, 1, November 12, 1922, sec. II, 3, and sec. III, 20, Nov. 19, 1922, sec. II, 1.

16. Frances Toor, *Mexican Popular Arts* (Mexico City: Frances Toor Studios, 1939), 10–11; Danly, *Casa Mañana*; Annie O'Neill, "Nelson A. Rockefeller: The Collector," in *The Nelson A. Rockefeller Collection of Mexican Folk Art* (San Francisco: The Mexican Museum, 1986), 26–27.

17. José Juan Tablada, "Mexican Painting of Today," *International Studio* 76 (January 1923), 276. On Tablada, see Ugalde, "Mexican Art in New York," 108–17.

18. Walter Pach, "Impresiones Sobre el Arte Actual en México," *México Moderno* 2 (October 1, 1922), 131–38.

19. Walter Pach, *Queer Thing Painting: Forty Years in the World of Art* (New York: Harper & Brothers, 1938), 283.

20. Ugalde, "Mexican Art in New York," 120–21; *Art News* 21 (March 3, 1923): 2; Thomas Craven, "The Independent Exhibition," *New Republic* 34 (March 14, 1923): 70–71.

21. Anita Brenner, "A Mexican Renascence," *The Arts* 8 (August 1925), 127–50. On Brenner, see Susannah Joel Glusker, *Anita Brenner: A Mind of Her Own* (Austin: University of Texas Press, 1998) and Susannah Joel Glusker, ed., *Avant-Garde Art and Artists in Mexico: Anita Brenner's Journals of the Roaring Twenties*, 2 vols. (Austin: University of Texas Press, 2010).

22. Karen Cordero Reiman, "Constructing a Modern Mexican Art," in James Oles, *South of the Border: Mexico in the American Imagination, 1914–1947* (Washington: Smithsonian Institution Press, 1993), 37.

23. Alon Bement to Charles R. Richards, September 21, 1927, Folder 724, Box 321, General Education Board Collection, Rockefeller Archive Center, Pocantico Hills, New York. See also Ugalde, "Mexican Art in New York," 176–81.

24. Alma Reed, *Orozco* (New York: Oxford University Press, 1956), 53. Orozco's complaint was probably due to the fact that some of the craft items were sold. The exhibit traveled to several American cities and to Canada, Denmark, and Sweden. See Alon Bement to Arthur G. Askey, October 25,

1928, and Alon Bement to Ernest A. Buttrick, December 10, 1930, Folder 724, Box 324, General Education Board Collection.

25. On the "Mexican Arts" exhibit, see Ugalde, "Mexican Art in New York," 189–211, and Anna Indych-López, *Muralism Without Walls: Rivera, Orozco, and Siqueiros in the United States, 1927–1940* (Pittsburgh: University of Pittsburgh Press, 2009), 75–138.

26. *Mexican Arts: Catalogue of an Exhibition Organized for and Circulated by the American Federation of Arts (1930–1931)* (Portland, Maine: Southwark Press, 1930), 42–43.

27. *New York Herald-Tribune*, October 12, 1930, sec. 8, 10.

28. *New York Times*, October 15, 1930, 22.

29. Indych-López, *Muralism Without Walls*, 126.

30. José Juan Tablada, "Orozco, the Mexican Goya," *International Studio* 78 (March 1924), 492–500; Anita Brenner, "A Mexican Rebel," *The Arts* 12 (October 1927), 201–209. Orozco's stay in New York, which embraced most of the years 1927–1934, is well documented. Reed's *Orozco* covers mainly the U.S. years while the artist's letters to Jean Charlot and to his wife have been published: José Clemente Orozco, *The Artist in New York: Letters to Jean Charlot and Unpublished Writings, 1925–1930*, trans. Ruth L. C. Simms (Austin: University of Texas Press, 1972), and *Cartas a Margarita, 1921–1949*, ed. Tatiana Herrera Orozco (Mexico City: Ediciones Era, 1987). General studies are Laurance P. Hurlburt, *The Mexican Muralists in the United States* (Albuquerque: University of New Mexico Press, 1989), 13–87; Alejandro Arneus, *Orozco in Gringoland: The Years in New York* (Albuquerque: University of New Mexico Press, 2001), and Renato González Mello and Diane Miliotes, eds., *José Clemente Orozco in the United States, 1927–1934* (Hanover, N.H.: Hood Museum, 2002).

31. Indych-López, *Muralism Without Walls*, 64.

32. Hurlburt, *Mexican Muralists*, 98–99.

33. "Hispano-American Art and Artists," *Bulletin of the Pan American Union*, 60 (April 1926), 359–67; *Los Angeles Times*, December 1, 1925, sec. 2, 12; *American Architect*, 135 (May 20, 1929), 672.

34. For Rivera's California murals, see Hurlburt, *Mexican Muralists*, 98–122. A more detailed account appears in Anthony W. Lee, *Painting on the Left; Diego Rivera, Radical Politics, and San Francisco's Public Murals* (Berkeley: University of California Press, 1999), 57–114.

35. Indych-López, *Muralism Without Walls*, devotes a chapter (pp.129–56) to this show. See also Ugalde, "Mexican Art in New York," 220–44.

36. Hurlburt, *Mexican Muralists*, 127–58.

37. Ugalde, "Mexican Art in New York," gives a detailed account of this well-known episode on 245–96.

38. Lee, *Painting on the Left*, 208. Lee discusses the mural on 207–15.

39. On Siqueiros, see Hurlburt, *Mexican Muralists*, 195–245; Ugalde, "Mexican Art in New York," 329–77; Shifra M. Goldman, "Siqueiros and Three Early Murals in Los Angeles," in Goldman, *Dimensions of the Americas: Art and Social Change in Latin America and the United States* (Chicago: University of Chicago Press, 1994), 87–100.

40. Hurlburt, *Mexican Muralists*, 222.

41. *New York Herald-Tribune*, January 29, 1928, sec. 7, 11.

42. Hurlburt, *Mexican Muralists*, 86.

43. *Art Digest*, 7 (June 1, 1933), 7. See also *New York Times*, June 10, 1933, 15, and Ione Robinson, "Fresco Painting in Mexico," *California Arts and Architecture*, 41 (June 1932), 36.

44. Robert Evans, "Painting and Politics: The Case of Diego Rivera," *The Masses*, 7 (February 1932), 25. For a discussion of the attitudes of the far left toward the muralists, see Andrew Hemingway, "American Communists View Mexican Muralism: Critical and Artistic Responses," *Crónicas* 8–9 (2005), 13–42.

45. On this exhibition, see Ugalde. "Mexican Art in New York," 396–459, and Indych-López, *Muralism Without Walls*, 157–85.

46. Jean Charlot, *Twenty Centuries of Mexican Art* (New York and Mexico City: Museum of Modern Art and Instituto de Antoropología e Historia de México, 1940), 141.

47. Ugalde, "Mexican Art in New York," 443.

48. Howard Cook, "The Road from Prints to Fresco," *Magazine of Art* 35 (January 1942), 4.

49. James Douglas Oles, "Walls to Paint On: American Muralists in Mexico, 1933–1936" (PhD diss., Yale University, 1995), 68.

50. Oles, *South of the Border*, 75.

51. Delpar, *Enormous Vogue*, 69.

52. Oles, *South of the Border*, 59, 108–109. On Biddle, see his *An American Artist's Story* (Boston: Little, Brown & Co., 1939).

53. Delpar, *Enormous Vogue*, 80; Oles, *South of the Border* 151, 154ff.

54. See Richard Cox, *Caroline Durieux: Lithographs of the Thirties and Forties* (Baton Rouge: Louisiana State University Press, 1977).

55. Oles, *South of the Border*, 179–85. The artist was born Paul Higgins in Utah but became known as Paul or Pablo O'Higgins in Mexico. See Oles, "Walls to Paint On," 201.

56. Most of the material in the next three paragraphs comes from Oles, "Walls to Paint On."

57. Oles, "Walls to Paint On," 47, 116.

58. Oles, "Walls to Paint On," 193–311. See also two articles in *Crónicas* 5–6 (2003): Elizabeth Fuentes Rojas, "El Abelardo Rodríguez, un Mercado del Pueblo y Para el Pueblo," 17–24, and Maricela González Cruz, "Isamu Noguchi en el Mercado Abelardo Rodríguez," 91–99.

59. Oles, "Walls to Paint On," 312–48.

60. Thomas Hart Benton, *An American in Art: A Professional and Technical Autobiography* (Lawrence: University Press of Kansas, 1969), 61–62. See also the catalogue of the MoMA exhibit "Murals by American Painters and Photographers" (May 1932), reprinted in *American Art of the Twenties and Thirties* (New York: Arno Press for The Museum of Modern Art, 1969).

61. Hurlburt, *Mexican Muralists*, 9.

62. Karal Ann Marling, *Wall to Wall America: Post Office Murals in the Great Depression* (Minneapolis: University of Minnesota Press, 1982), 42–49.

63. Lee, *Painting on the Left*. 134. Lee gives a detailed account of the Coit Tower murals and the surrounding turmoil on 129–59.

64. O'Connor, "Influence of Rivera," 174.

65. O'Connor, "Influence of Rivera," 167–70; Diana L. Linden, "Ben Shahn's New Deal Murals: Jewish Identity in the American Scene," in *Common Man, Mythic Vision: The Paintings of Ben Shahn*, ed. Susan Chevlowe (Princeton: Princeton University Press, 1998), 50–52.

66. Marling, *Wall to Wall America*, 57–58; Oles, "Walls to Paint On," 409.

67. Mary L. Meixner, "The Corn Mural," *Palimpsest* 66 (January–February 1985), 14ff.

68. Lizzetta LeFalle-Collins, "African-American Muralists and the Mexican Mural School," in LeFalle-Collins and Shifra M. Goldman, *In the Spirit of Resistance: African-American Modernists and the Mexican Muralist School* (New York: American Federation of Arts, 1996), 27–67; O'Connor, "Influence of Rivera," 178.

69. Steven Naifeh and Gregory White Smith, *Jackson Pollock: An American Saga* (New York: Clarkson N. Potter, 1989), 290. On the art refugees and the postwar avant-garde in the United States, see Dore Ashton, *The New York School: A Cultural Reckoning* (Berkeley: University of California Press, 1992), and Serge Guilbaut, *How New York Stole the Idea of Modern Art: Abstract Expressionism, Freedom and the Cold War*, trans. Arthur Goldhammer (Chicago: University of Chicago Press, 1983), which also discusses the political uses to which the new movement was put.

70. José Luis Cuevas, "The Cactus Curtain," *Evergreen Review* 7 (1959), 111–20. Tamayo's views are discussed in essays by Mary K. Coffey and Anna Indych-López in Diana C. DuPont, ed., *Tamayo: A Modern Icon Reinterpreted* (Santa Barbara, Cal.: Santa Barbara Museum of Art, 2007).

71. Rebecca M. Schreiber devotes a chapter to these artists in *Cold War Exiles in Mexico: U.S. Dissidents and the Culture of Critical Resistance* (Minneapolis: University of Minnesota Press, 2008), 27–57.

72. Shifra M. Goldman, "The Mexican School: Its African Legacy, and the Second Wave in the United States," in LeFalle-Collins and Goldman, *Spirit of Resistance* 69–82; Shifra M. Goldman, "Resistance and Identity: Street Murals of Occupied Aztlán," in Goldman, *Dimensions of the Americas: Art and Social Change in Latin America and the United States* (Chicago, Ill.: University of Chicago Press, 1980), 118–22.

73. *New York Times*, June 1, 1984, C1. See also Hurlburt, *Mexican Muralists*, 291, n.23.

74. *New York Times*, March 20, 1990, A14, October 29, 2002, E1; *Los Angeles Times*, September 19, 2010, A37.

75. Metropolitan Museum of Art, *Mexico: Splendors of Thirty Centuries* (New York: Metropolitan Museum of Art, 1990), vii–xi. See also Shifra M. Goldman, "Metropolitan Splendors" and "Three Thousand Years of Mexican Art," in Goldman, *Dimensions of the Americas*, 326–43. Two other exhibits in New York complemented the show at the Metropolitan: "Mexican Painting, 1950–1980" at the IBM Gallery of Science and Art and "Women in Mexico" at the National Academy of Design.

76. *Los Angeles Times*, October 9, 1990, 7.

77. *New York Times*, October 5, 1990, B1.

78. Ugalde, "Mexican Art in New York," 486–92.

79. Metropolitan Museum of Art, *Mexico: Splendors*, 554.

80. Joseph S. Nye, Jr., *Soft Power: The Means of Success in World Politics* (New York: PublicAffairs, 2004), 8, 89.

BIBLIOGRAPHY

American Architect, 135 (May 20, 1929): 672.

Arneus, Alejandro. *Orozco in Gringoland: The Years in New York*. Albuquerque: University of New Mexico Press, 2001.

Art News, 21 (March 3, 1923): 2.

Atl, Dr.. *Las artes populares en México*. Mexico City: Librería Cvltvra, 1921.

Bancroft, Hubert Howe. *The Book of the Fair*, 2 vols. Chicago: Bancroft Company, 1893.

Benton, Thomas Hart. *An American in Art: A Professional and Technical Autobiography*. Lawrence: University Press of Kansas, 1969.

Brenner, Anita. "A Mexican Rebel." *The Arts*, 12 (October 1927): 201–9

———. "A Mexican Renascence." *The Arts*, 8 (August 1925): 127–50.

Cahill, Holger. "Introduction." *American Folk Art: The Art of the Common Man in America, 1750–1900*. New York: Museum of Modern Art, 1932.

Cook, Howard. "The Road from Prints to Fresco." *Magazine of Art*, 35 (January 1942): 4–10.

Cosío Villegas, Daniel. *Memorias* [Memoirs]. Mexico City: Joaquín Mortiz, 1976.

Craven, Thomas. "The Independent Exhibition," *New Republic*, 34 (March 14, 1923): 70–71.

Cuevas, José Luis. "The Cactus Curtain." *Evergreen Review*, 7 (1959): 111–20.

Delpar, Helen. *The Enormous Vogue of Things Mexican: Cultural Relations between the United States and Mexico, 1920–1935*. Tuscaloosa: University of Alabama Press, 1992.

Evans, Robert. "Painting and Politics: The Case of Diego Rivera." *The Masses*, 7 (February 1932): 25.

Folgarait, Leonard. *Mural Painting and Social Revolution in Mexico, 1920–1940: Art of the New Social Order*. Cambridge, UK: Cambridge University Press, 1998.

"Furnishing the Modern Apartment with Distinction." *Arts & Decoration*, 20 (February 1924): 24–25.

General Education Board Collection. Alon Bement to Arthur G. Askey, October 25, 1928 and Alon Bement to Ernest A. Buttrick, December 10, 1930. Folder 724, Box 324. Rockefeller Archive Center, Pocantico Hills, New York.

———. Alon Bement to Charles R. Richards, September 21, 1927. Folder 724, Box 321. Rockefeller Archive Center, Pocantico Hills, New York.

Glusker, Susannah Joel. *Anita Brenner: A Mind of Her Own*. Austin: University of Texas Press, 1998.

———, ed. *Avant-Garde Art and Artists in Mexico: Anita Brenner's Journals of the Roaring Twenties*. Austin: University of Texas Press, 2010.

Goldman, Shifra M. *Dimensions of the Americas: Art and Social Change in Latin America and the United States*. Chicago: University of Chicago Press, 1994.

Hemingway, Andrew. "American Communists View Mexican Muralism: Critical and Artistic Responses." *Crónicas*, 8–9 (2005): 13–42.

"Hispano-American Art and Artists." *Bulletin of the Pan American Union*. 60 (April 1926): 359–67.

Hurlburt, Laurance P. *The Mexican Muralists in the United States*. Albuquerque: University of New Mexico Press, 1989.

Indych-López, Anna. *Muralism without Walls: Rivera, Orozco, and Siqueiros in the United States, 1927–1940*. Pittsburgh: University of Pittsburgh Press, 2009.

Ingle, Marjorie. *The Mayan Revival Style: Art Deco Mayan Fantasy*. Albuquerque: University of New Mexico Press, 1989.

Keppel Frederick P., and R. L. Duffus. *The Arts in American Life*. New York: McGraw-Hill Book Company, 1933.

Lee, Anthony W. *Painting on the Left: Diego Rivera, Radical Politics, and San Francisco's Public Murals*. Berkeley: University of California Press, 1999.

LeFalle-Collins, Lizzetta. "African-American Muralists and the Mexican Mural School." In *The Spirit of Resistance: African-American Modernists and the Mexican Muralist School*. ed. Lizzetta LeFalle-Collins and Shifra M. Goldman, pp. 27–67. New York: American Federation of Arts, 1996.

Linden, Diana L. "Ben Shahn's New Deal Murals: Jewish Identity in the American Scene." In *Common Man, Mythic Vision: The Paintings of Ben Shahn*. ed. Susan Chevlowe, pp. 37–65. Princeton: Princeton University Press, 1998.

Lopez, Rick A., "Lo más mexicano de México: Popular Arts, Indians, and Urban Intellectuals in the Ethnicization of Postrevolutionary Culture, 1920–1972." PhD diss., Yale University, 2001.

Los Angeles Times. December 1, 1925, sec. 2: 12.

Los Angeles Times. November 11, 1922, sec. II: 1.

Los Angeles Times. November 12, 1922, sec. II: 3; sec. III: 20.

Los Angeles Times. November 19, 1922, sec. II: 1.

Marling, Karal Ann. *Wall to Wall America: Post Office Murals in the Great Depression.* Minneapolis: University of Minnesota Press, 1982.

Marquis, Donald E. "Archeological Aspects of the Mayan Theatre of Los Angeles," *Art and Archaeology,* 29 (March 1930): 98–111.

Meixner, Mary L. "The Corn Mural." *Palimpsest,* 66 (January–February 1985): 14–16, 25–29.

"Mexican Art in New York." *New York Times,* October 8, 1916, sec. 5: 17.

"The Mexican Art Invasion." *Current Opinion,* 76 (March 1924): 305–07.

Mexican Arts: Catalogue of an Exhibition Organized for and Circulated by the American Federation of Arts (1930–1931). Portland, Maine: Southwark Press, 1930.

Thu Museum of Modern Art. "Murals by American Painters and Photographers." In *American Art of the Twenties and Thirties.* p. 173. New York: Arno Press for The Museum of Modern Art, 1969.

Naifeh, Steven and Gregory White Smith. *Jackson Pollock: An American Saga.* New York: Clarkson N. Potter, 1989.

New York Herald-Tribune. January 29, 1928, sec. 7: 11.

New York Herald Tribune. October 12, 1930, sec. 8: 10

New York Times. June 10, 1933: 15.

New York Times. October 15, 1930: 22

New York Times. October 4, 1925, sec. 13: 22.

Nye, Joseph S., Jr. *Soft Power: The Means of Success in World Politics.* New York: Public Affairs, 2004.

O'Connor, Francis. "The Influence of Diego Rivera on the Art of the United States during the 1930s and After." In *Diego Rivera: A Retrospective,* pp. 157–83. New York: Founders Society Detroit Institute of Arts, with Norton, 1986.

O'Neill, Annie. "Nelson A. Rockefeller: The Collector." In *The Nelson A. Rockefeller Collection of Mexican Folk Art.* pp. 1–6. San Francisco: The Mexican Museum, 1986.

Oles, James Douglas. "Walls to Paint On: American Muralists in Mexico, 1933–1936." PhD diss., Yale University, 1995.

―――. "Exhibiting Mexican Folk Art, 1820–1930." In *Casa Mañana: The Morrow Collection of Mexican Popular Arts,* ed. Susan Danly, pp. 11–29. Albuquerque: University of New Mexico Press, 2002.

Orozco, José Clemente. *The Artist in New York: Letters to Jean Charlot and Unpublished Writings, 1925–1930,* trans. Ruth L. C. Simms. Austin: University of Texas Press, 1972.

―――. *Cartas a Margarita, 1921–1949* [Letters to Margaret, 1921–1949]. ed. Tatiana Herrera Orozco. Mexico City: Ediciones Era, 1987.

Pach, Walter. "Impresiones Sobre el Arte Actual en México. [Views on Contemporary Art in Mexico.]" *México Moderno,* 2 (October 1, 1922): 131–8.

―――. *Queer Thing Painting: Forty Years in the World of Art.* New York: Harper & Brothers, 1938.

Porter, Katherine Anne. *Outline of Mexican Arts and Crafts.* Los Angeles: Young & McCallister, 1922.

Reed, Alma. *Orozco.* New York: Oxford University Press, 1956.

Reiman, Karen Cordero. "Constructing a Modern Mexican Art." In *South of the Border: Mexico in the American Imagination, 1914–1947.* ed. James Oles. pp. 11–46. Washington, DC: Smithsonian Institution Press, 1993.

Robinson, Ione. "Fresco Painting in Mexico." *California Arts and Architecture,* 41 (June 1932): 13–4, 36.

Rumford Beatrix T. "Uncommon Art of the Common People: A Review of Trends in the Collecting and Exhibiting of American Folk Art." In *Perspectives on American Folk Art,* ed. Ian M. G. Quimby and Scott T. Swank, pp. 13–53. Winterthur, De.: Henry Francis duPont Winterthur Museum, 1980.

Tablada, José Juan. "Orozco, the Mexican Goya." *International Studio,* 78 (March 1924): 492–500.

———. "Mexican Painting of Today." *International Studio,* 76 (January 1923): 267–76.

Toor, Frances. *Mexican Popular Arts.* Mexico City: Frances Toor Studios, 1939.

Twenty Centuries of Mexican Art. New York and Mexico City: Museum of Modern Art and Instituto de Antoropología e Historia de México, 1940.

Ugalde, Alejandro. "The Presence of Mexican Art in New York between the World Wars: Cultural Exchange and Art Diplomacy." PhD diss. Columbia University, 2003.

CHAPTER FOUR

BROWN, BLACK, AND BLUES
Miguel Covarrubias and Carlos Chávez
in the United States and Mexico
(1923–1953)

Mary Kay Vaughan and Theodore Cohen

INTRODUCTION

Scholars have paid considerable attention to the racially inclusive, democratic influence of Mexican revolutionary artists and intellectuals—Diego Rivera, José Clemente Orozco, and Anita Brenner—on cultural, political, and even entrepreneurial vanguards in the United States.[1] This essay examines similar contributions by artist and ethnographer Miguel Covarrubias (1904–1957) and composer Carlos Chávez (1899–1978). These young men grew up in the tumult of revolution as peasant armies, striking workers, and self-made army officers turned Mexico City into a cacophony of gunfire, street demonstrations, frenzied dance, and risqué floor shows. In 1923, Covarrubias and Chávez headed for New York. There they joined avant-garde circles, nourished by a New World spirit following the collapse of Europe in the World War, by an invigorated African American movement, by the Russian and Mexican revolutions, by new expressions of sexuality and bodily freedom, and by an effervescent popular culture of entertainment. Armed with aesthetic modernism's new notions of composition and embrace of the primitive and the popular, the tools of ethnography, and a sense of the potential of the mass media for disseminating artistic production to emerging mass societies, Covarrubias and Chávez gradually assembled new visual, musical, and literary modes to give positive representation to groups denigrated, despised, and excluded by nineteenth-century imperial conquest and Victorian mores in the United States, Mexico, and, more broadly, the Western Hemisphere.

In examining Covarrubias and Chávez in this exchange, we highlight intersections among art, race, class, and nation; between art and ethnography; and between nationalism and transnationalism in the creation of postcolonial identities north and south. We wish to create a dynamic conversation between brown and black, a dimension of the dialogue among U.S. and Mexican artists and intellectuals that has received little attention for this period. We refer to the construction of a "brown" Mexican nation, defined by the revolutionaries as a mixture of European (primarily Spanish) and indigenous peoples built on a Meso-American foundation. By "black" we begin with the discussion of Negro identity at play in the Harlem Renaissance. Miguel Covarrubias was the first artist to draw the Harlem Renaissance. He also illustrated a series of literary, musical, and ethnographic milestones in the African American struggle for equality. In 1937, he returned to Mexico to become a major ethnographer, archaeologist, painter, and publicist of Mexico's indigenous past and present. Carlos Chávez developed an awareness of black music in New York and in Latin America through his association with the International Composers' Guild and the Pan American Association of Composers. In New York he honed a modernist music with a Mexican Indian identity. Upon becoming virtual director of musical culture in Mexico in the 1930s, he furthered ethnographic exploration of regional music that led not only to the uncovering of indigenous/European traditions but to the discovery of African elements. In his promotion of an inclusive nationalist music expressing this vernacular repertoire, he drew support from his friend, U.S. composer Aaron Copland. In the midst of a decade of class strife in which workers, the rural poor, and racial/ethnic minorities struggled for their rights, both advocated a democratization of the content and accessibility of classical music.

In the vigorous period of Pan Americanism from the late 1930s into the 1950s, Covarrubias and Chávez furthered the study and dissemination of a cultural corpus of American identity, based on transnational exchanges and national mappings realized in the 1920s and 1930s. Although associated with Mexican *indigenismo*, they welcomed U.S. African American artists to Mexico, publicized the African in Mexican culture, and participated in the deepening of an understanding of the African Diaspora in the Americas.

YOUNG MEXICANS TAKE NEW YORK

In July 1924, Miguel Covarrubias wrote from New York to his friend, Carlos Chávez, then out of the city. "Dear Chavinski, I have received the score of Polígonos," he said referring to Chávez' latest abstract composition. He wanted the music to form part of a review "Americana" that would star Charlie Chaplin in comedy sketch, Margaret Severn in modern dance, an all-black jazz orchestra, the "negro actor" Paul Robeson, and a steam piano, "the kind that plays in the circus." In the middle of the stage, Covarrubias would build a platform that resembled a boxing ring that he would fill with "very modern" objects. We do not know if the performance ever took place: Covarrubias did note that Chaplin was very busy and hard to pin down.[2]

Sometime later, he wrote "Chavinski" from Paris. He sent him drawings for two ballets and asked him to compose the music. One would be a puppet show, a popular Mexican love story built around miracles performed by the Virgin of Guadalupe. The other concerned the beautiful and risqué model, Nahui Olin. The daughter of a Porfirian general, she had taken an Aztec name and gone mostly nude and notoriously photogenic in Mexico City in the 1920. The first they performed in New York. About the second, we have no knowledge. At the end of his letter, Covarrubias wrote of "la belle France":

> Paris strikes me as *altamente pinche* and intolerably bourgeois. In music,
> there is nothing interesting. I heard *Oedipus Rex*, Stravinsky's latest work,

and it struck me as stupid. . . . The Russian ballet was a big disappointment. Diagileff [sic] only wants to please rich old ladies. . . . In painting there is absolutely nothing new . . . Its musical reviews are infamously inferior. . . . The intellectual public is intolerable. . . . It is useless to create anything here. . . . The French invented the bourgeoisie and they still hold the record.

And with that, he announced he was leaving for North Africa to study *negritude*.[3]

Carlos Chávez and Miguel Covarrubias had come to New York from Mexico City in 1923. Chávez was twenty-four years old. Covarrubias was nineteen. Mexican poet and writer José Juan Tablada introduced them to the city's cultural life, enriched by scores of immigrants, refugees, and explorers of U.S. and foreign origin. Tablada had established himself and his Latin American bookstore on East 28th Street as springboards to counteract the stereotypization of Mexicans in the movies and popular press—the bandit, the greaser, the spitfire diva (in the real life form of the new Hollywood sensation, Lupe Vélez).[4] Chávez and Covarrubias charged in as iconoclasts and explorers. There would be no more European imitation. Mexico had to look inward to her own spiritual gifts. In 1921, José Vasconcelos had detonated the message as the first revolutionary Minister of Public Education. Chávez had turned from Claude Debussy to write what he imagined to be an Aztec ballet. Covarrubias had helped Adolfo Best Maugard organize the *Noche Mexicana*: they turned the once exclusive Chapultepec Park over to pretty women vending tacos, *aguas*, and enchiladas and to dancing *chinas poblanas* and *charros*, all in popular dress. Covarrubias also assisted in mounting the first exhibit of indigenous crafts, which heretofore had never passed as art.[5] His evenings were spent in the theater district and the cafés where the new artistic elite immersed themselves in the ribald entertainment.[6] He drew sketches on napkins and then published them in magazines like *El Ilustrado*, which declared itself a journal of genius against the establishment. For his part, Chávez hung out with the futurist Estridentistas who had declared "Death to Father Hidalgo!" and "Chopin to the electric chair!"[7]

These young men found Mexico City too small. In New York, they moved into poet Octavio Barreda's apartment along with designer Adolfo Best Maugard, painter Carlos Mérida, and writer Luis Cardoza y Aragón. Tablada presented them to New York trend setters. Carl Van Vechten, prolific critic who moved with ease from Diaghilev to the blues, loved Covarrubias' caricatures. He introduced him to Frank Crowninshield, director of *Vanity Fair*, a sleek new magazine combining upscale fashion with progressive politics as well as avant-garde and popular art. In the pages of *Vanity Fair*, Covarrubias' career took off with portraits of celebrities—politicians, athletes, movie stars, royalty, artists, and writers. Drawing from a long tradition of Mexican caricature, he developed a humorous, gentle style that marked the entire twentieth century in the United States.[8] With rhythmic Cubist lines and forms, he captured a personality or collective moment in elegant parody. Publishing books, exhibiting his work, he spent his free time in Harlem clubs enthralled by the dancers, musicians, and writers. For his part, Chávez found venues for his development of modernist composition in the International Composers' Guild, the Pan American Association of Composers, and the Copland-Sessions Concerts, which began in 1928.

MIGUEL COVARRUBIAS' NEGRO DRAWINGS AND BEYOND

We turn first Covarrubias' *Negro Drawings*, published by Alfred Knopf in 1927. Covarrubias went to the Harlem clubs—Small's Paradise, Happy Rhone's, the Cookery, the Savoy, the Kit Kat Club, and Leroy's—with fellow cartoonist Al Hirschfield, playwright Eugene O'Neil, Van Vechten, and later, Rose Roland, the sensational Broadway dancer who would become Covarrubias' wife.[9] He listened to Bessie Smith, Ethel Waters, and Alberta Hunter sing the blues and sketched the body-bending dancers. He met the young artists, writers, and political activists—Langston Hughes, Countee Cullen, Zora Neale Hurston, Guayana-born Eric Walrond, and NAACP secretary, Walter White. Covarrubias introduced them to Van Vechten, and Van Vechten introduced Covarrubias to the older NAACP leaders, W. E. B. Du Bois and James Weldon Johnson.[10] After he met the younger crowd, he launched a full-scale campaign to publicize them. In October 1924, Covarrubias showed him his Harlem drawings. Van Vechten showed them to Alfred and Mary Knopf.[11] In December, they appeared in *Vanity Fair*, with a text in popular dialect by Eric Walrond. They marked the first appearance of African Americans in the magazine.[12]

In 1925, Covarrubias contributed three drawings to *The New Negro*, the manifesto of the Harlem Renaissance, issued by Alain Locke, a Harvard Ph.D. in philosophy and the first African American Rhodes Scholar. In 1926, Covarrubias illustrated W. C. Handy's *The Blues: An Anthology*, published by Albert and Charles Boni. In this classical work, the blues composer, performer, and ethnomusicologist traced the history and provided the scores for compositions at a moment when the genre nourished mainstream popular song, dance, and classical music. Covarrubias' illustrations captured the rhythmic vigor, the contagious swing, the corporeal suppleness, and emotional power of the musicians, dancers, and singers. The same year, Covarrubias illustrated Langston Hughes' *Weary Blues* published by Knopf. Hughes' award-winning poem moved in uneven rhyme between his literary language and the vernacular verse of the old blues player he heard in Harlem. On the cover, Covarrubias drew the musician at his piano in the dark, his hands poised in midair to bear down on the keys, his face titled upward toward an old gas light.[13]

Covarrubias' *Negro Drawings* drew from these works. The book presented Harlem "types"—the fashionable couple, the dozing cab driver, the street dancer, the preacher, the somber worker; theater scenes of comedians, tap dancers, strutting dandies, and couples dancing the cake walk, the scrunch, the stump, and the double Charleston (Figure 1). The cabaret portraits featured an orchestra, the musicians and their horns, cymbals, and drums blending in one powerful rhythm (Figure 2). In *Rhapsody in Blue*, a female singer wrapped body, soul, and voice in plaintive song, seemingly unaware of the orchestra behind her and small audience around her (Figure 3).[14] The final section presented three Cuban women, drawn and painted during a recent trip Covarrubias and Rose had taken to the island. Many of these drawings exaggerated stereotypic features: huge lips and teeth, flattened nose, prominent buttocks, and, in dance, elongated hands, feet, arms, and legs to emphasize the body's elasticity. Covarrubias was a caricaturist. What he captured through exaggeration was dazzling rhythm and vitality worked through Cubist forms into unified compositions that Van Vechten said, let one "hear the music." Countee Cullen marveled at

Figure 1. *Double Charleston* by Miguel Covarrubias from Negro Drawings by Miguel Covarrubias, copyright 1927 by Alfred A. Knopf Inc. and renewed 1955 by Miguel Covarrubias. Used by permission of Alfred A. Knopf, a division of Random House Inc.

Figure 2. *Orchestra* by Miguel Covarrubias from Negro Drawings by Miguel Covarrubias, copyright 1927 by Alfred A. Knopf Inc. and renewed 1955 by Miguel Covarrubias. Used by permission of Alfred A. Knopf, a division of Random House Inc.

Figure 3. *Rhapsody in Blue* by Miguel Covarrubias from Negro Drawings by Miguel Covarrubias, copyright 1927 by Alfred A. Knopf Inc. and renewed 1955 by Miguel Covarrubias. Used by permission of Alfred A. Knopf, a division of Random House Inc.

his "special gift for capturing rhythm." Hughes told Covarrubias, "You are the only artist I know whose Negro things have a 'blues' touch."[15]

There was bound to be controversy. In the book's introduction, Frank Crowninshield lobbed the opening salvo. "How great is his understanding," he wrote, "How accurate his study of these Negro types. . . . the first important artist in America . . . to bestow upon our Negro anything like reverent attention—the sort of attention, let us say, which Gauguin bestowed upon the natives of the South Seas."[16] The debate hinged around interpretations of primitivism. W. E. B. Du Bois minced no words: "I could exist quite happily if Covarrubias had never been born."[17] For Du Bois, the leader of the African American civil rights movement, artists like Covarrubias and others associated with the Renaissance glorified atavistic elements that he associated with degeneracy, excess, and criminality. These nineteenth-century social Darwinist notions had plagued the African American struggle for rights. For Du Bois, political struggle required education, discipline, and refinement. While he published Renaissance writers in *Crisis*, the NAACP magazine, he asked if the movement was not a deviation from the political struggle just as it gathered momentum. Writer Benjamin Brawley, another Harvard graduate, agreed. For him the Renaissance artists perverted a rising black liberation movement with romanticism, a "disease that throws emphasis on sensational effects and abnormal states of mind," responding to a "popular demand for the exotic and exciting . . . with a perverted form of music originating in Negro slums and known as jazz." Moreover, the artists had abandoned canonical form.[18]

On the other side, Alain Locke lauded the artistic search for the primitive through their embrace of popular culture. A movement of spiritual emancipation, he called it—a deep engagement with Negro culture abandoned and despised by Negro elites who sought respectability on their white oppressors' terms. Locke used European modernism's cult of African art as a springboard for delving into the soul of the American Negro. He used the European affirmation in a way distinct from Piccaso's interest in African sculpture to solve technical problems. Locke's understanding was Bergsonian. Like many Mexican intellectuals and artists, he advocated the exploration of popular culture as a source of spontaneity, creativity, of primordial, natural expression. He advocated ethnography and its representation in art: the study of "folkways" in diverse languages—verbal, musical, corporeal, and visual.[19]

To a degree, the struggle within the African American movement was similar to conflicts between generations of Mexican artists and composers. In music, older Mexican composers, stuck in nineteenth-century European paradigms, opposed the new modernist aesthetics and its fascination with atonality, counterpoint, and the vernacular.[20] However, other concerns animated African American opposition to the celebration of Harlem's popular culture. Critics saw it as catering to white patrons interested in the exotic and primitive, not in African American equality.[21] Participant Langston Hughes later agreed.[22] At a moment in the 1920s when African Americans could not enter most hotels or restaurants, let alone the Algonquin Club where Van Vechten lunched, there was reason to question the white progressive intellectual. H. L. Mencken, leading critic and editor of *New Style,* asked in his review of Locke's *The New Negro* how far the black elite could go when "the vast majority of the people of their race are but two or three inches removed from gorillas."[23]

Yet, these white patrons gave visibility, stature, and respectability to contemporary African American artists as other U.S. patrons gave to Mexican muralists Diego Rivera and José Clemente Orozco. By the 1930s, as the African American struggle moved to the left and the locus of renaissance to Chicago, writer Richard Wright condemned the Harlem crowd as pandering, individualist, petty bourgeois lackeys. He committed himself to class struggle and the battle against racism. However, he carried the gifts of the Harlem Renaissance within him—a movement for democratic inclusion, an art that spoke the language of popular culture. So did African American plastic artists Aaron Douglas and Charles Aston as they painted the struggle against slavery and racism on public walls in the 1930s. They did so not with a private but a public patron. In its promotion of public and popular art, the U.S. government's Works Progress Administration modeled itself directly after the Mexican state program, and, not surprisingly, several African American artists found models in Diego Rivera and José Clemente Orozco.[24]

If Covarrubias suffered collateral damage from a struggle internal to the African American movement, he did not lose his commitment to a global antiracist initiative that had begun for him in Mexico and intensified in Harlem. He designed the scenery for the sensational *Revue Negre* that debuted at the Theatre des Champs Elysées in 1925 and made Josephine Baker the rage of Paris.[25] He illustrated the English translation of René Maran's novel, *Batouala* (1932). A black man from Martinique, Maran served in the colonial service in French Equatorial Africa. In his preface to the novel, he critiqued French colonial rule. He recounted how forced labor had reduced people to starvation, disease, and death. In 1921, *Batouala* won the Prix Goncourt, France's top literary prize. While many Frenchmen objected to his winning the prize for a "mediocre" novel that attacked the empire, the recognition stimulated investigation and denunciation of French colonial rule and swelled the movement for black civil rights within the French empire. African Americans from Locke to Du Bois took note. Du Bois became an active participant in the French-dominated Pan African movement.[26]

In 1937, Covarrubias illustrated Zora Neale Hurston's *Of Mules and Men*. This study of African American vernacular culture—of sermons, tales, games, songs, magic, and daily patter—drew from Hurston's field work in her native Eatonville, Florida, and New Orleans. Hurston's mentor at Columbia University, anthropologist Franz Boas, the "father" of cultural relativist challenges to social Darwinism, wrote the introduction. Covarrubias illustrated the lore: children in singing rhyme games, the adventures of 'Brer Gator, 'Brer Dog, and John Henry, men and women chewing the fat, an itinerant preacher assisted by two women, one banging the drums and the other raising her hands to God and singing, "You can't hide, sinners, you can't hide!"[27]

By the time he illustrated *Of Mules and Men*, Covarrubias himself had become a major ethnographer. He and Rose spent two years in Bali in the early 1930s immersed in what they saw as a communal culture integrated with nature, "primitive" in artifacts, in seminudity, and relatively open sexual relations, rich in an associational life and spectacular in its fine arts—dance, song, sculpture, theater, music, and opera.[28] *The Island of Bali*, published in 1937, included Miguel's drawings and paintings and Rose's photography. Miguel made a film to accompany it, and Knopf introduced it with such fanfare that it provoked a "Bali craze" in U.S. department stores.[29] No exotic travel account, the book was a serious ethnography based on academic sources and intense participant observation. As he grappled with the question of primitivism, Covarrubias showed a sophisticated understanding of historical change, of the relationship between space and power in an aggressive world, whether the aggression came from early or contemporary imperialisms or the modern marketplace. When he returned to Mexico in 1937, he dedicated himself to the archaeology, art history, and ethnography of Meso-America as a writer, painter, mapmaker, and promoter of the popular arts and modern dance. Knopf published his works for a U.S. audience. He wrote from a historical perspective typical of Mexican revolutionary intellectuals: the Spanish conquest had reduced the "high" ancient Meso-American cultures to miserable communities of chattel labor, and capitalism under the dictatorship of Porfirio Díaz had destroyed them further. However, like Alain Locke, who believed that slavery in the Americas had destroyed a refined African culture but created a rich array of everyday expressions, Covarrubias believed that living indigenous communities had cultivated the vernacular arts of craft- and costume-making, oratory, dance, music, and cuisine. His classic *Mexico South* illustrated his complex and sensitive understanding of the local-global interaction that created the conditions for particular artistic expressions.

CARLOS CHÁVEZ: NEW YORK, MEXICO, AND THE UNITED STATES

Carlos Chávez (Figure 4) arrived in New York in December 1923 after a brief stint in Europe. He stayed until March and returned in 1926 for two years. The skyscrapers, jazz clubs, orchestras, and avant-garde circles thrilled him. He arrived at a crucial moment in art music: Gershwin debuted his *Rhapsody in Blue*, and French expatriates Edgard Varèse, Dane Rudhyar, Ernest Bloch, and Carlos Salzedo launched the International Composers' Guild (1921) to patronize the birth of a new American music. The New World whirled

Figure 4. Carlos Chavez from Library of Congress, Prints & Photographs Division, Carl Van Vechten Collection [reproduction number, e.g., LC-USZ62-54231]

with sounds and rhythms that challenged European formalism and offered an antidote to the devastation of war: from the honking of taxicabs to Harlem tap dancers, from the whistles of great ships to the wailing of the blues, from the sleek vertical mass of the Metropolitan Life Tower to the teeming immigrant neighborhoods of the Lower East Side. Dissonance captured New World multiethnicity and energetic movement. "Dissonance is democracy," declared Dane Rudhyar.[30]

The International Composers' Guild provided a forum for Chávez. He composed a series of bold, dissonant, counterpunctual pieces: *Polígonos*, *Exágonos*, *36*, *Piano Sonata III*, and *Los Cuatro Soles*, an Aztec ballet. Abstract, even rigorously mathematical, his music was, to a degree, intended to be heard as Mexican—or more accurately as indigenous within the racialized stereotypes of the day. One of his biggest admirers, critic Paul Rosenfeld, heard his ballet and Sonata III as "undeluded [sic], bony and dry as his own high deserts and peppery as chilies . . . squat as Toltec divinities." He heard a "new American sound . . . a great creative talent, one of the few important composers this side of the Atlantic." "In place of the blazonry, sensuality and booze of the Russian music [Stravinsky]," he found in Chávez' compositions:

> . . . . an objective aristocratic remoteness . . . accommodation to a difficult nature. We have gained some new place. . . . It is no other than the shy certain heart of the Mexican American cosmos, the rocky, bare New World. . . . these exorable rhythms, pure severe contours, stony corners, crackling humors, rattlings, scrapings, arbitrary deceptions and withholdings, whipping dances of fire and ice, make us feel American.

He hailed it "an original classical music, a Pan American Renaissance! . . . . An integral New World based on the embryonic, wrecked with the Aztecs!"[31]

Leonora Saavedra argues that as imagined as this reading was, Chávez increasingly saw in modernist composition both the possibility of solving a technical and aesthetic crisis in Western music and integrating distinct sounds of the Mexican vernacular into a national music that would find its unique place in the cosmopolitan canon.[32] Such an integration of the vernacular took place around him as major composers from Gershwin to Milhaud to Copland worked with jazz. In New York, Chávez wrote about the popularity of African American music among modernists seeking to encounter the "primitive" and the possibilities that this quest opened for Mexican music.[33] He composed his own jazz-inspired *Cake Walk*, *Blues*, *Foxtrot*, and *Fox*. His exposure to vernacular-inspired composition deepened when he formed, with composers Henry Cowell, Charles Ruggles, and Emerson Whitmore, the Pan American Association of Composers. Successor to the International Composers' Guild, the Association presented experimental music from the Americas. Here Chávez met Cubans Amadeo Roldán, Alejandro Garcia Caturla, and Brazilian Heitor Villa-Lobos, all of whom embraced popular rhythms and instruments.[34]

Written and rewritten between 1926 and 1932, *Horse Power* (*HP*) became Chávez's signature piece. *HP* debuted in 1926 with the International Composers Guild. Chávez presented it again in 1928 at the ground-breaking Copland-Sessions Concerts, organized to introduce young U.S. composers. At the request of the Museum of Modern Art, he expanded the work.[35] In 1932, Leopoldo Stokowski, conductor of the Philadelphia Symphony Orchestra and an enthusiast of new Americanist music, presented *HP*, choreographed by Catherine Littlefield with scenery and costumes by Diego Rivera. In the Philadelphia performance, the languid, haunting strains of *La Sandunga* evoked the sensual tropics invaded by cold, mechanized U.S. commerce. Diego Rivera, Frida Kahlo, and Russian filmmaker Sergei Eisenstein had already iconized the dance and its performers, the Zapotec women of the Tehuantepec Isthmus, as the apex of primitive beauty (the *Sandunga* was in fact a nineteenth-century composition). In *HP*, Chávez used the *Sandunga* to primitivize a trope made famous by Uruguayan writer José Enrique Rodó in the aftermath of the U.S. seizure of Cuba and Puerto Rico in 1898. Rodó imagined the aggressive, industrial United States threatening the literary soul of Latin America. In place of Rodó's aristocratic spirituality, Chávez's popular, indigenous icon symbolized Latin American tropical sensuality. Diego Rivera designed great paper maché bananas, pineapples, and coconuts that danced across the stage. Chávez tread on dangerous ground as the trope affirmed Latin American exoticism and subordination to the more modern, enterprising United States. But Philadelphia critics read it both ways: one claimed it celebrated reciprocity, and another denounced it as anticapitalist subversion.[36]

Chávez' performances and associations in New York launched his career in Mexico. While visiting the United States regularly, he returned to Mexico to live in 1928. He had an ambitious agenda. In 1928, he formed the National Symphony Orchestra and became director of the National Conservatory of Music. He took charge of the Department of Fine Arts in the Ministry of Education from 1933 to 1934 and directed the new Institute of Fine Arts from 1947 to 1952. He came to control the production and performance of Mexican classical music.[37] He had been developing his agenda for some time, sweeping aside his opposition and his rivals (especially Julián Carrillo, who had introduced atonality to Mexico, and Manuel M. Ponce, who had incorporated vernacular melody into classical composition). Hoping to distance Mexican aesthetics from pre-revolutionary European sensibilities, he called for a modernist music inspired by the "very high degree of autochthonous culture" deriving from the grandeur of pre-Colombian societies."[38] His agenda resembled Alain Locke's for whom classical African art served as the source valorizing subsequent vernacular expression that had to be explored and articulated as art. Thus, like Covarrubias, Chávez turned to ethnography and history.[39]

Chávez trained young musicians José Pablo Moncayo, Blas Galindo, Daniel Ayala, and Salvador Contreras, who took their place beside the extraordinary Silvestre Revueltas, ethnomusicologist and composer Gerónimo Baqueiro Foster, and composer and choral arranger, Luis Sandi. By the 1930s, Chávez, like his friend, Aaron Copland, wanted to compose less abstract, more accessible work. Both composers sought a robust orchestral music that would capture popular motifs in modernist frames. Such music would explode with the energy, movement, and optimism of emerging New World mass societies. Both would stretch a huge canvas on which to etch the music of their nation's regions. Chávez' students traveled throughout Mexico to map the diversity of melodies, harmonies, rhythms, instruments, and their contextual uses. They expanded on ethnomusicological research begun in the early 1920s.[40] Within an evolutionist and a statist framework, this act of documenting carried dimensions of control, judgment and stylization. However, those engaged in it saw the possibility of giving voice to indigenous and mestizo communities in the making of an inclusive national culture.[41]

Ethnographers uncovered a rich musical complexity that broke the boundaries of an exclusive European-indigenous exchange. On the one hand, their findings complicated the stereotypized notion of a postconquest homogeneity of indigenous melancholy. On the other, they challenged the contention of postrevolutionary intellectuals that blackness was foreign to Mexico and a threat to its civilizing agenda. (Education Minister José Vasconcelos had claimed that Mexico was devoid of black blood that he condemned as "eager for sensuality, drunk of dances, and full of unbridled lust.")[42] In his research into the music of the Gulf Coast, Baqueiro Foster identified both colonial and contemporary contributions of African and Afro-Caribbean music to the Mexican repertoire.

Through fieldwork, composers integrated music across numerous divides of class, race, ethnicity, and place into a panoply of sounds they nationalized in compositions.[43] They did so within a Western framework. Despite his oft-expressed disdain for Europeanist notions, Chávez stuck to their stereotyped evolutionist understanding of the pentatonic scale as an essential marker of primitivism.[44] Exemplary of the juxtaposition between pentatonic and the Western twelve note system was his celebrated *Sinfonía India* (1935) in which he used contemporary instruments of the Yaqui, Seri, and Huichol peoples, made of deer hooves, butterfly cocoons, gourds, and clay rattles, to create a slow-gathering crescendo of percussive force.[45] Typically, Chávez did not build his compositions around whole vernacular melodies. An exception was his *Overtura Republicana* that included a revolutionary march, a Porfirian waltz, and a revolutionary corrido in a rousing celebration of a new nation coming of age.[46] Rather, Chávez, like Aaron Copland, used fragments of vernacular melody, rhythm, and instrumentation to create vast landscapes of mountains, deserts, and brush, animated by playful dances and deep drama, achieved through startling tonal clusters, palpitating counterpoint, and sweeping barrages of horns and commanding drums.

In the decade of the Depression, class conflict, and mass politics, artists and intellectuals in the United States turned to social questions that had for sometime concerned their Mexican counterparts.[47] Dozens became aesthetic ethnographers of poverty, class, and racial struggle, whether as photographers like Dorothea Lange and Tina Modotti, or novelists Richard Wright and John Steinbeck, or painters Pablo O'Higgins and Charles Alston, or choreographers Katherine Dunham and Anna Sokolow. In 1934, Charles Seeger, who would soon direct the WPA's Archive of the Folksong, wrote that an analysis of music through social conditions could balance the tensions between musical tradition and modernist aesthetics and overcome the fallacious bourgeois divisions among high culture, vernacular music, and proletarian music.[48]

Carlos Chávez, who composed his *Sinfonía Proletaria* in 1934, argued the new Mexican art music continued the Mexican Revolution's "liberating movement" that highlighted "the fight for the redemption of the oppressed classes and the fight against imperialist foreigners."[49]

But Chávez had no abiding interest in class struggle. He imagined a more just society where the proletariat and bourgeoisie functioned in harmony.[50] He did not seek a blurring between classical and vernacular music: he kept the distinction in the radio programming he oversaw as Director of Fine Arts in the Ministry of Public Education.[51] He was more concerned with the accessibility of music, classical and vernacular, to all sectors of society. He pursued the goal through vigorous touring with the national orchestra, his promotion of music over the radio, in film, dance, and recordings, and in his support for Luis Sandi's introduction of Mexican vernacular music and dance into the public school curriculum.[52]

He shared his commitment to the accessibility of art music with his friend Copland. Through Chávez, Copland turned in the 1930s from jazz to an interest in Latin America, particularly in Mexico and Cuba. At Chávez's invitation, he visited Mexico in 1932 for the first of many trips (1936, 1937, 1944, and 1962) and began to realize the larger differences between music in the Americas and Europe. He wrote:

> I'm left with the impression of having had an enriching experience. It comes, no doubt, from the nature of the country and the people. Europe now seems conventional to me by comparison. Mexico offers something fresh and pure and wholesome—a quality which is deeply unconventional-ized. The source of it I believe is the Indian blood which is so prevalent. I sensed the influence of the Indian background everywhere.[53]

Returning to Mexico in 1936, Copland completed his orchestral piece, *El Salón México*, named for a popular Mexico City dance hall. For the work, Copland drew from his obser-vations, his talks with Chávez and Anita Brenner, and his reading of Frances Toor's *Mexi-can Folkways,* a bilingual magazine that explored local culture, musical, literary, festive, etc. He wanted to translate "the spirit of the place," the vibrancy and fortitude of the Mexican people.[54] Chávez premiered *El Salón México* in Mexico City in 1937. Highlighting their friendship, Copland wrote of Chávez, "I know of no other fellow composer who has given me firmer support or more continuous encouragement in my work."[55]

El Salón México was Copland's first big hit in the United States. In his subsequent masterpieces of the U.S. west—the ballets *Billy the Kid* and *Rodeo*—he never lost sight of Mexico, and, unlike many Hollywood movies that likely inspired these ballets, his work did not denigrate Mexicans. *Billy the Kid* takes place on the border with Mexico and Copland was careful in introducing the outlaw as he was known to the Mexicans: "*Billy the Kid* con-cerns itself with significant moments in the life of this infamous character of the American Southwest," he wrote, "known to the Mexicans as 'El Chivato,' or simply, 'The Keed.'" Similarly, *Rodeo* in its title followed its original Spanish pronunciation.[56]

Copland was partially responsible for the prestige and visibility of Chávez in the United States where Mexican art music became nearly synonymous with Chávez. Chávez pre-sented his first symphony, *Antigona*, with the New York Stadium Symphony Orchestra in 1933 and *Sinfonia India* with the Boston, then the CBS Symphony Orchestra. In 1938, he replaced Arturo Toscanini as conductor of the NBC Symphony Orchestra for a period of time. In 1937, Norton published his *Toward a New Music: Music and Electricity*, a major work in modern musical thought. He guest conducted on many subsequent occasions, cut records with Columbia and Philips, and gave the Charles Eliot Norton lectures at Harvard in 1958.

PAN AMERICANISM: BROWN AND BLACK

In 1939, Carlos Chávez and Miguel Covarrubias approached Walt Disney to make a movie about the history of the Americas. Modernist music would illustrate the story of the Western Hemisphere from "the prehistoric to the historic world." They wanted to situate Mexico's pre-Conquest societies at the forefront so as to accentuate the primitivist understanding of native "subjects so full of the supernatural, of the fantastic, and of the absurd."[57] Walt Disney turned them down: *Fantasia*, then in production, already depicted the creation of the world through avant-garde music. Instead, Disney produced *Saludos Amigos* and *Los Tres Caballeros* to further inter-American understanding. These movies, particularly *Los Tres Caballeros*, have come to represent cultural Pan Americanism as a singular effort on the part of the U.S. government to mobilize Latin American support for the Allied cause in World War II and to further U.S. imperial designs on Latin America.[58]

This interpretation overlays an earlier phase of Pan Americanism with the full-blown U.S. Cold War policies that emerged in the mid-1950s. It overlooks critical dimensions of a movement that grew out of private initiative and exchange in the 1920s. In the 1930s, federal governments in the Americas supported the creation of national artistic repertoires that would be socially inclusive and multiracial.[59] Aaron Copland addressed the question of a national music in his Charles Eliot Norton lectures at Harvard in 1951:

> . . . in order to create an indigenous music of universal significance, three conditions are imperative. First, the composer must be part of a nation that has a profile of its own—that is the most important; second, the composer must have in his background some sense of musical culture and, if possible, a basis in folk or popular art; and third, a superstructure of organized musical activities must exist—that is, to some extent, at the service of the native composer.[60]

These conditions matured in the 1930s in various American countries, usually through state support. Cultural actors took a notion of primitivism adopted from European modernism and transformed it through ethnography and art into a cultural history of anticolonial struggle against oppression, exploitation, and racism. Indeed, this paradigm, however inchoate, contradictory, and evolutionist, became the script not only for artistic production but for historical research. Progressive artists and intellectuals, many allied with the Popular Front against Fascism, participated in the Pan American movement from 1938 through the early 1950s. In these remaining pages, we focus on Chávez and Covarrubias to uncover a portion of the progressive dialogue about blackness that took place among Mexican, North American, and Latin American actors in these years.

In 1940, the Mexican Department of Foreign Affairs and the New York Museum of Modern Art sponsored the monumental exhibit, *Twenty Centuries of Mexican Art.* It traced Mexico's history from pre-Colombian roots through European colonization to the contemporary period. Covarrubias curated the section on modern art, Chávez coordinated the music, and archaeologist Alfonso Caso organized the pre-Colombian material. In keeping with Covarrubias' long-standing conviction, the exhibit highlighted popular, "folk" art (Figure 5). Chávez formed an orchestra of local and Mexican musicians to perform a

Figure 5. Miguel and Rosa Covarrubias with Diego Rivera, Frida Kahlo, and friends. "Gathering at the Riveras' San Angel home," 1938/Unidentified photographer. Nickolas Muray Papers, Archives of American Art, Smithsonian Institution.

concert that would represent the historical scope and artistic breadth of Mexican music. To prepare, he had "directed expeditions to remote Indian villages . . . to find examples of musical material of the pre-Spanish and colonial periods." He had "superintended the reconstruction of archaeological flutes, drums, and wind instruments to provide as accurate an approximation as possible of music never heard before outside their original locales."[61] For the concert, he asked Baqueiro Foster to write an orchestral piece based on the *huapangos* of Veracruz. He well knew that Baqueiro Foster had overturned previous understandings of the huapango as an indigenous-Spanish melody to insist on its black elements introduced by African slaves.[62] Thus, through Baqueiro Foster's composition did blackness in Mexico—quite deliberately on the part of Chávez—enter the national self-representation in its most important international statement to date.[63]

Mexican ethnomusicologists' understanding of African-influenced music in Mexico and Latin America increased when Charles Seeger directed the Music Division of the Pan American Union from 1941 to 1953. Committed to furthering knowledge of Americanist music through research, publication, exchange, and performance, Seeger built on informal networks created in the 1920s and 1930s.[64] He saw the music of the Americas as a product of the "historical processes of acculturation among at least three great musical traditions—European, African, and American [indigenous]."[65] He sponsored the writing of national music histories, which, under the rubric of Pan Americanism, enriched understanding of transnational linkages. Mexican musicologists like Baqueiro Foster and Otto Mayer Serra began to link discussions of blackness in Mexican music with the findings of anthropologist Fernando Ortiz and writer and ethnomusicologist Alejo Carpentier for Cuba.[66]

Mexican composers and musicologists had shed their notion of black music as a foreign threat. In the 1940s, Cuban popular music poured out of the jukeboxes and dance halls of Mexico City and Veracruz and the capital embraced performers Celia Cruz, Pérez Prado, and others. In 1943, Mexicans enthusiastically welcomed contralto Marian Anderson to the city. Beloved in Europe, her fame leaped in 1939 when, barred by the Daughters of the American Revolution from singing in Constitution Hall, she sang from the steps of the Lincoln Memorial thanks to the intervention of First Lady Eleanor Roosevelt and NAACP Secretary Walter White. Thousands attended, and millions heard her over the radio. In 1947, Katherine Dunham arrived in Mexico City with her black dance troupe. Mexicans were so receptive she stayed for two months and returned in the early 1950s to televise performances.

Katherine Dunham brings our story full circle. She came out of the Chicago Renaissance, a vigorous movement of worker/race militancy and radical art. Comparing it with the Harlem Renaissance, poet Arna Bontemps said it lacked the "finger bowls" but had "increased power."[67] Dunham studied dance with the Russian ballerina Ludmila Speranzeva and choreographer Ruth Page: she got to know Spanish, Balinese, and Javanese dance. According to the artistic dictum of the day, she could not become a ballerina because the black body could not perform classical dance. A student at the University of Chicago, she found her opening when Robert Redfield, whose ethnography focused mainly on Mexico, introduced her to African anthropology and to Melville Herskovits, Northwestern University anthropologist of the African Diaspora, and author of a recent book on Haiti. With a Rosenwald Fellowship and Herskovits' letters of introduction, Dunham visited Jamaica, Martinique, and Trinidad and Tobago and settled in Haiti. It was 1935, shortly after the U.S. Marines ended their nineteen-year occupation. In Haiti, she immersed herself in native dance and religion.[68] She submitted her thesis, "Dances of Haiti, their Social Organization, Classification, Form and Function," and made a choice. Although later the founder of the field of dance anthropology, she left school to revolutionize U.S. modern dance through the incorporation of Afro-Caribbean movement and rhythm. Dance director of the WPA Negro Federal Theater Project in 1938, she soon found herself on Broadway and in Hollywood. Mexico was one of her first destinations in what became nonstop world touring in favor of art and civil rights. She did not forget Mexico. She incorporated Baqueiro Foster's *Huapangos*, renamed *Suite Veracruzana, No. 1* into her repertoire.[69]

Dance was perhaps the quintessential expression of modernism in both the United States and Mexico. In music, body movement, scenography, and costume, it broke free of nineteenth-century formal rigidities to express a new collective energy through its aestheticization of the vernacular and the natural. With dance, Carlos Chávez' and Miguel Covarrubias' collaborations had begun in New York and ended in Mexico City. As the head of the Institute of Fine Arts, Chávez in 1950 asked Covarrubias to direct the Department of Dance. For set design and costumes, they drew in major painters and composers, the older and the younger (Rufino Tamayo and Juan Soriano, José Pablo Moncayo and Carlos

Jiménez Mabarak). They called José Limón home from New York to teach and choreograph and engaged the young Guillermo Arriaga, who would later found the Folkloric Ballet of Mexico. Rose Roland, now Rosa Rolando, assisted and maverick painter Santos Balmori directed the Academy of Dance. Two and a half decades of ethnographic work, musical composition, and choreographic pioneering informed their productions. The themes were Mexican—*Zapata*, *La Manda*, and *Tonantzintla*. In two years, Covarrubias mounted 30 works. Never, wrote Elena Poniatowska, had Mexican dance been so spectacular.[70]

CONCLUSION AND EPILOGUE

Miguel Covarrubias died at the age of 54 in 1957. Carlos Chávez left public service in 1952 and briefly returned in the early 1970s. He continued to compose, conduct, write, and lecture in the United States. In 1973, he moved to New York. Shortly before he died in 1978, he conducted the National Symphony Orchestra in Washington, D.C. in the premiere of his *Concerto for Trombone and Orchestra*. These men belonged to a brilliant generation of artists and intellectuals, national and transnational actors in the creation of postcolonial identities north and south. With a maturing understanding of the rich potential of joining art to ethnography and reaching larger audiences, Chávez and Covarrubias, like so many of their cohort, gave voice and visibility to groups denigrated, despised, and excluded by nineteenth-century imperial conquest, racist ideology, and Victorian mores. Although their representations were necessarily interpretive within the cultural relations that shaped them and which they shaped, they were part of an ongoing conversation in the construction of nation, race, ethnicity, and class and the embrace of shared transnational identities in the Americas.

The progressive Americanism they created began to disintegrate in the early 1950s under the pressures of the Cold War. The U.S invasion of Guatemala in 1954 sparked strong anti-U.S. sentiment in Latin America, while the militant promotion of New York abstract painting in Latin America as a Cold War weapon against social art particularly grated in Mexico where social art achieved its greatest twentieth-century expression. By the mid-1950s, U.S. cultural policy in Latin America was virtually self-serving propaganda. Moreover, in the wake of the Second World War, New York reaffirmed the priority of its cultural relations with Europe and lost interest in the Americas just as Mexican artists and cultural policy makers, out of inclination and self-defense, renewed their interest in "la belle France." The rapprochement differed from relations before 1920: Mexicans and North Americans crossed the ocean with strong cultural repertoires of their own, jointly constructed in the interwar decades.

NOTES

1. See, among others, Alicia Azuela, *Arte y poder. Renacimiento artístico y revolución social, México 1910–1945* (Mexico City: Fondo de Cultura Económica, 2006); John Britton, *Revolution and Ideology: Images of the Mexican Revolution in the United States* (Lexington: University of Kentucky Press, 1995); Helen Delpar, *The Enormous Vogue of Things Mexican: Cultural Relations between the United States and Mexico 1920–1935* (Tuscaloosa: University of Alabama Press, 1995); Rick A. López, *Crafting Mexico: Intellectuals, Artisans, and the State after the Revolution* (Durham: Duke University Press, 2010); and James Oles, *South of the Border: Mexico in the American Imagination, 1914–1947* (Washington, D. C.: Smithsonian Institution Press, 1993).

2. Covarrubias to Carlos Chávez, February (n.d.), July 20,1924, Exp. 119 (Miguel Covarrubias), Vol. V, Caja Correspondencia 3, Sección Orquesta Sinfónica de México, Archivo General de la Nación-Fondo Carlos Chávez (hereinafter AGN-FCC).

3. Covarrubias to Carlos Chávez, July 20, 1927, Exp. 119 (Miguel Covarrubias), Vol. V, Caja Correspondencia 3, Sección Orquesta Sinfónica de México, AGN-FCC.

4. Adriana Williams, *Miguel Covarrubias* (Mexico: Fondo de Cultura Económica, 1999), 38–39. See also Esther Hernández Palacios, "José Juan Tablada en la Babilonia de hierro," in *De Coyoacán a la Quinta Avenida, José Juan Tablada, Una antología general*, ed. Rodolfo Mata, Esther Hernández Palacios, and Serge I. Zaitzeff (Mexico City: Fondo de Cultura Económica Fundación para las Letras Mexicanas, Universidad Nacional Autónoma de México, 2007), 457–82.

5. Rick A. López, "The Noche Mexicana and the Exhibit of Popular Arts: Two Ways of Exalting Indianness," in *The Eagle and the Virgin: Nation and Cultural Revolution in Mexico, 1920–1940*, ed. Mary Kay Vaughan and Steve Lewis (Durham, N. C.: Duke University Press, 2006), 32–42.

6. Elena Poniatowska, "Raoul Fournier, Carlos Solórzano, y Justino Fernández hablan de Miguel Covarrubias," *Novedades*, May 9, 1957, republished in *Miguel Covarrubias, vida y mundos*, by Elena Poniatowska (Mexico City: Era, 2004), 24–5, 123–5.

7. On Chávez in these years, see Alejandro Madrid, "Modernismo, futurismo, y kenosis canciones de Atropo Según Julian Carrillo y Carlos Chávez," *Heterofonía*, 33, no. 123 (2000): 89–100; and Marco Velázquez and Mary Kay Vaughan, "Mestizaje and Musical Nationalism in Mexico," in *The Eagle and the Virgin*, 95–118.

8. See Covarrubias caricatures at http://wn.com/Miguel_Covarrubias, particularly bands 1, 2.

9. Carl Van Vechten, *The Splendid Drunken Twenties: Selections from the Daybooks, 1922–1930*, ed. Bruce Kellner (Urbana: University of Illinois Press, 2003), 60–1; and Poniatowska, *Miguel Covarrubias*, 71–75; Williams, *Miguel Covarrubias*, 71.

10. Van Vechten, *Splendid*, 58–61.

11. Ibid, 57.

12. Williams, *Miguel Covarrubias*, 72.

13. See cover illustration at http://wn.com/Miguel Covarrubias, band 2.

14. Drawings of the orchestra, the drummer, the worker, the comedian, and the strut, as well as drawings of other dancers not published in *Negro Drawings*, can be viewed at http://wn.com/Miguel_Covarrubias, bands 1, 2, 4, 8, 9.

15. Van Vechten, *Keep A-Inchin' Along*, 52; Countee Cullen, "The Dark Towner," *Opportunity* 6, no. 2 (1928): 52; and Hughes as cited by Williams, *Miguel Covarrubias*, 74–75.

16. Frank Crowninshield, "Introduction," in *Negro Drawings*, by Miguel Covarrubias (New York: Knopf, 1927).

17. Du Bois, *Crisis*, April 1930, p. 129 cited in Williams, *Miguel Covarrubias*, 96–97.

18. Benjamin Brawley, "The Negro Literary Renaissance," in *The New Negro: Readings on Race, Representation, and African American Culture, 1892–1938*, ed. Henry Louise Gates, Jr., and Gene Andrew Jarrett (Princeton: Princeton University Press, 2007), 233–4.

19. Alain Locke, "The New Negro," "Note on African Art," "The American Negro as Artist," and "Negro Youth Speaks," in *The New Negro: Readings on Race*, 112, 118, 536–41, 542–6, 220–3. On new vernacular languages in African American art and literature, see also "Sterling Brown: The New Negro Folk-Poet," in *The New Negro: Readings on Race*, 119–22.

20. See Alejandro L. Madrid, *Sounds of the Modern Nation: Music, Culture, and Ideas in Post-Revolutionary Mexico* (Philadelphia: Temple, 2009), 111–37.

21. Henry Louise Gates, Jr., and Gene Andrew Jarrett, "Introduction," in *The New Negro: Readings on Race,* 14–17; and Claude McKay, "The New Negro in Paris," W. E. B. Du Bois, "Criteria of Negro Art," in *The New Negro: Readings on Race,* 146–8, 257–9.

22. He was particularly critical of Charlotte Mason, Hurston's patron. Langston Hughes, *The Big Sea* (New York: Hill and Wang, 1993), 315–7.

23. H. L. Mencken, "The Aframerican: New Style," in *The New Negro: Readings on Race,* 227.

24. Romare Bearden, "The Negro Artist and Modern Art," in *The New Negro: Readings on Race,* 554; David Driskell, "The Flowering of the Harlem Renaissance: The Art of Aaron Douglas, Meta Warrick Fuller, Palmer Hayden, and William Johnson," in *Harlem Renaissance: Art of Black America,* Introduction by Mary Schmidt B. Campbell, with essays by David Driskell, David Levering Lewis, and Deborah Willis Ryan (New York: The Studio Museum in Harlem and Harry N. Abrams Publishers, 1987), 111–2, 129–30, 153–4; and Deborah Cullen, "The Allure of Harlem: Correlations between *Mexicanidad* and the New Negro Movements," in *Nexus New York: Latin/American Artists in the Modern Metropolis,* ed. Deborah Cullen (New Haven: Yale University Press, 2009), 139.

25. Bryan Hammond and Patrick O'Connor, *Josephine Baker* (London: Jonathan Cope, 1988), 14–15.

26. Alice J. Smith, "René Maran's Batouala and the Prix Goncourt," *Contributions to Black Studies, A Journal of African and Afro American Studies* 4, no. 1 (2008): 18–34.

27. See illustrations at http://xroads.virginia.edu/~ma01/grand-jean/hurston/chapters/artist.html. Covarrubias illustrated other books about African Americans including Taylor Gordon's *Born to Be* (New York: Covici Friede, 1929) and Harriet Beecher Stowe, *Uncle Tom's Cabin* (New York: The Limited Editions Club, 1938).

28. Miguel Covarrubias, *The Island of Bali* (New York: A. Knopf, 1956, first published 1937), 27–28, 166, 195–6, 401–2.

29. Clips of the film and Bali paintings can be viewed at http://wn.com/Miguel_Covarrubias. On the Bali craze, see Williams, *Covarrubias,* 133–8.

30. Carol J. Oja, *Making Music Modern: New York in the 1920s* (Oxford: Oxford University Press, 2000), 101–5.

31. Paul Rosenfeld, *By Way of Art: Criticisms of Music, Literature, Painting, Sculpture, and the Dance* (New York: Coward McCann, 1928), 273–83.

32. Leonora Saavedra, "Of Selves and Others: Historiography, Ideology, and the Politics of Modern Mexican Music" (PhD diss., University of Pittsburgh, 2001), 314.

33. Carlos Chávez, "El arte popular y el no popular," July 7, 1929, Exp. 5 (Artículos Periodísticos, 1924–1934), Vol. 1, Caja 1, Sección Escritos, AGN-FCC.

34. On the Pan American Association, see Deane L. Root, "The Pan American Association of Composers (1928–1934)," *Anuario Interamericano de Investigación Musical,* 8 (1972): 49–70; and Stephanie N. Stallings, "Collective Difference: The Pan American Association of Composers and Pan American Ideology in Music, 1924–1945," (PhD diss., Florida State University, 2009).

35. Robert Parker, *Trece panoramas en torno a Carlos Chávez* (Mexico City: Conaculta, 2009), 50.

36. Herminio Portell Vita, "El estrena de 'H.P.' en Filadelfia," *Social* (June 1932), Exp. 2 (HP, 1926–1932), Vol. 1, Caja 2, Sección Escritos, AGN-FCC; Christina Taylor Gibson, "The Music of Manuel M. Ponce, Julián Carrillo, and Carlos Chávez" (PhD diss., University of Maryland, College Park, 2008), 201.

37. Alberto Rodríguez, "Nacionalismo y folklore en la Escuela Nacional de Música," in *Preludio y fuga: historias trashumantes de la Escuela Nacional de Música de la UNAM*, ed. María Esther Aguirre Lora (Mexico City: Universidad Nacional Autónoma de México, 2008), 375–418; and Ricardo Pérez Monfort, "Carlos Chávez en los años cuarenta: caudillo o cacique Cultural," in *Diálogo de resplandores: Carlos Chávez y Silvestre Revueltas*, ed. Yael Bitrán and Ricardo Miranda (Mexico City: Instituto Nacional de Bellas Artes, 2002), 174–81.

38. Carlos Chávez, "La importación en México" and "Sexto editorial de música," Exp. 5 (Artículos Periodísticos, 1924–1934), Vol. 1, Sección Escritos, AGN-FCC.

39. Exp. 9 (Nacionalismo en Latinoamérica), Vol. 1, Caja 1, Sección Escritos, AGN-FCC.

40. Pedro Michaca F. Domínguez, "Nuevas orientaciones sobre el folk-lore Mexicano. Tesis presentada en el Primer Congreso Nacional de Música en México, el Día 5 de Septiembre de 1926," Caja 1527—Congreso Nacional de Música (1o: 1926: México), Archivo Baqueiro Foster, Centro Nacional de Investigación, Documentación e Información Musical "Carlos Chávez" (hereafter CENIDIM-ABF); and Jesús C. Romero, *La historia crítica de la música en México* (Mexico: Taller Liñotipgrafico, 1927), Caja 1527—Congreso Nacional de Música (1o: 1926: México), CENIDIM-ABF.

41. See, for instance, Carlos Chávez, "La música y la raza," *El Nacional*, 1937, Exp. 20 (Sinfonía India, 1937–1946), Vol. 1, Caja 2, Sección Escritos, AGN-FCC.

42. José Vasconcelos, *La raza cósmica* (Mexico City: Colección Austral, 2002), 10, 31, 37, 148; and Rubén M. Campos, *El folklore y la música mexicana. una investigación acerca de la cultura musical en México (1525–1925)* (Mexico City: Publicaciones de la Secretaría de Educación Pública, 1928).

43. Velasquez and Vaughan, "Musical Nationalism," 95–118.

44. Carlos Chávez, "Entr'acte. Revolt in Mexico," *Modern Music* (April 1936), Exp. 1 (1935–Programas Actuaciones Boston, Ma.), Vol. 1, Caja 1, Sección Prensa Personal, AGN-FCC; and Saavedra, "Of Selves and Others," 234–7. For a discussion of the failure to remake Mexico's compositional system, see Alejandro L. Madrid, *Sounds of the Modern Nation*, 111–37.

45. The symphony can be heard at http://www.youtube.com/watch?v=w2AuobzcCTY.

46. The piece can be heard at http://www.youtube.com/watch?v=CYGMgEn3pRA.

47. For music, see Leonora Saavedra, "The American Composer in the 1930s: The Social Thought of Seeger and Chávez," in *Understanding Charles Seeger, Pioneer in American Musicology*, ed. Bell Yung and Helen Rees (Urbana: University of Illinois Press, 1999), 31; and Brunco Nettl, "The Dual Nature of Ethnomusicology in North America: The Contributions of Charles Seeger and George Herzog," in *Comparative Musicology and Anthropology of Music: Essays on the History of Ethnomusicology*, ed. Bruno Nettl and Philip V. Bohlman (Chicago: University of Chicago Press, 1991), 266–70.

48. Charles Seeger, "On Proletarian Music," *Modern Music*, 11 (March 1934): 122–4, qtd. 122; Saavedra, "The American Composer," 34–41; and Ann M. Pescatello, *Charles Seeger: A Life in American Music* (Pittsburgh: University of Pittsburgh, 1992), 136–72.

49. Exp. 6 (La Tesis Nacionalista de Ponce), Vol. 1, Caja 1, Sección Escritos, AGN-FCC.

50. Carlos Chávez, "El Arte Occidental," September 23, 1934, Exp. 69 (Arte Proletario), Vol. 5, Caja 5, Sección Escritos, AGN-FCC.

51. Joy Elizabeth Hayes, "National Imaginings on the Air: Radio in Mexico, 1920–1950," in *The Eagle and the Virgin*, 243–58.

52. While Director of Fine Arts in the Ministry of Education, Chávez secured the contract for Fred Zinneman, director, and Paul Strand, photographer, to make the profoundly aesthetic proletarian film, *Redes*, for which Silvestre Revueltas composed the score. See James Krippner-Martínez, "Traces,

Images, and Fictions: Paul Strand in Mexico, 1932–1934," *The Americas*, 63, no. 3 (2007): 359–83; and James Krippner et. al., *Paul Strand in Mexico* (New York: Fundación Televisa, 2010), 69–99.

53. Copland to Mary Lescaze, January 13, 1933, in *The Selected Correspondence of Aaron Copland*, ed. Elizabeth B. Crist and Wayne Shirley (New Haven: Yale University Press, 2006), 101.

54. Copland "The Story behind my *El Salón México*," *Tempo* 4 (July 1939): 2–3, qtd. 3; Gail Levin, "From the New York Avant-Garde to Mexican Modernists: Aaron Copland and the Visual Arts," in *Aaron Copland and his World*, ed. Carol J. Oja and Judith Tick (Princeton: Princeton University Press, 2005), 108.

55. Copland letter to Carlos Chávez (undated), Exp. 113 (Aaron Copland II 1937–1939), Vol. 5, Caja 3, Sección Correspondencia, AGN-FCC.

56. Copland quoted by Michael Steinberg in Aaron Copland the Populist, 1900–1990, Michael Tilson Thomas, San Francisco Symphony Orchestra, BMG Classics, 1999, 6, 8. Rodeo in Spanish is pronounced ro-day-o with an accent on each syllable; its U.S. pronunciation is ro-dy-o.

57. Carlos Chávez to Walt Disney, October 19, 1939, Exp. 42 (Walt Disney), Vol. 2, Caja 4, Sección Correspondencia, AGN-FCC; Parker, *Trece panoramas*, 79–81.

58. Amy Spellacy, "Mapping the Metaphor of the Good Neighbor: Geography, Globalism and Pan-americanism during the 1940s," *American Studies* 47, no. 2 (2006): 39–66; Julianne Burton-Carvajal, "Surprise Package: Looking Southward with Disney," in *Disney Discourse: Producing the Magic Kingdom*, ed. Eric Smoodin (New York: Routledge, 1994), 131–47; and Seth Fein, "Myths of Cultural Imperialism and Nationalism in Golden Age Mexican Cinema," in *Fragments of a Golden Age: The Politics of Culture in Mexico since 1940*, ed. Gilbert Joséph, Anne Rubenstein, and Eric Zolov (Durham: Duke University Press, 2001), 159–98.

59. For Brazil, see Daryle Williams, *Culture Wars in Brazil: The First Vargas Regime, 1930–1945* (Durham: Duke University Press, 2001).

60. Copland, *Music and Imagination* (Cambridge: Harvard University Press, 1952), 79.

61. "Museum of Modern Art Commissions Chávez to Arrange and Conduct Special Program of Mexican Music," May 1, 1940, Museum of Modern Art, Press Release Archives I (hereafter MoMA-PRA). See also "Series Arranged of Mexican Music," *New York Times*, May 1, 1940.

62. Gerónimo Baqueiro Foster, "El huapango," *Revista Musical Mexicana* 8, (April 21, 1942): 176–7, Exp. 99 (Gerónimo Baqueiro Foster), Vol. 4, Caja 1, Sección Correspondencia, AGN-FCC; and Baqueiro Foster y Saenz de Micra, "Notas acerca del folklore de los Estados de la República," Caja 2269 B1106, CENIDIM-ABF. See also Rolando Antonio Pérez Fernández, *La música afromestiza mexicana* (Jalapa: Universidad Veracruzana, 1990), 213.

63. Baqueiro Foster, "El huapango," *Revista Musical Mexicana*; and *Mexican Music: Notes by Herbert Weinstock for Concerts Arranged by Carlos Chávez* (New York: The Museum of Modern Art, May 1940), 19–21.

64. Charles Seeger, "Brief History of the Music Division of the Pan American Union," June 9, 1947, File Copy, February 5, 1951, Archives JX 1980.53.M75.B63, Organization of American States, Columbus Memorial Library (hereafter OAS-CML); Charles Seeger, "Review of Inter-American Relations in the Field of Music, 1940–1943," 1–8, 12, qtd. 4, Archives JX 1980.53.M75.S22, OAS-CML.

65. Seeger, "Forward to Original Edition," in *El estado presente de la música en México/The Present State of Music in Mexico,* by Otto Mayer-Serra, reprint of 3rd edition (Washington, D. C.: Pan American Union, 1960), xii, Archives JX 1980.58.M931,OAS-CML; and Seeger, "Review of Inter-American Relations," 8.

66. Baqueiro Foster, "La música en Cuba," *Diario del Sureste*, September 8, 1946, Cuaderno No. 4-G Baqueiro Foster Artículos, January 1, 1941, January 1950, RF-MF 17774, Archivo Gerónimo Baqueiro Foster, Fondos Especiales, Biblioteca de las Artes, Centro Nacional de las Artes; and Otto Mayer Serra, *Músico y músicos de Lationamérica A–J* (Mexico City: Editorial Atlante, 1947), 91, 254, 265; *K–Z* (Mexico City: Editorial Atlante, 1947), 865.

67. As cited by Joyce Aschenbrenner, *Katherine Dunham: Dancing a Life* (Urbana: University of Illinois, 2002), 19.

68. Katherine Dunham, *Island Possessed* (Chicago: University of Chicago, 1969).

69. Juan Vicente Melo, 'Una entrevista con Baqueiro Foster sobre los sones de Veracruz' por Juan Vicente Melo, Caja 0249 B0622, CENIDIM-ABF. On Dunham's life, see Aschenbrenner, *Katherine Dunham*.

70. Poniatowska, *Miguel Covarrubias*, 13–14.

BIBLIOGRAPHY

Aschenbrenner, Joyce. *Katherine Dunham: Dancing a Life*. Urbana: University of Illinois Press, 2002.

Archivo Gerónimo Baqueiro Foster, Centro Nacional de Investigación Musical Documentación and Información, "Carlos Chávez." Mexico City, Mexico.

Archivo Gerónimo Baqueiro Foster, Fondos Especiales, Biblioteca de las Artes, Centro Nacional de las Artes, Mexico City, Mexico.

Azuela, Alicia. *Arte y poder: Renacimiento artístico y revolución social, México 1910–1945* [Art and Power: Artistic Renaissance and Social Revolution, Mexico 1910–1945]. Mexico City: Fondo de Cultura Económica, 2006.

Bearden, Romare. "The Negro Artist and Modern Art." In *The New Negro: Readings on Race, Representation, and African American Culture, 1892–1938*, ed. Henry Louis Gates, Jr. and Gene Andrew Jarrett, pp. 554–7. Princeton, N.J.: Princeton University Press, 2007.

Beecher Stowe, Harriet. *Uncle Tom's Cabin*. New York: The Limited Editions Club, 1938.

Brawley, Benjamin. "The Negro Literary Renaissance." In *The New Negro: Readings on Race, Representation, and African American Culture, 1892–1938*, ed. Henry Louis Gates, Jr. and Gene Andrew Jarrett, pp. 233–7. Princeton, N.J.: Princeton University Press, 2007.

Britton, John. *Revolution and Ideology: Images of the Mexican Revolution in the United States*. Lexington: University of Kentucky Press, 1995.

Burton-Carvajal, Julianne. "Surprise Package: Looking Southward with Disney." In *Disney Discourse: Producing the Magic Kingdom*, ed. Eric Smoodin, pp. 131–47. New York: Routledge, 1994.

Campos, Rubén M. *El folklore y la música mexicana: una investigación acerca de la cultura musical en México (1525–1925)* [Folklore and Mexican Music: An Investigation about Musical Culture in Mexico (1525–1925)]. Mexico City: Publicaciones de la Secretaría de Educación Pública, 1928.

Chávez, Carlos. *Obertura republicana (OFUNAM)*. http://www.youtube.com/watch?v=CYGMgEn3pRA (accessed September 15, 2010).

Chávez, Carlos. *Sinfonia India. Part 1*. http://www.youtube.com/watch?v=w2AuobzcCTY (accessed September 15, 2010).

Columbus Memorial Library, Organization of American States, Washington, D.C.

Copland, Aaron. "Aaron Copland to Mary Lescaze, January 13, 1933." In *The Selected Correspondence of Aaron Copland*, ed. Elizabeth B. Crist and Wayne Shirley, p. 101. New Haven, Conn.: Yale University Press, 2006.

———. *Copland the Populist*. San Francisco Symphony Orchestra. Michael Tilson Thomas. CD, 6 and 8. BMG Classics, 1999.

———. *Music and Imagination*. Cambridge, Mass.: Harvard University Press, 1952.

———. "The Story behind My *El Salón* México." *Tempo*, 4 (July 1939): 2–4.

Covarrubias, Miguel. *The Island of Bali.* Originally published in 1937. New York: A. Knopf, 1956.

Crowninshield, Frank. "Introduction." In *Negro Drawings*, by Miguel Covarrubias. New York: Knopf, 1927.

Cullen, Countee. "The Dark Towner." *Opportunity*, 6, no. 2 (1928): 52–3.

Cullen, Deborah, "The Allure of Harlem: Correlations between *Mexicanidad* and the New Negro Movements." In *Nexus New York: Latin/American Artists in the Modern Metropolis*, ed. Deborah Cullen, 126–49. New Haven, Conn.: Yale University Press, 2009.

Delpar, Helen. *The Enormous Vogue of Things Mexican: Cultural Relations between the United States and Mexico 1920–1935.* Tuscaloosa: University of Alabama Press, 1995.

Driskell, David. "The Flowering of the Harlem Renaissance: The Art of Aaron Douglas, Meta Warrick Fuller, Palmer Hayden, and William Johnson." In *Harlem Renaissance: Art of Black America*, pp. 105–54. New York: The Studio Museum in Harlem and Harry N. Abrams Publishers, 1987.

Du Bois, W. E. B. "Criteria of Negro Art." In *The New Negro: Readings on Race, Representation, and African American Culture, 1892–1938*, ed. Henry Louis Gates, Jr. and Gene Andrew Jarrett, pp. 257–60. Princeton, N.J.: Princeton University Press, 2007.

Dunham, Katherine. *Island Possessed.* Chicago: University of Chicago Press, 1969.

Fein, Seth. "Myths of Cultural Imperialism and Nationalism in Golden Age Mexican Cinema." In *Fragments of a Golden Age: The Politics of Culture in Mexico since 1940*, ed. Gilbert Joseph, Anne Rubenstein, and Eric Zolov, pp. 159–98. Durham, N.C.: Duke University Press, 2001.

Fondo Carlos Chávez, Archivo General de la Nación, Mexico City, Mexico.

Gates, Jr., Henry Louis, and Gene Andrew Jarrett. "Introduction." In *The New Negro: Readings on Race, Representation, and African American Culture, 1892–1938*, ed. by Henry Louis Gates, Jr. and Gene Andrew Jarrett, pp. 1–20. Princeton: Princeton University Press, 2007.

Gibson, Christina Taylor. "The Music of Manuel M. Ponce, Julián Carrillo, and Carlos Chávez." PhD diss., University of Maryland College Park, 2008.

Gordon, Taylor. *Born to Be.* New York: Covici Friede, 1929.

Hammond, Bryan, and Patrick O'Connor. *Josephine Baker.* London: Jonathan Cope, 1988.

Hayes, Joy Elizabeth. "National Imaginings on the Air: Radio in Mexico, 1920–1950." In *The Eagle and the Virgin: Nation and Cultural Revolution in Mexico, 1920–1940*, ed. Mary Kay Vaughan and Steve Lewis, pp. 243–58. Durham, N.C.: Duke University Press, 2006.

Hernández Palacios, Esther. "José Juan Tablada en la Babilonia de hierro [José Juan Tablada in the Iron Babylon]." In *De Coyoacán a la Quinta Avenida, José Juan Tablada, Una antología general* [From Coyoacan to Fifth Avenue, José Juan Tablada, A General Anthology], ed. Rodolfo Mata, Esther Hernández Palacios, and Serge I. Zaitzeff, pp. 457–82. Mexico City: Fondo de Cultura Económica Fundación para las Letras Mexicanas, Universidad Nacional Autónoma de México, 2007.

Hughes, Langston. *The Big Sea.* New York: Hill and Wang, 1993.

Krippner, James, and Alfonso Morales, *Paul Strand in Mexico.* New York: Fundación Televisa, 2010.

Krippner-Martínez, James. "Traces, Images, and Fictions: Paul Strand in Mexico, 1932–1934." *The Americas*, 63, no. 3 (2007): 359–83.

Levin, Gail. "From the New York Avant-Garde to Mexican Modernists: Aaron Copland and the Visual Arts." In *Aaron Copland and his World*, ed. Carol J. Oja and Judith Tick, pp. 108–20. Princeton, N.J.: Princeton University Press, 2005.

Locke, Alain. "The American Negro as Artist." In *The New Negro: Readings on Race, Representation, and African American Culture, 1892–1938*, ed. Henry Louis Gates, Jr. and Gene Andrew Jarrett, pp. 541–6. Princeton, N.J.: Princeton University Press, 2007.

———. "Negro Youth Speaks." In *The New Negro: Readings on Race, Representation, and African American Culture, 1892–1938*, ed. Henry Louis Gates, Jr. and Gene Andrew Jarrett, pp. 220–3. Princeton, N.J.: Princeton University Press, 2007.

———. "The New Negro." In *The New Negro: Readings on Race, Representation, and African American Culture, 1892–1938*, ed. Henry Louis Gates, Jr. and Gene Andrew Jarrett, pp. 112–8. Princeton, N.J.: Princeton University Press, 2007.

————. "Note on African Art." In *The New Negro: Readings on Race, Representation, and African American Culture, 1892–1938*, ed. Henry Louis Gates, Jr. and Gene Andrew Jarrett, pp. 537–41. Princeton, N.J.: Princeton University Press, 2007.

————. "Sterling Brown: The New Negro Folk-Poet." In *The New Negro: Readings on Race, Representation, and African American Culture, 1892–1938*, ed. Henry Louis Gates, Jr. and Gene Andrew Jarrett, pp. 119–22. Princeton, N.J.: Princeton University Press, 2007.

López, Rick A. *Crafting Mexico: Intellectuals, Artisans, and the State after the Revolution.* Durham, N.C.: Duke University Press, 2010.

————. "The Noche Mexicana and the Exhibit of Popular Arts: Two Ways of Exalting Indianness." In *The Eagle and the Virgin: Nation and Cultural Revolution in Mexico, 1920–1940*, ed. Mary Kay Vaughan and Steve Lewis, pp. 23–42. Durham, N.C.: Duke University Press, 2006.

Madrid, Alejandro L. "Modernismo, futurismo y kenosis, canciones de Atropo Según Julián Carrillo y Carlos Chávez [Modernism, Futurism and Kenosis, Songs Atropo According to Julián Carrillo and Carlos Chávez]." *Heterofonia*, 33, no. 123 (2000): 89–110.

————. *Sounds of the Modern Nation: Music, Culture, and Ideas in Post-Revolutionary Mexico.* Philadelphia, Pa.: Temple University Press, 2009.

Mayer Serra, Otto. *Músico y músicos de Lationamérica* [Music and Musicians of Latin America], Vols. I and II. México, D.F.: Editorial Atlante, 1947.

McKay, Claude. "The New Negro in Paris." In *The New Negro: Readings on Race, Representation, and African American Culture, 1892–1938*, ed. Henry Louis Gates, Jr. and Gene Andrew Jarrett, pp. 141–8. Princeton, N.J.: Princeton University Press, 2007.

Mencken, H. L. "The Aframerican: New Style." In *The New Negro: Readings on Race, Representation, and African American Culture, 1892–1938*, ed. Henry Louis Gates, Jr. and Gene Andrew Jarrett, pp. 227–8. Princeton, N.J.: Princeton University Press, 2007.

Mexican Music: Notes by Herbert Weinstock for Concerts Arranged by Carlos Chávez. New York: The Museum of Modern Art, May, 1940.

"Miguel Covarrubias." *Mules and Men: An E-Text Edition.* http://xroads.virginia.edu/~ma01/grandjean/hurston/chapters/artist.html (accessed September 15, 2010).

Nettl, Bruno. "The Dual Nature of Ethnomusicology in North America: The Contributions of Charles Seeger and George Herzog." In *Comparative Musicology and Anthropology of Music: Essays on the History of Ethnomusicology*, ed. Bruno Nettl and Philip V. Bohlman, pp. 266–74. Chicago: University of Chicago Press, 1991.

Oja, Carol J. *Making Music Modern: New York in the 1920s.* Oxford, UK: Oxford University Press, 2000.

Oles, James. *South of the Border: Mexico in the American Imagination, 1914–1947.* Washington D.C.: Smithsonian Institution Press, 1993.

Parker, Robert. *Trece panoramas en torno a Carlos Chávez* [Thirteen Panoramas around Carlos Chávez]. México, D.F.: Conaculta, 2009.

Pérez Fernández, Rolando Antonio. *La música afromestiza mexicana* [Afromestiza Mexican Music]. Jalapa, Mexico: Universidad Veracruzana, 1990.

Pérez Monfort, Ricardo. "Carlos Chávez en los años cuarenta: caudillo o cacique cultural [Carlos Chávez in the Forties: Cultural Warlord or Chief]." In *Diálogo de Resplandores: Carlos Chávez y Silvestre Revueltas* [Dialogue of Splendors: Carlos Chávez and Silvestre Revueltas], ed. Yael Bitrán and Ricardo Miranda, pp. 174–81. México, D.F.: Instituto Nacional de Bellas Artes, 2002.

Pescatello, Ann M. *Charles Seeger: A Life in American Music.* Pittsburgh, Pa.: University of Pittsburgh, 1992.

Press Release Archives. Museum of Modern Art, New York, N.Y.

Poniatowska, Elena. *Miguel Covarrubias, vida y mundos.* México, D.F.: Era, 2004.

Rodríguez, Alberto. "Nacionalismo y folklore en la escuela nacional de música [Nationalism and Folklore at the National School of Music]." In *Preludio y fuga: historias trashumantes de la Escuela Nacional de Música de la UNAM* [Prelude and Fugue: Migrating Stories of the National School of Music of the UNAM], ed. María Esther Aguirre Lora, pp. 375–418. México: Universidad Nacional Autónoma de México, 2008.

Root, Deane L. "The Pan American Association of Composers (1928–1934)." *Anuario Interamericano de Investigación Musical,* 8 (1972): 49–70.

Rosenfeld, Paul. *By Way of Art: Criticisms of Music, Literature, Painting, Sculpture, and the Dance.* New York: Coward McCann, 1928.

Saavedra, Leonora. "The American Composer in the 1930s: The Social Thought of Seeger and Chávez." In *Understanding Charles Seeger, Pioneer in American Musicology,* ed. Bell Yung and Helen Rees, pp. 29–63. Urbana: University of Illinois Press, 1999.

———. "Of Selves and Others: Historiography, Ideology, and the Politics of Modern Mexican Music." PhD diss., University of Pittsburgh, 2001.

Seeger, Charles. "On Proletarian Music." *Modern Music,* 11 (March 1934): 121–7.

"Series Arranged of Mexican Music." *New York Times,* May 1, 1940: 30.

Smith, Alice J. "René Maran's Batouala and the Prix Goncourt." *Contributions to Black Studies, A Journal of African and Afro American Studies,* 4, no. 1 (2008): 17–34.

Spellacy, Amy. "Mapping the Metaphor of the Good Neighbor: Geography, Globalism and Panamericanism during the 1940s." *American Studies,* 47, no. 2 (2006): 39–66.

Stallings, Stephanie N. "Collective Difference: The Pan American Association of Composers, and Pan American Ideology in Music, 1924–1945." PhD diss., Florida State University, 2009.

Van Vechten, Carl. *Keep A-Inchin' Along: Selected Writings of Carl Van Vechten about Black Arts and Letters,* ed. Bruce Kellner. Westport, Conn.: Greenwood Press, 1979.

———. *The Splendid Drunken Twenties: Selections from the Daybooks, 1922–1930,* ed. Bruce Kellner. Urbana: University of Illinois Press, 2003.

Vasconcelos, José. *La raza cósmica* [The Cosmic Race]. Originally published in 1924. Mexico City: Colección Austral, 2002.

Velázquez, Marco, and Mary Kay Vaughan. "Mestizaje and Musical Nationalism in Mexico." In *The Eagle and the Virgin: Nation and Cultural Revolution in Mexico, 1920–1940,* ed. Mary Kay Vaughan and Steve Lewis, pp. 95–118. Durham, N.C.: Duke University Press, 2006.

Williams, Adriana. *Miguel Covarrubias.* México, D.F.: Fondo de Cultura Económica, 1999.

Williams, Daryle. *Culture Wars in Brazil: The First Vargas Regime, 1930–1945.* Durham, N.C.: Duke University Press, 2001.

World News, Inc. *Miguel Covarrubias.* http://wn.com/Miguel Covarrubias (accessed September 15, 2010).

CHAPTER FIVE

HOLLYWOOD VILLA AND THE VICISSITUDES
OF CROSS-CULTURAL ENCOUNTERS

Adela Pineda Franco

The first time, I was aboard the Guilio Césare, the next, I was in Paris.

In that city, spectacular *par excellence*, one would only think of going to the movies to rest or escape from the cold for an hour. During my month in Paris, I watched two movies exhibiting the cartoonish portrait of Mexico. Then, in Brussels, without intending to, I ended up seeing two more movies with the same dreadful propaganda . . . If Mexico were to send a spokesman to all European and American cities in order to speak in Mexico's defense, his or her success would be infinitesimal compared to the overwhelming accomplishments of the movies . . . It would be just as hopeless for Mexico to buy a newspaper space in each city of the world to counteract this derogatory campaign. Nothing can be said or written against that terrifying effectiveness of the image on the screen.[1]

These are words written by Gabriela Mistral during her stay in Mexico as a guest of President Álvaro Obregón. They show her concern with the emergence of Hollywood as an all-pervading transnational force shaping public opinion and as a powerful medium able to fabricate a nation's collective identity. Mistral was not alone. Her words reveal the historic prerogative of the Latin American *Lettered City* following the rise of the United States as a political and economic world power (1898–1930) and the appearance of modern mass media, which gave unparalleled access to new cultural forms. By and large, Latin American intellectuals would quickly come to be at odds with the universal grammar of American mass culture.

The foundation of this grammar was linked to the economic supremacy of the United States: its potential to control other markets, and its democratic dynamism, which came to replace Europe's cultural hegemony in the world. Popular film could communicate directly with mass audiences through a nonverbal medium. It rendered distant worlds closer, stripped the aura from cultural practices and had the potential to democratize the realm of culture and art. Without a doubt, some writers distrusted the liberating aspect of cinema, perceived by Walter Benjamin in the new principles of mass cultural reception and experience.[2] Behind the cinematic spectacle, they saw only a depravation of culture: an industry producing mechanized entertainment and banal amusement for the silent majorities. Most of all, intellectuals regarded popular cinema as a threat to their historic position as mediators between structures of power and subaltern groups within the plebeian public sphere.[3]

The case of Mexico is highly relevant because Hollywood productions constituted 97 percent of all films shown in that country and, since 1928, Mexico had become the sixth largest importer of Hollywood pictures.[4] During the years of national reconstruction (1925–1940), right after the Mexican Revolution (1910–1921), several regional identities were still resisting integration into the larger space of the nation, which was being broadly reconfigured in terms of a centralized government, a capitalist economy, and a state-sponsored nationalism promoting collective unity. Intellectuals, who took it on themselves to voice the popular consciousness born out of the Revolution, regarded Hollywood not only as a symbol of mass culture and modernity but also as a source of cultural and political interventionism.[5] The press was these intellectuals' main forum; through it their Hollywood critique found their most direct utterance before mass audiences, giving them their first encounter with the movies outside the theater.[6]

Notwithstanding, the relationship between lettered intellectuals, Mexican nationalism, and Hollywood as the paradigm of cultural interventionism was far more complicated during the years of national reconstruction in Mexico, when Hollywood aimed at ameliorating previous stereotypical depictions of Mexicans following the vogue for Mexico's cultural renaissance in the United States, with films like *Viva Villa!* a David O. Selznick and Metro Goldywin Meyer (MGM) production, which was released in 1934. The story of this film (its making and reception) reveals not only the role of lettered intellectuals as mediators between Hollywood and mass audiences but also the ambivalent politics of collaboration between the Mexican State and Hollywood in the crafting of the Revolution's memory. This collaboration was hindered by unexpected circumstances that set off a transnational debate about the cultural image of Mexico brought about by the Mexican Revolution.

This chapter documents the film's reception in Mexico and abroad as reported by the press, showing that it elicited antagonistic views on Villa. It relates this discordant reception to the peculiar use of cinematic genre conventions that the film displays. On the one hand, the film articulates an illusionistic reality effect built around the epic story of Villa; on the other, it has a comic subtext that contradicts the epic visual regime. This generic hybridity may be interpreted as the result of multiple factors: an economic strategy on the part of the studio system willing to please a mixed audience by not taking sides with respect to Villa; a consequence of Hollywood's political calculations to comply with Mexico's official cultural politics regarding Villa's diminished historic memory at a moment of national reconfiguration; the outcome of the troublesome incidents surrounding the film's production; and, finally, a deliberate strategy exercised by the makers of the film (particularly the scriptwriter Ben Hecht) in order to produce a mock epic, that is, a parody of journalistic representation and of the epic film genre in the context of the depression years.

During the month of November 1933, several newspapers, particularly *El Universal*, documented the events surrounding the making of *Viva Villa!* Initially, these newspaper accounts were meant to raise expectations about the film. Photographs, advertisements, and feature articles publicized the one million dollar production as an epic biopic of General Villa. Filmed on location, one hundred kilometers from the capital at the hacienda of the actor Julio Saldívar, the film was acclaimed for its historical accuracy and critics predicted that it would become the greatest cinematic success of the following year. Attention was focused on the film's title role actor, Wallace Beery, one of Hollywood's top 10 box office performers at the time.[7] According to a commentator in *El Universal*, Beery's robust virility made him ideal for the epic role of Villa, and to promote the film, a gun-toting Beery appeared at the Balmori Theater in Mexico City dressed in a cowboy outfit as Pancho Villa during the premiere of another of his movies, *Tugboat Annie*[8] (Figure 1).

"Viva Villa"

Figure 1. Cartoon by Santiago Corredor-Vergara. Used with permission.

As a star, Beery combined the filmic persona of both the villain and the comedian with a peculiar off-screen personality: a tough, ugly guy, at times clumsy but always charming who began his career as a circus elephant trainer and whose adventurous drive lead him to fame and success.[9] A *New York Times* article from 1924 eloquently described the characters played by Beery and synthesized his Hollywood personality: "His villains have a sense of humor, something that every really successful villain should never be without; they have a sense of romance and they are human, which, of course, means that somewhere down deep they are illuminated by a spark of kindliness."[10] The film provides repeated visual evidence of Villa's harmless villainy, as is the case with Villa's currency deploying a severe face framed by two peaceful pigeons on each side (Figure 2).

How might this comical, "celebrated villain" (as the *New York Times* called him) play Villa? Such a "picturesque villain" could not help but embody an ideologically ambiguous Villa. The film was advertised as a historical epic of the life and times of Pancho Villa, one whose purpose was to ameliorate Villa's reputation as the infamous raider of Columbus, New Mexico, or the mischievous bandit of previous screen incarnations.[11] The danger was that Beery, as actor, would threaten Villa's epic stature and risk turning him into a buffoon. For how could Beery play a laudable—rather than a laughable or fearful—Villa if, according to the *New York Times,* he had been a first-rate villain for more than a decade with a talent "for sinister flirtations, and cold-blooded murders"?[12] In bringing a national figure within the reach of people's senses and emotion, the risk was that he would bring out a comic demeanor, a donjuanesque personality, and a confusing mix of violence and generosity. In a word, Villa's fictional character as hero appeared to be at odds with Beery's popular image as villain and comedian. Indeed, since the outset, when MGM's producers were evaluating character treatment, plot development, and film adaptation of the novel *Viva Villa!,*[13] there was already concern over the dubious match between Villa, epic hero, and Beery, profit-making luminary. An insightful MGM-commissioned reader commented in

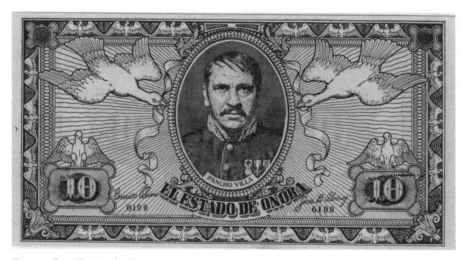

Figure 2. Villa's Bill (Selznick Collection, Harry Ransom Center).

CHAPTER FIVE

his evaluation of the film's preliminary outlines: "the character of Villa has been subdued for the sake of Beery's personality, and once more as in the past history of motion pictures, we find ourselves losing the full value of a tremendous story, for the sake of adapting it to a big star."[14] After the release of the film, reviewers in both countries were still puzzling over the hazy message behind Beery's Villa.[15]

As for Mexican audiences, they were confronting a historic film expensively produced by foreigners, one which marketed Villa for transnational, indiscriminate mass consumption. At the Balmory, so we read in *El Universal*, Beery was going to speak in English to the Mexicans with Mona Maris (a supporting Argentine actress in the film) as his interpreter. Judging from the press, Beery's distinctive face and voice were never quite convincing to Mexicans. An anonymous commentator in *El Ilustrado* doubted that the film, advertised as truly historical, could be taken as "accurate," in part because Villa's memory was still alive in the recollections of many Mexicans.[16] Whether or not they remembered Villa, Mexican audiences would not have been amused by the music Hollywood used for the Villista anthem. . . . "La cucaracha"![17] Such excessive Mexicanness must have been a disappointment for many.

"La cucaracha" notwithstanding, within the Mexican cultural and political hegemonic context of those years, Beery's ambiguous, comical-epic Villa may not have been completely out of place and might even have been useful to the Mexican government. During the twenties and early thirties, *villismo* remained a political threat to the centralized Mexican State. Since Villa's death in 1923, besides violent repression, the State resorted to the realm of culture in order to neutralize any possible villista uprising, diminishing the importance of Villa and his movement within the official memory of the revolution.[18] Ironically, it is during these years, that Villa gains unprecedented cultural appeal in Mexico and abroad.[19] Historical accounts are everywhere, in popular culture and literary discourse, but, at the same time, a hegemonic cultural apparatus does its best to channel divergent views of Villa into a homogenizing national narrative. This narrative presents Villa as a popular subject born out of the revolution but, at the same time, as an irrational demon, in sum, as the bandit.[20]

Other films reinforced that image. The trope of banditry often appeared in the pages of *El Universal* in connection with the energetic promotion of *El Tigre de Yautepec*, a Mexican movie by Fernando de Fuentes, who was to become one of the most prominent Mexican directors of the following decade. Commentaries on the filming of *Viva Villa!* appeared alongside news of *Tigre*, which examined the bloody legacy of the nineteenth-century *Plateados*, using the trope of banditry to represent the demonical force of liberal discourse.[21] Although *Plateado* banditry was far from resembling villismo, talk of banditry in these two movies in *El Universal* probably contributed to the ambivalent reception of *Viva Villa!* whose protagonist was perceived as the social bandit *par excellence*. Judging from coverage in *El Universal*, two interests came together: Hollywood's economic expectations meshed with Mexico's institutionalized cultural politics regarding Villa's diminished historic relevance.

During those years, the Mexican postrevolutionary State was resorting to a particular reading of the revolution to ground its legitimacy, a reading based on a coherent yet fictitious linkage between the grassroot uprisings (such as Zapatismo and Villismo) and the bourgeois, lettered ones, mainly represented by Maderismo. The film was very much in accord to this reading, at least from the point of view of V. G. Hart, one of the Production Code Administration employees who, after having previewed the film, stated that: "It is an outstanding production. . . . with particular attention to the scene with Villa, where Madero, determined to free Mexico of the yoke of aristocracy, convinces the wild bandit of his wrong attitude in his cruel banditry, winning over the ignorant savage, to his way of thinking, and making him a loyal, true friend."[22] The collaboration between Hollywood and the Mexican State is also brought up by one of Villa's widows, who addressed a complaint to MGM in May 1934 on what she considered defamatory and denigrating treatment of her belated husband, ". . . making him appear as a drunkard, ignorant and coward, vulgar assassin." She explicitly states: "It is to be regretted that in this production the technical advisors were two Mexicans and it might be true that one of the Mexicans was the originator of the defamatory scenes that as poison have soiled the picture. I mean Mr. Carlos Navarro whose family by tradition have been Villa's enemies."[23] No surprise then, that, despite its heavy-duty stereotypes, *Viva Villa!* was praised initially by a frontline newspaper like *El Universal* as an outstanding super production and, having passed censorship from both, Hollywood's Production Code and the Mexican State, the film was receiving full governmental support.[24]

By November 21, however, with the movie several weeks into production, *El Universal* changed its tune, publishing articles, editorials, and cartoons that expressed frank opposition toward the film. What triggered that sudden change happened offscreen. On November 19, actor Lee Tracy, an important member of the movie cast, appeared naked and drunk on the balcony of his hotel room in *Reforma* Avenue, shouting obscenities at the crowd and urinating on the cadets of Colegio Militar (the West Point of Mexico) during the anniversary parade—no less!—of the Mexican Revolution.[25]

At the same time, the writer and dancer Nellie Campobello began a fiery campaign against *Viva Villa!* Concerned with the emergence of Hollywood as an all-pervading transnational medium able to fabricate a nation's collective identity, she used journalism to mediate—culturally and politically—between mass audiences and the American film industry. Campobello did not comment on the public spectacle given by Tracy; instead, she attacked the film's derogatory treatment of revolutionary Mexico and Hollywood's image of Villa, whose troubled relationship with the United States and the American industry had a long history. Hollywood was up to its ears in the politics—both American and Mexican—of Villa and the Revolution. According to Campobello, the movie was meant to incite hatred among American audiences by reminding them of Villa's infamous raid on Columbus.[26]

It is worth mentioning that, in her articles, Campobello did not treat villismo as a regional entity, something she had done in her collection of short stories *Cartucho* (1931), her literary attack on the Mexican State's official memory of villismo. In the public forum of the press and facing what she believed to be cultural intervention from across the Río Grande, she came decisively forward as a legitimate guardian of the national patrimony, treating Villa as a national icon and his life story as the history of the revolution.

Anticipating the alienating effect of the film, Campobello urged the Mexican government to confiscate the reels at the border before they could leave Mexican territory. In a detailed review, with plot summary and representative dialogue, prepared after she had previewed several scenes, Campobello objected to the stereotypical depictions of the popular insurgency and its national icons Madero and Villa. When Villa joins the national movement led by Madero, the film treats this merely as passage from small-scale to national banditry: if he joins Madero, Villa can kill more hacendados.[27] The film, Campobello points out, makes Villa into a brute who callously cleans his boots in the presidential chair or collaborates shamelessly with a shrewd American journalist who forges Villa's image in the American press and, worse, manipulates Villa's decision-making process. In the film, the journalist was played by none other than Lee Tracy, whose public behavior in Mexico was stirring commotion.

In his statements to the press, Tracy asserted that his public behavior was a meaningless, isolated incident.[28] However, for Mexicans who scrutinized him in the newspapers, this "incident" revealed something of the imperialistic "essence" of Tracy as Hollywood star. Inside and outside *Viva Villa!* he had begun to represent America's contempt for Mexico's sovereignty. A witty cartoon in *El Universal* clearly established the connection between Tracy's performance image in *Viva Villa!* and his disgraceful public act on November 19[29] (Figure 3).

After his brief incarceration and subsequent escape to the United States, Tracy's contracts with MGM were canceled in their entirety. However, such measures were not enough to stop the public scandal that followed, putting *Viva Villa!* under close scrutiny up until February 1934, when the last version of the film was previewed for Mexican authorities before its release in the United States in April 1934.

The Tracy incident and the accidental loss of some footage in an airplane crash[30] affected *Viva Villa!*'s production, distribution, and future presentation in Mexico. Location filming was discontinued,[31] the film was recast almost in its entirety,[32] several sequences were rewritten,[33] and Jack Conway replaced Howard Hawks as director. The premiere in Mexico was far from successful, with a group of resentful spectators throwing firecrackers into the crowded theater and wounding three women, an incident that resulted in a temporary prohibition of the film.[34] From all that has been said, despite the strong support on the part of Mexican government to have the movie filmed in Mexico, it is clear that through the network of subsidiary circulation in Mexico, and with the intermediation of intellectuals like Campobello and of print journalism, spectators had their first negative encounter with *Viva Villa!* long before it was released.

Whatever its shortcomings, *Viva Villa!* cannot be considered a failure in terms of profit, popularity, or critical assessment. Box office returns exceeded the high costs of its production.[35] The film received positive reviews in the United States, was nominated for several awards, and appeared as one of the best films of the year in more than one rating guide.[36] In subsequent decades, it became the primary source for other shows and movies on Villa, and, in the sixties, when the circumstances of production and the change of directors, from Hawks to Conway had been all but forgotten, it was praised by auteur criticism in *Cahier du Cinema* as a remarkable film worthy of Howard Hawks' talent.[37] Still, it is difficult to

DE NUESTRO CONCURSO DE CARICATURAS

CINE AMERICANO EN MEXICO

De qué manera interpretarían a nuestros personajes históricos, los artistas de Hollywood.

Figure 3. "De Nuestro Concurso de Caricaturas. Cine Americano en México" *El Universal*, November 22, 1933, 5.

sustain that director Hawks retained authorship and thus control of *Viva Villa!* under the eventful circumstances of its production. As has been said, Jack Conway took over the direction of the film after the Tracy episode, making it difficult to differentiate his footage from that of Hawks.[38] Its final structure was determined by the context of the diplomatic tension between the United States and Mexico, and the troublesome incidents surrounding its production could have altered the traffic of ideas through which the film was made. *Viva*

Villa! is thus the site of several economic, social, and political forces at work. In any case, the film's international success and positive reception in the United States points to its ability to express audience desires while fulfilling Hollywood's economic interests within the larger context of American culture. Now the question is why and how *Viva Villa!* would express themes and conflicts that preoccupied American audiences during the depression years.

Viva Villa! was released when Mexico became culturally fashionable in the United States.[39] This vogue was made possible by a particular political and economic scenario. The United States' geopolitical interest in Latin America (including Mexico) after World War I generated production of cultural and scientific knowledge and enabled intellectual and diplomatic exchange. Mexico's social and economic retreat from revolutionary action, government control of opponents, and abandonment of agrarian reform seemed to promise a climate favorable to foreign economic and cultural investment. Hollywood, the most efficient mass producer of a social reality woven from dream, contributed to the materialization of Mexico as a system of representations framed by such political and economic forces, nurturing the decade's utopian drive toward revolution and its nostalgia for a primordial past.

"Amid the uncertainties of the present, we turn to something we can trust, and in the unchangeable facts of history we find relief from our burdens," wrote journalist Alice Rogers Hager in the *New York Times* in 1934. With Pancho Villa riding the border, Rogers stated, "the sunstruck pages of the past lie before our magicked vision."[40] For the price of admission, spectators could fantasize about a new mythical frontier, breaking through "the sudden and terrifying apparition of limits" brought about by the depression years.[41]

Hollywood's stereotypical depiction of Mexico had a long history of its own and led to a diplomatic crisis in 1921, when the Obregón administration banned motion pictures with derogatory Mexican images.[42] Oddly enough, despite Beery's dubious characterization of Villa, the film attempts to restore Hollywood's reputation as a factory of Mexican stereotypes, particularly that of the vengeful greaser. Influenced by the documentary imagery produced during the armed phase of the revolution, showing Villa on horseback in the heat of battle, some sequences attempted to remain faithful to observed reality, a technique traditionally used in documentary photography. These sequences recall the photographic archive produced during Villa's victorious campaign in 1914.[43]

The film draws, too, on the cultural ideology of *indigenismo* and the visual archive of a cosmopolitan nationalist art, produced in Mexico and abroad. The superb cinematography of James Wong Howe, director of photography, captures scenes of timeless agrarian communities untouched by the mechanized rhythm of industrialization. These images may have reminded the American spectator of the "Machineless" *Tepoztlan*, recently popularized by Stuart Chase in his bestseller *Mexico. A Study of Two Americas*, which was illustrated by Diego Rivera. However, more than the nostalgic longing for the unmediated authenticity of peasant life, *Viva Villa!* plays with the spark of social revolution; the film indulges in expressive shots of death and rebirth complemented by the savage cry of "Viva Villa!"

James Wong Howe's stylized sketches in ink of desert landscapes, sombreros, cactus, marching bare feet, and carcasses are evidence of his great familiarity with the Revolution's visual archive[44] (Figure 4). This remarkable cinematographer used the image of the Mexican sombrero as a metonymy of the revolutionary peasantry. He also made intelligent use

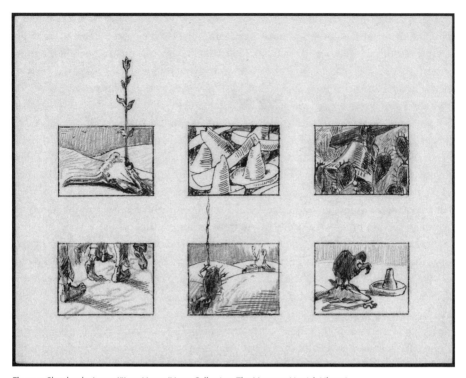

Figure 4. Sketches by James Wong Howe (Howe Collection, The Margaret Herrick Library).

of deep focus in order to draw spectators' attention to the revolutionary action performed not only by Villa but also by the Mexican people, who were portrayed by the camera as the legitimating force of the revolution. Normally, Howe wrote, "one makes close-ups with a two- or three-inch lens, subordinating the background to the more important action of the close-up . . . I did exactly the reverse on *Viva Villa!* . . . . There was a definite, photo-dramatic reason for this treatment: The audience could not forget that Mexico was there, overshadowing even Villa himself."[45]

Apparently, the film sided with participatory American journalism and literary radicalism, of the sort that John Reed heralded in revolutionary Mexico in 1914. Specifically, the film was inspired by the recently published novel, written by Edgcumb Pinchon, a leftist sympathizer of the agrarian revolution, who claimed to be well acquainted with the literary and historical sources of the revolution and who was assisted by Odo B. Stade. Pinchon wrote the novel in a faulty but highly effective realist style in order to contradict the negative perception of Villa in the United States, previously forged by the American Media.[46]

In fact, willing to participate actively in the making of the film, Pinchon portrayed himself before the Hollywood studio and the American Press as a "friendly interpreter between the United States and our neighbor to the South." He claimed that his first book, *The Mexican People, Their Struggle for Freedom* (1914), coauthored with Lázaro Gutiérrez de Lara, a member of Mexico's radical Liberal Party, had been the first historical defense of the

1910 revolution written in English, that it had been read in manuscript form by President Woodrow Wilson, and, consequently, had "done much toward establishing a sympathetic policy toward Mexico as a definite part of our [American] national outlook and foreign policy."[47]

Both novel and film were epics based on the narrative of social banditry.[48] However, the film clearly elicited the novel's explicit vindication of Villa against the Mexican State by superimposing other genre conventions over the epic plot. At the end of the novel, the narrator clearly demands national recognition for Villa, whose memory has been sent into exile by the current Mexican State.[49] Most importantly, it defies the Mexican political status quo by suggesting that Villa's killer Jesús Salas Barraza acted on behalf of the repressive apparatus of the State.[50] In the film, Villa's death follows the formula common in movie Westerns: a Hacendado kills Villa in retaliation for having killed his sister. Understandably, Hollywood would have not received full governmental support for filming *Viva Villa!* on location if Villa's death had been portrayed as in Pinchon's novel.

Surprisingly, Pinchon himself, who more than a genuine revolutionary was an adept opportunist, reformulated his interpretation before the MGM studio executives by later saying that Salas Barraza was a mere lunatic whose "distorted mind has decided that the man who kills Pancho Villa will be famous throughout the world."[51] In March 1933, Pinchon came to an agreement with the Production Code Administration in order to work out a script that would satisfy the requirements of the Mexican government. The Hollywood censors argued that the "securing of such satisfaction would be essential in dealing as it [the story] does with the rise of the revolutionary party of Mexico. . . . the men involved in the process, most of whom are at present powerful in the politics and administration of the country, would be very sensitive about the story of Villa as it is told in this book."[52]

Several drafts of the script attest the difficulties in finding a coherent resolution to the story.[53] The Western formula of revenge did not solve the political problem in its entirety because the vengeful killer had to be somewhat connected to the web of intrigue that put an end to the villista revolution. In one of the earlier versions of the script, Villa was killed by one of his youngest, most truthful, and yet disappointed followers, the bugler boy, for having executed Felipe Ángeles and for having sent the Spanish residents in Chihuahua into exile. This script clearly portrayed Villa as the dark side of an enlightened revolution. In his vehement desire to acquire Hollywood status as a writer, Pinchon did not only diminish Odo B. Stade's role in the writing of the novel[54] but also changed his own interpretation of villismo in accordance to the political apparatus of the Mexican State and Hollywood's economic interests.

In terms of filmic presentation style, the epic and Indianist quality of Howe's cinematography did not prevent stereotype use. Several sequences framing Villa recapture racial, psychological, behavioral, and ideological connotations derived from previous Hollywood stereotypes of "el mexicano." Other sequences interpret journalistic and fictional discourse, reproducing salient traits of Villa's legend as avenger, bandit, macho man, and womanizer. On one hand, *Viva Villa!* was promoting an epic based on postrevolutionary nationalism; on the other, it was exporting the cartoonish portrayal of Mexico to which intellectuals like Campobello and Mistral so deeply objected. As I noted earlier, this paradoxical visual regime lies in Mexican cultural politics regarding Villa, and in State censorship. According to Ronald Haver, MGM's secret negotiator before the Mexican Government, Carlos Navarro, managed to get the screenplay approved in the summer of 1933 with the promise of some changes regarding the portrayal of Villa, "making him more of a brutal, groveling peasant, taking away some of the mythos with which Hecht, Selznick, and Pinchon had invested him."[55]

Although this disparity in the characterization of Villa could have engendered paradoxical feelings of repulsion and fascination in American audiences as well, a reviewer in *The New York Times* took it as a marketing strategy. Because Villa had had a reputation as the "bad man" in the American imaginary, partly because of Columbus but also because of a negative image previously forged in the media, producers at MGM lacked confidence in him as a box-office drawing card, and spiced up the movie with scenes of unnecessary brutality.[56]

To sum up, the ambiguous portrayal of Villa through this combination of epic and comic elements was the result of an economic strategy on the part of the studio system willing to please a mixed Mexican/American audience, a consequence of Hollywood's political calculations to avoid State censorship in Mexico, and the unintentional outcome of production turmoil in Mexico. The clash between the prerogatives of the studio system and the aesthetic expectations of its makers, as well as the diplomatic pressure between the United States and Mexico altered the initial aesthetic and ideological framework of the film.

Yet, there is another way to look at this juxtaposition of the epic and the comic in *Viva Villa!* Peter Wollen contends that Howard Hawk's films are structured by "a contrast between his adventure dramas (which always had a comic subtext) and his comedies (which always parodied his dramas)."[57] Although Hawks did not direct the entire film, one of the fundamental features of *Viva Villa!*'s narrative structure can probably be related to one of Hawk's closer collaborators, the screen writer Ben Hecht, who unlike Hawks, worked on *Viva Villa!* until the very end and was asked to write more scenes after the Tracy incident.[58]

Within the economic and political constraints described above, Hecht did his best to surmount the negative representations of Villa, previously forged by the American media. He also solved the dilemma of successfully adapting Pinchon's novel into a coherent screen play in political terms. His strategy was less politically fervent and more cynical than the novel, and, surely, a lot sharper than Pinchon's first ungainly versions of the script. The film articulates two modes of representation: an illusionistic reality effect built around the epic story of Villa and a sarcastic style that lays bare the politics behind that pseudodocumentary reality. On one hand, the film purports to document actual events, and, on the other, it illustrates the way actual events are fabricated by the capitalist demands of American journalism. The film presents Villa's actions within the solemn background of Howe's imposing cinematography; it resorts to certain melodramatic twists to build suspense for Villa's adventure drama, and it simultaneously parodies the pathos of this drama with a comic subtext. The core of this comic subtext lies in Hecht's creation of the character Johnny Sykes, the American reporter who accompanies him until his death and who writes Villa's revolution for the American public, manipulating Villa's actions in favor of the marketability of his journalistic discourse. It is worth noting that this character does not appear in Pinchon's earlier versions of the script.[59] In his screenplay, Hecht satirizes not only Villa and his Dorados but also Johnny Sykes.

The final scene of the film clearly exemplifies this narrative logic. In response to Villa's dying request, Johnny advances his future eulogy on Villa's death. Speaking flamboyantly on behalf of Villa, Johnny resorts to the symbolic repertoire of an epic revolutionary narrative that fits within the ideological framework of both Mexican official cultural politics and American liberal discourse, apologizing for Villa's "dark side" as a barbarous being. However, Villa resists Johnny's appropriation of his identity by interrupting his speech, avoiding closure and concluding the film with an open question: "what have I done wrong, Johnny?"[60]

The character of the newsman as "the most hardboiled of cynics," ready to act unethically in order to get a story, was not an isolated creation in *Viva Villa!* It was embedded in the mood of the time and underwent many dramatic uses in films ranging from *The Front Page* (1931) to the acclaimed *Citizen Kane* (1941). Hecht is responsible for its development within a genre closely related to the screwball comedy, which is the newspaper film.[61] Having been a journalist in Chicago with unfulfilled literary expectations, Hecht wrote fast-paced scripts with a distinct witty language and with an unmistakable urban satirical style for Hollywood.[62] The idealized vistas of rural Mexico in *Viva Villa!* bear that urban mark of Hecht's skeptical and humorous style.

Intellectuals like Nelly Campobello, and surely many other sympathizers of villismo, could not have taken *Viva Villa!* with humor in the context of Mexican cultural politics and under the geopolitical relationship between Mexico and the United States. In the mind of many Mexicans, Johnny Sykes (who was played by Stuart Erwin) was too easily identifiable with Lee Tracy, swaying drunkenly on the balcony of the Regis Hotel, raining on the parade of an unfinished revolution. For Americans, the Mexican Revolution seemed remote from their political immediate concerns. It could only be lived as a cinematic spectacle of exhilarating otherness and sentimental sameness. It could be consumed as the decade's romantic drive toward primitive landscapes and utopian revolutions. Although Johnny Sykes was there to remind audiences how Hollywood and nationalism shape our dreams of the subaltern other, nobody was willing to pull aside the curtain that conceals the logic of power relations.

NOTES

1. In Jason Borge, *Avances de Hollywood: Crítica Cinematográfica en Latinoamérica, 1915–1945* (Rosario, Beatriz Viterbo Editora, 2005), 105 (my translation).

2. "The Work of Art in the Age of Its Technological Reproducibility" in *The Work of Art in the Age of Its Technological Reproducibility and Other Writings on Media*, ed. Michael W. Jennings et al. (Cambridge: Harvard University Press, 2008), 19–55.

3. On Latin American intellectuals and their relationship with popular culture, and particularly Hollywood, see Jason Borge, *Latin American Writers and the Rise of Hollywood Cinema* (New York: Routledge, 2008), 1–17; and Jesús Martín Barbero, *De los Medios a las Mediaciones: Comunicación, Cultura y Hegemonía* (Bogotá, Convenio Andrés Bello, 1998), 3–112.

4. Gaizka S. de Usabel, *The High Noon of American Films in Latin America* (Ann Arbor, Mich.: UMI Research Press, 1982), 53.

5. The involvement of the American film industry in the Mexican Revolution since the armed conflict's eruption in 1910 was to have lasting effects in the Mexican reception of American movies on revolutionary Mexico produced at a later date. On this subject, see Margarita Orellana, *Filming Pancho: How Hollywood Shaped the Mexican Revolution*, trans. John King (New York: Verso, 2009).

6. On journalism as a site of intellectual mediation between Hollywood and the audience see Borge, *Latin American Writers*, 9.

7. Nicols [sic], *El Universal*, November 1933; Emegere "De Charla con Wallace Beery," *El Ilustrado. Semanario Artístico Popular*, November 9, 1933, 21, 42; A.F.B, "Dos días viendo filmar a Pancho Villa" *El Ilustrado. Semanario Artístico Popular*, November 16, 1933, 6, 39, 42; "Viva Villa!" Motion Picture Daily's Hollywood Preview, *Motion Picture Daily*, March 27, 1934, 8.

8. "Wallace Beery se presenta en público," *El Universal*, November 1933. The reviews of *Tugboat Annie* and the commentaries on the making of *Viva Villa!* appeared side by side in *El Universal*. In *Tugboat Annie*, Beery played a character highly associated with his Hollywood persona: a clumsy drunkard but good natured husband who learned the meaning of true commitment in the high seas as the drama of his family life unfolded. On this movie, see Mordaunt Hall, "Marie Dressler and Wallace Beery in a Picture of Life Aboard a Pacific Coast Tugboat," *The New York Times,* August 12, 1933, 14.

9. "Who's Who in the Films," *New York Times*, December 18, 1932, X6; "Bos'N Beery, Elephanteer," *The New York Times*, December 26, 1926, X3.

10. "Successful Villainy," *New York Times*, August 17, 1924, X2.

11. "'Viva Villa!' Outstanding Triumph of Showmanship," *The Hollywood Reporter*, March 26, 1934, 3.

12. "Successful Villainy," X2.

13. Edgcumb Pinchon, *Viva Villa!* (London: Cassel and Company, 1933).

14. Unsigned reader report addressed to MGM producer John Considine, June 13, 1933, 4; *Turner/MGM Scripts Collection*, 3597–f356 at the Margaret Herrick Library, Academy of Motion Picture Arts and Sciences.

15. "Los Últimos Estrenos," *El Redondel*, 303 (September 9, 1934), 6; "The Cutting Room: *Viva Villa!*," *Motion Picture Herald*, February 10, 1934, 39; "Reviews of the New Features," *The Film Daily*, April 12, 1934, 10.

16. "Pancho Viva Made in USA," *El Ilustrado. Semanario Artístico Popular,* November 23, 1933, 5, 35.

17. Alejandro Aragón, "¡'Muera Villa'!" *El Ilustrado. Semanario Artístico Popular*, April 16, 1934, 20.

18. Friedrich Katz, *The Life and Times of Pancho Villa* (Stanford, California: Stanford University Press, 1998), 769–70.

19. Max Parra, *Writing Pancho Villa's Revolution: Rebels in the Literary Imagination of Mexico* (Austin, University of Texas Press, 2005), 13–22.

20. The case of literature is paradigmatic. The canonization of Mariano Azuela's *The Underdogs* (1915) after 1924 entailed a specific reading of the novel that favored the myth of the revolution as State. According to this reading, Demetrio's irreducibility to the rationale of the State, that is, the protagonist's inability to elucidate why he ventured into a lawless life provides evidence of his prepolitical condition as bandit. Demetrio's death facilitates the lettered agency of the postrevolutionary intellectual, who then gives a full account of the bandit's life and shortcomings (Juan Pablo Dabove, *Nightmares of the Lettered City: Banditry and Literature in Latin America, 1816–1929* (Pittsburgh, University of Pittsburgh Press, 2007), 253). Martín Luis Guzmán's *The Eagle and the Serpent* (1928) could be read within similar parameters. For this intellectual, Villa is the popular subject born out of the revolution, but he is also the opposite of reason. These two novels had already been translated into English and enjoyed considerable popularity at the time *Viva Villa!* was filmed. Edgcumb Pinchon listed these works as important sources for his novel *Viva Villa!*, which was the inspiration of the MGM movie.

21. *El Universal*, November 18, 1933, 4; November 20, 8; November 21, 7; November 22, 7.

22. V. G. Hart, April 12, 1934, *History of Cinema. Series 1, Hollywood and the Production Code: Selected Files from the Motion Picture Association of America Production Code Administration Collection*, reel 10, Woodbridge, Conn., Primary Source Microfilm, 2006.

23. The letter is unsigned but because the *Turner/MGM Scripts Collection* also contains an agreement between MGM and Luz Corral, signed in May 1934, acknowledging specific changes to meet her expectations, one may assume that this complaint must have come from Corral, who saw previews of the movie before its release. Her main objections were the portrayal of Villa as being extremely cruel (having his enemy Pascal being eaten alive by ants); disgracefully weak (crawling cowardly to his knees in front of his executioner); ridiculous and brute-like (wearing a big sombrero sunk to his ears while taking an open bath in a train), and scandalously donjuanesque, "he was besought by women and not the opposite." *Turner/MGM Scripts Collection*, 3598–f368.

24. In a letter signed April 4, 1934, and addressed to MGM executive L. B. Meyer, Joseph I. Breen, who presided over the Hollywood Production Code Administration, acknowledges having reviewed the movie, deeming it satisfactory under the Code. He also writes that "we understand that you have received an official clearance from the Mexican Government," *History of Cinema. Series, Hollywood and the Production Code*, reel 10.

25. The Mexican reaction to this incident is vividly narrated in an unsigned letter addressed to "Howard" (most likely Strickling): "The crowds in the street were in an uproar and the cadets were on the point of coming after Tracy en masse. By the time I got to his room he was just throwing out the first of the many policemen who eventually arrived . . . Then all the cops in town began to arrive, until eventually there were probably thirty . . . uniformed men and detectives. By this time Lee had passed out cold in his room while we were holding the cops in the hall; it was a blessing, because they were all for beating him to a pulp and throwing him in jail pronto," *Ronald Haven Collection*, U 74 Box 2, at the Margaret Herrick Library, Academy of Motion Picture Arts and Sciences. See also Robert M. W. Vogel's remarks (who was head of the International Department at the Studio) in *An Oral History with Robert M. W. Vogel Interviewed by Barbara Hall*, Oral History Program (Beverly Hills, California: Margaret Herrick Library, Academy of Motion Picture Arts and Sciences, 1991), 114; and "Lee Tracy rumbo a Estados Unidos," *El Universal*, November 22, 1933, 1, 5; "Lee Tracy Flees Mexico by Plane, *The New York Times*, November 22, 1933, 23.

26. Nellie Campobello, "La Película *Viva Villa* es Insultante para México," *El Universal*, November 21, 1933, 1, 5; Nellie Campobello, "A Propósito de la Película "Viva Villa." Una Rectificación de Nellie Campobello," *El Ilustrado*, December 7, 1933, 41. In his suggestions on the script the novelist Edgcumb Pinchon includes the Columbus raid; however, he sets the episode as an ambush from Carranza against Villa (*Turner/MGM Scripts Collection*, 3596–f347). By June 1, 1933, Mexico's Secretary of the Interior Eduardo Vasconcelos wrote Carlos Navarro issuing the Mexican permit for filming *Viva Villa!*, provided that scenes relative to the Benton case and the expedition of Columbus would be removed because "these scenes are entirely secondary and might revive hostile sentiments in our country" (*Turner/MGM Scripts Collection*, 3597–f353). Campobello may have read versions of the script that still contained reference to Columbus.

27. "La Película *Viva Villa*," 5.

28. "Tracy Seized in Mexico. Movie Actor is Accused of Insulting Government," *The New York Times*, November 21, 1933, 22; "Denies He Insulted Cadets," *The New York Times*, November 23, 1933, 23.

29. "De Nuestro Concurso de Caricaturas. Cine Americano en México" *El Universal*, November 22, 1933, 5.

30. An airplane carrying the negatives from Mexico to El Paso, Texas, crashed and caught fire. "Making *Viva Villa!* Relating Some of the Obstacles Faced by Film Company in Mexico," *New York Times*, April 15, 1934, X4.

31. The movie was completed in California, except for a second shooting unit that stayed in Mexico until December 1933 ("Viva Villa" Exterior Unit Remains Three Weeks," *The Hollywood Reporter*, November 29, 1933, 3).

32. In addition to Tracy, who was replaced by Stuart Erwin, all the principal actors in Hawks's cast except Joseph Schildkraut and Beery were replaced. Fay Wray replaced Mona Maris in the role of Teresa; Donald Cook replaced Donald Reed in the role of Don Felipe, and Leo Carrillo replaced Irving Pichel in the role of Sierra.

33. Hecht wrote new sequences in mid-February 1934 ("Hecht on Rewrite Job for MGM's 'Viva Villa,'" *The Hollywood Reporter*, February 15, 1934, 1).

34. "Explosions Halt Film," *The New York Times*, September 7, 1934, 25.

35. It returned the movie's cost and made a profit of eighty thousand dollars. Ronald Haver, *David O. Selznick's Hollywood* (New York: Bonanza Books, 1985), 152.

36. "Critics of Nation Pick Best Films," *The New York Times*, January 3, 1935, 25; "A Backward Look at the 1934 Cinema," *The New York Times*, December 30, 1934, X5.

37. On a 1957 musical by Matt Dubey and Harold Karr, based on the movie, see "Musical Planes on Pancho Villa," *The New York Times*, November 19, 1957, 37. On auteur criticism regarding the film, see "Viva Villa!" *Cahier du Cinema*, 139 (January 1963): 18–19.

38. After the Tracey incident, Selznick appointed Conway as director, but he also commissioned Dick Rosson to film several sequences in Mexico, such as the death of the bugler boy during the heat of a battle and Villa's magnificent entrance into Mexico City "with several cameras and getting as many exciting production shots as possible . . . since the Mexican government is particularly anxious that we show Mexico City in all is glory in these shots." See several notes on retakes dating from February 1934 in *James Wong Howe Papers*, 15-f.166–168, Margaret Herrick Library, Academy of Motion Picture Arts and Sciences.

39. Helen Delpar situates the peak of this vogue between 1927 and 1935. Consult chapter 2 of *The Enormous Vogue of Things Mexican. Cultural Relations between the US and Mexico 1920–1935* (Tuscaloosa: University of Alabama Press, 1992).

40. Alice Rogers, "Movies Reflect Our Moods," *The New York Times*, April 22, 1934, SM22.

41. In 1932, James Rorty, a dispirited radical journalist from New York, addressed the loss of faith in the American Dream: "There is a great wall facing America . . . a rather sudden and terrifying apparition of limits" (in Richard H. Pells, *Radical Visions and American Dreams. Culture and Social Thought in the Depression Years* (Middletown, Conn.: Wesleyan University Press, 1973), 99).

42. Usabel, *High Noon of American Films*, 40.

43. Zuzana M. Pick, *Constructing the Image of the Mexican Revolution: Cinema and the Archive* (Austin: University of Texas Press, 2010), 49.

44. *James Wong Howe Papers*, 15-f.169.

45. James Wong Howe, "Upsetting Traditions with 'Viva Villa!'" *American Cinematographer* 15, no. 2 (1934): 71–72.

46. A review in the *New York Times* remarks Pinchon's "positive" use of mythology regarding Villa, by comparing his work to that of John Reed, the forger of Villa's legend as Robin Hood ("Villa, the Mexican Robin Hood," *The New York Times*, March 19, 1933, BR5).

47. Pinchon to MGM Story Editor Samuel Marx, February 28, 1933, 1–2 in *Turner/MGM Scripts Collection*, 3596-f.345

48. Both tell the story of a peon who becomes an outlaw in the presence of local injustice and who, subsequently, becomes a patriot when his actions as bandit intersect with the overarching demands of the national movement led by Madero.

49. Pinchon, *Viva Villa!*, 376.

50. Ibid, 375.

51. "Story Treatment by Pinchon," March 28, 1933, *Turner/MGM Scripts Collection*, 3596-f.347.

52. James Wingate to Thalberg, March 4, 1933, *History of Cinema. Series 1, Hollywood and the Production Code*, reel 10.

53. Ann Cunningham, Wallace Smith, Oliver H. P. Garret wrote the preliminary outlines and drafts, with Edgcumb Pinchon's collaboration, between March and July 1933. See *Turner/MGM Scripts Collection*, 3596-f344, 3597-f354, 3598-f361, and 3598-f362.

54. In a letter addressed to MGM Editor Samuel Marx, dated March 24, 1933, Odo B. Stade sent three pages of corrections for the script, claiming that he did not see neither galley nor page proofs of the novel. He also asked Marx not to tell Pinchon of these corrections because "I have declared peace, and I would not want the present smooth surface of our relationship to be ruffled again." Stade also claimed to be an expert on things Mexican, claiming that "the idea of the book originated with me" and that "I had to get all of the material, enhanced by my thorough knowledge of Mexico, and things Mexican. I am of course very anxious that the film version follow the facts in so far as this will be found possible" *Turner/MGM Scripts Collection* 3596 –f343.

55. Ronald Haver, *David O. Selznick's Hollywood*, 134.

56. Mordaunt Hall, "Wallace Beery as Pancho Villa in a fictionalized film biography of the bandit," *The New York Times*, April 11, 1934, 25.

57. *Howard Hawks, American Artist*, ed. Jim Hillier and Peter Wollen (London: BFI Publishing, 1996), 2.

58. Hecht was paid by producer Selznick ten thousand dollars for the script plus a bonus of five thousand dollars if he completed the work in fifteen days (Haver, *David O. Selznick's Hollywood*, 13).

59. The first draft of Johnny Sykes characterization appears in an outline by Ben Hecht dated September 11, 1933 (*Turner/MGM Scripts Collection* 3598-f363, p 18).

60. It is worth mentioning that these last words did not appear but in the very last versions of the script. There was a lot of discussion among the producers and Hecht in how to conclude the scene. In February 23, 1934, Villa's final words were meant to be: "Johnny, don't let Rosita find that bathrobe." See *James Wong Howe Papers* 15-f.164.

61. The newspaper films written by Hecht are *Roadhouse Nights* (1939), *Freedom Ring* (1939), *Foreign Correspondent* (1940), *Roman Holiday* (1953), *The Front Page* (1931), *Nothing Sacred* (1937), *Comrade X* (1940), *His Girl Friday* (1940), and *Roxie Hart* (1942).

62. Jeffrey Brown Martin, *Ben Hecht, Hollywood Screenwriter* (Ann Arbor, Mich.: UMI Research Press, 1985), 42.

BIBLIOGRAPHY

"A Backward Look at the 1934 Cinema." *New York Times*, December 30, 1934: X5.

A. F. B. "Dos Días Viendo Filmar a Pancho Villa [Two Days Watching Filming Pancho Villa]." *El Ilustrado. Semanario Artístico Popular*, November 16, 1933: 6, 39, 42.

Aragón, Alejandro. "¡Muera Villa! [Die Villa!]" *El Ilustrado. Semanario Artístico Popular*, April 16, 1934: 20.

Barbero Martín, Jesús. *De los Medios a las Mediaciones: Comunicación, Cultura y Hegemonía* [Communication, Culture and Hegemony: From the Media to Mediations]. Bogotá: Convenio Andrés Bello, 1998.

Benjamin, Walter. "The Work of Art in the Age of its Technological Reproducibility." In *The Work of Art in the Age of its Technological Reproducibility and Other Writings on Media*, ed. Michael W. Jennings, and Brigid Doherty, pp. 19–55. Cambridge, Mass.: Harvard University Press, 2008.

Borge, Jason. *Avances de Hollywood: Crítica Cinematográfica en Latinoamérica, 1915–1945* [Hollywood Moves: Film Criticism in Latin America, 1915–1945]. Rosario, Argentina: Beatriz Viterbo Editora, 2005.

———. *Latin American Writers and the Rise of Hollywood Cinema*. New York: Routledge, 2008.

"Bos'N Beery, Elephanteer." *New York Times*, December 26, 1926: X3.

Brown Martin, Jeffrey. *Ben Hecht, Hollywood Screenwriter*. Ann Arbor, Mich.: UMI Research Press, 1985.

Campobello, Nellie. "A Propósito de la Película 'Viva Villa.' Una Rectificación de Nellie Campobello [Purpose of the Film 'Viva Villa.' A Rectification by Nellie Campobello]." *El Ilustrado*, December 7, 1933.

———. "La Película Viva Villa es Insultante para México [The Film Viva Villa Is Insulting to Mexico]." *El Universal*, November 21, 1933, 1, 5.

"Critics of Nation Pick Best Films." *The New York Times*, January 3, 1935: 25.

"The Cutting Room: *Viva Villa!*" *Motion Picture Herald*, February 10, 1934: 39

Dabove, Juan Pablo. *Nightmares of the Lettered City: Banditry and Literature in Latin America, 1816–1929*. Pittsburgh: University of Pittsburgh Press, 2007.

Delpar, Helen. *The Enormous Vogue of Things Mexican: Cultural Relations between the US and Mexico 1920–1935*. Tuscaloosa: University of Alabama Press, 1992.

"De Nuestro Concurso de Caricaturas. Cine Americano en México [From Our Cartoon Contest. American Cinema in Mexico]." *El Universal*, November 22 1933: 5.

"Denies He Insulted Cadets." *The New York Times,* November 23, 1933: 23.

Emegere. "De Charla con Wallace Beery [Chat with Wallace Beery]." *El Ilustrado. Semanario Artístico Popular*, November 9, 1933: 21, 42.

"Explosions Halt Film." *The New York Times*, September 7, 1934: 25.

Hall. Barbara. "An Oral History with Robert M. W. Vogel." In: *Oral History Program*, p.114. Beverly Hills, Ca.: Margaret Herrick Library, Academy of Motion Picture Arts and Sciences, 1991.

Haver, Ronald. *David O. Selznick's Hollywood.* New York: Bonanza Books, 1985.

"Hecht on Rewrite Job for MGM's 'Viva Villa,'" *The Hollywood Reporter*, February 15, 1934: 1.

Hillier Jim and Peter Wollen, eds. *Howard Hawks, American Artist*. London: BFI Publishing, 1996.

History of Cinema. Series 1, Hollywood and the Production Code: Selected Files from the Motion Picture Association of America Production Code Administration Collection. Reel 10.Woodbridge, Conn.: Primary Source Microfilm, 2006.

Howe, James Wong. "Upsetting Traditions with 'Viva Villa.'" *American Cinematographer*, 15.2 (1934): 71–72.

James Wong Howe Papers. Margaret Herrick Library, Academy of Motion Picture Arts and Sciences, Beverly Hills, Ca.

Katz, Friedrich. *The Life and Times of Pancho Villa*. Stanford, Ca.: Stanford University Press, 1998.

"Lee Tracy Flees Mexico by Plane." *The New York Times,* November 22, 1933: 23.

"Lee Tracy Rumbo a Estados Unidos [Lee Tracy for the United States]." *El Universal*, November 22, 1933: 1, 5.

"Making *Viva Villa!* Relating Some of the Obstacles Faced by Film Company in Mexico." *New York Times*, April 15, 1933: X4.

Mordaunt, Hall. "Marie Dressler and Wallace Beery in a Picture of Life aboard a Pacific Coast Tugboat." *The New York Times,* August 12, 1933: 14.

———. "Wallace Beery as Pancho Villa in a Fictionalized Film Biography of the Bandit." *The New York Times*, April 11, 1934: 25.

Orellana, Margarita. *Filming Pancho: How Hollywood Shaped the Mexican Revolution.* Trans. John King. New York: Verso, 2009.

"Pancho Viva Made in USA." *El Ilustrado. Semanario Artístico Popular.* November 23, 1933: 5, 35.

Parra, Max. *Writing Pancho Villa's Revolution: Rebels in the Literary Imagination of Mexico.* Austin: University of Texas Press, 2005.

Pells, Richard H. *Radical Visions and American Dreams: Culture and Social Thought in the Depression Years.* Middletown, Conn.: Wesleyan University Press, 1973.

Pick, Zuzana M. *Constructing the Image of the Mexican Revolution: Cinema and the Archive.* Austin: University of Texas Press, 2010.

Pinchon, Edgcumb. *Viva Villa!* London: Cassel and Company, 1933.

"Reviews of the New Features." *The Film Daily*, April 12, 1934: 10.

Rogers, Alice. "Movies Reflect our Moods." *The New York Times*, April 22, 1934: SM22.

Ronald Haven Collection. Margaret Herrick Library, Academy of Motion Picture Arts and Sciences, Beverly Hills, Ca.

"Successful Villainy." *The New York Times*, August 17, 1924: X2.

"Tracy Seized in Mexico. Movie Actor is Accused of Insulting Government." *The New York Times,* November 21, 1933: 22.

Turner/MGM Scripts Collection. Margaret Herrick Library, Academy of Motion Picture Arts and Sciences, Beverly Hills, Ca.

"Los Últimos Estrenos [The Latest Releases]." *El Redondel*, September 9, 1934: 6.

Usabel, Gaizka S. de. *The High Noon of American Films in Latin America.* Ann Arbor, Mich.: UMI Research Press, 1982.

"Villa, the Mexican Robin Hood." *The New York Times*, March 19, 1933: BR5

"Viva Villa!" *Cahier du Cinema,* 139 (January 1963): 18–19.

"Viva Villa" Exterior Unit Remains Three Weeks," *The Hollywood Reporter*, November 29, 1933: 3

"'Viva Villa!' Motion Picture Daily's Hollywood Preview." *Motion Picture Daily*, March 27, 1934: 8.

"'Viva Villa!' Outstanding Triumph of Showmanship." *The Hollywood Reporter*, March 26, 1934: 3.

"Wallace Beery se Presenta en Público [Wallace Beery Appears in Public]." *El Universal*, November 2, 1933: 5.

"Who's Who in the Films." *The New York Times*, December 18, 1932: X6.

CHAPTER SIX

FALLEN UTOPIAS

The Mexican Revolution in Katherine Anne Porter's
María Concepción and *Flowering Judas*

Jaime Marroquín Arredondo

Just like love always fails in Katherine Anne Porter's fiction about Mexico, so does revolution. This essay analyzes Porter's critique of the Mexican Revolution in two of her most famous "Mexican" short stories: *María Concepción* and *Flowering Judas*. Porter's fiction is not only one of the first critiques to the nowadays well-documented political and economic shortcomings of the Mexican Revolution. In her short stories, revolutionary failure questions the very validity of the philosophical and moral values that inform modern Western civilization's continuous attempts to construct a future Utopia through arms and reason.

As John Britton documents, for young American intellectuals and artists such as Carleton Beals, Anita Brenner, Edward Weston, and Katherine Anne Porter, Mexico in the 1920s was a country experiencing a rapid social and cultural change that attempted to favor the claims for land and education of its dispossessed Indian and Mestizo population. Some of them were particularly interested in the cultural aspects of a self-proclaimed socialist Revolution. As Britton states, "Beals, Porter, and Weston shared a sense of alienation from the middle-class materialism that dominated the United States in the 1920s."[1] Looking at "the other" for political and even existential answers was a common attempt among Western intellectuals and artists at the time. There was a widespread discomfort and anxiety regarding the very definition of Western culture and civilization. World War I had left a feeling of people living, as Katherine Porter would write years later, "in a falling world."[2] Nine million deaths caused by war made it hard for any lucid mind to keep the faith in the Hegelian logic of constant human progress.

In the United States the first two decades of the twentieth century were also a time of a growing uncertainty that would reach its climax during the great 1929 crisis. Richard Pells notices that there was a growing discomfort among the intellectual elite about the way the national economy was being conducted as well as about the cultural and material consequences of capitalism gone amok.[3] Radical individualism, capitalist ethics based on greed, increasing standardization of products and management techniques and the economic predominance of immensely powerful trusts, had created a longing among artists and intellectuals for a different set of social values. Public intellectuals like Waldo Frank and Lewis Mumford thought that the essence of the problem was moral and spiritual. America's commercial devotion had destroyed the old sense of community and the population was emotionally and spiritually impoverished. There was a growing homogenization of taste and behavior and the American people had lost any intimate connection with their natural environment. Artists and intellectuals attempted to use art as a stronghold for political resistance, progressive social influence, and even as the means for a secular, utopian, vision of a new and better society.

In search for answers, several young American intellectuals traveled to Mexico during its great revolution. As Helen Delpar has explained, for them the Mexican Revolution was more than an attempt to change political, economic, and social structures; "their concept of revolution envisioned psychological and aesthetic transformation as well, a transformation that would alter the consciousness and values of both masses and elites."[4] Thus, as John Reed would rediscover communal living while traveling with the Pancho Villa Army, Katherine Anne Porter would find beauty in Mexico. In "The New Man and the New Order," an article published shortly after her arrival to Mexico in 1920, Porter wrote that beauty in Mexico had the green color of plants and the copper color of human things not yet completely corrupted by civilization.[5]

Upon her arrival, Porter did not speak Spanish or know much about Mexican history and culture. Her first encounters with the Mexican Indians took her by surprise and her reactions oscillated between extremes, as seen in two of her earliest essays about Mexico: *Fiesta de Guadalupe* and *The Children of Xochitl*. In the former, she is shocked by the profound and premodern religious faith of the pilgrims who visited the sanctuary of the Virgin of Guadalupe on December 12. She concludes this essay with revolutionary fervor, hoping that the Indian religious alienation would end soon, because men will not always live dreaming. On her second essay about Mexican Indians, *The Children of Xochitl*, Porter describes the Indian town of Xochimilco and its ancient canals as the last remnants of a recently lost yet recoverable paradise. For Porter, Indians there lived away from the modern world and their Catholic faith only imperfectly covered their ancient deities, some of them truly benevolent, like *Xochitl*: Porter's own version of an Aztec goddess of the earth and fertility. In Xochimilco, the poor smile because they have enough money to be free, and a young woman in front of her house moves in a sort of trance, a kind of "prenatal dream."

In her two most celebrated short stories about Mexico, *María Concepción* and *Flowering Judas*, Porter expands and refines her contrasting views about Mexico during its revolution; still, some of her early impressions would remain. Like other modernist writers, Porter anticipates some of Martin Heidegger's philosophical conclusions about the roots of Western civilization's crisis, which he would synthesize in his famous *Being and Time*, published in 1927. Heidegger affirms there that Western culture started with the forgetting of Being. Knowledge abandoned Parmenides' considerations about the totality of Being, favoring instead the study of concrete and particular entities. Heidegger considered that Greek culture began with the ancient consciousness of totality slowly sinking into oblivion. It was gradually replaced by a strict separation of nature into clearly differentiated objects and entities.

Because of this shift, Western civilization became the culture of science and logical reason. Instead of the predominance of the poetic and mythical intelligence, which opened human mind to the consciousness of the Absolute, it gave priority to logical reason, which imposes limits and classifies everything it discovers in the natural world. The mystical dimension of nature gradually became superstition or pure speculation, since it proved impossible to verify and classify.[6]

MARÍA CONCEPCIÓN

Similar ideas inform Porter's early views about Mexico and its revolution. In her first published short story, *María Concepción*, she attempted to understand and recreate the consciousness of a young Mexican Indian woman whose closeness to nature as both, Indian and woman, is the crux of the story. Almost everything takes place in a small indigenous town in Mexico, near Teotihuacán. María Concepción is a strong, fiercely independent Indian woman who is married to a happy and careless fellow named Juan. They have a good social status in the village and at the beginning of the story she is pregnant and feeling in harmony with herself and the natural world. Porter writes that:

> "Instinctive serenity softened her black eyes (. . .) She walked with the free,
> natural, guarded ease of the primitive woman carrying an unborn child.
> The shape of her body was easy, the swelling life was not a distortion, but
> the right inevitable proportions of a woman. She was entirely contented."[7]

This instinctive serenity is soon shattered as she discovers that her husband is cheating on her with another woman from the village, María Rosa, a seductive and sweet beekeeper. The lovers flee the village to work as soldiers in the Revolution, and María Concepción's serenity is further destroyed when her baby dies just four days after being born. At that point, Porter writes, she becomes a knot of pain, silent and gaunt, taking refuge in her work by selling chicken so diligently that "her butchering knife was scarcely ever out of her hand."[8] A year goes by this way when one day Juan and María Rosa return home. They got tired of military life, and María Rosa is about to give birth to their first child. When Juan goes back to his old home for the first time, drunk, to reestablish himself as the man of the house, María Concepción does not submit to him in any way. She does not allow him to beat her. Instead, she cries out her pain alone under the shadow of a thorny bush. Suddenly, she thoughtlessly walks toward María Rosa's place and furiously stabs her to death. Juan and the village women instinctively recognize, without any rational explanation, that Maria Concepción had the right to kill María Rosa, and they decide to save her from the police. Nobody saw anything; they all confirm to the police that she is a good woman who took her husband back without turmoil. There is also no opposition to María Concepción adopting María Rosa's newborn baby. Later that same night, Juan wonders why he has saved his wife from the police. He begins to realize that his days of careless freedom with María Rosa are over and that he has to go back to "dull and endless labor."[9] He feels overwhelmed with melancholy. He is now the one thrown away from serenity, since "there was nothing in him except a vast blind hurt like a covered wound."[10] In contrast, María Concepción rediscovers peace and harmony with the natural world. Before she fell asleep, "the silence overfilled the world, the skies flowed down evenly to the rim of the valley, the stealthy moon crept slantwise to the shelter of the mountains (. . .) [and] she dreamed that the newly born child was her own, and she was resting deliciously."[11] The story ends by telling us that even "as she was falling asleep, head bowed over the child, she was still aware of a strange, wakeful happiness."[12] Despite Porter's assumption that in a Mexican Indian town it was possible to be at peace with nature and oneself, she does not portray a world without political and religious conflicts. Cultural imperialism and labor exploitation are implicit in her portrayal of Givens, the American anthropologist in charge of the Teotihuacán dig who "liked his Indians best when he could feel a fatherly indulgence for their primitive childish ways."[13] The ideological power of the Catholic Church is also present; María Concepción enjoys a privileged status at the beginning of the story because of her ability to pay for a wedding inside the church, and people from the village sympathize with her after Juan's departure. They witness her regularly visiting the church, "lighting candles before the saints, kneeling with her arms spread in the form of a cross for hours at a time."[14] However, these conflicting social realities are not strong enough to overpower the mythical world that Porter recreates in her story. Jane Krause has written that *María Concepción* can be read as the eternal feminine principle, the Great Mother, a primal goddess whose purpose is the continuation of human life and who only needs man for fertilization. According to Krause, María Concepción kills María Rosa in order to reestablish her fertility and regain her sexual power of attraction, stolen by her rival. María Concepción represents some of the most ancient human views about the feminine character of nature: a benign goddess of fertility as well as an uncontrollable, hostile force. The usually careless Juan is simply awed by María Concepción after she kills María Rosa: "He stared at her as at a creature unknown to him, who bewildered him utterly, for whom there was no possible explanation."[15] She even appears to him almost as a supernatural being:

> The light from the charcoal burner shone in her eyes; a yellow phosphorescence glimmered behind the dark iris. (. . .) He could not fathom her, nor himself, nor the mysterious fortunes of life grown so instantly confused where all had seemed so gay and simple. He felt too that she had become invaluable, a woman without equal among a million women, and he could not tell why.[16]

It is interesting to notice that Mexican Indians' ideas are barely articulated in the story. Not surprisingly, it is written from the point of view of an omniscient narrator. There is nothing close to a stream of consciousness of an Indian character, and it is even hard to find concrete or abstract thoughts in their portrayal. For example, when Juan leaves with his lover to fight in the Revolution, we never know what María Concepción, the main character, thinks. We know that she did not weep, that she went to church regularly, lighting candles and kneeling for hours. We also do not know what she thinks when she accepts Juan back without submitting to his beating. And in the climax of the story, before her impulsive killing of María Rosa, the narrator tells us that "all her being was a dark confused memory of grief burning in her at night, of deadly baffled anger eating at her by day."[17] After her crime, we can read one of María Concepción's thoughts, which follows a very simple logic: the killing was justifiable because "María Rosa had eaten too much honey and had had too much love. Now she must sit in hell crying over her sins and her hard death forever and ever."[18] At the end of the story, after she is safe and has become the adoptive mother of María Rosa's baby, she is aware of a strange happiness that she cannot explain.

Instincts rule over logic in the Indian village. Juan, for example, is simply overwhelmed by the power of nature, always seen as a feminine principle who likes to hide an unreachable secret, the effects of which we can see but whose causes always remain obscure.[19] In Porter's short story, the feminine, archetypical force of nature imposes its mysterious power over a conventional human law that is not yet strong enough to dominate the premodern consciousness of Mexican Indians. While the village inhabitants recognize the overwhelming power of María Concepción's actions and her need to eliminate the source of her estrangement and alienation from society and herself, they are unable or unwilling to put this realization into words. María Concepción's return to a state of wholeness is the triumph of premodern values over both Christian and secular modern morality. Interestingly, the triumph of the feminine, natural principle does not bode well with men, because at the end of the story it is Juan who feels trapped and anguished, perhaps suggesting the impossibility of reconciling not only morality and natural instincts but masculine and feminine profound needs and desires as well.

In this mythical world, the Mexican Revolution is only a temporary distraction. History itself appears as something intrinsically false. The armed struggle does not mean anything significant for the village. It changes nothing: Ancient customs and social practices remain untouched. For Juan and María Rosa the Revolution appeared to be the possibility to escape from the town's conventions and to live their love freely. However, the revolutionary libertarian impulse wears out rather soon, in part because of María Rosa's pregnancy. In the end the Revolution only gives Juan material symbols of social status. He gets "new and handsome clothes" including a hat "of unreasonable dimensions and embroidered with silver thread."[20] The Revolution has not only political but erotic value in the story, challenging the village's sexual conventions for a while. María Rosa, the erotic female figure, the sweet and seductive beekeeper, follows her man while carrying the blankets, cooking pots, and her own rifle on her back. They make love between battles, marching, and quarrelling. Thanks to the Revolution she can have a rifle and participate in the struggle as any other fighting man or woman. Still, she has to carry with her the bed and the kitchen and when she talks too much, Juan simply slaps her and says: "Silence, thou simpleton!"[21] The return home is not only a return to traditional values but also a return to a primordial matriarchal world. The ire of María Concepción—modern goddess of nature, earth and fertility—is the force that triumphs and dominates in the end. The Revolution was just a temporary diversion from primordial and almost unchanging realities.

FLOWERING JUDAS

Flowering Judas, the most famous of Porter's Mexican-based fiction, is almost an antithesis of *María Concepción*. Self-fulfillment and the search for harmony with oneself, nature and society are also at the center of the story. Here, however, the main character is not a Mexican Indian, close to nature and far from logical reasoning, but an American woman in love with rigorous rational thinking. Also, in *Flowering Judas* the Mexican Revolution is not a remote and rather unimportant passing event but an ever-present reality that determines the faith of every single character. Finally, the narration is not in the past tense, like in *María Concepción*, but in the present.

The story takes place in a single day. Braggioni, one of the powerful revolutionary generals who ruled Mexico at the time, pays a visit to one of his employees, Laura, a young, beautiful and idealist American who is in Mexico working for the success of a utopian social revolution. Braggioni has temporarily left his wife and home—annoyed by the endless crying about his constant infidelities—and is living in a hotel. He is patiently trying to seduce the pretty American woman in her apartment, singing traditional romantic Mexican songs for her with his guitar.[22] Braggioni is a man of the flesh, a cruel and dominant revolutionist who is already abusing his new found power, toying with subordinates, seducing women and being "cruel to everyone, with a kind of specialized insolence."[23] He is in love with his new found status of power and wealth and shows it by wearing a lavender collar, a purple necktie held by a diamond hoop, an ammunition belt of tooled leather worked in silver and glossy, as well as yellow leather shoes. He appears to be the embodiment of Porter's views about the Revolution's limitations and corruption, although he is also portrayed as a man full of wit, intelligence, and life experience.

Laura, on the other hand, is an idealist Christian who went to Mexico to work for the success of a social revolution. Apparently, she belongs to an anarchist group who believes in Kropotkin's original promachine ideas, because the narrator writes that: "in her special group the machine is sacred and will be the salvation of the workers."[24]

Laura teaches English to a group of Indian children but is unable to understand or identify with them and only likes "their round hands and their charming opportunist savagery."[25] She tries to be useful to a couple of political agitators, one Romanian and the other Polish, but she knows that both lie to her and hate each other. She also visits political prisoners who spend their time counting cockroaches or writing memoirs and political manifestos. If the prisoners she visits become utterly helpless, she smuggles them their favorite narcotics. In her free time she "goes to union meetings and listens to busy important voices quarreling over tactics, methods, internal politics."[26] Laura tries hard to be useful to a good cause but appears to fail every time, and she knows it.

She is beautiful. Everybody praises her gray eyes, looks at her sensual way of walking and dreams about her "great round breasts"[27] and "long, invaluably beautiful legs"[28] that she tries to hide under modest and "sound blue serge."[29] Laura keeps trying to convince herself that she has renounced vanities in the name of a moral principle of the highest order. The narrator writes that "she wears the uniform of an idea" and has "encased herself in a set of principles."[30] Mexican men want the distant, beautiful, and exotic American with vehement ardor. At least three of them attempt to seduce her, but Laura rejects everybody. She appears to have repressed love and sexual desire and protects herself with a strong will to negate everything that might harm her, even her most basic desires. Laura thinks she made a mistake having thrown a flower to the young man who was singing at her window; yet, "she is pleasantly disturbed"[31] by his eyes following her all the time. She considers a young Zapatista captain who declared his love to her as a simpleton, a man-child whom she might give a box of color crayons as an adequate present. Yet, she tries "to forgive herself for having spurred her horse at the wrong moment,"[32] just as the captain was trying to help her dismount. Laura also despises Braggioni and tenaciously resists his seduction attempts but not without experiencing a certain fascination for him. She obeys him when he asks her to clean and oil his pistols, an obvious symbol of male sexual power. She also feels a faintness slowly rise and subside in her when Braggioni talks about love and sex, and he asks her why she works so hard for the Revolution without loving a man who is a true revolutionist.[33] Could it be true that nobody loves her? Even a legless female beggar has a faithful lover, Braggioni explains to her. Yet, Laura resists every man's seduction attempt, striving to cultivate a stoicism that will allow her to protect herself against that disaster she fears, though cannot name.

At her crucial meeting with Braggioni, she is in a state of alienation and loneliness. "She is not at home in the world," the narrator explains.[34] Laura has lost her religious faith. She was born Roman Catholic, and sometimes she still tries to pray at church while hiding from all her comrades. However, "it is no good," and she often finds herself distracted, feeling "tender about the battered doll-shape of some male saint."[35] She has promised herself to Mexico, but she does not even know the motives for her revolutionary devotion or her obligations toward it. She is conscious that nobody invited her and that everyone smiles at her participation in it. Even her anarchist comrades laugh at her romanticism, which, they claim, prevents her from understanding reality as it is. She is appalled to find that, to them, cynicism is what passes for "a developed sense of reality."[36] In short, Laura has a strong puritanical distaste for the reality that surrounds her and refuses to live her life outside the frame of her own preconceived idea of what life should be. For her, a revolution should follow abstract, Christian-like virtues. Her utopian views are strongly tainted by her religiosity and that is why she especially resents the anti-Christian ways of Braggioni.

While visiting a prison, Laura finds Eugenio, a young political prisoner, going into a stupor because he swallowed all the sleeping pills she had smuggled for him. She tells Braggioni that he refused to allow her to call the doctor to save his life. Laura obeyed and let him die. Braggioni is deeply touched by Eugenio's suicide; so much that he hastily leaves Laura's apartment and returns home after being away a whole month. There, his wife has no reproach, only the look of grief stamped on her face. She even unlaces her husband's shoes and wants to wash his feet in an obvious allusion to the anti-Christian ways of Braggioni. When her eyes meet her husband's, he is moved to the point that he starts to cry tears of repentance.

There is no such consolation for Laura. When she is finally alone and goes to bed, guilt and desperation visit her during her sleep. Eugenio appears in her dream and invites her to death. "Murderer—he says—follow me, I will show you a new country, but it is far away and we must hurry."[37] Laura obeys and climbs to the Judas tree outside her window, which takes her "to the rocky ledge of a cliff, and then to the jagged wave of a sea that was not water but a desert of crumbling stone."[38] The ocean, common symbol of death and totality, has a jagged wave and even transforms itself into a desert, similar to the faithless wasteland of T. S. Eliot.[39] Eugenio then gives her the flowers of the Judas tree, which she eats greedily, for they satisfy both hunger and thirst. As West wrote in his seminal work about *Flowering*

Judas, Laura's eating of the Judas flowers is a negative sacrament. Instead of a sacrament of love, she eats Eugenio's flowers of despair, cowardice, and death. She has also betrayed life, by allowing a man to die, and has betrayed herself by repressing her desire for love and sex. Laura finally awakes, trembling and, fittingly, screaming a single word: No!

The Mexican Revolution in *Flowering Judas* is an omnipresent reality that determines in part the life of all the characters in the story. Both the narrator and Laura see and describe it with pessimism not exempt of irony.[40] The story invites the reader to consider Braggioni as a symbol of the Mexican Revolution leaders, that is, corrupt and selfish to great extremes. When he was younger, we read, he was a thin, idealist poet; at the time of the story Laura considers that his "gluttonous bulk (. . .) has become a symbol of her many disillusions."[41] The narrator does not spare negative adjectives to describe Braggioni throughout the story. He is cruel, insolent, vain, corrupt, insensitive, callous, malicious, wicked, incomplete . . . However, he understands his own reality and is even aware of the shortcomings of the Revolution. "I am disappointed in everything as it comes," he explains.[42] He even has an articulate and cynical awareness of the Revolution's demagogic justifications. He recites to Laura that

> "Nothing shall survive that the stiffened hands of poverty have created for the rich and no one shall be left alive except the elect spirits destined to procreate a new world cleansed of cruelty and injustice, ruled by benevolent anarchy."[43]

Braggioni's revolution has a few redeeming qualities, such as his own social mobility and the political actions of his wife, who works hard for the good of factory girls. Braggioni explains to Laura that the Revolution is always about both self-interest and love. Everyone looks out for his own interests; the same people he tries to help would kill him for nothing if he does not protect himself. He has accepted and embraced corruption and sin. "What are Laura's motives," he wonders.[44]

The Mexican Revolution becomes futile and radically inexplicable to all the "professional revolutionists," the ones who had a preconceived idea of what a revolution should be. The anarchists and the political prisoners in the story all appear as detached from reality as Laura but without even being aware of it. While in jail, some of them count cockroaches and start losing themselves, confusing day with night and even dying of boredom. In Laura's case, the Revolution loses its meaning because it does not follow her own utopian, Christian-like moral values. She is proud that she does not surrender to the real-world politics and keeps living for the sake of the ideals that dominate her life and which have left "no detail or gesture of personal taste untouched."[45] However, preconceived ideas cannot guide her on concrete situations or on the way she should behave for the good of the Revolution in practical terms. Afraid of reality, she maintains her distance with all revolutionist without exception. "The very cells of her flesh reject knowledge and kinship in one monotonous word. No. No. No."[46]

Laura hates everything that is impure. Political and sexual violence terrify her. She is also never in the present, always worried about her "remembered afflictions," and her "uneasy premonitions of the future."[47] She has tried to embrace a secular, godless faith and longs for a religious meaning that is now lost for her. She has projected her puritanical longing for order, spirituality, and neatness onto a violent and spontaneous revolution that so obviously refuses to be clean and comely.

Laura follows the long Western tradition of considering rationality and personal freedom as the most precious of human achievements, a tradition perhaps started by Socrates in the fifth century B.C.[48] She is a radically modern character: intelligent, lonely, alienated, and immersed in an endless and fruitless search for an absolute meaning that cannot be found through rationality and abstraction. In the end, she betrays her own ideal by letting a man die of boredom, allowing him do what she does not dare, as revealed by her dream. As Vanashree wrote in regard to *Flowering Judas*, Laura's puritanical mind regards as a "horrible confusion" the inherent and inevitable contradictions of the human condition.[49] She finds it "monstrous to confuse love with revolution, night with day, life with death."[50] Behind an apparent mask of progressive, democratic, and utopian ideals, Laura hides puritanical hypocrisy. It confuses revolution with moral abstraction and political ideals with repressed violence.

CONCLUSIONS

Katherine Anne Porter trip to revolutionary Mexico in search for political, material, aesthetic, and psychological answers to the American and Western crisis of the beginning of the twentieth century ends in disappointment. Her brief belief in a coming Utopia very soon turned into a detailed critique of the Mexican revolutionary failure.

In *María Concepción*, an archetypical, primitive, female figure, recovers her lost "instinctive serenity" by faithfully following her primordial instincts. Porter explored an Indian Mexican community inserted in a complex and modern national and global historical reality. In this world, nature, emotions, and myth still can triumph over rationality and law. Porter portrays a cruel and remorseless mythical world where personal well-being can still be conquered through force and domination. This mythical Indian community is influenced by Western hegemonic modernity but still the possessor of a largely premodern mentality that focuses most of its energies in the present, remains in touch with nature, and still considers violence, death, and contradiction as a common part of life. For this mythical world, the Mexican Revolution was nothing more than a temporary distraction, an unimportant disturbance that did not affect in any significant way the material, cultural, or spiritual life of Mexican peasants.

In contrast, Laura, the main character in *Flowering Judas*, is a modern and feminist character who loses herself in rationality and idealism. Revolutionary Mexico, seen and judged through Christian moral paradigms, is a fallen world. For Laura, the Revolution itself appears as an absurd and corrupt aberration, a grotesque mirror image of what a preconceived rational, aseptic, and utopian social movement should be.

María Concepción and *Flowering Judas* share a profound distrust in human reason's ability to explain and guide individual and social conduct. Both short stories appear to doubt the incessant modern rational quest to build Utopia in an improbable future. They question modernity's faith in revolution and progress. Progress, reason, and Christian ethical values are the implicit parameters against which María Concepción's social transgression and Laura's disenchantment with herself and the Revolution are measured. Those parameters still guide political theory. In Porter's Mexican fiction, myth, emotions, dreams, and sexual desire appear as the most fundamental components of human actions, politics, and language. Nature imperatively refuses to be hidden by faith and reason. It demands its lost place in history, philosophy, and politics.

NOTES

1. John Britton, *Revolution and Ideology. Images of the Mexican Revolution in the United States* (Lexington: The University Press of Kentucky, 1995), 54–55.

2. The expression belongs to Katherine Anne Porter, who writes it in her essay about Gertrude Stein. I personally found it in the article by Janis Stout, "Between Two Wars in a Breaking World," *Cather Studies* 6.1 (2006): 70–91.

3. Richard H. Pells, *Radical Visions and American Dreams. Culture and Social Thought in the Depression Years* (New York: Harper and Row, 1973).

4. Helen Delpar, *The Enormous Vogue of Things Mexican. Cultural Relations between the United States and Mexico, 1920–1935* (Tuscaloosa: University of Alabama Press, 1992), 24.

5. All of Porter's nonfictional works can be found in *The Collected Essays and Occasional Writings of Katherine Anne Porter* (New York: Delacorte Press, 1970).

6. Martin Heidegger, *El Ser y el Tiempo*, trans. José Gaos (Mexico City: FCE, 1967).

7. Katherine Anne Porter, *Flowering Judas and Other Stories* (New York: Random House, 1940), 3.

8. Porter, *Flowering Judas*, 10.

9. Porter, *Flowering Judas*, 20.

10. Porter, *Flowering Judas*, 21.

11. Porter, *Flowering Judas*.

12. Porter, *Flowering Judas*.

13. Porter, *Flowering Judas*, 7.

14. Porter, *Flowering Judas*, 9.

15. Porter, *Flowering Judas*, 15.

16. Porter, *Flowering Judas*, 15–16.

17. Porter, *Flowering Judas*, 13.

18. Porter, *Flowering Judas*, 17.

19. An excellent summary of western ideas about nature can be found in Pierre Hadot's *The Veil of Isis: An Essay on the History of the Idea of Nature* (Cambridge, Mass.: Belknap Press of Harvard University Press, 2006).

20. Porter, *Flowering Judas*, 10.

21. Porter, *Flowering Judas*, 12.

22. Thomas F. Walsh has identified one of the songs that Braggioni sings to Laura. It is, "A la orilla de un palmar" by Manuel M. Ponce. Found in *Katherine Anne Porter and Mexico. The Illusion of Eden* (Austin: University of Texas Press, 1992). Interestingly, in the story the narrator says that Braggioni sings that he is an orphan, while the song is about an orphan girl. Walsh thinks that Porter consciously changed the song's subject. Another possibility is that Porter simply did not understand Spanish well enough. One of the few words she writes in Spanish, *gringuita*, is mistakenly spelled gringita.

23. Porter, *Flowering Judas*, 90.

24. Porter, *Flowering Judas*, 92.

25. Porter, *Flowering Judas*, 97.

26. Porter, *Flowering Judas*, 94.

27. Porter, *Flowering Judas*, 97

28. Porter, *Flowering Judas*.

29. Porter, *Flowering Judas*, 92.

30. Porter, *Flowering Judas*.

31. Porter, *Flowering Judas*, 96.

32. Porter, *Flowering Judas*.

33. An interesting study on the subtle ritual of sexual seduction and domination between Laura and Braggioni is Mary E. Titus' "The 'Booby Trap' of Love: Artist and Sadist in Katherine Anne Porter's Mexico Fiction," *Journal of Modern Literature* 16 (Spring 90): 617–35.

34. Porter, *Flowering Judas*, 97.

35. Porter, *Flowering Judas*, 92.

36. Porter, *Flowering Judas*, 91.

37. Porter, *Flowering Judas*, 102.

38. Porter, *Flowering Judas*.

39. T. S. Eliot's influence on *Flowering Judas* was noticed in the seminal essays of both Ray B. West and Leon Gottfried. West noticed that Eliot's poem "Gerontion" also uses the tree's blossoms as a substitute for the host, and Gottfried observes that the landscape of Laura's dream is somehow similar to "The Waste Land." (Ray B. West, "Katherine Anne Porter: Symbol and Theme in *Flowering Judas*," and Leon Gottfried, "Death's Other Kingdom: Dantesque and Theological Symbolism in *Flowering Judas*." Both essays can be found in Virginia Spencer Carr's critique of *Flowering Judas* (New Brunswick, N. J.: Rutgers University Press, 1993).

40. There is a curious overlapping between the narrator and Laura's consciousness. After describing Braggioni's personality and personal habits, the narrator writes that Laura *knows* and *thinks* those things about him.

41. Porter, *Flowering Judas*, 91.

42. Porter, *Flowering Judas*, 93.

43. Porter, *Flowering Judas*, 100.

44. Perhaps it is worth mentioning that despite its many shortcomings, the Revolution slightly improved the material conditions of the poorest sectors of society, generated vast social mobility, included the Indians into the national project for the first time since the Colonial period, promoted national art and culture and attempted—unsuccessfully—to free the country from the economic imperialism of the United States and Europe. Three classic books about revolutionary Mexico are *Historia de la Revolución Mexicana* by Lorenzo Meyer (México: Colegio de México, 1995), *Revolutionary Mexico* by John M. Hart (Berkeley: University of California Press, 1997) and Alan Knight's *The Mexican Revolutio* (New York: Cambridge University Press, 1986).

45. Porter, *Flowering Judas*, 92.

46. Porter, *Flowering Judas*, 97.

47. Porter, *Flowering Judas*, 91.

48. An excellent book that touches on early feminism's reliance on Hegel is Carol McMillan's *Women, Reason and Nature. Some Philosophical Problems with Feminism* (Princeton, N. J.: Princeton University Press, 1982).

49. Vanashree, *Feminine Consciousness in Katherine Anne Porter's Fiction* (New Delhi: Associated Publishing House, 1991).

50. Porter, *Flowering Judas*, 101.

BIBLIOGRAPHY

Britton, John. *Revolution and Ideology: Images of the Mexican Revolution in the United States.* Lexington: The University Press of Kentucky, 1995.

Delpar, Helen. *The Enormous Vogue of Things Mexican: Cultural Relations between the United States and Mexico, 1920–1935.* Tuscaloosa: The University of Alabama Press, 1992.

Gottfried Leon, "Death's Other Kingdom: Dantesque and Theological Symbolism in *Flowering Judas.*" In *Flowering Judas,* ed. Virginia Spencer Carr. New Brunswick, N.J.: Rutgers University Press, 1993.

Heidegger, Martin. *El Ser y el Tiempo* [Being and Time], trans. José Gaos. México: Fondo de Cultura Económica, 1967.

Pells, Richard H. *Radical Visions and American Dreams. Culture and Social Thought in the Depression Years.* New York: Harper and Row, 1973.

Porter, Katherine Anne. *Flowering Judas and Other Stories.* New York: Random House, 1940.

———. *The Collected Essays and Occasional Writings of Katherine Anne Porter.* New York: Delacorte Press, 1970.

Stout, Janis, "Between Two Wars in a Breaking World." *Cather Studies,* 6.1 (2006): 70–91.

Titus, Mary E., "The 'Booby Trap' of Love: Artist and Sadist in Katherine Anne Porter's Mexico Fiction," *Journal of Modern Literature,* 16 (Spring 90): 617–635.

Vanashree. *Feminine Consciousness in Katherine Anne Porter's Fiction.* New Delhi: Associated Publishing House, 1991

Walsh, Thomas F. *Katherine Anne Porter and Mexico: The Illusion of Eden.* Austin: University of Texas Press, 1992.

West, Ray B. "Katherine Anne Porter: Symbol and Theme in *Flowering Judas.*" In *Flowering Judas,* ed. Virginia Spencer Carr. New Brunswick, N.J.: Rutgers University Press, 1993.

CHAPTER SEVEN

ANITA BRENNER AND THE JEWISH ROOTS OF MEXICO'S POSTREVOLUTIONARY NATIONAL IDENTITY

Rick A. López

In the United States and Mexico the public has a confident sense of how "authentic Mexico" sounds, looks, and tastes. It is women dancing *ballet folklorico* in colorful dresses; roving *mariachi* musicians dressed in *charro* pants and wide brimmed hats; indigenous vendors offering gaily-colored handicrafts; and a cuisine borne of peasant food, with emphasis on such native ingredients as corn, *chile*, and tomato. I have shown elsewhere that this definition of *mexicanidad* did not emerge organically out of Mexico's past, as is often presumed.[1] Instead, it took form after the Revolution as part of a transnational push to culturally integrate the nation around an ethnicized, or Indianized, collective identity. In this essay, I address how the Jewish experience became one of the prisms through which this transnational search for a Mexican national identity was refracted.

Anita Brenner, in the late 1920s, coined the term "Mexican Renaissance" to describe the cultural florescence the emerged from the revolution. Participants in this renaissance claimed that "Indian Mexico" had survived despite hundreds of years of efforts to extirpate it. Brenner likened it to "idols behind altars," arguing that, behind a veneer of acculturation, an authentic, hidden, indigenous soul endured, and stood ready be taken up as the basis for Mexico's regeneration. The renaissance that Brenner described was already underway when she arrived in 1923. It was spearheaded by the likes of the nationalist anthropologist Manuel Gamio, the educator Moisés Sáenz, the intellectuals José Vasconcelos and Rafael Pérez Taylor, and the artists Diego Rivera and Gerardo Murillo. Shortly after her 1923 arrival, Brenner became a central contributor to this renaissance as she moderated how it was perceived domestically and internationally.

In 1928, Brenner summarized in her personal journal what she saw as the impetus behind this renaissance: "Revolution takes on a new meaning, for as in all times, great tragedy here gives birth to great art. The tragedy is four hundred years old, for since the conquest of Mexico by the Spaniards, it has been a land divided against itself, endlessly struggling to unite. The Indian layer, majority of the population, passively resisting European culture, imperceptibly proving it [European culture] out of place, and surging, slowly, upward to assert itself, physically in revolution, spiritually in arts."[2] For Brenner and others, this repressed indigenous culture comprised the heart and soul of the real Mexico that needed to be recovered.

Scholars have noted in passing that Anita Brenner was Jewish, but they have not recognized that it was her complex relationship to her own Jewish heritage that attuned her to Mexico's denigrated indigenous traditions (what she would term "idols behind altars") and inspired her to elevate even the Indian's lowly *petate* (woven reed sleeping mat) to national prominence.[3] Anita Brenner's diaries, correspondence, and publications reveal a woman who feels herself the outsider desperate to become an insider. She was born in 1905 in Aguascalientes to European Jews who had arrived in the United States in the 1880s, married in Chicago, and moved to Mexico where they became wealthy landowners. In 1916, after fleeing the violence of the revolution, the family resettled in San Antonio, Texas. She would spend most of the early part of her life caught between her dueling identities as a Mexican Bohemian, a Jewish woman, and a privileged *estadounidense* (someone of the United States).

Raised and educated in the Lone Star State after the family's flight from Aguascalientes, Anita Brenner always felt out of place in both the Jewish and the non-Jewish communities. She completed a semester of university education at Our Lady of the Lake College in San Antonio and then transferred to the University of Texas (UT) at Austin, where, she explained, she suffered the sting of anti-Semitism, yet felt alienated from the small Jewish community. After two semesters, she quit UT Austin, moved to Mexico City in 1923, and enrolled in the National University. Her protective father allowed her to go only after Joseph Weinberger of the Mexico City branch of the Jewish service organization B'nai B'rith promised to keep an eye on her. Upon Brenner's arrival, Weinberger's wife Frances Toor introduced her into the capital's Jewish community and then into Mexico's international circle of Bohemian artists, intellectuals, and political refugees.

After years of alienation, Anita Brenner was beside herself about suddenly finding herself at the center of these circles. She wrote to her childhood friend Jerry Aron about what it was like after Toor started taking her to breakfasts at Sanborn's in the Casa de los Azulejos:

> [Sanborn's] is quite fashionable, particularly [at] tea-time. But at breakfast it is different. You lounge through your meal, and interesting people whom you know—or ought to know, drop along and talk—oh, books and politics and the theater and gossip—over the cigarettes and the coffee. There is Goopta, Hindu revolutionist, who teaches Sanskrit in the University and also teaches in the public schools, who is famous and intriguing and delightful. There are the Wolfs, communists, avid readers, satisfying and quite charming, particularly the lady. There are lots of others—everybody who has any sort of claim to intellectual-ism(?) is sort of loosely bound into it. Artist[s], sculptors, writers, socialists, musicians, poets—intelligentzia[sic], but not the imitation of it that we have, Jerry. They are not a bit startling. That love is free is a matter so accepted that no one ever thinks to bother

to state so. They all speak the same language, that is, all understand each other, whether they all approve or not. But not literally, for French, German, It[a]lian, English, and of course, Spanish, play around quite congenially. Of course I bask in it. And everybody nearly gives me advice, and Panchita, even if she is Mrs. Weinberg. Of course I appreciate it, all of it, and I can't help wondering why they bother about anything so un-achieved as me. But that is just it. We are quite on a level, here. No snobbishness, prejudice, of any sort—racial, monetary, apparent—As to racial, there couldn't be. There are too many of skin and flag represented.[4]

Soon Brenner was typing essays for Diego Rivera, who converted her to his pro-indigenous vision of Mexican culture, while Carleton Beals helped her enter the publishing world. In 1925, she got a job as Ernest Gruening's research assistant. She helped with his upcoming book, introduced him into Mexico's intellectual circles, and set up his interviews. By 1926, thanks in large part to the French expatriate Jean Charlot, who had become a Mexican citizen, an assistant to Rivera, and a master artist in his own right, Brenner had established herself as a major figure in the cultural scene, hosting large dinner parties whose attendees read like a who's who list. Within the cosmopolitan circle of foreign and Mexican artists and intellectuals in the capital city, Brenner for the first time felt comfortable in her own skin as a transnational Jewish intellectual woman.

Brenner was thrilled when her bohemian friends took an interest in her Jewish heritage. Embarrassed by her inability to answer their questions about Judaism, she set out to learn more about her religion and history, to study Hebrew, and to consider what it meant to her, personally, to be a Jew. After a job at a Protestant girls' school did not work out, she went to work for the B'nai B'rith, meeting Jewish refuges at the port of Veracruz, helping them with their paper work and transportation to Mexico City, settling them in Mexico City, and prolifically publishing in Jewish newspapers and news services about the plight of these refugees. This was the birth of her lifelong career as a researcher and reporter. Her accounts touted Mexico as a land open to settlement and as an ideal location for Jewish newcomers. Her own past experience of alienation from the Jewish community in the United States prompted her to take offense when Mexico's old Jewish families' rejected the flood of newcomers. She responded by trying to facilitate communication and cooperation between the established community and newcomers.[5]

Brenner also delved into the history of Jews in Mexico, passing many hours in the archives following leads about crypto-Jews persecuted in colonial New Spain. One of the first cases to catch her attention was the execution of Tomás Treviño de Sobremonte in 1649 by the Office of the Inquisition. As someone fleeing Texas anti-Semitism, she identified with the stories of these persecuted refugees. As she pieced together their stories, she also patched together an understanding of herself as a transnational Jew and relished discovering how, even in the face of persecution, the people she studied established themselves as a permanent fixture of Mexican society.

Even as she reveled in her reclaimed Jewish identity, she was pleased to no longer be stigmatized as a Jew everywhere she went, as she felt she had been in the United States. She claimed that she felt liberated by what she described as Mexicans' "splendidly indifferent to 'Jewishness' as a class distinction." A heritage that had always seemed to her a burden now struck her as romantic: "I recovered some of the feeling of romance and glamour from them [the recent Jewish immigrants], and when genial little clumps of peddlers began filtering through Mexican streets, I became vastly and actively interested in them, and through them, in other things openly and interestingly Jewish."[6] This newfound pride gave her a different perspective from which to view her previous experiences. She began an autobiographic manuscript titled "A Race of Princes," an excerpt from which won a prize and was published in the *The Jewish Daily Forward* in 1925. She confessed in her manuscript that, having grown up as an outsider to both Jewish and non-Jewish communities, "I had no friends. I was too proud to seek much intimacy where I felt undesired, and too queer for my own people. I got a good deal of rather dolorous ironic joy out of that phrase [my own people]."[7] In Mexico, she at last had learned to embrace her Jewishness, even peppering her letters to Jewish friends with her recently acquired Yiddish terms.[8]

As she came to terms with herself as a Jew, she found herself drawn even more deeply into the historical archives. She became convinced that "there were many more Jews than is generally admitted in the story of the conquest and colonization of Spain's empire." Her previous interest in the narratives of persecution gave way to a fascination with how these Jews of the past struggled over whether to be or not to be Jewish in this new context, and the range of things that meant for them. She particularly delighted in the seditious idea that all "the Jews of the period were of course apparently Catholic as to their religious ideas."[9] This, perhaps, was her first formulation of the tantalizing notion that, behind Christian altars, a group might have preserved their non-Christian faith and practices.

A historical figure with whom she developed a particular bond was the sister of Luis Carvajal. In the sixteenth century, Luis Carvajal had settled part of northern Mexico with a colony of Iberian Jews. He enjoyed great economic and political power until his enemies deposed him by exposing him to the Office of the Inquisition as a Jew. His sister Doña Guiomar, according to Brenner, was

> one of the great heroines of all time, and one of the most attractive figures, humanly speaking. She is torn between two loyalties: her brother, whose views she respects, and her son (Carvajal's heir), who has become a Jewish crusader so eloquent and zealous that, as an Inquisition prisoner, he converted to Judaism a friar who had been put in his cell for the purpose of converting him. But Doña Guiomar's situation is even more complicated. She has one sone[sic] who became a monk (and his conflict is difficult indeed!). She has younger children whom she can save from physical and social suffering by the simple expedient of being a good Catholic. She has on the other hand, her own conscience, and it can be inferred, from bits and pieces of her story as it comes out in the questioning, that she has slowly and painfully been arriving at a faith (adonoi Israel, adonoi echod) on which rock she must stand, at whatever cost, and this is the teaching

she transmits to her children, who like her, behave with almost incredible courage under torture.[10]

Brenner felt that her own struggles over her identity paralleled that of Doña Guiomar, and she drew strength from the latter's resilient adherence to her Jewish faith despite the costs.

Brenner was fascinated also by the accusation that revolutionary leader Francisco Madero was a closet Jew. She drew strength from the thought that Madero, whom she considered "the first wedge in the heartbreaking revolution that tore Mexico from feudalism into socialism," might have struggled over how to balance his Jewishness with his Mexicanness. With her newfound sense of Jews as deeply rooted in Mexican history, and her suspicion that perhaps even the revolution itself had emerged from the ideals of a Jew, she felt that she at last could shed her sense of shame and insecurity until "after a time I strutted my hooked nose again."[11]Along the same vein, Brenner loved to quote Diego Rivera's claim that "Every native Mexican has Jewish blood in his veins."[12] Perhaps it was Rivera, during those early months she spent listening to his lessons on Mexican culture, that first inspired her with the notion of "idols behind altars." Her attempt to understand her Jewish heritage informed her understanding of the Mexican revolution as a rupture that lifted the mask of Spanish Catholicism to reveal Mexico's authentic indigenous face. "Idols behind altars" therefore invoked for Brenner the idea of Judaism secretly preserved despite public conversion, as well as indigenous culture hiding behind a façade of Catholicism and Spanish civilization.

Even as Anita Brenner reveled in at last uniting her dual identities as a Mexican and a Jew, she could escape neither the sting of anti-Semitism nor the presumption that her Jewishness marked her as an outsider to the Mexican nation. We see this, for example, in her relationship to the artist José Clemente Orozco. Though he would become one of Mexico's great masters, at that time, Orozco still was a relative unknown, bitterly laboring in Rivera's shadow. Brenner made it her mission to win him recognition by promoting his work in the United States. When she organized an exhibition to promote Orozco's work in New York City, her efforts received a scathing critique by W. Salisbury, published in *Art Digest*, in early 1928. His review went beyond the art to attack her directly, stating: "It is not enough to say that you do not understand art or art criticism—you do not understand the English language. Perhaps this is partly explained by the fact that the Semitic race has never done anything in art except as a result for contact with the Aryan race."[13] As upsetting as this was to her, she felt shielded by her inclusion within Mexican circles. But Orozco knew her weakness and exploited it. Angered by her refusal to denounce Rivera, Orozco hurt her by telling anti-Semitic jokes and drawing anti-Semitic cartoons.[14] Anita Brenner's response to Salisbury made clear that she knew to harden herself against people like him, but she perhaps was at a loss when humiliated from within what she treasured as her safe space, her own intimate community. She tried to make light of Orozco's insults by playing along. On one occasion she even hung one of his anti-Semitic cartoons on her apartment wall in an effort to make light of it. But, as much as she tried to play it off, it no doubt stung.

At times she sank into fits of depression over slights of this kind. On one occasion she asked her diary: "1. Why am I so often fool enough to believe that I matter to anybody?

2. Why are we obliged to count with all the traditional 'Jew-faults.' If I like the color yellow it is avarice—if I lose a dear painted scarf it is the price I weep for—if the material a friend needed hinders my work and I am thoroughly molested it's the value of it that angers—and so forth. ¿What?"[15] Anti-Semitism and the separation she felt as a Jew at times tested her relationships. One of her closest friendships, with Nahui Olin, for instance, was strained by the fact that Olin's lover was Gerardo Murillo, a father of the Mexican Renaissance, a vocal anti-Semite and a fascist.[16] And Anita Brenner's desire to marry her lover Jean Charlot was thwarted by their religious difference. So frustrated was she, that she almost converted to Catholicism so as to marry him. She pondered the benefits: marriage to her lover and a sense of no longer feeling the outsider. In the end, she concluded that she could not convert because "I don't know enough about Judaism to continue into Catholicism"; that is, she was not confident that she could preserve her Jewish identity behind a façade a Catholic façade.[17]

A few years later, in 1929, she published her book *Idols behind Altars* as the first major account of what she coined the "Mexican Renaissance" and the clearest statement of her thinking about what she saw as Mexico's repressed authentic self. In the book, Brenner wrote that "in the span of one generation Mexico has come to herself" and has "discovered the suffering and hopes of its own people."[18] Behind a Hispanic veneer, she argued, lay the uncontaminated indigenous culture that was the real Mexico. She recounts how, on the heels of the Spaniards' conquest of the Aztec empire, the monks who were zealously working to convert the indigenous population to Christianity tried to transfer natives' religious loyalties from idols to Jesus, Mary and the saints by burying native idols and planting "crosses on their graves." But instead of abandoning their idolatry, the Indians, she argued, pretended to worship the cross when, in fact, they were worshipping the idols buried beneath the foot of the cross, hidden behind it, or incorporated directly into the altar's foundation stones.[19]

The revolution, she argued, at last demolished the façade of Hispanic and Catholic culture. Following the lead of Manuel Gamio and other nationalist intellectuals, she contended that indigenous peoples' vernacular art offered the most sincere expression of this secreted worldview. She insisted that this repressed worldview was the true soul of nation and that it needed to serve as the foundation for the Mexico's own brand of modernity. Brenner had arrived at this interpretation by way of her recovery of her own Jewish roots. It was a declaration that both the Jewish and the indigenous experience, despite centuries of repression, were integral parts of the modern Mexican nation.

From the late 1920s through the 1940s, foreign researchers and scholars fanned out across Mexico to conduct well-funded field research. Their publications circulated widely within Mexico and internationally, and they enjoyed influence as mediators of what counted as authentically Mexican, unabashedly favoring indigenous and peasant sectors over the Hispanic urban middle class. Though these foreigners borrowed their basic narrative from their Mexican colleagues, their growing influence as promoters of this interpretation of the national culture prompted a nationalist backlash. Mexicans called for better research support from their government, and systematically erased signs of the foreign-Mexican collaboration that over the previous two decades had consecrated an ethnicized identity for the postrevolutionary nation.[20] They replaced these signs of collaboration with the illusion that Mexican culture was the organic culmination of the nation's history, nurtured by nationalist intellectuals and artists as against the despoiling Gringo invader.

In the process of erasing this history of transnational collaboration, nationalists also erased Brenner's attempt to create space for Judaism within the nationalist narrative. Later in her life—after her long career as an anthropologist, art historian, reporter, tourism promoter, and defender of the rights of Jews—the Mexican government offered her the Aztec Eagle award, the highest honor offered to a foreigner. According to her daughter, Susannah Joel Glusker, Anita rejected the award on the grounds that she was a Mexican, not a foreigner.[21] Though Brenner did not elaborate about her rejection of the award, perhaps she also was concerned that her acceptance of an honor reserved for foreigners might reinforce the presumption that the Jewish experience was separate from authentic *mexicanidad.*

As this essay has argued, Brenner's promotion of indigenous culture as the foundation for Mexico's postrevolutionary culture was born out of her own search for a Mexican Jewish identity. It is ironic therefore that though her Jewish heritage inspired Brenner to formulate her ideas about the role of indigenous culture in Mexico's renaissance, Judaism remains, even today, outside of mainstream views of what comprises authentic *mexicanidad.*

NOTES

1. Rick A. López, *Crafting Mexico: Intellectuals, Artisans, and the State after the Revolution* (Durham, N. C.: Duke University Press, 2010).

2. Anita Brenner, journal from 1928, quoted in Susannah Joel Glusker, *Anita Brenner: A Mind of Her Own* (Austin: University of Texas Press, 1998), 96.

3. Anita Brenner, "The Petate, A National Symbol," *Mexican Folkways* 1(1) (June–July 1925): 26–27.

4. Anita Brenner to Jerry Aron, September 24, 1923, Folder 3, box 52, series III, Anita Brenner Archives, Harry Ransom Humanities Research Center, University of Texas at Austin.

5. Anita Brenner, "Mexico—Another Promised Land," typescript of an article for *Menorah Journal*, February 1928

6. Quoted in Glusker, 152.

7. Quoted in Glusker, 152.

8. See, for example, correspondence between Brenner and Frances Toor, folder 4, box 71, series III, Brenner Archives.

9. Brenner, "The Carvajal Story," typescript, folder 2–5, box 1, Series I, Brenner Archives.

10. Brenner, "The Carvajal Story," typescript, folder 2–5, box 1, Series I, Brenner Archives.

11. Quoted in Glusker, 152.

12. Anita Brenner, folder 3, box 4, series I, Brenner Archives.

13. Anita Brenner to W. Salisbury, February 19, 1928, folder 3, box 52, series III; and Anita Brenner, personal diary entry Saturday, February 25, 1928, page 63, folder 3, box 121, series IV, Brenner Archives.

14. Glusker, 49–50.

15. Anita Brenner, personal diary entry, January 16, 1926, page 55, folder 5, box 120, series VI, Brenner Archives.

16. Brenner diaries, August 21, 1927; and Anna Indych-López, *Muralism without Walls: Rivera, Orozco, and Siqueiros in the United States, 1927–1940* (Pittsburgh, Pa.: Pittsburgh Press, 2009), 47.

17. Quoted in Glusker, 126.

18. Brenner, *Idols behind Altars* (New York: Payson & Clark, 1929), 314.

19. Brenner, *Idols behind Altars*, 142–5.

20. This encounter is discussed and analyzed in my book, López, *Crafting Mexico.*

21. Glusker, 11, 17. This claim is repeated often but always by reference to Glusker and never with clarity about what year is said to have occurred. While there is no reason to doubt the claim, I have been unable to verify it with a separate, independent source.

BIBLIOGRAPHY

Anita Brenner Archives, Harry Ransom Humanities Research Center, University of Texas at Austin.
Brenner, Anita. *Idols behind Altars.* New York: Payson & Clark, 1929.
————. "The Petate, a National Symbol," *Mexican Folkways* 1 (June–July 1925): 26–27.
Glusker, Susannah. *Anita Brenner: A Mind of Her Own.* Austin: University of Texas Press, 1998.
Indych-López, Anna. *Muralism without Walls: Rivera, Orozco, and Siqueiros in the United States, 1927–1940.* Pittsburgh, Pa.: University of Pittsburgh Press, 2009.
López, Rick A. *Crafting Mexico: Intellectuals, Artisans, and the State after the Revolution.* Durham, N.C.: Duke University Press, 2010.

SECTION II

LIVING BORDERS

CHAPTER EIGHT

MEXICAN AMERICANS AND THE NOVEL OF THE MEXICAN REVOLUTION

Yolanda Padilla

In her memoir of the Mexican Revolution (1910–1920), written during the 1920s and entitled *La Rebelde*, Leonor Villegas de Magnón strove to provide a different perspective from the one that was already congealing in official versions of the war. Magnón devoted much of her life to the Revolution, first as an active participant through the female nursing corps she founded, La Cruz Blanca, and then through the years she spent trying to find a publisher for her narrative. She was born on the U.S.-Mexico border, in Nuevo Laredo, Tamaulipas, Mexico, in 1876, the same year that Porfirio Díaz began his thirty-six year dictatorship of the country. Although she was born into an affluent and cultured family that was part of the Mexican frontier's "rural aristocracy," Magnón's unhappiness with the inequalities of the Mexican social order and the political corruption that undergirded them prompted her to risk her family wealth by participating in the overthrow of the Díaz regime. What followed was a series of remarkable exploits, as she tended to injured revolutionary soldiers, housed political exiles, engaged in numerous acts of political intrigue, and rubbed shoulders with the likes of Pancho Villa, Álvaro Obregón, and Emiliano Zapata. Moreover, she became an important confidante and advisor to Venustiano Carranza, a future Mexican president, and the person who urged her to write down and publish her experiences of the Mexican Civil War.

While her experiences were extraordinary, Magnón's goal in writing her memoir was to show that she was part of a larger group of politically and socially engaged border Mexicans, one that included women along with men, and whose contributions to Mexican history were in danger of being forgotten before the war's last bullets had even been fired. She makes this aim explicit:

> . . . history has assumed responsibility for documenting the facts, but it has forgotten the important role played by the communities of Laredo, Texas, and Nuevo Laredo, Tamaulipas and other border cities which united themselves in a fraternal agreement.[1]

In speaking about the border region, Magnón often singles out her hometown of Laredo, as she elaborates on the rich intellectual and political culture produced by the city's Mexican Americans and proto-Mexican Americans. She details their active participation in the Revolution, both as direct participants in the war, and as commentators who felt that their opinions should carry weight despite their marginalized positions north of the border. Pushing back against Mexican narratives that either ignored the border region completely or showed great disdain for its people, Villegas de Magnón produces a narrative that refuses to honor the dividing line between the United States and Mexico or to allow the borderlands to continue as a forgotten zone for both countries.

Villegas de Magnón's memoir has several qualities that are common among Mexican American responses to the Revolution: She corrects a faulty historiography that excludes Mexican Americans from the narrative of the Revolution, she chastises those who view the people of the border with contempt, and she understands Mexicans in the United States to constitute the continuation of Mexican history north of the border. In what follows, I will examine how early twentieth-century Mexican American writers responded to the Mexican Revolution, arguing that, like Villegas de Magnón, they grappled with the war's meanings and consequences in ways that were shaped by their positions as border subjects marginalized by and alienated from the national cultures of both Mexico and the United States. I read these Mexican American engagements with the war as part of the preeminent Mexican narrative thematic, the novel of the Revolution. Mexican American writers such as Villegas de Magnón, Conrado Espinoza, Josefina Niggli, Luis Pérez, Américo Paredes, and José Antonio Villareal all wrote versions that share many of the key concerns of the Mexican tradition, including an emphasis on the betrayal of the Revolution. However, as I argue, while narratives written south of the border express a largely national orientation, those written to the north express a fundamentally transnational orientation, one that asserts the centrality of Mexican Americans to the Revolution, and thus to the emerging Mexican national narrative. Mexican Americans produce, then, what I call "the 'other' novel of the Revolution" narratives that insist that Mexicans in the United States be accounted for in the Mexican national project. In so doing, they emplot issues into the Mexican tradition that reflect their local conditions as members of an emerging and embattled ethnic group and that consequently point to and critique the neocolonial relationship between Mexico and the United States. Such issues include dispossession, racial and ethnic conflict, and debates about cultural integrity. In what follows, I will sketch out the defining characteristics of this "other" novelistic tradition and will then provide examples through readings of Josefina Niggli's *Mexican Village* and Américo Paredes' novel *The Shadow*.

In order to understand the significance of including Mexican American texts as part of the tradition of the novel of the Revolution, one must have some familiarity with the place of northern Mexico in the Mexican imaginary, which, in turn, introduces issues of nation and region and how they are treated in the novel and its scholarship. Numerous scholars have noted the contempt and deep suspicion with which the Mexican center has historically regarded the northern frontier, as it has viewed the region as a "cultural desert"[2] and, even more, as an untamable zone of rebellion inassimilable into the national body.[3]

Martín Luis Guzmán indicates this view in his great novel of the Revolution, *El Águila y la Serpiente* (1928), when he complains of the "barbarous" Sonoran desert, a "savage region" populated by men of "uncontrolled passions" who respond to "none but the zoological stimuli."[4] María Socorro Tabuenca Córdoba notes that the "barbaric" cultural desert in the Mexican imaginary includes the U.S. Southwest along with northern Mexico.[5] Córdoba calls this deeply rooted attitude "North of the Borderism," which she argues is in part the result of a "Mexican centralist necessity to possess a 'national identity' inherited from the 19th century. In the wake of the loss of more than half of Mexico's territory, 'national unity' urgently erected a retaining wall of mexicanidad (Mexicanness) at the border."[6] North of the Borderism, then, combines a historical disdain of fronterizos with an anti-imperial impulse to look inward, to sever the story of the Mexican nation from that of those Mexicans who were sacrificed to U.S. imperial expansion.

Some literary critics have credited the canonical novels of the Revolution—especially Mariano Azuela's *Los de Abajo* (1915)—with playing a part in rehabilitating the Mexican north in the national imaginary. Adalbert Dessau has argued that novels of the Revolution participated in the formation of a national consciousness based on perceived Mexican values and traditions as an anti-imperial stance.[7] These novels, which were often set in the north, replaced the urban with the rural and crafted peasant protagonists.[8] In the case of Azuela, in particular, scholars have noted such qualities as his use of the popular expressions of the *campesinada* and the appropriateness of speech to social class.[9] This attention to the culture of the northern peasantry was one of the qualities that lead Luis Leal to assert that Azuela had "broken with European tradition to forge a genuinely American novel," one that was "admirably adopted to his theme."[10]

Such analyses commend the novelists of the revolution for making the peasantry visible within the national narrative and for making that visibility the basis for an autochthonous, authentically Mexican nationalism and literary tradition. Others, however, have criticized these narratives precisely for their complicity—intentional or not—with nation-building strategies that gestured toward the recognition of long-marginalized groups as heroes of the revolution, only to use that superficial recognition to obscure the neglect and oppression in which they continued to exist. As Alicia Schmidt Camacho has noted, the revolutionary constitution of 1917 "hailed the peones of Mexico's historical division of labor as citizens and patriots, and it made land reform a reward for their sacrifices in battle to the modern nation."[11] Not only did the revolutionary state break such promises, but it also initiated an often contradictory strategy that continued to promote peones as national heroes while simultaneously blaming them and their "backwardness" for the nation's belatedness in becoming fully modern.[12] Max Parra locates these contradictory impulses in the "master narratives" of the novel of the Revolution. As he asserts, they celebrate nonurban, popular subjects as "the proud source of Mexican 'values' and identity"; at the same time, those subjects are seen to be "frightfully violent, backward, and antimodern, lacking the intellectual and moral attributes necessary to lead the nation into the future." Parra further avers that such portrayals of the rural masses were "sustained on the tenets of urban citizenship," tenets that included "social discipline, literacy, individualistic bourgeois morality, and the subordination of the countryside to the city." By cultivating such values, however inadvertently, these writers became "unofficial advocates of the modernizing, middle-class project of nationhood promoted by the postrevolutionary regimes."[13]

As critics such as Parra and Jean Franco have argued, representations of popular violence have been of particular importance in the process of "Othering" the rural masses. One sees this even in the narratives of such seemingly distinct writers as Azuela and Guzmán. While traditionally they have been understood to have divergent agendas, with Azuela's classic novel sympathetic toward and focused on the peasantry, and Guzmán's work generally interested in elite political leaders, both portray the Revolution as an irrepressible force fueled by the incomprehensible rage and violence of the rural masses—a rage that the peasants themselves fail to understand. By abstracting the violence from actual peasant grievances, these writers depoliticize and dehistoricize that violence.[14] Many of these novels fall under the category of "Villista" literature, narratives that view the war either directly or indirectly through the lens of the rebel Pancho Villa. These texts are set in Mexico's northern environs, where Villa's "Division of the North" famously was based, and thus their vision of the irrational and unfathomable violence of the Revolution perpetuates the view of the "barbaric North" along with that of the primitive peasantry. In the end, we come full circle: While the novel of the Revolution initially seems to valorize the long-maligned rural masses and to privilege the Mexican north for its potential as the site of an "authentic" Mexican culture, ultimately, it reconsolidates traditional views of the barbarous north and the civilized center, and, as Bruce Novoa argues, fundamentally supports a centralist position and an authoritarian national government.[15] However, such was not the case with all novels of the Revolution. The works of Azuela and Guzmán become the "master narratives" of the Revolution's literary tradition in part precisely because of their nationalist and centralizing imperatives, qualities that traditional studies of revolutionary literature privilege in their analyses. Parra uses a "regionalist" approach to examine marginalized works that constitute what he calls "an alternative genealogy" of literature of the Revolution.[16] Texts such as Nellie Campobello's *Cartucho* and Rafael Muñoz's *Vámonos con Pancho Villa!* are regionalist in their "self-conscious, cultural, political, and emotional attachment to a specific territorial homeland within the space of the nation, sometimes called 'patria chica.'"[17] As Parra argues, attending to the regionalist sensibilities that mark these narratives "places subaltern insurgencies in their own unique revolutionary dynamic, rooted in local historical processes and cultural practices" and elucidates "how regional rebels define themselves and their participation in the war."[18] One example of such distinctions comes in the representation of violence. In contrast to Azuela's and Guzman's severing of popular violence from historical and cultural contexts, Campobello and Muñoz provide what Parra calls an "ethics of violence," one in which violence is always contextualized, is inseparable from struggles for social liberation, and is culturally specific. Seen in this light, representations of violence in the Mexican north become snapshots of human reality, not examples of the region's savagery.

The Mexican American novel of the Revolution shares much with the regionalist tradition Parra identifies. Like the narratives of Campobello and Muñoz, those by Mexicans in the United States foreground local conditions and cultural values in their responses to the war. They show a cultural, political, and emotional attachment to their "patria chica," the northern borderlands constituting a region that transgresses the U.S.-Mexico border. And while they do not represent inordinate amounts of violence, they also undermine the center's ideas regarding the primitive and violent north. Together with the regionalist narratives, they comprise a literary tradition in contradistinction to the centralizing imperatives of the canonical novels, one that valorizes the peripheral north while humanizing and historicizing the experiences and actions of the region's revolutionaries.

At the same time, there are significant differences between the regional and Mexican American novels of the Revolution stemming from the latter's emergence north of the border. First, the regional novelists do not feel compelled to argue for the cultural authenticity of the region and people they represent. Mexican Americans, however, are rendered culturally suspect by their contact with the United States, an issue that the narratives raise and often refute to varying degrees. Villegas de Magnón, for example, explicitly repudiates the idea of cultural inauthenticity in her memoir. Chastising those who view the people of the border with contempt, she asserts that the *fronterizos* are examples of the so-called "Pochos who are so scorned by the Mexican capital, and who guard with tightly held hands the honor and international decorum of an incomprehensible and grand psychology."[19] The term "pocho" was an insult directed at border dwellers to indicate that they were tainted by their proximity to the United States and thus were not "real" Mexicans. Villegas de Magnón turns ideas about Mexican authenticity on their head by asserting that the *fronterizos* safeguard the honor and cultural integrity of the Mexican people, while in the Mexican capital one finds nothing but corruption.[20]

This point leads to a more significant difference between the regional and Mexican American novels of the Revolution: While regional versions show little concern in positioning their subjects within Mexico's national paradigms, Mexican American examples often explicitly grapple with the place that Mexicans in the United States might occupy in the Mexican national narrative. This is not to say that the regional novels are irrelevant to discussions of national culture; on the contrary, any engagement with the regional calls forth a dialogue with the nation. Moreover, with the outbreak of the war, the fighting peasantry so often portrayed in novels of the Revolution instantly gained a place—however vexed—in the national imaginary. Such was not the case for Mexicans in the United States, as writers such as Villegas de Magnón lamented and protested. Pushing back against Mexican narratives that either ignored the border region completely or showed great disdain for its people, Mexican American novels of the Revolution often locate the epicenter of the war on the U.S.-Mexico border, and thus position border Mexicans at the center of the defining event of twentieth-century Mexican history. Such narratives refuse to honor the dividing line between the United States and Mexico or to allow the borderlands to continue as a forgotten zone for both countries.

Their efforts to grapple with the Revolution's meanings and consequences meant that they probed the revolutionary plan from a transnational perspective and that they consequently attempted to reshape a Mexican national narrative that had rendered them either invisible or as a threat to Mexican cultural and national integrity. Following David Luis-Brown, I use the term "transnational" to denote "modes of affiliation that elude the national and activities beyond the purview of the state."[21] For many Mexican American writers, such activities included producing knowledge that was informed by a transnational imaginary and thus refuses a nation-based logic that would sever the history of Mexican-Americans from that of Mexico. Whether the authors I study are writing the story of the Revolution or querying its legacies, they do so first and foremost from the perspective of Mexican America, engaging such questions through transnationally informed perspectives and modes of analysis. This is the case despite the fact that these writers encompassed an array of backgrounds as migrants, immigrants, exiles, and longtime residents who traced their family lines back to when the U.S. Southwest was still the Mexican north. Moreover, and following from such differences in background, the period in which they wrote, and their class positions, their sense of identity varied greatly. Thus, while Américo Paredes and José Antonio Villareal self-identified in ways that we feel comfortable calling "Mexican American" today, Leonor Villegas de Magnón, who was a lifelong resident of the borderlands, considered herself to be Mexican, while Josefina Niggli resisted identifying with either nation-state, focusing instead on her position as an outsider deeply versed in the culture of the border.

For all of their differences, these Mexican American and proto-Mexican American writers shared an imaginary that was shaped by their maintenance of strong, ongoing connections both to Mexico and to the United States, as well as a collective memory of a time when the U.S. Southwest was Mexican land and of a later period when the border was relatively unregulated. For some, such as Villegas de Magnón and Luis Pérez, this prompted an understanding of Mexican American identity and everyday life that emphasized two-way movements across a relatively fluid national border. For others, such as Niggli and Paredes, it meant interrogating and elucidating larger U.S.-Mexico relations from the vantage point of Mexican America. For all, it led to an insistence that they marked the continuation of Mexican history in the United States, a position that compelled them to write from perspectives on the margins of nations and which informed their understanding of national projects as transnational processes.

Such perspectives provide a stark contrast to the classic novels of the Revolution. While many of the war's battles occurred on the northern frontier and at times spilled over into the United States and while significant numbers of Mexicans north of the border participated in the war in a variety of ways, including as soldiers and as intellectuals who tirelessly weighed in on the proceedings, the novels of the Revolution that emerged from Mexico ignored the transnational dynamics that played a part in fueling the upheaval and made no room for Mexican Americans or proto-Mexican Americans in their visions of national and cultural integrity. This was the case despite the fact that some of the most prominent Mexican novels were initially published in Spanish-language newspapers in the United States. *Los de Abajo*, critically acclaimed as the first and most important of the novels of the Revolution, appeared in serial form in El Paso del Norte in 1915. Guzmán's *La Sombra del Caudillo* was published in 1929, both by San Antonio's *La Prensa* and Los Angeles' *La Opinión*. Yet their place of publication had no bearing on their content, as they engage the Revolution from a fundamentally national perspective, focusing on domestic contexts and problems in their treatments of the war. The same is true of those novels that feature characters that end up in the United States, including again *Los de Abajo, La Sombra del*

Caudillo, and Guzmán's *El Aguila y la Serpiente*. The United States is nothing more than an escape valve for these characters, with no influence on their subjectivities or on their sense of the Revolution itself. As Bruce-Novoa has argued, their escape to the United States indicates a pessimistic view of the Mexican future and a narrative closure rather than an entry into a renewed analysis.[22]

The transnational imaginary, then, distinguishes the Mexican American from the Mexican novel of the Revolution, a difference one immediately sees by comparing the protagonists of each tradition. The classic examples from Mexico focus on the fighting peasantry (Azuela's *Los de Abajo*, 1915; Campobello's *Cartucho*, 1931), military and political leaders (Guzmán's *El Aguila y la Serpiente*, 1928 and *La Sombra del Caudillo*, 1929), intellectuals (Vasconcelos' *Ulisis Criollo*, 1935), and the disaffected middle class (Azuela's *Andrés Pérez, Maderista*, 1911), all of whom find a place within the Mexican national narrative. In contrast, those written by Mexicans north of the border take as their protagonists the border subject (Villegas de Magnón's *La Rebelde* and Paredes's *The Shadow*), the migrant (Pérez's *El Coyote, the Rebel*), the immigrant (Villareal's *Pocho*), the exile (Espinoza's *Under the Texas Sun*)—in short, the refuse of imperial incursions, failed nationalist projects, and revolutionary ambitions. Such figures always threaten to rupture the imagined community of the nation and are normally contained at least in part through renewed national narratives that elide or subordinate them.

Josefina Niggli responds to such elisions in her masterwork, the 1945 novel *Mexican Village*. She insists on writing the story of the border subject into the Revolution, doing so by focusing on the legacies of the war and on the long history of U.S.-Mexico contact and conflict that played a part in fueling its outbreak and that continues to shape the Mexican future. She takes as her protagonist the mixed-race, dispossessed, and proto-Mexican American Tejano Bob Webster, positioning him at the center of a national allegory that queries the raced-based nation-building strategies that originated during the Revolution and were aggressively promoted by state intellectuals. I see Niggli's choice of hero first and foremost as her orchestration of a "return of the repressed," as the postrevolutionary government's nation-building paradigm must account for those Mexicans who ended up on the other side, whether because the border had crossed them in the aftermath of the Mexican-American War or because they had crossed the border in search of the economic and social stability that revolutionary Mexico could not provide. Like Villegas de Magnón, then, Niggli refuses to allow Mexican Americans to be cut loose by the Mexican nationalist project, insisting on writing them into the story of the nation in ways that combine an emerging ethnic history with the larger history of U.S.-Mexico relations.

Niggli was born in Monterrey, Nuevo León, in 1910, the year the Revolution began. Her American father was the chief manager of the foreign-owned quarry that was the economic center of the small village of Hidalgo where he lived with his family.[23] The quarry's preeminence in the town's economic life was not unusual; by the time of the Revolution's outbreak, millions of acres of Mexico's most valuable land were foreign-owned. But the circumstance was a profound source of conflict—both in Hidalgo and elsewhere—that many point to as the final spark that ignited the revolution. Years later, Niggli took her experience of the transnational undercurrents that permeated Hidalgo as her point of departure for

Mexican Village, depicting the role encroaching multinationals played in the everyday lives of rural Mexicans. Linking such neocolonial practices to the outbreak of the rebellion, she showed the war to be a profoundly transnational event that could not be understood fully without taking into account the shaping influence of the United States as a neo-imperial power. Moreover, those connections between neocolonialism and the Revolution come to reveal a much longer history of transnational contact, conflict, and interdependence between Mexico and the United States.

Through her focus on the border subject and U.S. neocolonialism, Niggli crafts a narrative of the Revolution that directly conflicts with the Mexican government's vision of an autochthonous Mexican nationhood, especially as enunciated by Manuel Gamio and José Vasconcelos, luminaries of the Mexican revolutionary and postrevolutionary periods. They initiated the institutionalization of the Revolution by crafting narratives that positioned nation-building as its ultimate goal, consequently, obscuring the war's agrarian origins and demands. At the heart of such narratives were their influential ideas regarding revolutionary mestizaje, a fraught concept that argues for the achievement of national consolidation through racial miscegenation.[24] Proponents of mestizaje believed that Mexico's Indians were the primary impediment to the country's unification and subsequent entrance into modernity. Their solution was to celebrate Mexico's indigenous heritage as central to the nation while insisting on the imperative of Indian assimilation through mixing with Mexican Creoles, who were considered to be "white." Under this plan, the Indian would eventually be racially and culturally "whitened," disappearing under the banner of the mestizo, the nation's ideal citizen for the future.[25] Among the numerous implications of this vision of nationhood was that it promoted a community strictly imagined along Spanish-Indian racial and cultural lines and that it vigilantly contained that community within the confines of its borders.

In Mexican Village, Niggli tests the possibilities of a Mexican nation constituted by the mestizo citizen through an allegorical narrative. The great Castillos have ruled the border region outside of Monterrey for centuries but are facing a moment of crisis, as the Revolution has dismantled the cacique system that has historically ordered Mexican society. In the midst of the crumbling of the Castillo power, Don Saturnino, the family patriarch, believes that he has only to find the proper heir in order to restore his family to its place of preeminence. True to the state's vision for the future, that heir turns out to be a mestizo. However, and in keeping with the focus on dispossession that I am identifying as a hallmark of these "other" novels, Niggli features Bob Webster at the center of her nation-building allegory, thus undoing her national allegory at its very initiation by virtue of her impulse to examine the situations of those subjects on the borders of nations.

Bob is the illegitimate product of an affair between a Mexican maid and her Anglo Texas boss. His father cruelly rebuffs him, exclaiming "admit an Indian is a son of mine? Damn it, I'm a white man!"[26] In response, Bob eventually chooses to live in Mexico, the country that his grandmother endlessly spoke of when he was a child and where he hopes his "blood will be a pleasure rather than a disgrace"[27] Through this scene of paternal rejection, one that haunts Bob throughout the narrative, and the move to Mexico in which it results, Niggli foregrounds issues of race in ways that introduce ethnic conflict faced by proto-Mexican American border subjects in the United States, while also raising the specter of Mexican dispossession in what is now the U.S. Southwest. Moreover, by accentuating such racial divides, Niggli instantly denaturalizes U.S. conceptions of race, first by foregrounding Indian-Mexican-White relations as opposed to the Black-White binary that dominates the U.S. racial imaginary, and second, by having Bob reject the segregationist U.S. racial paradigm governed by its "one drop rule" and fleeing to Mexico where he hopes to find acceptance through its integrationist model of racial mestizaje.

However, in having Bob reject the United States for Mexico, Niggli does not romanticize revolutionary mestizaje. In fact, she begins the novel with an extensive depiction of the outsider status of the village's Indian population, suggesting that the reality of mestizaje is one of rhetorical force over material benefit for the Indians who form its symbolic foundation. Rather, she employs this racial formation in order to highlight U.S.-Mexico contact as an integral part of Mexican history, and she does so in a manner that conflicts with the use of mestizaje to craft a "foundational fiction" understood exclusively in Spanish-Indian terms. Specifically, the narrative foregrounds Bob's mixed-race status at the same time that it positions him as the primary candidate to become the next heir of the Castillo estate. The result in terms of the national allegory would be to make a mestizo the inheritor of the Mexican national patrimony and to dramatize the state's ideal of a nation founded on the principle of mestizaje. However, the fact that he is a mestizo from the United States confounds his ability to act as the symbol of an autochthonous national identity; his is an identity that spills across national borders, makes manifest political, cultural and racial histories that have constituted the border region, and reveals the mutually shaping relationship between the border and the nation.

Bob's disarticulation of the national allegory begins with his arrival in Hidalgo, even before the narrative has initiated its nation-building themes. The book begins by revealing the region to be a fluid and deeply transnational space economically sustained by a foreign-owned quarry. Significantly, Bob enables this revelation when he appears as the new *patrón*, for his very presence animates the region's profound but obscured history of transnational contact, especially as it centers on the quarry. He is the latest in a long line of foreign quarry masters dating back to 1903 (the novel opens in 1920), and which have included a "martinet German," a "casual Irishman," a "homesick Englishman," an "excitable Frenchman," and a "drunken Italian."[28] This last met his end in 1913, when the rebels found him, demanded that he reveal the whereabouts of Don Saturnino and then hanged him when he could not oblige them with the information. Bob's arrival kindles these dormant memories, which allude to the tensions raised in the northern Mexican countryside by the policies of Mexican dictator Porfirio Díaz. Díaz's aggressive program of land expropriation meant that by 1910 ninety-eight percent of the agrarian working classes were landless, resulting in a profound transformation of the rural Mexican economy and way of life.[29] This program culminated with the dictator's increasingly urgent courting of foreign investors, a move that made it impossible for local elites to compete for resources, ultimately prompting their alliance with the peasantry and providing yet another impetus for the outbreak of the Revolution. As a number of historians have posited, the exploitation of the Mexican countryside by U.S. entrepreneurs was the final spark that ignited the rebellion and that informed its often nationalist and anti-imperial forms.[30]

By reanimating the obscured geopolitical and transnational origins of the Revolution, Bob's arrival shows that it is the "provincial" village that spearheads the revolutionary events that upset the neocolonial milieu of the region, consequently making visible its penetration by foreign interests and the role that that penetration played in shaping everyday life. These revelations go beyond merely representing Hidalgo as the victim of *yanquí* imperial incursions. Rather, the portrait of the foreign-owned quarry and its collision with Mexican history reveals an asymmetrical power structure that nonetheless could be and was attacked and at least temporarily dismantled from below. Circumscribed neither by Mexico nor the United States, Hidalgo has been constituted in part by the fitful and uneven interplay between the two, all the while remaining a somewhat autonomous border culture.

Bob's role in shedding light on this ongoing history of contact, antagonism, and ambivalent adaptation does not come about simply because he is the most recent foreigner in Hidalgo. Unlike those foreign bosses who preceded him, Bob's personal history is implicated in the violence and foreign domination his presence reveals and in ways that reflect the emergence of Mexican American racial and cultural identities on the U.S.-Mexico border. He has both suffered and benefited from the legacy of United States imperial and neocolonial practices in the borderlands and as a consequence occupies a vexed insider/outsider position in the village, one that contributes to the thematization of the Mexican frontier's transnational formation. Thus the novel's representation of autochthonous Mexican nation-building ultimately is undermined by its protagonist precisely because of his association with the United States. As a subject of the border, Bob reveals the deep history of transamerican contact that has defined the very Mexican region on which Niggli centers her narrative of national achievement. *Mexican Village*, then, marks the excess of history embodied by the border subject as represented through Bob. In turn, that subject undermines the project of national sovereignty, putting in motion instead a repetition of the cycle of transnational contact that has defined the history of the U.S.-Mexico borderlands.

Articulations of mestizaje elided the web of entanglements that proceeded from Mexican-U.S. contact. Through its Tejano protagonist, who is constituted by those elided histories, *Mexican Village* tells a different story, one that founds its version of mestizaje on a history of miscegenation that includes the Anglo-American along with the Spaniard and Indian. This alternative narrative uses the rhetoric of Mexican liberal nationalism against itself, challenging its forging of an originary myth that occludes the much more expansive transnational history that played a key role in shaping the Mexican nation. The major implication that follows is that the longer history of violent contact, resistance, and adaptation between Spain and Mexico remains important but recedes to the background, acting as the canvas on which Niggli draws the similar and more recent historical process involving the United States and Mexico. This change in emphasis focuses attention on the newer circumstance of U.S. neocolonial imperialism as an integral part of Mexico's future, a situation Niggli saw all too clearly during her time in Texas.[31] The transnational state both embodied and augured by the proto-Mexican American protagonist produces a narrative that focuses less on building a race-based mythology of national origins than on bringing into prominence the history of national permeability that will continue to shape the Mexican future.[32]

Roughly ten years after *Mexican Village* was published, Américo Paredes would also produce a novella that insists on writing Mexican Americans into the Revolution. Paredes is most renowned for his studies of racial conflict and Mexican border culture north of the Rio Grande. More recently, however, scholars such as Juan Alonso, Ramón Saldívar, and Alicia Schmidt Camacho have analyzed his work in more broadly transnational terms, especially with regard to his keen observations of developments in postrevolutionary Mexican society and their significance for Mexicans in the United States.[33] Paredes's novella, *The Shadow*, written during the 1950s but not published until 1998, is of particular relevance for such transnationally informed critical scholarship.[34] The narrative is set in northern Mexico in the late 1930s, the period when, as Saldívar puts it, "the fervor and idealism of revolutionary struggle begin to settle into their institutionalized forms."[35] The protagonist, Antonio Cuitla, is a former member of Pancho Villa's famed Division of the North, at one time Mexico's most feared rebel army. His courageous exploits in battle, which exceed even those of his former friend and rival leader, Jacinto Del Toro, prompt one of his men to name him "the bravest man in the whole Division of the North"[36] and underwrite his position as president of the *ejido* (a small collective landholding) that is at the center of the novel's action.

The novel opens during a moment of great tension between the workers and the former local *hacendado* (hacienda owner), Don José María Jiménez. Spurred by Del Toro, the workers increasingly voice their unhappiness at the way in which agrarian reform has been implemented, as Jiménez has retained the most arable lands, while the *ejido* is at a distance from the fertile banks of the river. The situation reaches a breaking point when Del Toro talks of taking all the land up to the river's edge and driving the landowners out. In response to such ideas, "the men of the colony, discontent with their high, dry soil, tired of grubbing trunks out of the ground and living in the *jacales* they had made with their own hands, looked greedily at the cleared farms, the neat houses and the planted fields of the people along the river."[37] Cuitla finds himself caught between his loyalty to the peasant community from which he comes and his attraction to the imperatives of modernization and progress represented by Jiménez. He enters into an uneasy alliance with the former *hacendado*, working to diffuse the rising tensions and to convince his men that they should abide by the reform policies. All the while, he is unaware that Jiménez has decided that both Cuitla and Del Toro pose a threat to his interests in commercial agriculture and that he is plotting to have the former revolutionaries killed. Jiménez hires an assassin, Gerardo Salinas, who succeeds in murdering Del Toro. Cuitla subsequently kills Salinas. After the killing, he encounters a dark mass, "the shadow" of the novella's title, which he believes is the man's departing spirit, succumbs to fright and dies.

This brief synopsis of the plot raises a number of issues, but for the purposes of this essay I will focus on how the novel's concern with Mexicans north of the border shapes it treatment of Mexican land reform. Paredes is not the only writer who produced a searing critique of postrevolutionary agrarian reform policies. As Juan Alonso has also noted,[38] Paredes's narrative in many ways recalls Juan Rulfo's "Nos han Dado la Tierra," which appears in his classic short story collection *El Llano en Llamas* (1953). Like the peones in *The Shadow*, those in Rulfo's story are given land in an area so hot and dry that "just a few lizards stick their heads out of their holes, and as soon as they feel the roasting sun [they] quickly hide themselves again in the small shade of rock."[39] The men protest to a government representative about the gross inadequacy of what they have been given but are silenced by the massive government bureaucracy in charge of reapportionment: "You can state that in writing," retorts the government official to their complaints, "and now you can go."[40] Similarly, *The Shadow* opens by elaborating on the complicated bureaucratic process the peones must undergo in order to be awarded the land for their *ejido*. They are successful in their petitions but are so far behind schedule as a result that they "work against time" plowing "the rapidly drying earth" in the fury of the noonday sun.[41]

Both narratives, then, thematize the government practice of giving the worst farmland to the poorest people under the banner of revolutionary land reform. Both are also examples of the tradition of the regional novel of the Revolution identified by Parra. But there are also important differences between the two, differences that I argue are rooted in the imperative Mexican Americans felt to emplot issues into the Mexican tradition that reflected their local conditions in the United States. In *The Shadow*, this process is not explicit, as the narrative takes place entirely in northern Mexico, with only fleeting references to the United States. However, as Camacho notes, the novella "conforms to Paredes's inclination toward the long, historical view of border conditions," and with its attention to local conflicts over land appropriations in the border state of Tamaulipas "he clearly seeks to address the formation of the migrant, transnational stream at its inception—in the campesinos' incomplete transition from revolutionary to national subjects.[42]

In part, then, Paredes provides a prehistory of the migrants who sustain the transnational labor markets of the developing agricultural economy between Mexico and the United States. As Camacho so aptly puts it, the *ejidatarios* of *The Shadow* are not so much "new national subjects as future emigrants, captured in the moment of their final dislocation from the revolutionary project."[43] This is a point I will return to, but first I want to note that Paredes also asserts the significance of transnational contact in the initial moments of revolutionary fervor. As Alonzo suggests, the novel's imagined geographic setting foregrounds the importance of agrarian revolt twenty years earlier:

> The communal farm is on the south bank of the Rio Grande, across from the fictive town of Jonesville-on-the-Grande (22). The village's proximity to the city of Morelos is also an artistic conceit, for there is no such city near the U.S. border. Still, the reference to Morelos signals the violent conflicts of the revolution and the agrarian reform movement. For example, Jan Bazant recounts that land disputes between hacendados and peones were 'particularly bad in the state of Morelos . . . where recent increases in sugarcane cultivation had induced local hacendados to seek more land.[44]

Morelos, of course, was the home state of Emiliano Zapata and the center of operations for the peasant revolt he led. But the revolutionary ambitions of the peasantry in *The Shadow* are not simply examples of homegrown insurgency. Cuitla, Del Toro, and others were first schooled in revolution in their previous lives as transnational migrant laborers. We learn of this after Cuitla has killed Salinas, the assassin who murdered Del Toro. Going through

Salinas's wallet, he finds a newspaper clipping "about the coming cotton season in Texas and the need for pickers, the high wages being offered."[45] Cuitla sighs and thinks of himself, remembering that "he too had gone to Texas when he was young."[46]

As we learn, Texas was of great significance in the men's eventual development as revolutionaries:

> It was in Texas he first heard men talk of revolution, men of his own sort, talk about striking off their chains, and of the imprisonment of starvation. Yes, he had got most of his education in Texas. In the cotton fields and the coal mines.
>
> And Del Toro, too. He also received his education there, especially at the Huntsville prison farm. Texas had a lot to teach the Mexican peon turned migrant laborer, who looked across the border for a new kind of life.[47]

Saldívar and Camacho read the political awakening of the men as a result of their exploitation in the racial economies of Texas agriculture. As Saldívar puts it, "through the reification of their subjectivities into racialized objects of labor, the 'Mexican peon turned migrant laborer' attained class consciousness and became an agent of history."[48] Along with the racialization of the peones turned migrant laborers, I want to add a brief consideration of the other men Cuitla met in Texas, those "men of his own sort" who talked of "striking off their chains."[49] Who were those men, and what might be the significance of their role in Cuitla and Del Toro's politicization?

By virtue of their time in the United States, we can think of Cuitla and Del Toro as *norteños*, a group that Juan Mora-Torres describes as Mexican migrants who came into contact with U.S. society and then returned to their homeland. As Mora-Torres explains, while we know little about the norteños or who they came into contact with, we have tantalizing hints that they played an important role in sparking the Revolution.[50] Agustín Yañez provides a snapshot of these migrants in his classic novel of the Revolution, *Al Filo del Agua* (1947). In the chapter entitled "Los Norteños," we hear the complaints of disembodied village voices intermingling:

> It's hard to say which is worse, their absence or their return . . . It's worse when they come back, most people say . . . Even those who come back with money aren't satisfied here any longer. Many of them don't want to work anymore; they just strut around, air their opinions and criticize everything. They're a bad example, making fun of religion, the country, the customs. They sow doubt, undermine patriotism, and encourage others to leave this filthy, poverty-stricken country. They're the ones who spread ideas of Masonry, Socialism, and Spiritism. They've no respect for women.[51]

One norteño responds, "No . . . I'm sorry to say so, but when we come back, we realize what the people here have to put up with: the injustices and living conditions. Why should a man have to sweat all day to earn a few centavos?"[52] Along with their racialization in the United States, the norteños also became politicized through their contact with an array of groups pressing for social justice for laborers, including the Partido Liberal Mexicano and the

International Workers of the World, as well as individual labor organizers.[53] These groups included Mexican Americans and proto-Mexican Americans, people of Mexican ancestry whose identities had been shaped by their positions as subjects of the United States. Men such as Nicolás and Clemente Idar, who lived in Laredo, Texas, and were deeply involved in labor activism for most of their lives, were especially committed to helping Mexicans who crossed the border in search of work. Villegas de Magnón specifically cites Clemente's work in an early draft of her memoir, writing that "he gained international fame for his efforts in support of Mexican workers established in the United States," and his "notable efforts earned him the esteem of Samuel Gompers, President of the American Federation of Labor, and William Green, leader of the United States Labor Union, both of whom Idar represented in important commissions."[54] While Idar is an extraordinary case, many Mexican Americans worked as labor organizers. They were part of the larger movements for labor rights of the period; in turn, these Mexican Americans played an important role in influencing Mexican migrants who would return to Mexico before the Revolution. After all, and as Mora-Torres reminds us, before the strikes in Mexico that highlighted the politicization of the working class, there were strikes by Mexicans in the United States, such as the one in Bisbee, Arizona in 1903.

What I want to suggest, then, is that when Cuitla speaks of the "men of his sort" who educate him in Texas, at least some of those men are Mexican Americans, and that through this brief but resonant reference, Paredes hints at the significance of Mexican Americans for the Revolution through their contact with norteños. This is not to suggest by any means that the Revolution was wholly instigated by norteños but rather that they were one of a number of segments of Mexican society that sparked the war—especially in particular regions—and that their contact with Mexican Americans was a crucial aspect of their politicization. In this way, and like Villegas de Magnón and Niggli, Paredes attempts to reshape the faulty historiography that occludes the role Mexican Americans played in shaping the Revolution and thus in shaping twentieth-century Mexican history. Moreover, through such engagements with the past, Paredes elucidates the relationship between the local specificities of borderlands histories and larger global designs and world historical events.

By examining Mexican American literary engagements with the Mexican Revolution, I hope to make at least two broad critical interventions in the fields of transnational American studies and border studies. Generally speaking, transnational American studies have focused on U.S. economic and political dominance in the hemisphere, resulting in an exciting body of work that has oriented American studies toward transnational analyses. However, that work has also been criticized from a Latin Americanist perspective because of its tendency to treat Latin America as little more than a recipient site of U.S. policies and aggressions.[55] By focusing on Mexican American engagements with the Revolution, this essay foregrounds Mexico's role as a protagonist in the story of Mexican Americans, not simply as a victim of U.S. rapaciousness. This emphasis on some of the ways that the Revolution's literary, political, and social legacies unfolded in Mexican American culture becomes a means of tracking the active presence of Latin American politics and culture in the United States, forcing a recognition of what Paula Moya and Ramón Saldívar have characterized as the influence of "competing nationalisms . . . within the borders of the nation," and thus an attention to the roles that other national projects play in the U.S. national-cultural space.[56]

Even more central to the story I am telling is the fact that Mexican Americans were not simply acted on by these Mexican ideologies—on the contrary, they actively responded to the Revolution, attempting to shape many of its most important political and social currents and in ways that would subsequently inform their struggles for social justice in the United States. In so doing, they asserted themselves as active agents within Mexican history even as they attempted to make lives for themselves north of the border. Situating segments of Mexican American culture in this way has implications for border studies, a field that rightly emphasizes Mexican American cultural autonomy in the borderlands as well as the local conflicts that give rise to them. As invaluable as this focus on the local is, it can inadvertently obscure the continuing persistence and relevance of state-national power in regions/communities that are resistant toward national centers, while also overlooking the relationships among local conflicts, national projects, and transnational currents. Using a transnational approach allows for a continued examination of how Mexican Americans have been excluded from the United States but adds a focus on how they operate as dynamic parts of multiple nations and of transnational phenomena. While the Mexican nation largely ignored them, these Mexican American writers asserted their own stories and perspectives as part of the story of the Revolution—even after they had long been settled in the United States—and thus as part of the Mexican nation's unfinished business.

NOTES

1. Quoted in Clara Lomas, *Introduction to the Rebel* by Leonor Villegas de Magnón, ed. Clara Lomas (Houston: Arte Público Press, 1994), xxxix.

2. Victor Zuñiga, "El Norte de México como Desierto Cultural: Anatomía de una Idea," *Puentelibre* 1 (1995): 18–23.

3. Ana María Alonso, *Thread of Blood: Colonialism, Revolution, and Gender on Mexico's Northern Frontier* (Tucson: University of Arizona Press, 1995), 18.

4. Martín Luis Guzmán, *The Eagle and the Serpent*, trans. Harriet de Onis (New York: Knopf, 1930), 46–47.

5. The Mexican politician and intellectual José Vasconcelos had an even more expansive conceptualization of what Tabuenca calls the "North of the Borderism" view, writing in the second volume of his memoir that everything from the northern Mexican environs to New York was a "no man's land of the spirit, a desert of the soul." Quoted in Zuñiga, 19.

6. María Socorro Tabuenca Córdoba, "Sketches of Identities from the Mexico–US Border (or the Other Way Around)," *Comparative American Studies* 3.4 (2005): 498.

7. Adalbert Dessau, La Novela de la Revolución Mexicana (Mexico City: Fondo de Cultura Económica, 1972), 10.

8. Silvia Lorente-Murphy, "La Revolución Mexicana en la Novela," *Revista Iberoamericana* 55 (1989): 848–49, 851.

9. Marta Portal, *Proceso Narrativo de la Revolución Mexicana* (Madrid: Espasa-Calpe, 1980), 63.

10. Luis Leal, *Mariano Azuela: Vida y Obra* (Mexico City: Ediciones Andrea, 1961).

11. Alicia Schmidt Camacho, *Migrant Imaginaries: Latino Cultural Production in the U.S.–Mexico Borderlands* (New York: New York University Press, 2008), 97.

12. For more on how this process worked with regard to Mexico's indigenous populations through the concepts of "revolutionary *indigenismo*" and *mestizaje*, see Cynthia Hewitt de Alcántara, *Anthropological Perspectives on Rural Mexico* (London: Routledge, 1984), 10–13; Guillermo Bónfil Batalla, *México Profundo: Reclaiming a Civilization*, trans. Philip A. Dennis (Austin: University of Texas Press, 1996), 113; and María Josefina Saldaña-Portillo, *The Revolutionary Imagination in the Americas and the Age of Development* (Durham, N. C.: Duke University Press, 2003), 206–12.

13. Max Parra, *Writing Pancho Villa's Revolution: Rebels in the Literary Imagination of Mexico* (Austin: University of Texas Press, 2005), 138.

14. As Franco puts it in writing about Guzmán, "the abstraction of violence from any context that could serve to explain it obscures an important relationship between violence and the human exploitation that gave rise to it." Jean Franco, "Dominant Ideology and Literature: The Case of Post-Revolutionary Mexico" in *Critical Passions: Selected Essays*, edited with an introduction by Mary Louise Pratt and Kathleen Newman (Durham, N. C.: Duke University Press, 1999), 456.

15. Juan Bruce-Novoa, "La Novela de la Revolución Mexicana: La Topología Final," *Hispania* 74.1 (March 1991), 36.

16. Parra, *Writing Pancho Villa's Revolution*, 6.

17. Ibid.

18. Ibid.

19. Quoted in Lomas, Introduction to *The Rebel*, xli.

20. Ibid., 56.

21. David Luis-Brown, *Waves of Decolonization: Discourses of Race and Hemispheric Citizenship in Cuba, Mexico, and the United States* (Durham, N. C.: Duke University Press, 2008), 245.

22. Bruce-Novoa, "La Novela de la Revolución Mexicana," 38.

23. For more on Niggli's life, see Elizabeth Coonrod Martínez, *Josefina Niggli, Mexican American Writer: A Critical Biography* (Albuquerque: University of New Mexico Press, 2007); and William Orchard and Yolanda Padilla, "Introducing Josefina Niggli" in *The Plays of Josefina Niggli: Recovered Landmarks of Latino Literature* (Madison: University of Wisconsin Press, 2007).

24. See Hewitt de Alcántara, *Anthropological Perspectives on Mexico*; and Bonfil Batalla, *México Profundo*.

25. See Saldaña-Portillo, *The Revolutionary Imagination in the Americas*, 206–12; and Bonfil Batalla, *México Profundo*, 113.

26. Josefina Niggli, *Mexican Village* (Albuquerque: University of New Mexico Press, 1994), 453.

27. Ibid., 470.

28. Ibid., 18.

29. John Mason Hart, "Social Unrest, Nationalism, and American Capital in the Mexican Countryside, 1876–1920" in *Rural Revolt In Mexico: U.S. Intervention and the Domain of Subaltern Politics*, ed. Daniel Nugent (Durham, N. C.: Duke University Press, 1998), 73.

30. For examples of such scholarship, see the essays in Daniel Nugent, ed., *Rural Revolt in Mexico: U.S. Intervention and the Domain of Subaltern Politics* (Durham, N. C.: Duke University Press, 1998), especially John H. Coatsworth, "Measuring Influence: The United States and the Mexican Peasantry," 64–71; Hart, "Social Unrest, Nationalism, and American Capital in the Mexican Countryside,

1876–1920," 72–88; and Rubén Osorio, "Villismo: Nationalism and Popular Mobilization in Northern Mexico," 89–103.

31. Rita Keresztesi similarly notes Niggli's attention to neocolonial imperialism. See Rita Keresztesi, "Romancing the Borderlands: Josephina Niggli's Mexican Village," in *Doubled Plots: Romance and History*, ed. Susan Strehle and Mary Paniccia Carden (Jackson: University of Mississippi Press, 2003), 107–26.

32. For a much more expansive version of this argument, see Yolanda Padilla, "The Transnational National: Race, the Border, and the Immigrant Nationalism of Josefina Niggli's Mexican Village," *CR: The New Centennial Review* 9.2 (Fall 2009), 45–72.

33. Juan J. Alonso, "Américo Paredes's The Shadow: Social and Subjective Transformation in Greater Mexico," *Aztlán* 27.1 (Spring 2002), 27–57; Ramón Saldívar, *The Borderlands of Culture: Américo Paredes and the Transnational Imaginary* (Durham, N. C.: Duke University Press), 2006; and Alicia Schmidt Camacho, *Migrant Imaginaries: Latino Cultural Production in the U.S.–Mexico Borderlands* (New York: New York University Press, 2008).

34. Saldívar includes Paredes's engagements with postwar Japan in his examination of the transnational imperatives that inform Paredes's work.

35. Saldívar, *Borderlands of Culture*, 403.

36. Américo Paredes, *The Shadow* (Houston: Arte Público Press, 1998), 83.

37. Ibid, 29.

38. Alonso, "Américo Paredes's The Shadow," 35–36.

39. Juan Rulfo, "They Gave Us the Land," in *The Mexico Reader: History, Culture, Politics*, ed. and trans. Gilbert M. Joseph and Timothy J. Henderson (Durham, N. C.: Duke University Press, 2005), 466.

40. Ibid., 468.

41. Paredes, *The Shadow*, 1.

42. Camacho, *Migrant Imaginaries*, 101.

43. Ibid., 97.

44. Alonso, "Américo Paredes's The Shadow," 31.

45. Paredes, *The Shadow*, 61.

46. Ibid.

47. Ibid., 62.

48. Saldívar, *Borderlands of Culture*, 418.

49. Paredes, *The Shadow*, 62.

50. Juan Mora-Torres, "The Migration Revolution: The Role of Migration during the Mexican Revolution, 1910–1930," unpublished manuscript, 3.

51. Augustin Yáñez, *At the Edge of the Storm*, trans. Ethel Brinton (Austin: University of Texas Press, 1963), 135.

52. Ibid.

53. Mora-Torres, "The Migration Revolution," 19. Mora-Torres's work in progress has influenced deeply my analysis of *The Shadow*. I am grateful to him for sharing his research with me.

54. Quoted in Lomas, Introduction to *The Rebel*, xl.

55. Claudia Sadowski-Smith and Claire F. Fox, "Theorizing the Hemisphere: Inter-Americas Work at the Intersection of American, Canadian, and Latin American Studies," *Comparative American Studies* 2.1 (2004), 7.

56. Paula M. L. Moya and Ramón Saldívar. "Fictions of the Trans-American Imaginary," *Modern Fiction Studies* 49.1 (2003), 4. See also Sandhya Rajendra Shukla and Heidi Tinsman "Across the Americas" in *Imagining Our Americas: Toward a Transnational Frame* (Durham, N. C.: Duke University Press, 2007), 11.

BIBLIOGRAPHY

Alonso, Ana María. *Thread of Blood: Colonialism, Revolution, and Gender on Mexico's Northern Frontier.* Tucson: University of Arizona Press, 1995.

Alonzo, Juan J. "Américo Paredes's *The Shadow*: Social and Subjective Transformation in Greater Mexico." *Aztlán*, 27, no. 1 (Spring 2002): 27–57.

Azuela, Mariano. *Los de Abajo* [The Underdogs]. Originally published in 1915. Madrid: Espasa-Calpe, 1930.

Bonfil Batalla, Guillermo. *México Profundo: Reclaiming a Civilization.* Trans. Philip A. Dennis. Austin: University of Texas Press, 1996.

Bruce-Novoa, Juan. "La Novela de la Revolución Mexicana: La Topología Final [The Novel of the Mexican Revolution: The Final Topology]." *Hispania*, 74.1 (March 1991): 36–44.

Camacho, Alicia Schmidt. *Migrant Imaginaries: Latino Cultural Production in the U.S.-Mexico Borderlands.* New York: New York University Press, 2008.

Campobello, Nellie. 1931. *Cartucho.* Austin: University of Texas Press, 1988.

Coatsworth, John H. "Measuring Influence: The United States and the Mexican Peasantry." In *Rural Revolt in Mexico: U.S. Intervention and the Domain of Subaltern Politics*, ed. Daniel Nugent, pp.64–71. Durham: Duke University Press, 1998.

Córdoba, María Socorro Tabuenca. "Sketches of Identities from the Mexico-US Border (or the Other Way Around)." *Comparative American Studies*, 3.4 (2005): 495–513.

Dessau, Adalbert. *La Novela de la Revolución Mexicana* [The Novel of the Mexican Revolution]. México: Fondo de Cultura Económica, 1972.

Franco, Jean. "Dominant Ideology and Literature: The Case of Post-Revolutionary Mexico." In *Critical Passions: Selected Essays*, ed. Mary Louise Pratt and Kathleen Newman. Durham, N.C.: Duke University Press, 1999: 447–60.

Gamio, Manuel. *Forjando Patria: Pro Nacionalismo* [Forging Fatherland: Pro Nationalism]. Mexico City: Libreria de Porrúa Hermanos, 1916.

Guzmán, Martín Luis. 1928. *El Aguila y la Serpiente* [The Eagle and the Serpent]. Mexico City: Editorial Porrúa, 1987.

———. *The Eagle and the Serpent.* Trans. Harriet de Onis. New York: Knopf, 1930.

Hart, John Mason. "Social Unrest, Nationalism, and American Capital in the Mexican Countryside, 1876–1920." In *Rural Revolt in Mexico: U.S. Intervention and the Domain of Subaltern Politics*, ed. Daniel Nugent, pp. 72–88. Durham, N.C.: Duke University Press, 1998.

Hewitt de Alcántara, Cynthia. *Anthropological Perspectives on Rural Mexico.* London: Routledge, 1984.

Keresztesi, Rita. "Romancing the Borderlands: Josephina Niggli's *Mexican Village*." In *Doubled Plots: Romance and History*, ed. Susan Strehle and Mary Paniccia Carden, pp. 107–26. Jackson: University of Mississippi Press, 2003.

Leal, Luis. *Mariano Azuela: Vida y Obra* [Mariano Azuela: Life and Work]. Mexico: Ediciones Andrea, 1961.

Lomas, Clara. "Introduction." In *The Rebel* by Leonor Villegas de Magnón, pp. xi–li. Houston: Arte Público Press, 1994.

_____. "Introducción." En _La Rebelde_ de Leonor Villegas de Magnón, xv–lxii. Houston: Arte Público Press and Conaculta, INAH, 2004.

Lorente-Murphy, Silvia. "La Revolución Mexicana en la Novela. [The Mexican Revolution in the Novel.]" _Revista Iberoamericana_ ,55, nos. 148–149 (1989): 847–57.

Luis-Brown, David. _Waves of Decolonization: Discourses of Race and Hemispheric Citizenship in Cuba, Mexico, and the United States._ Durham, N.C.: Duke University Press, 2008.

Martínez, Elizabeth Coonrod. _Josefina Niggli, Mexican American Writer: A Critical Biography._ Albuquerque: University of New Mexico Press, 2007.

Mora-Torres, Juan. "The Migration Revolution: The Role of Migration during the Mexican Revolution, 1910–1930." Unpublished manuscript.

Moya, Paula M. L. and Ramón Saldívar. "Fictions of the Trans-American Imaginary." _Modern Fiction Studies,_ 49.1 (2003): 1–18.

Niggli, Josefina. _Mexican Village._ Originally published in 1945. Albuquerque: University of New Mexico Press, 1994.

Nugent, Daniel, ed. _Rural Revolt in Mexico: U.S. Intervention and the Domain of Subaltern Politics._ Durham, N.C.: Duke University Press, 1998.

Orchard, William and Yolanda Padilla. "Introducing Josefina Niggli." In _Introduction to The Plays of Josefina Niggli: Recovered Landmarks of Latino Literature,_ ed. William Orchard and Yolanda Padilla, pp. 3–33. Madison: University of Wisconsin Press, 2007.

Osorio, Rubén. "Villismo: Nationalism and Popular Mobilization in Northern Mexico." In _Rural Revolt in Mexico: U.S. Intervention and the Domain of Subaltern Politics,_ ed. Daniel Nugent, pp. 89–103. Durham, N.C.: Duke University Press, 1998.

Padilla, Yolanda. "The Mexican American Novel of the Mexican Revolution." In _Lenguaje, Arte y Revoluciones Ayer y Hoy: New Approaches to Hispanic Linguistic, Literary, and Cultural Studies,_ ed. Alejandro Cortazar and Rafael Orozco, pp. 73–86. Newcastle-upon-Tyne, UK: Cambridge Scholars Publishing, 2011.

_____. "The Transnational National: Race, the Border, and the Immigrant Nationalism of Josefina Niggli's _Mexican Village._" _CR: The New Centennial Review,_ 9.2 (Fall 2009): 45–72.

Paredes, Américo. _The Shadow._ Houston: Arte Público Press, 1998.

Parra, Max. _Writing Pancho Villa's Revolution: Rebels in the Literary Imagination of Mexico._ Austin: University of Texas Press, 2005.

Portal, Marta. _Proceso Narrativo de la Revolución Mexicana_ [Narrative Process of the Mexican Revolution]. Madrid: Espasa-Calpe, 1980.

Rulfo, Juan. 1953. "Nos Han Dado la Tierra [They Gave Us the Land]." Originally published in 1953. In _El Llano en Llamas_ [The Burning Plain], pp. 9–15. Mexico City: Fondo de Cultura Económica, 1994.

_____. "They Gave Us the Land." In _The Mexico Reader: History, Culture, Politics,_ ed. Gilbert M. Joseph and Timothy J. Henderson, pp. 465–9. Durham, N.C.: Duke University Press, 2005.

Sadowski-Smith, Claudia, and Claire F. Fox. "Theorizing the Hemisphere: Inter-Americas Work at the Intersection of American, Canadian, and Latin American Studies." _Comparative American Studies,_ 2, no. 1 (2004): 5–38.

Saldaña-Portillo, María Josefina. _The Revolutionary Imagination in the Americas and the Age of Development._ Durham, N.C.: Duke University Press, 2003.

Saldívar, Ramón. _Chicano Narrative: The Dialectics of Difference._ Madison: University of Wisconsin Press, 1990.

_____. _The Borderlands of Culture: Américo Paredes and the Transnational Imaginary._ Durham, N.C.: Duke University Press, 2006.

Shukla, Sandhya Rajendra and Heidi Tinsman. "Across the Americas." In _Imagining Our Americas: Toward a Transnational Frame,_ pp. 1–33. Durham, N.C.: Duke University Press, 2007.

Villegas de Magnón, Leonor. *La Rebelde* [The Rebel]. Houston: Arte Público Press and Conaculta, INAH, 2004.

Yañez, Augustin. *At the Edge of the Storm*. Trans. Ethel Brinton. Originally published in 1947. Austin: University of Texas Press, 1963.

Zuñiga, Victor. "El Norte de México Como Desierto Cultural: Anatomía de una Idea [Northern Mexico As Cultural Desert: Anatomy of an Idea]." *Puentelibre*, 1 (1995): 18–23.

CHAPTER NINE

CHARTING THE LEGACY OF THE REVOLUTION
How the Mexican Revolution Transformed
El Paso's Cultural and Urban Landscape

David Dorado Romo

"El Paso, Texas, is the Supreme Lodge of the Ancient Order of Conspirators of the World. The personnel changes from year to year; but its purpose is always the same—to destroy the existing government of Mexico. In every hotel and lodging-house a junta is in session at all hours of the day and night—revolutionary juntas, counter-revolutionary juntas and counter-counter revolutionary juntas."
—John Reed, "El Paso"

INTRODUCTION
During the turn of the twentieth century, El Paso, Texas, was an ideal launching pad for a revolution in Mexico. Having the largest ethnic Mexican population in the United States and located at the crossroads of major binational railroad lines made it the most strategic site along a 1,900-mile border from which to carry out arms smuggling, espionage, recruitment, and the publication of newspapers denouncing the dictatorial regime of Porfirio Díaz. Although no military engagements were fought in El Paso during the Mexican Revolution, the city was a zone for many other kinds of battles. El Paso newspapers—both in Spanish and English—carried out the struggle at the ideological level. Photographers and filmmakers were on the front lines of the image and propaganda war. The city was the base for smuggling and intelligence wars that often had a huge impact on the outcome of insurrectionary movements launched from the border. Often the behind-the-scenes battles waged in El Paso determined the success or failure of the "real" battles waged on Mexican soil. My microhistorical study of El Paso's built environment explores not only the central role that this American border city played in helping to spark the Mexican Revolution but how the upheaval across the international line profoundly transformed its sociocultural and urban landscape.

By focusing on small-scale analysis and examining data that traditional historiography has often considered marginal or insignificant, microhistory attempts to uncover previously overlooked clues that provide new insights into broader historical developments. Historic buildings and sites of memory serve as the primary source documents, so to speak, for my investigation. They offer new directions for research that may not have been as evident through traditional methodologies based exclusively on textual analysis. I have identified 130 buildings and sites of memory in El Paso with narratives connected to the Mexican Revolution—84 of these structures are still standing while 46 have been demolished.[1] This paper will focus only on some of the more significant sites. Many of them are plotting grounds that New York journalist John Reed wrote about when he visited the U.S.-Mexico border in search of Pancho Villa in 1914. Others include radical newspaper offices, headquarters for the various factions involved in the military conflict, arms and munitions stores, espionage agencies, and homes where revolutionaries in exile lived or gathered.

The historical narratives of buildings in South El Paso are intricately connected to the often much broader global trajectories of their inhabitants. They tell the story of the legacy and impact of the Mexican Revolution on immigration, public health policies, arms smuggling, militarization, media and image wars, and other issues that continue to have resonance today beyond the borderlands. Most of these sites of memory, unfortunately, have yet to be designated as official historic landmarks despite their importance to the city's international cultural heritage. In 2006, the City of El Paso approved an urban redevelopment plan that envisioned the future demolition of dozens of these buildings and their subsequent replacement by big box retail stores, shopping centers, and high-rise apartments in downtown and South El Paso.[2] Many critics of the city's urban renewal project in South El Paso raised the issue of the destruction of historical sites of memory as part of their opposition to the plan. The questions of historic preservation and urban erasure are not entirely within the scope of this paper, but they indeed add an extra layer to our understanding of the ongoing significance of Mexican Revolution sites to the *fronterizo* community.

METHODOLOGIES

Both old and new cartographical methodologies using Sanborn insurance maps, Google Earth, city zoning maps, and multilayered GIS (Geographic Information Systems) maps have been fundamental tools of my research. One of the most important uses of these mapping technique is a means of tracing and documenting networks among the various revolutionary factions that used El Paso as a base of operations during the revolution. New Web-based cartographical tools make it easier to record demographic changes and ethnic concentrations over time. El Paso's population nearly doubled due to a heavy inflow of Mexican refugees during the revolution. Between 1910 and 1920 the population figures went from 39,279 to 77,560.[3] Multilayered maps help document qualitative information as well. Color-coded Sanborn maps created during the turn of the twentieth century, for example, have helped chart the transformation of the built environment in South El Paso from an area with a predominance of adobe buildings to one with mostly brick buildings. The maps illustrate the effects of racialized public health and urban removal policies carried out by both city and military officials during the revolution that resulted in the massive demolitions of adobe homes in the city's ethnic Mexican neighborhoods.[4]

Maps that chart geographical trajectories sometimes provide unexpected insights. For instance, they allow us to illustrate how tuberculosis contamination flowed from predominantly Euro-American sectors of El Paso toward predominantly ethnic Mexican neighborhoods. During the early twentieth century the El Paso Chamber of Commerce carried out national advertising campaigns in major Eastern cities in the United States promoting the border city as an ideal location for those suffering from tuberculosis. Multilayered GIS cartography illustrates how, contrary to popular notions, tuberculosis rates of infection were substantially higher in wealthier Anglo neighborhoods until the 1930s when the levels of contamination began to spread southward into the Mexican American communities.[5] A classic example of this kind of cartography is Dr. John Snow's map of the London cholera outbreak in 1854. Spatial humanities scholars have described his map, which traced the outbreak to a single water pump in the city, as a precursor of GIS cartography that helps us discover hidden relationships and spatial patterns in the urban landscape.[6]

There are several other ways in which research methodologies that focus on space and the built environment have helped uncover previously undocumented histories of the Mexican Revolution. Although the buildings are the primary source material, there are also many other texts and documents related to them that are important for the recuperation of urban history. These include census records, tax rolls, property deeds, title abstracts, architectural designs, city council minutes, planning documents, city directories, and other notarial records. They offer valuable information for historians that is often difficult to retrieve from other sources.[7] Late nineteenth- and early twentieth-century city directories listed the occupation as well as ethnicity of city residents. Title abstracts that include the name of spouses sometimes provide other potentially useful information such as divorce agreements and interfamily property disputes. The data gathered from these types of documents can be extremely useful for the recuperation of silenced histories of women, ethnic communities, and other subaltern groups.

MEXICAN REVOLUTION SITES: RECONSTRUCTING THE NARRATIVES

My study focuses primarily on a one-square-mile section of South El Paso known as the Second Ward, or Segundo Barrio. It is one of the oldest predominantly Mexican American neighborhoods in the United States, often referred to as the "Ellis Island of the border." In 1900, of the four American cities with an ethnic Mexican population of 5,000 or more, only El Paso had 10,000—and most of them lived in the Segundo Barrio.[8] A large portion of the Segundo Barrio lies within the disputed Chamizal territory that originally belonged to Mexico until the river shifted course in the 1860s and became part of the United States. Some of the major protagonists of the Mexican Revolution who used South El Paso as base of operations or hiding place include Francisco Madero, Pancho Villa, Ricardo and Enrique Flores Magón, Praxedis Guerrero, Teresita Urrea, and Pascual Orozco. Thousands of other Mexican refugees moved to the Second Ward to flee violence across the border between 1910 and 1920. The names of the today's streets bear witness to their presence. El Paso's Chihuahua, Durango, and Sonora Streets were named after the respective Mexican states of origin of the refugee groups who lived there during the revolution. While the Segundo Barrio housed mostly working-class refugees, the more affluent Mexican exile community lived in the Sunset Heights area of El Paso north or the railroad tracks.

One of the sites in South El Paso that best exemplifies the impact of the Mexican Revolution on the city's cultural terrain is the historic building that currently houses the Pablo Baray apartments on 609 South Oregon Street. Constructed in 1910, this structure is arguably one of the most important sites connected to revolutionary journalism and literature north of the border. It was the site of the *El Paso del Norte* press (Figure 1), also known as the "Imprenta Moderna." *The El Paso del Norte*—printed six times a week—was one of the more than 40 Spanish-language newspapers published in El Paso between 1890

Figure 1. *El Paso del Norte* ad, 1915. (Courtesy of Special Collections Department, University of Texas at El Paso Library.)

and 1925.[9] These periodicals provided a counternarrative of the border not found in the mainstream press on either side of the line. They printed not only news and political manifestoes but serial novels, poetry, essays, and other literary works as well. The cultural milieu created by a large inflow of political refugees and exiles—which included some of Mexico's best journalists and writers—set the stage for a renaissance of Spanish-language journalism and literature not seen before in the history of the border.

Mariano Azuela wrote *Los de Abajo* (*The Underdogs*), considered the preeminent novel of the Mexican Revolution, in the press offices of the *El Paso del Norte* newspaper on 609 South Oregon Street—where it was published in serial form in November 1915. Azuela used a typewriter made available to him by Fernando Gamiochipi, editor of *El Paso del Norte*, to complete the last third of the novel.[10] *Los de Abajo* received little attention at first until the mid-1920s when Mexico City literary critics declared it among the most important works of Mexican literature and was later translated into dozens of languages. Azuela was a former Villista doctor who fled to El Paso after Pancho Villa's troops suffered major defeats at the hands of general Álvaro Obregón. He was unable to practice medicine in the United States but a $3 weekly salary he received from Gamiochipi while writing *Los de Abajo* helped him survive financially.[11] Despite his difficult economic situation, Azuela still had positive memories of his exile in South El Paso decades after his novel was published. "I even remember fondly those five-cent loaves of bread and those pints of refrigerated milk as a blessing from heaven in El Paso, Texas, after my journey through mountainous areas of Jalisco and Zacatecas, eating roasted cow's meat with no salt," he wrote. "El Paso endures in my memory as a paradise for gluttons."[12]

Fernando Gamiochipi helped many other revolutionary exiles as well. He was a well-connected intellectual—and the childhood friend of future president Plutarco Elias Calles—who emigrated to El Paso from Guaymas, Sonora, after "suffering countless persecutions" for his political beliefs. One contemporary observer noted that "there was no revolutionary leader or even sympathizer of the Revolution who did not stop by the offices of Gamiochipi, some of them to greet him, others, to obtain advice and not a few to get money and help."[13] When Pancho Villa approached Gamiochipi at his newspaper offices in February 1913 asking for financial support to launch an armed movement against the Huerta regime, he raised more than $2000 to help Villa launch what scholars have called one of the most extraordinary military and political comebacks in Mexican history.[14] Two of Gamiochipi's children were writers as well. His daughter Elisa wrote an autobiographical novel based on her family's experiences in El Paso, titled *Luz y Sombra*, that was published by San Antonio's *La Prensa* in the 1930s.[15] Fernando's son, Alberto, was a poet as well who continued to run the press after his father's death in 1920.[16]

Another writer whose personal biography was intimately connected to the building on South Oregon Street is Elias L. Torres, assistant editor of *El Paso del Norte*. According to city property records, Torres helped finance this building beginning in 1914.[17] He was a civil engineer, contractor, and the owner of several properties in El Paso. He was also a former *porfirista* who in 1911 had tried to kill Octavio Paz Solórzano—the father of the Nobel Prize recipient and a supporter of the revolutionary forces of Emiliano Zapata.[18] Torres and his family—originally from an affluent neighborhood in the outskirts of Mexico

City—relocated themselves to the Sunset Heights neighborhood in El Paso in 1914 when Pancho Villa's military fortunes were on the rise. Torres subsequently became a good friend of Pancho Villa and authored several books and articles about him.[19] In 1921, Torres acted as an intermediary during the peace negotiations between Villa and the Mexican government. A few years later he became Mexican Consul in San Antonio for the Obregón government.[20]

Elias Torres was the father of Olga Beatriz Torres, a writer whose work has recently been rediscovered. In 1919, while still a teenager, she published a memoir of her family's exile in El Paso titled *Memorias de mi Viaje* as a series of epistolary letters in *El Paso del Norte*. Her work was mostly forgotten until 1995, when Chicana scholar Juanita Luna-Lawn translated and republished her account as *Recollections of my Trip*. Scholars have described the book as the first literary work about the Mexican diaspora in the United States during the revolution written by a woman. They also characterize Olga Beatriz Torres, whose writings explored "the psychological impact of transculturation," as a forerunner of Chicana writers.[21] Apparently, no scholar who has written about *Memorias de mi Viaje* has been aware of the father-daughter relationship between Olga Beatriz and Elias Torres, a fact that undoubtedly contributes to a fuller understanding of her autobiographical account. This family connection, however, is not obvious by concentrating exclusively on the literary texts. It emerged in my own research by focusing on the built environment and individuals associated with the *El Paso del Norte* printing press.

There were several other noteworthy books published by the El Paso del Norte press with wider implications beyond South El Paso. One of them was *¿Quien es Pancho Villa?* (*Who is Pancho Villa?*) by John Kenneth Turner. Turner was the author of the highly acclaimed *Barbarous Mexico* that did much to turn U.S. public opinion against the Porfirio Díaz regime when it was published in 1910. Five years later, he wrote his critical biography of Villa with funding from Venustiano Carranza.[22] Carranza, like other revolutionary leaders including Villa, knew the value of having good writers on his payroll as part of the international propaganda war. The pro-Carrancista *El Paso del Norte*, which by then had turned solidly against Pancho Villa, was in many ways situated in the front line of this ideological battle on American soil.

After Fernando Gamiochipi's death, Pablo Baray—the former mayor of Bachiniva, Chihuahua—bought the building. In 1924, Baray constructed new apartment buildings on two adjacent lots that he joined to the original structure by adding a new facade wall prominently displaying his own name.[23] Baray's ownership of the building on 609 South Oregon Street further complicates the "revolutionary" narrative of this historic site. Pablo Baray, as Ana Alonso has written, was one of the most hated caudillos of Chihuahua before the revolution.[24] There is evidence he was involved in the 1893 massacre of the villagers of Tomóchic on the side of the Porfirista federal forces.[25] The Porfirista governor of Chihuahua Enrique Creel appointed Baray mayor of Bachiniva in 1906. As mayor, Baray was accused of a wide range of abuses on the local populace including terror, torture, and the dispossession of entire villages in order to sell their lands to the highest bidder. Armed insurgents deposed him from his position and raided his home at the outset of the Maderista revolution in January 1911.[26] He fled to Chihuahua City then joined the Villistas two years later.

In 1914, Baray sought refuge in El Paso where he reinvented himself as a real-estate agent and owned dozens of properties. Oddly, he listed his occupation as "special police agent" in a border-crossing manifest he filled out in the 1920s.[27] There is not sufficient evidence to verify Baray's claim of being a special police agent. El Paso, however, was indeed a place with extremely high levels of espionage activity during the revolution. It was somewhat like Berlin during the Cold War—a center for hundreds of spies, double agents, and even triple agents.[28] A printing press and apartment complex that historically served as a gathering place and residence for writers and politically active exiles would have certainly served as a good location from which to carry out such surveillance on the border city's refugee community.

Examining the narratives associated with the *El Paso del Norte* printing press shows how a detailed analysis of a single space can suggest multiple directions for further historical research. Yet there are several other sites with similar stories to tell of the complex and multilayered world of literary and journalistic production on the border. The newspaper press of the *El Paso Times*, located just two blocks north of the Pablo Baray apartments, is one such site. During the revolution the editors of *El Paso del Norte* bitterly criticized the *El Paso Times* for its pro-Villista bias. During the revolution the *El Paso Times* published a Spanish-language section aimed at the city's rapidly growing Mexican exile community. It was managed by Ramón Prida, a former judge from Veracruz and eminent historian who was openly sympathetic to Pancho Villa. In 1915, mayoral candidate Tom Lea Sr. accused the paper of having received $10,000 in bribes for favorable coverage of Pancho Villa's movement.[29] But the *El Paso Times'* reputation for sympathizing with revolutionary movements in Mexico had begun at least a decade and a half earlier during antigovernment uprisings in northern Chihuahua. In 1893, the government of Porfirio Díaz denounced the *El Paso Times* for running a story on the massacre at Tomóchic by federal soldiers and publishing a manifesto written by the survivors of the raid. The Porfirista regime branded the El Paso paper as a "hostile paper" and banned it from Mexico.[30]

Besides printing presses, about forty other Mexican Revolution sites of memory are located along South Oregon and South El Paso streets alone. These two streets lie within the 30-acre area in the Segundo Barrio that the City of El Paso has targeted for urban renewal. Both of these streets were particularly well-situated for underground revolutionary activity because of their proximity to the railroad tracks and two international bridges. When the anarchist newspaper editors Enrique and Ricardo Flores Magón and their followers concentrated in El Paso to launch an insurrectionary attack on Ciudad Juárez in October 1906, most of the *magonistas* hid in rooming houses along these two streets.[31] Their plan was that if the revolutionary plot succeeded, they would swarm into Juárez across the international bridges. If it did not, then the railroad would provide a quick escape route for them.

Many of the hardware stores that sold arms and ammunition were similarly located near the Rio Grande and railroad tracks. The Ketelsen & Degetau Store on 801 S. El Paso Street had a platform in the rear adjacent to the Santa Fe railroad lines. It was an important hardware and ammunition supplier for all factions of the revolution in the border area. Max Weber, the German vice consul in Juárez, worked for Ketelsen & Degetau beginning in the 1880s. After the Battle of Juárez of 1911, the pro-Porfirista consul helped the defeated federal general Juan Navarro escape to El Paso.[32] The building was not only associated with international arms smuggling. There is evidence that the *magonistas* may have used this building to plot their attack on Juárez in 1906. Another major weapons supplier, located on 301 South El Paso Street, was the Shelton-Payne Arms Company. In December 1910, Mexican government agents reported that Abraham González ordered 60,000 cartridges from the Shelton-Payne Arms Company and sent them across the border to the Maderista *insurrectos*.[33] Archival records show that the company had assets exceeding $1,100,000 dollars in 1913.[34] The U.S. Bureau of Investigations, forerunners of the FBI, allowed Mexican government spies to openly operate in El Paso. The spies were permitted to follow and search anyone who bought arms and ammunition at places such as the Shelton-Payne Arms Company. El Paso Chamber of Commerce president Adolph Krakauer also profited greatly from the violence across the border. He and his hardware company, Krakauer, Zorke and Moye, found ways of doubling their profits by selling all the barbed wire in stock to the federal government troops and all the barbed wire cutters to the revolutionaries.[35] Thanks to the Mexican Revolution El Paso's economy boomed. The city's bank deposits increased eighty-eight percent between 1914 and 1920.[36] El Paso's built environment literally expanded during this period as well due to a construction boom throughout the city.

As a result of the highly profitable business of the Mexican Revolution, three floors were added to the Popular Dry Goods Company building on 301 San Antonio Street in 1916. The Popular was owned by Jewish-Hungarian immigrant Adolph Schwartz—who chose not to sell arms during the revolution, although he did sell other merchandise to both government and antigovernment forces. At one point, both the rebels and the *federales* were in the store simultaneously shopping for their respective troops. Pancho Villa visited the store in 1911 and years later put an order for $50,000 worth of khaki uniforms. The Popular building also served as a hiding place for the much hated General Juan Navarro after the Battle of Juárez. The federal general hid in the basement of the Popular when Villa and Orozco called for his court martial after his surrender. On May 14, 1911, the *New York Times* reported that Navarro hid in the cellar of the Popular Dry Goods Company, "a large department store in El Paso, where he is guarded by United States Secret Service Agents."[37] Despite the protection of the secret service agents, Navarro was immediately whisked away when a group of Popular employees, most of them sympathetic to the rebels, began to jeer and taunt the general.

Beyond selling weapons, uniforms, and other supplies to the various warring factions, El Paso property owners and merchants found other creative ways to make a profit from the violence across the line. Many offered the rooftops of their buildings as ringside seats to watch armed clashes across the Rio Grande (Figure 2), often charging between twenty five cents to a dollar per spectator—with money back guaranteed if the battles did not materialize. The El Paso Laundry building, just a few hundred yards away from the Santa Fe international bridge, is the only observation point that still has bullet holes on its walls from the revolutionary period. During the Battle of Juárez of 1911, an unexploded mortar shell landed a few feet away from the El Paso Laundry, where scores of sightseers including former El Paso mayor Joseph Sweeney stood on the rooftop.[38] Local newspapers reported that five El Pasoans were killed and 18 wounded on the American side of the line during

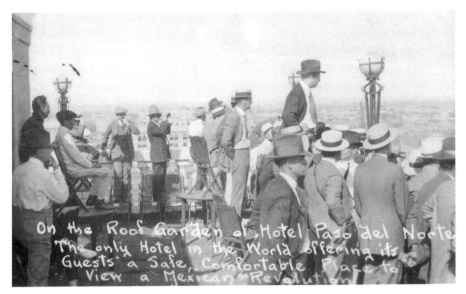

Figure 2. El Paso del Norte Rooftop Garden, "A Safe and Comfortable Place to Watch a Mexican Revolution," c. 1913. (Courtesy of the El Paso County Historical Society.)

the 1911 battle. A year later, stray bullets from Juárez into El Paso during other armed skirmishes between the followers of Pascual Orozco and federal troops prompted Texas Governor Oscar Colquitt to denounce United States President Howard Taft for supposedly not doing enough to protect American citizens from the violence across the river.[39]

The El Paso del Norte Hotel was another site that advertised itself as a "safe and comfortable place to watch a Mexican Revolution." But this hotel was an important site of revolutionary activities in other ways as well. The list of prominent guests connected to the revolution that has stayed at the El Paso del Norte Hotel includes Álvaro Obregón, Venustiano Carranza, John Pershing, and Plutarco Elias Calles. In 1916, Obregón used his chambers in the hotel to carry out diplomatic negotiations with General Hugh Scott on the issue of the Punitive Expedition, when the American forces under Pershing giving chase to Pancho Villa had worn out their welcome in Mexico. Former Chihuahuan governor Luis Terrazas and his family stayed in this hotel during his brief exile in the city. Terrazas was by far the richest man in Chihuahua and owned 6.25 million acres of land. When Villistas began expropriating Terrazas' properties in 1914, the multimillionaire rented the entire top floor of this luxurious hotel for his family and his 27 servants.

The El Paso del Norte Hotel, which cost 1.5 million dollars to construct in 1912, was too luxurious for Pancho Villa's taste. The swanky hotel was more appropriate for those he called the *perfumados*—sweet-smelling dandies—like Terrazas. The "Centaur of the North" preferred the more modest Roma Hotel on the corner of South Santa Fe and Second Street. He stayed here after escaping from a Mexico City prison during his exile in El Paso in 1913. According to oral history sources, Villa met at a bar inside the South El Paso hotel with German agent Maximilian Kloss, who allegedly tried to make a deal with him in exchange for German submarine bases off the coast of Baja California.[40] In 2003, this historic building was razed and replaced with a Burger King.

Fortunately, one of the most important structures in El Paso related to the Mexican Revolution, the Caples Building (Figure 3), has not yet been torn down. In January 1911, after moving to El Paso from San Antonio, Francisco Madero established the international offices of his revolutionary movement in this centrally located five-story buildings. During the initial stages of the revolution, Francisco Madero's calls for an armed uprising against the dictatorship of Porfirio Díaz mostly petered out everywhere except in northern Chihuahua. When Madero moved to El Paso he established his offices in room 507–508 of the Caples Building and declared them the International Headquarters of the Revolutionary Junta.[41] Provisional Chihuahua Governor Abraham González, who was in charge of the El Paso junta, recruited both Pancho Villa and Giuseppe Garibaldi, the grandson of the liberator of Italy. Garibaldi came to the Caples Building to offer his services but González initially hesitated to incorporate a foreigner into "insurrecto" ranks, wishing to avoid charges of filibustering. But the third-generation freedom fighter was hard to resist, especially given the paucity of experienced soldiers in the rebel army. When the U.S. government put out a warrant for both González and Madero in February 1911, both leaders decided to cross into Mexican territory. They left behind a skeleton staff at the Caples

Figure 3. Caples Building, International Headquarters of the Maderista revolutionary junta, El Paso, Texas, 1911. (Courtesy of El Paso Public Library.)

CHAPTER NINE

to be in charge of the recruitment of troops, the purchase of munitions, and the relaying of information.

Not all revolutionary headquarters were as accessible or centrally located as those of the Madero insurrection—a movement which was extremely popular among major sectors of the El Paso community. As early as 1896—when Teresita Urrea inspired an insurrection-ary movement out of her Segundo Barrio home—dozens of buildings throughout El Paso served as residences or bases of operation associated with different revolutionary factions. The most prominent ideological factions who used El Paso as a base of operations included Villistas, Orozquistas, Carrancistas, Magonistas, Teresistas, and Huertistas.

But there were other sites in El Paso with connections to the Mexican Revolution that at first glance may not be as obvious as those housing revolutionary headquarters or anti-Porfirista newspapers that were nevertheless also an integral part of the historical developments of the period. One such space is the disinfection plant at the Santa Fe Street International Bridge linking Juárez to El Paso. This particular structure for the "physi-cal inspection of aliens" in many ways epitomizes the medicalization of the U.S.-Mexico border during the Mexican Revolution (Figure 4). The architectural blueprint of the Santa Fe bridge disinfection plant provides an extremely useful document for the microhistorical study of small-scale urban spaces. The El Paso disinfection chamber diagram (Figure 5),

Figure 4. Physicial inspections of Mexican border crossers at the Santa Fe International Bridge, El Paso, Texas, 1917. Previously published in David Dorado Romo's *Ringside Seat to a Revolution* (El Paso, Tex.: Cinco Puntos Press, 2005).

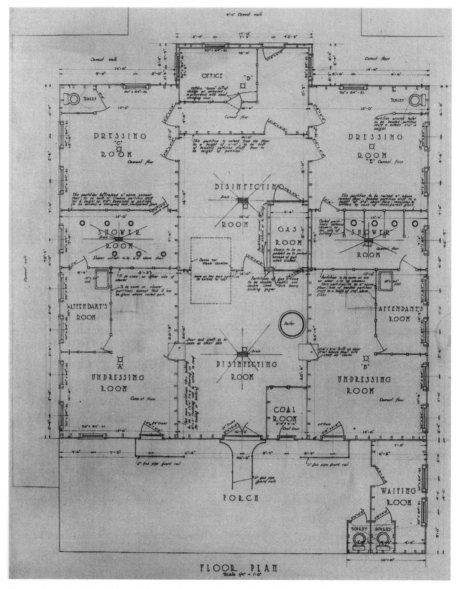

Figure 5. Blueprints of the El Paso Delousing Plant, 1916. Previously published in David Dorado Romo's *Ringside Seat to a Revolution* (El Paso, Tex.: Cinco Puntos Press, 2005).

which shows the spatial arrangements for the delousing process—including the "gas rooms" for the sterilization of clothes where Zyklon-B was later used as a pesticide—can only be understood by contextualizing it within larger narratives.[42]

The fumigations arose within the historical context not only of the Mexican Revolution but also of WWI, Progressive Era public health and social control policies, and international eugenics (racial hygiene) movements.[43] Beginning in 1917, Mexicans crossing from

Juárez to El Paso deemed to be "second class" by U.S. public health officials were forced to strip completely, turn in their clothes and baggage to be steam dried and fumigated with hydrocyanic acid, and stand before a customs inspector who would check his or her "hairy parts"—the scalp, armpits, chest, pubic area, and anus—for lice. Those found to have lice were required to shave their head and body hair with No. 00 clippers and apply a mix of kerosene and vinegar on their body. The humiliating delousing process experienced by 127,173 Mexican border crossers at the Santa Fe International Bridge in 1917 continued in El Paso until the mid-1930s.[44]

In 1937, Dr. Gerhard Peters wrote an article for a German pest science journal, *Anzeiger für Schädlinskunde*, which included two photographs of the El Paso delousing chambers at the international line.[45] Dr. Peters used these two fumigation structures on the U.S.-Mexico border to demonstrate how effective hydrocyanic acid, or Zyklon-B, was as an agent for killing unwanted pests. He became the managing director of Degesch, one of two German firms that acquired the patent to mass-produce Zyklon-B in 1940. In his patent application for a new "exterminating agent for vermin" Peters explained, "My invention relates to the extermination of animal pest-life of the most varied kinds, for instance, warm-blooded obnoxious animals and insects."[46] During WWII, Gerhard Peters was the major supplier of Zyklon-B to Nazi concentration camps.[47] The Germans used Zyklon-B in concentrated doses in the gas chambers to exterminate millions of human beings whom they considered "pests" and "parasites." Peters was tried and convicted at the Nuremberg trials for his role in the mass exterminations but was later retried and found not guilty.[48]

Of course, there were major differences between the *Desinfektionskammern* (disinfection chambers) in Germany and those in El Paso that Gerhard Peters included in his 1937 study. To begin with, Zyklon-B was not put to use at the El Paso-Juárez crossing to physically eliminate unwanted people by intentionally killing them as it was in Nazi Germany. However, the events in Germany did not take place in a historical vacuum. There were important connections between the discourse of eugenics, immigration control, and the racialized politics of public health underlying the disinfection chambers in both parts of the world that historians have thoroughly documented.[49]

A different South El Paso site related to counterhegemonic narratives of healing was the building on 500 South Oregon Street that served as the residence of the revolutionary *curandera* Teresita Urrea. The twenty-two-year-old healer and her family exiled themselves to El Paso's Segundo Barrio in 1896 after president Porfirio Díaz banished her from Mexico for her role in inspiring several antigovernment uprisings in northern Mexico including the revolt of Tomóchic. Thousands of fronterizo residents camped in front of Teresita's South El Paso home waiting to be cured by her.[50] She practiced indigenous herbal medicine that she learned from a Yaqui curandera in Sonora. Teresita was also a spiritualist whom her followers believed possessed miraculous healing and prophetic powers. At her South El Paso residence, she saw about 250 patients a day, taking male patients in the morning and women and children in the afternoon. "She never charged for her services," one El Paso newspaper wrote. "If a rich patron donated money to her, she would distribute it among the poor."[51]

Together with Lauro Aguire, Terresita Urrea was listed as the coeditor of Spanish-language newspaper titled *El Independiente* that denounced the dictatorship of Porfirio

Díaz and promoted a vision for a new spiritualist society that called for the end to all hierarchies based on class, race, and gender. Both Urrea's spiritualist ideas and her natural healing practices provided alternative visions of modernity that countered top-down discourses of order, progress, and medicalization by elites on both sides of the border. A few months after several armed attacks on northern Mexican towns along the border by followers of Teresita Urrea, the young curandera was the victim of three assassination attempts in her South Oregon Street residence. She boarded a train at the Union Depot and left the border city in the summer of 1897.

Other historic sites in El Paso not directly related to the armed conflict in Mexico tell the story of other types of battles waged on the cultural terrain during the revolution or that show the impact of the demographic changes on the urban landscape. More than a dozen movie theaters were constructed in El Paso between 1910 and 1920 that catered mainly to the thousands of Mexican refugees who crossed the line to flee the chaos in their homeland.[52] Movies shown at these theaters about the Mexican Revolution and the border were sometimes part of image and propaganda battles taking place on the US side of the line. The Imperial Theater on Alameda Street owned by Felix Padilla, himself a refugee from the revolution, regularly projected movies subtitled in both English and Spanish that included newsreels and fictionalized accounts of the armed conflict in Mexico. In September 1917, "a moving picture play" titled *The Battle of Carrizal* was shown at Padilla's theater. The film depicted the June 21, 1916, battle in northern Chihuahua where Carranza's forces soundly defeated General Pershing's African American 10th Calvary. The *El Paso Herald* reported that the predominantly ethnic Mexican audience at the Imperial Theater cheered loudly during the scenes depicting Carrancista soldiers capturing or killing Pershing's troops.[53]

In the early 1930s, Félix Padilla and his son Edmundo created a film with bilingual subtitles entitled *La Venganza de Pancho Villa* (*Pancho Villa's Revenge*). The Padillas made their film by reediting footage appropriated from anti-Mexican Hollywood propaganda movies known as "greaser films" and splicing in original footage they themselves shot in El Paso.[54] By doing so, the El Paso father and son team appear to have unwittingly become the first Mexican American filmmakers in the United States. The moving picture, with both English and Spanish subtitles, depicted Villa as a complicated figure who was neither a savage bandit nor an entirely heroic Robin Hood figure. Film scholars argue that their bilingual cinematic montage was a precursor of Border Cinema and was in many ways ahead of its time. *La Venganza de Pancho Villa* was lost to the public until Mexico City documentary filmmaker Gregorio Rocha "rediscovered" it in 2001 in the University of Texas at El Paso (UTEP) Special Collections archives. He also came upon other "lost" silent films that included fragments of the Mutual Film Corporation's *The Life of General Villa* (1914). The films of the revolution era had been stored away for decades in the basement of the Padilla family in El Paso.

PUBLIC MEMORY AND URBAN SPACE

Like the "lost" films by Félix and Edmundo Padilla, it was not until the twenty-first century that most of the Mexican Revolution sites of memory in this study were "rediscovered" by the El Paso community. Yet even today, hardly any of these buildings have local, state, or national historic landmark designation. Official historic preservation efforts in the city have almost entirely ignored vernacular structures with narratives connected to working-class and other subaltern communities. The Segundo Barrio, despite being the oldest neighborhood in El Paso, has not been designated as an historic district—unlike relatively newer, yet more affluent, districts.[55] Similarly, although El Paso played a central role in helping to spark the first major social revolution of the twentieth century, its legacy in the urban landscape has for the most part not been acknowledged by city elites.

Local business and political leaders, instead, have emphasized historical narratives that promote El Paso as an "Old West town." Gunfight reenactments that glamorize "Wild West outlaws" such as John Wesley Hardin were, and still are, a popular staple of local heritage tourism.[56] Other public history projects that have received substantial funding from the City of El Paso, such as a large-scale bronze sculpture walk known as the Twelve Travelers Memorial, highlight the role of Spanish and Anglo hegemony and colonization in the region. Scholars and community activists have criticized these monumental projects, such as the erection of the huge equestrian statue honoring Don Juan de Oñate, not only for their antiquated "Great Man" visions of history but for ignoring the historical agency and contributions of Mexican American and indigenous communities that make up more than eighty percent of El Paso's population.[57]

Political discourses that seek to portray the Mexican American population in the United States as recent immigrants with few or no roots on the U.S. side of the line have been boosted by the politics of urban and cultural erasure. In a twenty-year period alone—between 1960 and 1980—the City of El Paso systematically removed 14,700 people (six out of ten residents) from the Segundo Barrio through a series of urban renewal projects, sanitation campaigns, road constructions, tenement eradications, park expansions, commercial zonings, housing code enforcements, and eminent domain expropriations.[58] In 1963, the binational Chamizal Settlement between the United States and Mexico resulted in the loss of almost one third of the Segundo Barrio's territory, the displacement of more than 5,600 Southside residents, and the destruction of hundreds of homes, apartments, and buildings.[59] A large number of these razed buildings were constructed during the late nineteenth and early twentieth century. The long history of urban removal in South El Paso during the twentieth century has contributed to the disconnection between the Mexican American community and the historical knowledge of its own geography.

In 2010, as part of the one-hundred-year anniversary of the Mexican Revolution, scholars and members of the fronterizo community initiated a project to recuperate some of the city's forgotten and silenced narratives connected to this period. They created the *Museo Urbano: An Indoor/Outdoor Exhibit of the Mexican Revolution* to highlight the revolution's impact on El Paso's urban and cultural landscape.[60] One component of this project, developed by UTEP's Department of History, was an exhibit entitled "El Paso: The Other Side of the Revolution."[61] It was displayed at the El Paso Museum of History between November 2010 and July 2011. The multimedia exhibition explored the role of image and propaganda wars carried out in the cultural terrain—in film, photography, music, journalism, and literature—during the revolutionary period. Text and photography panels also documented the important urban sites of cultural production associated with revolutionary activity in this border city.

The outdoor component of the *Museo Urbano* includes a walking tour of twenty of the most significant Mexican Revolution sites of memory in downtown and South El Paso. As part of an ongoing project funded by UTEP and Humanities Texas, several of these buildings will have banners on their exterior walls bearing historic photographs. In the summer and fall of 2011, the building at 500 S. Oregon Street also served as a welcoming room for the self-guided walking tour.[62] At distinct times during the turn of the twentieth century, this South El Paso building functioned as the Mexican Preparatory School, a Chinese laundry, an African American brothel, and a Ladies Hospital, as well as the residence of the revolutionary healer Teresita Urrea. The temporary museum at this site featured an exhibit on Teresita Urrea and curanderismo as well as an exploration of the transnational histories connected to South El Paso. The display was curated by a team of historians, UTEP graduate students, artists, and barrio residents.

This building and its multilayered history lies within the "redevelopment zone" that the city targeted as site of major demolitions in 2006. Both local opposition and global economic recession, however, have put a temporary stop to large-scale urban removal projects in South El Paso. For now, this and other sites of memory within the Segundo Barrio are still standing. But the neighborhood that helped spawn the Mexican Revolution continues to be a zone of contested narratives and disputed territories.

CONCLUSION

My study, focusing on the recuperation of narratives of revolution and counterrevolution linked to El Paso's built environment, has allowed me to uncover information that may not have been readily apparent by an exclusively thematic or chronological approach. GIS maps and Web-based cartography tools such as Google Maps or HyperCities have made it easier to chart historical patterns and changes of the built environment through time. For this particular study, these tools made it possible to tag and group historical sites based on their connection to the various revolutionary factions operating on the border. They also helped to categorize Mexican Revolution sites of memory according to the types of activity connected to them. These locations include espionage agencies, recruitment centers, arms suppliers, military camps, commercial enterprises, printing presses, labor organizations, bars/meeting places/plotting grounds, newspaper offices, cultural sites, observation points, film and photography studios, and sites dedicated to other revolutionary activities. The proximity of both revolutionary and counterrevolutionary activity within the same street block—or sometimes within the same building—adds new layers and dimensions to our understanding of historical developments.

Revolution, like business, is to a large degree about location. It is somewhat paradoxical that a transnational periphery became the central spawning ground for the Mexican Revolution. The revolution's major developments, especially in the initial stages, did not take place in the capital or other major cities—unlike what occurred during the Russian or French revolutions—but on Mexico's northern border. The border, both as contact zone and as fault line where many different worlds collide and come together, was the epicenter for a series of revolutionary and counterrevolutionary movements that emerged during the early twentieth century. The revolution was literally everywhere in El Paso's urban landscape. In a sense, it permeated the totality of space.

Today, the tendency of contemporary scholarship is to dematerialize the border and transform it into an ubiquitous metaphor. Indeed, the border is a series of overlapping spaces with boundaries that are not always sharply defined. However, it is important not to lose sight of the very real, concrete spaces these metaphors are built on. Those particular spaces have much to teach us about the social, political, military, economic, and cultural histories of the U.S.-Mexico borderlands. Perhaps the most fruitful approach to the study of these historical developments is through a process that combines both fission and fusion. One approach is to proceed as if there is no such thing as the history of a city, or a country, or a continent but rather only a series of microhistories—of zones, streets, buildings, and individual rooms. Every building, as Camille Wells puts it, "can be understood in terms of power or authority—as efforts to assume, extend, resist, or accommodate it."[63] On the one hand, sometimes what transpires within a single room, such as the offices of the *El Paso del Norte* in South El Paso, makes a profound impact on cultural and historical developments far beyond its wall. On the other hand, one cannot fully understand what takes place in a space such as the disinfection chambers of the Santa Fe International Bridge without contextualizing it within much broader narratives. In this case, in order to fully understand the history of a single building, one must understand the history of the world. Ultimately, microhistory and macrohistory are inextricably intertwined.

NOTES

1. I have charted most of these sites on Google Maps as part of an ongoing University of Texas at El Paso public history project and urban museum exhibit I am currently curating in collaboration with Dr. Yolanda Chávez Leyva. See Mexican Revolution Sites of Memory map, http://maps.google.com/maps?hl=en&tab=nl (accessed December 15, 2010).

2. The City of El Paso/Paso Del Norte Group/SMWM, "El Paso Downtown 2015 Plan," September 2006. http://www.ci.el-paso.tx.us/downtownplan/_documents/El_Paso_Report_060920.pdf#view =fitH (accessed February 20, 1012).

3. Census figures quoted in R. E. Alexander, Urban Development Manual for the City of El Paso, 1968. In 1916, the U.S. government ordered a "special census" in El Paso that for the first time counted "persons of Mexican descent" as a separate category. The U.S. Census Bureau counted 32,737 persons of Mexican descent, 27,358 Whites (other than Mexican), 1,514 Negroes, 243 Chinese, 41 Japanese, 5 Indians, 6,554 Mexican refugees, and 482 White refugees.

4. City and military authorities razed hundreds of Mexican adobe homes facing the Rio Grande—mostly along South Santa Fe, South Oregon, Ninth Street, and the Guerrero Alley. Photographs in the El Paso Times of the Second Ward in 1916 show city blocks that seemed to have suffered bombardments or the devastation of war. In a sense, they had. El Paso Herald, June 16, 1916. See David Dorado Romo, *Ringside Seat to a Revolution: An Underground Cultural History of El Paso and Juárez, 1893–1923* (El Paso: Cinco Puntos Press, 2005), 235.

5. See Anne Gabert, "Defining the Boundaries of Care: Local Responses to Global Concerns in El Paso Public Health Policy, 1881–1941" (Ph.D. diss., University of Texas at El Paso, 2006).

6. David Bodenhamer et al., ed., *The Spatial Humanities: GIS and the Future of Humanities Scholarship* (Bloomington: Indiana University Press, 2010), vii.

7. The categories of historical documentation of particular buildings include original date of construction, architect, architectural description, city directory, and census information related to the building's owners and residents, as well as the building's current use, occupants, and owner.

8. Oscar Martinez, *Border Boom Town: Ciudad Juárez since 1848* (Austin: University of Texas Press, 1978), 34.

9. For a list of El Paso Spanish language newspapers during the revolution, see Romo, *Ringside Seat to a Revolution*, 284.

10. Stanley Robe, *Azuela and the Mexican Underdogs* (Los Angeles: University of California Press, 1979), 67.

11. Azuela Robe, 67. As his final payment, received 1,000 copies of his novel that went on sale for thirty cents each. One month after his novel came out, he was only able to sell five copies.

12. Robe, *Azuela*, 67.

13. Elias Torres, *Twenty Episodes in the Life of Pancho Villa* (Austin: Encino Press, 1973), 9. Originally published as *20 Episodios Vibrantes de la Vida de Villa* in 1934.

14. Torres, *Twenty Episodes*, 9.

15. Susie Aquilina, "Public History Walkthrough," unpublished public history paper, El Paso: University of Texas at El Paso, Public History of the Mexican Revolution, December 2009.

16. Aquilina, "Public History Walkthrough."

17. Release, Grantor: Elias L. Torres, Granee: Fernando and Juana Gamiochipi, July 7, 1917, El Paso County Clerk's Records; Release Satisfaction: Grantee: Elias Torres, Grantor: Texas Bank and Trust Company of El Paso Texas, June 26, 1917, El Paso County Clerk's Records. Fernando Gamiochipi paid installments of $700, $900, and $1,700 for the building on Lot 6 and southerly nine feet of Lot 7 in the 101 Campbell's Addition. Sam Gillet was the notary public. Juana de Gamiochipi bought the building on March 30, 1914.

18. La Patria, June 13, 1911.

19. Torres' books included *20 vibrantes episodios de la vida de Villa* (1934), *La Cabeza de Villa* (1947), *Como Murio Pancho Villa* (1954), and *Vida y Hazáñas de Pancho Villa* (1959).

20. San Antonio Light, November 20, 1920.

21. Jadwiga Maszewska, "Chicana Texts? Postcolonial Theory? Olga Beatriz Torres's Memorias de mi viaje/Recollections of my Trip," paper presented at International Symposium: Migrating Words, at Chiva University, Japan, June 12, 1910. http://migratingwords.com/proceedings/Maszewska-Abstract-Proceedings.pdf (accessed December 15, 2010).

22. Paul Moeller, "John Kenneth Turner: Early Twentieth-Century Regime Change and Support through the Pen," http://knol.google.com/k/paul-karl-moeller/john-kenneth-turner/3pj5r6n3 uurvd/3 (accessed December 15, 2010). As part of a secret agreement, Carranza paid Turner $2,000 for "writing in favor of his constitutional rule."

23. Warranty Deed, Grantor: W. R. Franklin, Grantee: Pablo Baray, November 1, 1921, Block 101 of Campbell Addition, lot 6 southerly nine feet of Lot 7 County Clerk's Office Records; Warranty Deed, Grantor: Francisco Ruiz, Grantee: Pablo Baray, Block 101 of Campbell Addition, seventeen feet of Lot 7 and 18 feet of Lot 8, November 18, 1921. County Clerk's Office Records.

24. Ana María Alonso, *Thread of Blood: Colonialism, Revolution, and Gender on Mexico's Northern Frontier* (Tucson: The University of Arizona Press, 1995), 199; Friedrich Katz, *Life & Times of Pancho Villa* (Palo Alto, Cal.: Stanford University Press, 1998) 294–95. Katz writes about Baray's motives for joining the Villistas: "In his eyes, fighting for the revolution was the good life, and he proudly stated that during his army service his weight had increased from 64 to 75 kilos."

25. Scott Comar, "Public History Walkthrough," unpublished public history paper, University of Texas at El Paso, December 2009.

26. Alonso, *Thread of Blood*, 199.

27. Manifest, U.S. Department of Labor, Immigration Service, Port of El Paso, June 9, 1923.

28. "Mexican Spies Overrun El Paso" *El Paso Herald*, July 19, 1912. In 1912, when Mexican Consul Enrique Llorente headed the Madero secret service agency in El Paso, he had a half-million dollar budget to pay his spies. At one point, there were more than 200 Mexican secret agents working within El Paso.

29. *El Paso Herald*, July 14, 1916.

30. "Hostile Paper," *El Paso Times*, December 21, 1893.

31. *El Paso Herald*, October 20, 1906.

32. Oscar Martinez, *Fragments of the Mexican Revolution: Personal Accounts from the Border* (Albuquerque: University of New Mexico Press, 1993), 90; For a more thorough history of the Ketelsen & Degetau site, see also Scott Comar, "Public History Walkthrough," unpublished paper, University of Texas at El Paso, December 2009.

33. Romo, *Ringside Seat*, 270. In a two-year period, 10 million rounds of ammunition, 40,000 rifles, and 500 tons of dynamite were sent through El Paso into Mexico. An arms smuggler could buy 1,000 cartridges of ammo for $30 in El Paso and sell them for $50 in Juárez.

34. Zork Hardware Company Archives, Special Collections, University of Texas at El Paso.

35. Charles Harris and Louis Sadler, *The Secret War in El Paso: Mexican Revolutionary Intrigue, 1906– 1920* (Albuquerque: University of New Mexico Press, 2009), 144–5.

36. Michelle Lorraine Gomilla, "Los Refugiados y los Comerciantes: Mexican Refugees and Businessmen in Downtown El Paso," (M.A. thesis, University of Texas at El Paso, 1990), 49.

37. *New York Times*, May 14, 1911.

38. Joseph Sweeney to Jack Sweeney, May 12, 1911, in Martínez, *Fragments of the Mexican Revolution*, 79.

39. Charles Harris and Louis Saddler, *Texas Rangers and the Mexican Revolution: The Bloodiest Decade, 1910–1920* (Albuquerque: University of New Mexico Press, 2004), 89.

40. Jessica Peterson and Thelma Knoles, *Pancho Villa: Intimate Recollections by People Who Knew Him* (New York: Hastings House, 1977), 186–187.

41. For a more detailed account of the Madero headquarters in the Caples Building, see Mardee De Witter, "Revolutionary El Paso, 1910–1917" (M.A. thesis, Texas Western College, El Paso, 1946).

42. Surgeon J. R. Hurley to Surgeon General, January 19, 1929. NACP, USPHS, RG 90, File 1960 (245–184), Box 249. On January 19, 1929, J. R. Hurley, the medical officer in charge of the El Paso delousing station, put in a requisition for $25 worth of Zyklon-B as the fumigation agent of choice.

43. See Alexandra Minna Stern, *Eugenic Nation: Faults & Frontiers of Better Breeding in Modern America* (Los Angeles: University of California Press, 2005).

44. *El Paso Herald*, March 7, 1918.

45. Gerhard Peters, "Durchgasung von Eisenbahnwagen mit Bläusare [Fumigation of Railroad Cars with Hydrocyanic Acid]," *Anzeiger für Schädlinskunde* 13, 3, (1937), 35–41.

46. Quoted in Scott Christianson, *The Last Gasp: The Rise and Fall of the American Gas Chamber* (Los Angeles: University of California Press, 2010), 131.

47. Chistianson, *Last Gap*, 131.

48. "Poison Gas Maker Convicted," *New York Times*, March 29, 1949; Alexander Cockburn, "Zyklon B on the Border," *The Nation*, June 21, 2007.

49. See Edwin Black, *War against the Weak: Eugenics and America's Campaign to Create a Master Race* (New York: Four Walls Eight Windows, 2003).

50. *El Paso Herald*, June 16, 1896; *El Paso Times*, September 30, 1896.

51. *El Paso Herald*, July 1, 1896.

52. These movie theaters included the Alhambra, Colón, Crystal, Estrella, Hidalgo, Ideal, Majestic, Rex, the Alameda, and the Imperial Theaters.

53. *El Paso Herald*, September 10, 1917.

54. See Gregorio Rocha, "La Venganza de Pancho Villa: A Lost and Found Border Film" in ed. Alexandra Juhasz and Jesse Lerner, *F is for Phony: Fake Documentary and Truth's Undoing* (Minneapolis: University of Minnesota Press, 2006), 50–58.

55. "Whose History?: The Politics of Historic Preservation and Urban Removal in El Paso," UTEP Border Public History Web site. http://academics.utep.edu/LinkClick.aspx?link=Neighborhoods%2FPolitics_of_Preservation__1.pdf&tabid=55450&mid=123747 (accessed February 20, 2012).

56. David Burge, "John Wesley Hardin's Legend Lives in Concordia Show," *El Paso Times*, August, 18, 2011. http://www.elpasotimes.com/news/ci_18704175 (accessed February 20, 1012).

57. Ginger Thompson, "As a Sculpture Takes Shape in Mexico, Opposition Takes Shape in the U.S." *New York Times*, January 17, 2002; Ralph Blumenthal, "Still Many Months Away, El Paso's Giant Horseman Keeps Stirring Passions," *New York Times*, January 10, 2004.

58. According to Federal Census figures, there were 24,200 people living in South El Paso in 1960. By 1980, only 9,500 residents remained.

59. See City of El Paso Department of Planning, "South El Paso: A Study of Tenement Housing and the Preliminary Redevelopment Plan, 1967."

60. The *Museo Urbano* project was conceived and developed as part of a graduate-level public history course taught by Dr. Yolanda Leyva, UTEP borderlands history department chair, in 2009.

61. Chris Lechuga, "UTEP History Department Exhibit Brings Mexican Revolution to Life," November 29, 2010. http://admin.utep.edu/Default.aspx?tabid=67628 (accessed February 20, 2012).

62. John Hall, "Museo Urbano Opens: Museum Dedicated to El Paso's Segundo Barrio," *El Paso Times*, May 9, 2011. http://www.elpasotimes.com/news/ci_18019051 (accessed February 20, 1012).

63. Quoted in Dolores Hayden, *The Power of Place* (Cambridge: The MIT Press, 1999), 30.

BIBLIOGRAPHY

Alonso, Ana María. *Thread of Blood: Colonialism, Revolution, and Gender on Mexico's Northern Frontier.* Tucson: University of Arizona Press, 1995.

Azuela, Mariano. *Los de Abajo: Novela de la Revolución Mexicana* [The Underdogs: A Novel of the Mexican Revolution]. New York: Penguin Books, 2008.

Black, Edwin. *War against the Weak: Eugenics and America's Campaign to Create a Master Race.* New York: Four Walls Eight Windows, 2003.

Bodenhamer, David, John Corrigan, and Trevor Harris, eds. *The Spatial Humanities: GIS and the Future of Humanities Scholarship.* Bloomington: Indiana University Press, 2010.

Christianson, Scott. *The Last Gasp: The Rise and Fall of the American Gas Chamber.* Los Angeles: University of California Press, 2010.

De Witter, Mardee. "Revolutionary El Paso, 1910–1917." Master's thesis. Texas Western College, El Paso, 1946.

Gabert, Anne. "Defining the Boundaries of Care: Local Responses to Global Concerns in El Paso Public Health Policy, 1881–1941." PhD diss., University of Texas at El Paso, 2006.

Gomilla, Michelle. "Los Refugiados y los Comerciantes: Mexican Refugees and Businessmen in Downtown El Paso." M.A. thesis, University of Texas at El Paso, 1990.

Harris, Charles, and Louis Sadler. *The Secret War in El Paso: Mexican Revolutionary Intrigue, 1906–1920.* Albuquerque: University of New Mexico Press, 2009.

Hayden, Dolores. *The Power of Place.* Cambridge, Mass.: The MIT Press, 1999.

Juhasz, Alexandra, and Jesse Lerner, eds. *F is for Phony: Fake Documentary and Truth's Undoing.* Minneapolis: University of Minnesota Press, 2006.

Katz, Friedrich. *The Life and Times of Pancho Villa.* Stanford, Ca.: Stanford University Press, 1998.

Martinez, Oscar. *Border Boom Town: Ciudad Juárez since 1848.* Austin: University of Texas Press, 1978.

———. *Fragments of the Mexican Revolution: Personal Accounts from the Border.* Albuquerque: University of New Mexico Press, 1993.

Peters, Gerhard. Durchgasung von Eisenbahnwagen mit Bläusare [Fumigation of Railroad Cars with Hydrocyanic Acid]," *Anzeiger für Schädlinskunde,* 13 (3): 35–41.

Peterson, Jessica, and Thelma Knoles. *Pancho Villa: Intimate Recollections by People Who Knew Him.* New York: Hastings House, 1977.

Robe, Stanley. *Azuela and the Mexican Underdogs.* Los Angeles: University of California Press, 1979.

Robert E. Alexander and Associates. *Urban Development Manual for the City of El Paso.* Los Angeles: R. E. Alexander, 1968.

Romo, David Dorado. *Ringside Seat to a Revolution: An Underground Cultural History of El Paso and Juárez, 1893–1923.* El Paso, Tex.: Cinco Puntos Press, 2005.

Stern, Alexandra M. *Eugenic Nation: Faults and Frontiers of Better Breeding in Modern America.* Los Angeles: University of California Press, 2005.

Torres, Elias. *Twenty Episodes in the Life of Pancho Villa.* Austin, Tex.: Encino Press, 1973.

CHAPTER TEN

ON THE BANKS OF THE FUTURE
Ciudad Juárez and El Paso in the Mexican Revolution

Oswaldo Zavala

As noted by historian Alan Knight, the majority of the historiography of the Mexican Revolution begins with the celebrations of the centennial of the War for independence in 1910. Coinciding with Porfirio Díaz's eightieth birthday and his seventh reelection, the centennial festivities were more than anything a Mexico City affair, with its lavish parades, newly unveiled monuments, expensive banquets, and even the inauguration of an asylum for mental patients.[1] "Yet the real Mexico, and in particular the Mexico of the Revolution, was provincial Mexico," explains Knight.[2] As it was the case with the 2010 celebration of the bicentennial of the Independence in the capital, the states in the Republic hardly joined the commemoration of 1910. In some small towns, writes Knight, the anniversary was completely ignored, as most citizens were occupied with the tasks of daily survival or had their attention diverted by the passing of Halley's comet. As was repeated by President Felipe Calderón in 2010, public spending for the nationalist celebrations a century ago was principally a matter of *capitalinos* and their illegitimate dictator. The historical narratives of the Revolution that seek to emphasize the relevance of Mexico's provinces in the conflict, however, often underestimate the importance of one of the landmarks of the revolt. I am referring to the battle for Ciudad Juárez, which took place between May 8 and 10, 1911. During those three days, Francisco Villa, Pascual Orozco, and Giuseppe Garibaldi—grandson of the Italian liberator—dismissed the orders of Francisco I. Madero and independently decided to take the city by assault in order to force the resignation of Díaz. Jesús Silva Herzog summarizes the episode in a single paragraph of his *Breve historia de la Revolución Mexicana* (1960).[3] In their *In the Shadow of the Mexican Revolution* (1989), Héctor Aguilar Camín and Lorenzo Meyer simply transcribe the three lines that historian François Xavier Guerra dedicates to the fight.[4] Even Alan Knight, despite considering it a crucial battle, discusses it in less than a page in the first of the two volumes of *The Mexican Revolution* (1986).[5]

It is not a coincidence that the two books that offer greater attention to the battle are the profuse biographies of Francisco Villa written by historian Friedrich Katz and novelist Paco Ignacio Taibo II. In addition to propelling Madero toward his triumphant entrance into Mexico City and his election to the presidency, the battle of Ciudad Juárez also made a hero of Villa, who, in turn, grew in influence owing to Madero's political and military ineptitude. With the surrender of General Juan Navarro, official commander of the border city, "the revolutionaries achieved their greatest and decisive victory."[6] The federal army's defeat represented a symbolic reversal of a pompous and celebrated official meeting that Díaz held in Ciudad Juárez on October 16, 1909, with the U.S. President William Taft. Ultimately, it would be the indispensable factor that would produce the overthrowing of the dictator. Only in this context is it possible to fully comprehend Alfonso Reyes' analysis of the end of Porfirian Mexico: "An invisible crack, a slight opening through which fresh air from the outside suddenly began to find its way in, and that stubborn chamber, incapable of pumping oxygen, exploded like a bomb."[7]

But in spite of its importance for the success of Madero's campaign and the initial stage of the Revolution,[8] the battle of Ciudad Juárez has only been studied in depth in a recent work by border historians Miguel Ángel Berumen and Pedro Siller. Edited originally in two volumes, this investigation recovers an impressive photographic archive overlooked by most historians until its publication in 2003. Berumen drew from more than 200 collections in 50 archives in Mexico and the United States. His selection forms an integral view of rebel activity on the northern border that substantially differs from that of the widely known Casasola archive.[9] Most iconographic images of the Revolution have traditionally been drawn from the work of the Casasola brothers and that of other photographers included in the same archive, focusing on subsequent episodes of the conflict. Berumen argues that this collection "gradually filled in the absence of a graphic memory of [border] inhabitants with a national iconography that had little to do [. . .] with the photographic phenomenon of Madero's movement in the [border] area."[10] Along with the research of other cultural historians and writers such as David Dorado Romo and Charles Bowden that I will discuss later, the last decade has seen a complex process of recovery of the borderland's historical memory. In particular, the task of reconstructing and fully appreciating the relevance of the battle of Ciudad Juárez sheds an unprecedented light on the history of the first major social and political revolution of the twentieth century. More than an alternative political and military account, these recent investigations reveal that Ciudad Juárez and El Paso have been the privileged site of transcendental historical events from both countries. The borderland was in 1910 and is again in 2010 the ground zero of social unrest where two histories collide and affect one another. The "deep, horizontal comradeship"[11] of the imagined community that collectively constructs a national identity, as theorized by Benedict Anderson, comes to a contradictory halt when confronted with the unusual social dynamics of the border. As Anderson explains, one of the characteristics of an imagined community is the emergence of a fraternity "willingly to die for such limited imaginings"[12] as nationalism. In the border region, those communal imaginings involve an ironic intertwining of relations continually shifting the very concept of national identity. As I will argue in what follows, the unexpected power vectors at the border radicalize theorizations of the region's "cultural difference"[13] or of its mechanisms of "border thinking,"[14] as conceptualized respectively by Homi Bhabha and Walter Mignolo. Finally, I propose to explore how the shifting sands surrounding anomalous places such as Ciudad Juárez and El Paso have, in fact, become a metaphor of their own desert nature: a paradigm in constant movement, producing an irreducible conundrum where hegemony and resistance are not the typical polarities at stake. In this sense, I will analyze the historical force of Villa's image as it is embodied in the contemporary figure of the border inhabitant and crosser, as portrayed by Charles Bowden in his recent accounts of immigration. Thus, following his essays, I will approach the phenomenon of migration as a modern exodus from Mexico that has produced an alternative way of living that represents a direct reaction to the failed social reforms of the 1910 Revolution.

INVENTING THE REVOLUTION

The first edition of *1911. La batalla de Ciudad Juárez* circulated in its two-volume format primarily in the border region. In 2009, Berumen reedited a condensed version containing most of the photographic material from the first edition and his essay on the work of news photographers, national and foreign, who covered the battle. Berumen and Siller's careful edition presents a focalized analysis, recovering the graphic documentation that makes explicit the radical significance of this historical happening. Among his findings, for example, Berumen compares two photographs of Villa taken at Madero's camp, the so-called "House of Adobe" that served as the headquarter for the rebels located on the banks of the Río Bravo (Río Grande). In the first image, taken on April 26, 1911, when he was promoted to the rank of colonel, Villa appears dressed in simple clothes: a black suit with a wide brimmed *charro* hat. In the second picture, dated May 5 during the celebration of the anniversary of the battle of Puebla, three days before the assault on Ciudad Juárez, Villa stands with a light color jacket, dress pants, and the beige American hat that he would be wearing from then on as seen in his most iconic images. Berumen explains: "These changes were very noticeable, especially with regard to the link between people's clothes, their trades, and their social conditions."[15]

The border had already been the scenario of a first rebel uprising led by Abraham González on February 5, 1911. Pedro Siller recalls that González, appointed by Madero as provisional governor of the state of Chihuahua, managed to unite the two fundamental factions of the Revolution: Madero's democratic movement and the strong men that would soon become the protagonists of the armed conflict, namely, Villa and Orozco.[16] Persecuted and with his troops dispersed, Madero found in Ciudad Juárez a disciplined group with powerful and charismatic leaders who commanded authority among the rebels and who had earned the sympathy of citizens from both sides of the Río Bravo, the natural border between the two countries. The leaders of the liberating army signed the communiqué officially establishing the camp "on the banks of the Río Bravo, facing Ciudad Juárez," on April 16, 1911.[17] This location granted unprecedented advantages to the Revolution. The most basic was that the rebels had immediate access to weapons and an escape route into the United States. Also, the U.S. telephone company Bell provided a line out from El Paso to Juárez, directly into that modest barracks to allow Madero an immediate and international means of communication. And there were other advantages:

> In front of the House of Adobe there was a suspension bridge from which one could cross to El Paso [. . .] On the northern shore of the bridge there

used to pass an electric tramway that went all the way into downtown El Paso. El Pasoans, among whom there were many Mexicans, were not shy in showing their sympathy to the revolutionary soldiers; they would cross the bridge over the river to meet and salute the rebel commanders and the rest of the troops. They brought them clothes, food, guns and ammunition.[18]

By the end of April, other Madero followers and even family members started arriving, including his father and brother Gustavo. Díaz sent envoys to negotiate the peace; they were prepared to concede to any rebel demand with the exception of the dictator's resignation. To ease the anxiety of the troops who were beginning to show signs of exasperation for his postponing the attack, Madero organized a ceremony on April 26 to recognize and decorate his military chiefs. He appointed Orozco to be his major general while Villa and Garibaldi were promoted to colonels.[19] Twenty-five hundred rebel soldiers witnessed the military ritual that was documented by the renowned British photojournalist Jimmy Hare, who had reported on the 1898 Spanish-American war and the 1904 Russo-Japanese conflict for the illustrated magazine *Collier's*. Arriving to the border more than a month earlier than most Mexican journalists, Hare became one of the central photographers shooting the battle of Juárez with his German camera and his automatic Kodak.[20] Hare also captured images of the May 5 celebration, another of Madero's tactics to appease his army anxious for action. Various amateur photographers soon flooded the rebel camp. Some waited hours under the burning sun to shake Villa's hand and take a picture with him. Alan Knight highlights that, indeed, "Juárez conferred prestige and publicity"[21] to the rebels who quickly became adept at using the attention of foreign and national journalists covering the conflict.

Although the reasons why Madero decided to call off the attack on Ciudad Juárez on May 7 are not entirely clear, that same day Porfirio Díaz issued a national message in which he assured that

> he will indeed remove himself from power, but when his conscious tells
> him that by doing so he will not deliver the country into anarchy, and that
> he will do it with décor in the interest of the Nation and as it is proper
> of a dignitary that may have without doubt incurred in mistakes but that
> in contrast also knew how to defend his homeland and to serve it with
> loyalty.[22]

Siller conjectures that this ambiguous resignation of Díaz influenced Madero's decision to leave Ciudad Juárez untouched. Katz, on the other hand, hypothesizes that Díaz's emissaries had convinced Madero that an assault on the border city could result in U.S. intervention. Villa and Orozco, writes Katz, agreed that withdrawing from Ciudad Juárez would boost the morale of the federal troops while discouraging the rebels: "The main military leaders of the Revolution, Orozco and Villa, now decided that the time had come for insubordination,"[23] explains Katz. They ordered the attack to begin on the morning of May 8 without informing Madero, correctly assuming that once initiated, the political leader of the movement would be unable to stop it.

Soldiers loyal to Villa and Orozco provoked the first gunfights with the federal troops. Porfirian General Navarro, taken by surprise, communicated with Madero, who, in turn, assured him—because he honestly believed it to be so—that the shooting was accidental and that he would order an immediate cease-fire. As Orozco and Villa had predicted, no one listened. And as Knight bluntly explains, "whatever the cause, Madero was powerless to halt the attack."[24] General Navarro was instructed by Díaz not to shoot back: he still feared that a stray bullet killing a U.S. citizen could be used by the neighbor to the north as an excuse for an intervention.

A story by *El Paso Herald* reporter Timothy Turner, unearthed by David Dorado Romo in his *Ringside Seat to a Revolution, An Underground Cultural History of El Paso and Juárez: 1893–1923* (that I will discuss in detail later), confirms the unique opportunity of the siege and the unusual strategy adopted by the rebels:

> The attack was made slowly and surely, and each man acted as a center. There were no orders. The Federals fought as a machine. The rebels as individuals. Every man did as he pleased, and used his own head. Therein was the victory. The loss of all the officers does not entirely destroy the fighting efficiency, as it does in some European armies, where the men are not allowed to think. This holds, as well, in Mexico. The rebel soldiers think; the federals do not.[25]

According to this account, Villa's soldiers were capable of spontaneously inventing their own way of fighting, of organizing decentered tactics that prevailed and that were not comparable to other military strategies in America or Europe. Rebel troops thus advanced southward at a rapid pace. Three days later, three photographs by Jimmy Hare sum up the end of the battle: in the first image, Hare captures the entrance of Madero and Villa into the recently-seized city.[26] Paco Ignacio Taibo II comments on this image, which he consulted in Berumen's book for the writing of his biography of Villa:

> [Villa] returns to the House of Adobe to inform Madero of the news. "¿What are you telling me, Pancho," Francisco Madero would ask, inquiring about a victory he did not seek to win, that he does not deserve. And he cannot believe the news [. . .] [Hare's photograph] shows impetuous soldiers on horseback riding among the trees: [. . .] Madero with a hat, and to his right Pancho Villa wearing his Sunday best (he had finally slept) with two cartridge belts over his jacket, advancing toward the city.[27]

In the second photograph, defeated General Navarro converses with Madero, both of them looking at the ground, as if both had been defeated by the same army. In the third image, soldiers step over trash, soiled uniforms, and debris. A truck collects the dead bodies.[28] Abraham González calculates that 302 people were killed and wounded in the fight; 100 federal soldiers and 15 revolutionary fighters were among the dead.[29] Katz recalls that after the successful assault of Ciudad Juárez, military general Victoriano Huerta tried to convince Díaz to send him to the border city with 2,000 soldiers to defeat the rebels once and for all. Instead, heeding finance minister José Yves Limantour's advice, Díaz decided to resign the presidency. Katz states that the end of the dictatorship was mainly due to "an exaggerated fear of U.S. intervention and a realistic appraisal of the military situation in Chihuahua, with its social and political consequences."[30]

THEORIZING THE BORDER EVENT

The battle of Ciudad Juárez serves as a multilayer symbol of border dynamics. As a vehicle to analyze it, I turn to Alberto Moreiras' concept of "subaltern negation." He defines this term as "a kind of resistance" to hegemonic control.[31] He then applies this notion to his reading of a tense confrontation between Zapatistas (the rebel army from the south led by Emiliano Zapata) and Villistas, taken from an episode of Martín Luis Guzmán's *El Águila y la Serpiente* (1928), a novel based on the author's personal experience of the Revolution. In this scene, soldiers loyal to Villa mock a group of drunken Zapatistas in control of the National Palace in Mexico City. Instead of starting a gunfight, the Zapatistas simply ignore the mockery and continue their drinking. Moreiras attributes here to the Zapatista army a "secret triumphant redemption" emanating from "an alternative understanding of the political"[32] vis-à-vis the Villistas, who are seen as representing the hegemonic group among the armed rebels. I contend, however, that the first and most decisive "subaltern negation" actually occurred at the beginning of the Revolution, with the ascension of the Villistas during the Battle of Ciudad Juárez. Their intervention implied a more effective understanding of the political than what Moreiras attributes to the Zapatistas. Facing the hegemonic power of the Porfirian government in 1911, Madero capitulated. Refusing to conform, Villa and Orozco comprehended the political ineptitude of Madero's decision, when he unilaterally ordered the rebel army out of Ciudad Juárez. They clearly understood the consequences of not taking the city and, contrary to Moreiras' formulation, enacted what may be called a radical subaltern *affirmation* by seizing Ciudad Juárez from federal control. This same radicalization affects what Homi Bhabha calls the "act of writing the nation,"[33] introducing in this episode of Mexico's history a type of discontinuity into the homogenizing constructs of nation, national culture, and the centralized flow of power. Bhabha sees "the nation as the measure of the liminality of cultural modernity,"[34] as discourses of nationalism are the platform for the unfolding of modernity. In this sense, the reach of modernity is at the same time the reach of the idea of a nation. In the paradigm operating in Ciudad Juárez in 1911, nevertheless, the very idea of nation and its apparent liminality—the geopolitical border as the material limit of the nation—become superfluous. What is articulated, instead, seems to be an unprecedented emergence of an ad hoc horizontal alliance between subalterns who not only seized the city but also the very core of hegemonic power, reconfiguring from the margin the mainstream historical narration of Mexico.

Walter Mignolo envisions a possibility for subaltern emancipation through the conceptualization of "border thinking," an epistemological tool that, he suggests, produces a specific "subaltern knowledge."[35] He locates "border thinking" originally in the forced interaction of American indigenous populations and enslaved Africans with European frameworks of knowledge.[36] Setting a precedent to resistance movements and cultural agency within the restrictions of imperial domination, "border thinking" explores subalternities produced both in the interior and the exterior borders of what Mignolo calls the "modern/colonial world system."[37] Mignolo's idea of border thinking is similar to Néstor García Canclini's analysis of Latin American modernity. Like Mignolo, García Canclini envisions "contrasting conceptions of modernity"[38] that may be resisted through strategies that encourage a deliberate abandoning of hegemonic conceptions of modernity. Beyond the programmatic structures of these theorizations of counterhegemonic agency in Latin America, the Battle of Ciudad Juárez in the Mexican Revolution offers a material and factual model for resisting hegemonic power. I propose, therefore, to analyze this concrete materiality as an *event*, following Alain Badiou's understanding of the term. He defines an event as an anomalous happening within a rigorously normalized network of power that "compels us to decide a *new* way of being."[39] Facing the event, there is an urgent call for a *decision* that projects an opening to a process leading to the finding of a *truth*, in which the individual pledges a *fidelity* to follow through with the ethical imperatives of this finding. Badiou explains the process to attain such a truth:

> To be faithful to an event is to move within this situation that this event has supplemented, by *thinking* (although all thought is a practice, a putting to the test) the situation 'according to' the event. And this, of course —since the event was excluded by all the regular laws of the situation—compels the subject to *invent* a new way of being and acting in the situation.[40]

Villa and Orozco's decision is not simply an act of insubordination but implies a radical break with the very logic of the revolutionary movement followed until then; this event allows us an integral understanding of the border region and its dynamics of power. These military leaders acted on an independent plan that reveals the conditions that made possible Madero's revolution, that is, an insurgence produced by an interrupted democratic process that could be disarmed with the simple promise of a transparent and effective presidential election. Risking the anachronism of the following example, I find it productive to follow as well Slavoj Žižek's analysis—appropriating Badiou's concepts—of world *slums* such as Ciudad Juárez as "authentic 'evental sites' in contemporary society."[41] As regions of extreme neglect that become "a necessary product of the innermost logic of global capitalism,"[42] the *slums*—"the crucial geopolitical event of our times"[43]—seek an alternative way of subsisting. In this sense, Žižek finds a polemical but assertive model in Hugo Chávez's 1998 presidential election in Venezuela: "he *grabbed* power"[44] in a way that may produce "the political mobilization of new forms of politics."[45] Chávez represents for Žižek the exemplary decision made within an event and its subsequent fidelity.[46] Certain characteristics of Ciudad Juárez in 1911 make it a predecessor of modern slums: its constant flow of immigrants, marginal settlements in extreme poverty, brothels serving a dissipated U.S. clientele, and the brutal and repressive politics that attempted to control the crossing of the border to the north. Thus, Žižek's analysis can be extended to Moreiras' criticism of the historical Zapatistas versus the Villistas. The Battle of Ciudad Juárez is, in fact, Villa's fidelity to the authentic revolutionary event: the complete overthrowing of the old order and the *invention* of a new beginning, even if such an event was ultimately betrayed by most revolutionaries in the course of the following decade.

Immediately after the victory, Madero spent his time organizing his cabinet and practicing politics. He responded too slowly to the desperate needs of his troops, who had not eaten properly and who required clothes and the money to buy them. The tension escalated when Madero, again unilaterally, decided to spare General Navarro's life. Villa and Orozco decided to speak to Madero on behalf of the troops, but the meeting quickly turned into an argument that almost ended in their insurrection.[47] Madero's political operatives and representatives of Porfirio Díaz met at the old Customs building to sign the peace treaty by night. They found the building closed and in darkness. Most rebels, especially those who did not take part in the fight at all, were celebrating the victory inside the Juárez Theatre. The personal physician of Díaz, Madero supporter Francisco Vázquez Gómez writes in his *Memoirs*:

> Thus at eleven, on the night of May 21st, 1911, on the street where the Customs office is located in Ciudad Juárez, by the light of matches and car headlights and on the back of one of the people present, the Treaty of Ciudad Juárez was signed.[48]

An unverifiable but often quoted incident supposedly occurred during the victory banquet held in the same Customs building a few days before the signing of the peace treaty. While Madero's wealthy friends and family dined and congratulated each other for a battle, they did not fight, "Maderito" (as Villa used to call him) engaged the General in a conversation concerning the battle. Charles Bowden recreates the scene from Villa's perspective:

> Then Madero said to me, 'And you, Pancho, what do you think? The war is over; aren't you happy? Give us a few words.' I didn't want to say anything, but Gustavo Madero [the president's brother], who was sitting at my side, nudged me, saying, 'Go ahead, chief, say something.' So I stood up and said to Francisco Madero, 'You, sir, have destroyed the revolution.' He demanded to know why, so I answered, 'It's simple: this bunch of dandies has made a fool of you, and this will eventually cost us our necks, yours included.' Madero kept on questioning me. 'Fine, Pancho, but tell me, what do you think should be done?' I answered, 'Allow me to hang this roomful of politicians and then let the revolution continue.' Well, seeing the astonishment on the faces of those elegant followers, Madero replied, 'You are a barbarian, Pancho. Sit down, sit down.'"[49]

Echoing Villa's intuition in this romanticized anecdote, historian Mauricio Tenorio explains that the Treaty of Ciudad Juárez was, in fact, a brilliant and secret negotiation of Mexican *Realpolitik* at its best that "worked despite the explosion of violence."[50] By appointing Porfirian minister Francisco León de la Barra as the provisional president while demanding the immediate disarming of all rebel forces, Katz suggests that the official negotiation was a final attempt to hijack the victory from the rebels and gradually "revive the Porfirian state."[51] Héctor Aguilar Camín and Lorenzo Meyer point out that the treaty, a clear betrayal of Madero's revolutionary principles, such as the promise of land reform, went unquestioned by the political leaders of the rebellion, focused as they were on his road to the presidency:

To obliterate its own origin, demobilize its forces, and take preventive measures to avoid being scratched by the tiger's claws that it had unleashed proved to be a historic plan in Madero's rise to power. Confined by the old legality, he wanted to put to rest the agitation and expectations that had been awakened in the country he wanted to govern, in order to establish in the republic undergoing convulsive spasms a new government, not a new order. He seemed to want his movement to correspond to the impulse of a nineteenth-century political rebellion, and not the first thrusts of a twentieth-century social revolution.[52]

Madero left Ciudad Juárez on June 2 at 10:30 a.m., the same day Porfirio Díaz embarked to Paris in exile. Deliberately or not, Madero's presidency boiled down to an electoral matter. In that sense, summarizing his legacy with the slogan popularized during his political and military campaign, "sufragio efectivo, no reelección" (Effective Suffrage, No Re-election), is not entirely unfair. At the same time, Pancho Villa's role, especially during this first stage of the Revolution, cannot be understated. He followed his revolutionary instinct to take Ciudad Juárez and together with Orozoco finally brought down a thirty-year-old dictatorship that had survived decades of fierce political opposition and several insurrections. For all its importance, however, it must be highlighted that Villa's *fidelity* to the event was not maintained. At least not while remaining faithful to Madero's political cause: as Katz remarks, Villa returned to the fight during a new uprising of Orozco and Zapata against Madero as the sole *caudillo* still willing to defend his old commander from the Ciudad Juárez days of 1911.[53] As it is recorded in Salvador Toscano's documentary *Memoirs of a Mexican* (1950),[54] Villa wept before Madero's tomb.

THE RETURNING SPECTER OF VILLA

From the northern side of the Rio Grande, David Dorado Romo wrote a cultural history of the border region chasing the historical *specter* of Pancho Villa that reveals the crucial relevance and specificity of the metroplex (or borderplex) formed by Juárez and El Paso. I am invoking here Derrida's notion of the "specter" as a figure of resilient opposition that defies a hegemonic system that in turn "organizes the repression and thus the confirmation of a haunting."[55] Thus, Dorado Romo's investigation is "about insurrection from the point of view of those who official histories have considered peripheral to the main events."[56] A sort of recalcitrant specter, the border citizen's living conditions are very different from those in either country: "Fronterizos, people who live on the border, are unclassifiable hybrids. They are not exactly immigrants. Immigrants don't cross back and forth as much. Border crossers are a people on the margin. Not real Americans. Nor real Mexicans for that matter."[57] Dorado Romo's reconstruction of the battle of Juárez sheds light especially on the peculiar circumstances on the U.S. side of the border:

> While the Mexicans were waging revolution, the Americans were running around trying to figure out how to make a quick buck from it —selling everything from commemorative Madero spoons, to postcards, to military

supplies and ammunition. [. . .] The Mexican Revolution on the border was not televised, but it was photographed, filmed and commodified.[58]

His valuable archival work on the library records of El Paso's newspapers and periodicals completes the history written by Berumen and Siller, recovering more photographs that were virtually unknown. Among his findings, Dorado Romo traces the impact of Spanish-language periodicals on the border that were used as vehicles of political resistance, printing anything from political manifestoes to serial works of fiction, such as the iconic case of Mariano Azuela's *Los de Abajo* (*The Underdogs*) (1915), the most emblematic novel of the Mexican Revolution. With the unprecedented situation in which many of Mexico's best journalists and writers were living at the border as political refugees and exiles, Dorado Romo argues that these newspapers "set the stage for a renaissance of Spanish-language journalism and literature never before seen in the history of the border."[59] Furthermore, at the textual level, I argue that the memory of the Revolution operates as a "haunting" and is thus relocated to a true in-between space where alternative forms of action are spontaneously structured. In a "spectral" dimension, migration and ordinary life at the border become a resilient effect of that haunting in the context of contemporary border life. The constant apparition of undocumented immigrants and the paradoxical existence of border crossers become manifestations of national identities under the imminent process of dispersion. Each of these individuals, like the rebel fighters of Ciudad Juárez in 1911, is, in fact, (re)generating a contingent type of collective revolution.

Present-day Ciudad Juárez is haunted by Pancho Villa's specter and example. *Exodus/Éxodo* (2008), an essay by Charles Bowden with images by Juárez photojournalist Julián Cardona, elaborates on the complexity of undocumented migration from Mexico into the United States as a direct by-product of the failed Revolution of 1910. Bowden makes the bold assertion that the phenomenon of immigration reactivates many of the unfulfilled promises of social change of the Revolution. The book follows *Juárez: The Laboratory of Our Future* (1998), in which Bowden and Cardona, together with other local photographers, explore the realities of today's border city. After the guest worker programs that supplied much needed manpower to the United States ended in the mid-1960s, an era of industrialization swept Mexico. During the same decade, the first manufacturing plants or *maquiladoras* became the massive workplaces that have provided low-paid employment for thousands of Juarenses ever since. The city expanded without any possibility of order or planning due to the constant influx of this floating population and the lack of government resources and infrastructure to support them. A study produced in 2004 by a federal government commission to eradicate violence against women found that fifty percent of the streets of Juárez are unpaved; the city suffers a deficit of eighty percent of green areas; over 200,000 families live in high-risk zones. As the U.S. economy entered a period of recession in 2000, global capital found cheaper labor force in impoverished third-world countries. Not surprisingly, close to 100,000 maquiladora jobs were lost by 2002, doubling the city's poverty levels. Eighty percent of crimes are never reported to the police, and yet the local prison that houses both federal and state detainees is overpopulated. It was built for 1,800 inmates but currently holds over 4,000, with frequent riots protesting the inhumane living conditions.[60]

Ciudad Juárez, the city of immigrants, of everlasting hope for a job opportunity, the vestibule to the United States and the American dream, the natural environment for the trafficking of drugs, arms, and people, is still the location of Villa's revolution. According to Bowden, Villa "is still out there, embodied in this new strange revolution called illegal immigration, an act by which poor Mexicans go from doom to a future, a movement which has enhanced the lives of poor people more than any policy attempted by either the U.S. government or the Mexican government."[61] Or, as Bowden himself foresaw in his 1998 book, the sign greeting people at the entrance of Juárez should read: "Welcome to the laboratory of our future."[62] His analysis seems to be corroborated by the current state of drug-related violence that has already produced in Mexico more than 50,000 killings (about one-fifth in Ciudad Juárez alone) since 2008, when President Felipe Calderón ordered an open "war" against drug cartels.[63] Bowden explains the current state of exception at the border:

> Government here and in my own country increasingly pretends to be in charge and then calls it a day. The United States beefs up the border, calls in high-tech towers, and tosses up walls, and still, all the drugs arrive on time and all the illegal people make it into the fabled heartland and work themselves into a future.[64]

Pondering the dramatic events of 1910 onward, Mexican *homme de lettres* Alfonso Reyes writes that "history that just occurred is always the least appreciated. [. . .] A certain dose of ungratefulness is the law of all progress, of all process."[65] In part, I have tried to analyze some of the key aspects of these corrective accounts that seek to mitigate history's "ungratefulness" with regard to the border's involvement in the Mexican Revolution. Among other works that I could not address here for lack of space, I wish to highlight the 2003 exhibit *Las luces de la batalla* ("The Lights of the Battle"), curated in Ciudad Juárez by Willivaldo Delgadillo and Fausto Gómez Tuena.[66] Of equal interest and innovation is Miguel Ángel Berumen's photographic archival investigation *La cara del tiempo* (2002) ("The Face of Time"). Along with the books examined here, the fog of oblivion erasing the border protagonists of both countries' histories has already begun to fade.

Alan Knight argues that when people from the capital say that "outside Mexico City it's all Cuautitlán,"[67] what, in fact, is enunciated is a limited and revealing *capitalino* mentality. This is why he insists that a true comprehension of the complexities of the Revolution is possible only when the complexities of the provinces are also understood. The border region of purported "marginality" is, nevertheless, the space where the narrative of the armed conflict relocates many of its transcendental historical episodes. One hundred years later, Ciudad Juárez and El Paso are once again that space where misery and violence converged in an explosive reaction, perhaps foreshadowing the emergence of a new postnational order. Beyond the reaches of tragedies old and the new, the border serves as a constant reminder that all cultural processes in formation must be examined within their local and regional specificities and not simply as the liminal symbols of a nation's inconsistent modernity. Claudio Lomnitz writes that in Mexico the reflection on what is only problematically called "national culture" has always been accompanied by a process of deep social change, since the War of Independence to the Revolution. Although this reflection operates as an act of deconstruction, it has yet to corrode "the cultural bases that suggest the existence of national culture."[68] Thus, the description of any dimension of such imagined national culture "has generated a circular dialectic, a vicious cycle that is built on the tensions that occur between the maze of social relations that exist within the national space and the ideologies regarding a common identity, a shared sense of the past, and a unified gaze towards the future."[69] The latent and persistent conditions of possibility of the spectral life at the border are at the same time the dismantling conditions of *impossibility* of normalized hegemonic centers on either side of the Río Bravo/Rio Grande. Each migrant crossing the border, legally or not, carries the specter of Pancho Villa and the unfinished revolution that began with the Battle of Ciudad Juárez, reproducing the ongoing border event.

NOTES

1. Porfirio Díaz was born on September 15, 1830. Some historians inaccurately state that the centennial festivities were scheduled the day before Miguel Hidalgo y Costilla's historic call to Independence on September 16, 1810, in order to make the date coincide with the dictator's birthday. The fact is that the earliest commemoration of the Independence held on September 15 dates to 1825, five years before the birth of Díaz. See Carmen Nava and Isabel Fernández, "La Campana de Dolores en el Imaginario Patriótico," *Boletín del Archivo General de la Nación* 2, 6a serie (2003): 127.

2. Alan Knight, *The Mexican Revolution.* Vol. I. *Porfirians, Liberals and Peasants* (Lincoln: University of Nebraska Press, 1986), 1.

3. Jesús Silva-Herzog, *Breve historia de la Revolución Mexicana. Los antecedentes y la etapa maderista*, Vol. 1 (México, D.F.: FCE, 2010), 207. In his account, Silva-Herzog argues that the battle began spontaneously due to isolated quarrels between rebels and federal soldiers. As it will be discussed later, this is the excuse that Villa and Orozco gave Madero, whereas the attack, in fact, was deliberately orchestrated by both commanders.

4. Héctor Aguilar Camín and Lorenzo Meyer, *In the Shadow of the Mexican Revolution* (Austin: University of Texas Press, 1993), 30–31. Aguilar Camín and Meyer cite an extensive paragraph of François Xavier Guerra's text without a proper bibliographic reference.

5. Knight, *The Mexican Revolution,* 203. See particularly the chapter "The Madero Revolution."

6. Friedrich Katz, *The Life and Times of Pancho Villa*, (Stanford, Calif.: Stanford University Press, 1998), 111.

7. Alfonso Reyes, "Pasado inmediato," in *Obras completas*, Vol. XII (México, D.F.: FCE, 1967), 185. All translations are mine unless otherwise indicated.

8. In his "Plan de San Luis" Madero called for the nullification of Díaz's reelection and for Mexican citizens to take up arms against the dictatorship on November 20, 1910. I consider Madero's rise to power as a separate and initial stage of the Revolution, following Alan Knight's analysis of what he terms "The Madero Revolution." After the demise of Madero's presidency, a second stage of the Revolution began with Victoriano Huerta's usurpation, or as Knight names it, the "counter-revolution." Knight, *The Mexican Revolution*, vols. 1–2.

9. This archive, compiled by brothers Agustín Víctor Casasola and Miguel Casasola, contains over 800,000 photographs spanning from 1900 to 1970. The archive is housed at Mexico's National Institute of Anthropology and History.

10. Miguel Ángel Berumen, *1911. La batalla de Ciudad Juárez. II. Las imágenes*, (Ciudad Juárez: Cuadro por Cuadro, 2003), 23. Berumen refers here to the fact that the Mexican Revolution was the first large-scale conflict photographed and filmed in the twentieth century. The Battle of Ciudad Juárez, as we will see, received an extraordinary level of attention by national and foreign correspondents and photographers.

11. Benedict Anderson, *Imagined Communities* (New York: Verso, 2006), 7. It is worth mentioning that Anderson exemplifies his analysis of nationalism in Mexico through his reading of José Joaquín Fernández de Lizardi's novel *El periquillo sarniento (The Itching Parrot)* (1816).

12. Anderson, *Imagined Communities*, 7.

13. Homi Bhabha, "DissemiNation," in *The Location of Culture* (New York: Routledge, 2005), 201.

14. Walter Mignolo, *Local Histories/Global Designs. Coloniality, Subaltern Knowledges, and Border Thinking* (Princeton, N. J.: Princeton University Press, 2000).

15. Berumen, *1911*, 28–29.

16. Pedro Siller and Miguel Ángel Berumen, *1911. La batalla de Ciudad Juárez. I. La historia* (Ciudad Juárez: Cuadro por Cuadro, 2003), 50.

17. Berumen, *1911*, 38.

18. Siller, *1911*, 109. In his extraordinary film archive of the Revolution, Salvador Toscano (1872–1947) captured images of the House of Adobe and the suspension bridge across the Río Bravo. Along with the "humble shack that served as the National Palace" for the rebels, Toscano also managed to record images of some of the destruction in the aftermath of the battle. Other scenes show a city hospital where the wounded were being treated, parts of Madero's victory speech, and a conversation between Madero and Venustiano Carranza outside of the old Customs building where the peace treaty was signed. Toscano's archive, edited by his daughter as the narrative documentary *Memoirs of a Mexican*, was released in 1950. Today, it stands as a filmic monument of the history of the Mexican Revolution.

19. Siller, *1911*, 117–18.

20. Berumen, *1911*, 173.

21. Knight, *The Mexican Revolution*, 203.

22. Siller, *1911*, 140.

23. Katz, *Pancho Villa*, 109.

24. Knight, ibid.

25. Dorado Romo, *Ringside Seat to a Revolution*, 99.

26. Berumen, *1911*, 196–97.

27. Paco Ignacio Taibo II, *Pancho Villa. Una biografía narrativa* (México, D.F.: Planeta, 2006), 104.

28. Berumen, *1911*, 198, 200–201.

29. Siller, *1911*, 198.

30. Katz, *Pancho Villa*, 116.

31. Moreiras, *The Exhaustion of Difference*, 122.

32. Moreiras, *The Exhaustion of Difference*, 126.

33. Bhabha, "DissemiNation," 201.

34. Bhabha, "DissemiNation," 201.

35. Mignolo, *Local Histories/Global Designs*, 39.

36. Mignolo, *The Idea of Latin America* (Oxford: Blackwell, 2005), 9.

37. Mignolo, *Local Histories/Global Designs*, 11.

38. Néstor García Canclini, *Hybrid Cultures. Strategies for Entering and Leaving Modernity* (Minneapolis: University of Minnesota Press, 1995), 6.

39. Alain Badiou, *Ethics. An Essay on the Understanding of Evil* (New York: Verso, 2002), 41.

40. Badiou, *Ethics*, 41–42. Emphasis in the original.

41. Salvoj Žižek, *In Defense of Lost Causes* (New York: Verso, 2008), 424–5.

42. Žižek, *In Defense of Lost Causes*, 424.

43. Žižek, *In Defense of Lost Causes*, 424.

44. Žižek, *In Defense of Lost Causes*, 427.

45. Žižek, *In Defense of Lost Causes*, 427.

46. Žižek compares Chávez's aggressive political tone to what he deems the ineffective leadership of Subcomandante Marcos in the Mexican southern state of Chiapas. Žižek notes that while Chávez has managed to successfully oppose Western practices of political domination, the 1990s Zapatista movement seems to have been neutralized and his leader mocked as "Subcomediante Marcos." Žižek, Ibid, 425.

47. Villa and Orozco settled on a fragile promise of civility that the latter did not hesitate to break when Madero became president, taking up arms against the democrat that he had helped put in power. Siller, *1911*, 205.

48. Siller, *1911*, 218.

49. Charles Bowden and Julián Cardona, *Exodus/Éxodo* (Austin: University of Texas Press, 2008), 94.

50. Mauricio Tenorio Trillo, *Historia y celebración. México y sus centenarios* (México, D.F.: Tusquets, 2009), 76.

51. Katz, "El fin del viejo orden en las haciendas de México, 1911–1913," in *Nuevos ensayos mexicanos*, (México, D.F.: Era, 2010), 194. Katz cites a letter written by Pancho Villa to Rodolfo Chávez, one of the richest men in the northern state of Chihuahua, where Ciudad Juárez is located. In it, Villa accurately analyzes Victoriano Huerta's *coup d'état* that ended Madero's presidency with his assassination. The oligarchy involved in the *coup*, writes Villa referring to Chávez and others in his social position, "did not understand that [Madero's] government was not getting in [the oligarchy's] way and that [the oligarchs] would have been able to still be the masters, because Maderito's family and he himself had ties to all of the high aristocracy." Katz, Ibid, 231.

52. Héctor Aguilar Camín and Lorenzo Meyer, *In the Shadow of the Mexican Revolution*, 22.

53. Katz, *Pancho Villa*, 119.

54. See note 20 regarding Toscano's film.

55. Jacques Derrida, *Specters of Marx* (New York: Routledge, 2006), 46. Derrida refers here to the manifested spectral presence of Marxism in the age of postindustrial neoliberalism.

56. David Dorado Romo, *Ringside Seat to a Revolution, An Underground Cultural History of El Paso and Juárez: 1893–1923* (El Paso, Tex.: Cinco Puntos Press, 2005), 10.

57. Dorado Romo, *Ringside Seat to a Revolution*, 11.

58. Dorado Romo, *Ringside Seat to a Revolution*, 83.

59. Dorado Romo, *Ringside Seat to a Revolution*, 18.

60. Comisión para prevenir y erradicar la violencia contra las mujeres en Ciudad Juárez, "Informe de gestión, noviembre 2003–abril 2004," (México, D.F.: Segob, 2004), 13.

61. Bowden and Cardona, *Exodus*, 3.

62. Bowden, *Juárez, The Laboratory of Our Future* (New York: Aperture, 1998), 117.

63. In reality, writes Bowden in a recent book chronicling the current state of violence, "the war is *for* drugs, for the enormous money to be made in drugs, where the police and the military fight for their share, where the press is restrained by the murder of reporters and feasts on a steady diet of bribes, and where the line between government and the drug world has never existed." Bowden, *Murder City: Ciudad Juárez and the Global Economy's New Killing Fields* (New York: Nation Books, 2010), 18.

64. Bowden, *Murder City*, 22.

65. Reyes, "Pasado inmediato," 182.

66. In addition to the exhibit showcased between May and August 2003, this project produced an eponymous short film directed by Ángel Estrada with a script by local author and activist Williwaldo Delgadillo. The film was shown in 2004 at the Museum of the Former Customs Office, the same site where the Treaty of Ciudad Juárez was signed to end Porfirio Díaz's regime in May of 1911. See http://docentes2.uacj.mx/museodigital/investigacion/las%20luces%20WEB/Luces%20Batalla.htm.

67. Knight, *The Mexican Revolution*, 2.

68. Claudio Lomnitz-Adler, *Exits from the Labyrinth: Culture and Ideology in the Mexican National Space*, (Berkeley: University of California Press, 1992), 3.

69. Lomnitz-Adler, *Exits from the Labyrinth*, 3.

BIBLIOGRAPHY

Aguilar Camín, Héctor, and Lorenzo Meyer. *In the Shadow of the Mexican Revolution: Contemporary Mexican History 1910–1989*, trans. Luis Alberto Fierro. Austin: University of Texas Press, 1993.

Anderson, Benedict. *Imagined Communities*. New York: Verso, 2006.

Badiou, Alain. *Ethics. An Essay on the Understanding of Evil*, trans. Peter Hallward. New York: Verso, 2002.

Bhabha, Homi. "DissemiNation." In *The Location of Culture*. New York: Routledge, 2005.

Berumen, Miguel Ángel. *1911. La batalla de Ciudad Juárez. II. Las imágenes* [1911. The Battle of Ciudad Juarez. II. The Images]. Ciudad Juárez: Cuadro por Cuadro, 2003.

———. *1911. La batalla de Ciudad Juárez en imágenes* [The Battle of Ciudad Juarez in Images]. Revised Edition. México, D.F.: Océano and Cuadro por Cuadro, 2009.

Bowden, Charles. *Juárez: The Laboratory of Our Future*. New York: Aperture, 1998.

———. *Murder City: Ciudad Juárez and the Global Economy's New Killing Fields*. New York: Nation Books, 2010.

Bowden, Charles, and Julián Cardona. *Exodus/Éxodo*. Austin: University of Texas Press, 2008.

Comisión para prevenir y erradicar la violencia contra las mujeres en Ciudad Juárez. "Informe de Gestión, Noviembre 2003–Abril 2004 [Commission Report, November 2003–April 2004]." México, D.F.: Segob, 2004.

Derrida, Jacques. *Specters of Marx*, trans. Peggy Kamuf. New York: Routledge, 2006.

Dorado Romo, David. *Ringside Seat to a Revolution, An Underground Cultural History of El Paso and Juárez: 1893–1923*. El Paso: Cinco Puntos Press, 2005.

García Canclini, Néstor. *Hybrid Cultures. Strategies for Entering and Leaving Modernity*, trans. Christopher L. Chiappari and Silvia L. López. Minneapolis: University of Minnesota Press, 1995.

Katz, Friedrich. "El fin del viejo orden en las haciendas de México, 1911–1913 [The End of the Old Order in the Haciendas of Mexico, 1911–1913]." In *Nuevos ensayos mexicanos* [New Mexicans Essays], trans. Paloma Villegas, pp. 191–231. México, D.F.: Era, 2010.

———. *The Life and Times of Pancho Villa.* Stanford, Calif.: Stanford University Press, 1998.

Knight, Alan. *The Mexican Revolution.* Vol. I., *Porfirians, Liberals and Peasants.* Lincoln: University of Nebraska Press, 1986.

Lomnitz-Adler, Claudio. *Exits from the Labyrinth: Culture and Ideology in the Mexican National Space.* Berkeley: University of California Press, 1992.

Mignolo, Walter. *Local Histories/Global Designs. Coloniality, Subaltern Knowledges, and Border Thinking.* Princeton, N. J.: Princeton University of Press, 2000.

———. *The Idea of Latin America.* Oxford: Blackwell, 2005.

Moreiras, Alberto. *The Exhaustion of Difference: The Politics of Latin American Cultural Studies.* Durham, N. C.: Duke University Press, 2001.

Nava, Carmen, and Isabel Fernández. "La campana de Dolores en el imaginario patriótico [The Bell of Dolores in the Patriotic Imaginary]." *Boletín del Archivo General de la Nación* 2, 6a serie (2003): 123–42.

Reyes, Alfonso. "Pasado inmediato" [Immediate Past]. In *Obras completas* [Complete Works]. Vol. XII, 182–216. México, D.F.: FCE, 1967.

Siller, Pedro, and Miguel Ángel Berumen. *1911. La batalla de Ciudad Juárez. I. La historia* [1911. The Battle of Ciudad Juarez. I. The History]. Ciudad Juárez: Cuadro por Cuadro, 2003.

Silva Herzog, Jesús. *Breve historia de la Revolución Mexicana. Los antecedentes y la etapa Maderista* [Brief History of the Mexican Revolution. The Background and the Maderista Stage]. Vol. 1. 1960. México, D.F.: FCE, 2010.

Tenorio Trillo, Mauricio. *Historia y celebración. México y sus centenarios* [History and Celebration. Mexico and its Centennials]. México, D.F.: Tusquets, 2009.

Taibo II, Paco Ignacio. *Pancho Villa. Una biografía narrativa* [Pancho Villa. A Narrative Biography]. México, D.F.: Planeta, 2006.

Žižek, Slavoj. *In Defense of Lost Causes.* New York: Verso, 2008.

CHAPTER ELEVEN

REVELING IN PATRIOTISM
Celebrating America on the U.S.–Mexico Border
during the Mexican Revolution

Elaine A. Peña

REVELING IN PATRIOTISM

On January 1, 1914, soldiers fighting under Venustiano Carranza attacked the federalist army in Nuevo Laredo, Tamaulipas. The battle was bloody; both sides suffered horrendous losses and the city was left in shambles.[1] Directly across the U.S.–Mexico border, residents in Laredo, Texas, were not having trouble following the realities of warfare or absorbing the gravity of that conflict. *La Crónica*, *El Demócrata Fronterizo*, the *Laredo Weekly Times*, and other Laredo-based newspapers offered details of the horrible scenes at hospitals; they named the wounded and often gave play-by-play accounts of the battle and its aftermath. Violence and suffering in Nuevo Laredo dominated news coverage, particularly during those first few weeks of 1914. But Laredoans could also be heard discussing another critical issue: should the city of Laredo continue its tradition of commemorating George Washington's Birthday on February 22? Should they organize historical reenactments, watch dazzling pyrotechnic displays, sing the Star Spangled Banner, and adorn municipal buildings with American flags? Should the city revel in patriotism amid the loss of human life, extensive collateral damage, and impending violence across the border?

It could. And it did. But analyzing the backstage logistics that supported the impulse to celebrate America communicates something more. The city's collective self-doubt, if only momentary, pinpoints a powerful moment of identity negotiation in U.S.–Mexico borderlands history. Although formally separated by the Treaty of Guadalupe Hidalgo in 1848, Nuevo Laredo and Laredo maintained strong socio-economic and kinship ties—transregional links that a geopolitical boundary could weather but not dissolve.[2] When confronted with the realities of the Mexican Revolution, however, U.S.-based border residents seemed to have reached an impasse. Exceptional local residents like Leonor Villegas de Magnón, also known as "La Rebelde," rushed to help injured soldiers from both political factions.[3] She and her fellow White Cross volunteers set up makeshift emergency rooms in

Laredo—in the kindergarten classroom where she taught and in a hall owned by the fraternal group "los Hijos de Juárez" (the Sons of [Benito] Juárez). In addition to co-founding *La Liga Femenil Mexicanista* (The League of Mexican Women) in 1911, Jovita Idár used media outlets like *La Crónica* to critically engage the realities of the Revolution. But many border residents chose to pause and direct their gaze inward—toward celebrating America's past and the promise of its greatness.

Although scholars of Laredo history and the Mexican Revolution's impact on U.S. border towns have offered insightful analyses of that tumultuous period,[4] many studies elide a critical discussion of collective patriotic representations. Using the George Washington's Birthday Celebration as an optic, the following examines how forging ahead with nation-building performances created a parallel focal point for border residents—one that not only reinforced distinctions between American and Mexican interests but also determined the limits of bi-national solidarity. It argues those seemingly anodyne discussions actually generated a differentiation strategy that preserved and strengthened American identity in that embattled environment.

CELEBRATING GEORGE ON THE U.S.–MEXICO BORDER: BACKSTAGE LOGISTICS

The city of Laredo had commemorated George Washington's Birthday as early as 1870[5] but it was the Improved Order of Red Men (est. 1834)—a fraternal group whose ideological antecedents include the Sons of Liberty—that institutionalized the custom in 1898. Like other brotherhoods operating during the nineteenth century, Improved Order of Red Men members moved their aspirations westward, established outposts or "hunting grounds," and practiced hyper-patriotic rituals that evinced their belief in America. Driven by the fact that many Mexican holidays but "no American memorials were considered seriously,"[6] members of Laredo's elite socio-political class established a chapter of the fraternity in 1897 and organized the Washington's Birthday Celebration the next year. The inaugural cohort used spectacle to remind border residents that the soil underneath their feet was indeed American. They staged eccentric performances like George Washington crossing the Delaware (using the Rio Grande) and reenacted the Boston Tea Party. Other popular events included a mock battle on city hall in which fraternity brothers dressed as Native Americans and "played Indian."[7] Those exuberant representations inspired candid headlines: "Red Men Are Rustlers and Doing Grand Work in Laredo: They Will Awaken Patriotism on the Border and Make us Realize That we Live in the United States."[8]

Residents from both sides of the border contributed to the popularity of the burgeoning tradition as participants, consumers, and witnesses. Ushered in by the National Lines of Railways of Mexico, the Missouri Pacific Lines, and the Texas-Mexican Railway Company, those patriotic gatherings attracted thousands of spectators from as far away as Monterrey, Nuevo León and San Antonio, Texas.[9] But it was local Improved Order of Red Men members who oversaw the most critical moments of the festivities. Using fraternal codes, reenactments of iconic moments in American history, invented rituals, political finesse, and municipal funds,[10] Laredo-based Red Men accomplished the unimaginable. They made their vision of America palatable and legible for a bi-national, multiethnic, and multi-lingual audience. And they did so in spite of competing intrafraternity affiliations and extrafraternity interests. Several members of the inaugural 1898 cohort, for example, were naturalized U.S. citizens born in Italy, Germany, France, and Canada. Some were birthright U.S. citizens of Mexican descent. They spoke different languages and followed distinct cultural logics. They approximated Native American cosmologies to venerate George Washington but also identified as Protestants, Catholics, or Jews. Two common denominators helped them assuage those differences: capital and power.

Amador Sánchez, for example, acted as Mayor of Laredo and then Webb County Sheriff; R. McComb-Mayor; H. Ligarde-Tax Collector; J. F. Mullally-Judge of the 49th Judicial District of Texas; J. A. Rodriguez-County Clerk and County Judge; J. A. Ortiz-City Treasurer; J. Agan-alderman; M. G. Benavides-Chief Deputy Sheriff; L. J. Christen-City Superintendent of Schools; and J. A. Valls-Webb County District Attorney. Also, Red Men members such as J. Alexander of J. Alexander Clothier and Furnisher; A. W. Wilcox, Laredo National Bank, Board of Directors; G. R. Page, Laredo Machine Made Brick; J. Netzer, Joseph Netzer Hardware Company; S. N. Johnson, Wholesale Dealer of Budweiser, Coca-Cola, and the leading bottler in Laredo, among others, were prominent businessmen. Chronicler of Laredo history and fraternity brother J. W. Falvella became City Editor of the *Laredo Times* in 1914.[11] The point here is to foreground the idea that as Laredo's political and economic elite, Red Men members were able to publically coalesce and actively promote a sense of American identity in a bi-national environment.

Considering their collective clout, it is hardly surprising then that the question of celebrating Washington's Birthday shared print space with coverage of the Mexican Revolution. The January 4, 1914, edition of the *Laredo Weekly Times*, for example, published two news stories side by side: "Saw Some Horrible Sights: Massacre of Bunch of Rebels Witnessed by Men Who Later Saw How Federals Treated Dead" and "Will Meet Tuesday Afternoon: Matter of Whether or Not Washington Birthday Celebration Will Occur Will Be Decided." The latter was brief and persuasive:

> [...] It is imperative that those who favor the celebration being staged
> attend this meeting, as there is an inclination on the part of some to pass
> it up this year on account of the unsettled conditions prevailing across the
> river, but as this is a celebration of a strictly American character com-
> memorating an important event in American history, others are inclined to
> have the celebration as usual. Nuevo Laredo contributes very little to these
> celebrations, outside of the people of the city coming over here to enjoy the
> festivities, hence there is no reason for not having the celebration.[12]

In light of the *Times*' editorial staff, such a justificatory tone was to be expected. But even then, publications without overt ties to the fraternity such as *El Demócrata Fronterizo* also entertained those discussions.[13] Offering print space to both topics created an analogous focal point for Laredo's reading public. And while news of the revolution lingered, Laredoans decided on the fate of the Washington's Birthday Celebration rather swiftly. It was a topic and plan of action that they could control.

Shortly after the *Laredo Weekly Times* published this announcement, Laredoans decided it was acceptable to continue observing Washington's Birthday.[14] The *Times* reported a week later, the "unanimous opinion seems to prevail that Laredo should endeavor to make the celebration next month [Feb. 1914] bigger and grander than ever before."[15] And they did. Joseph Netzer, chairman of the events committee, decided to raise the stakes. He not only approached Fort McIntosh authorities Colonel Blockson and Major Caldwell for permission to continue the tradition of staging a spectacular mock battle on City Hall but also contacted military authorities in Nuevo Laredo, specifically Generals Guardiola and Quintana, to procure their support. Guardiola and Quintana actually entertained the idea of participating. They endeavored to "have the military band sent to this city [Laredo] to furnish music during the celebration provided the United States government allowed them to come to this side. This matter will be taken up with Washington."[16] In the end, the First Battalion Band of Nuevo Laredo did not lend their services to the festivities because of a "misconstruction of the request made to the [U.S.] war department."[17] Regardless of the outcome, those conversations are noteworthy because they offer a glimpse of the bi-national backstage logistics supporting the George Washington's Birthday Celebration. But in order to understand the deeper implications of Nuevo Laredoans' non-participation that year, we must recognize that exchange as forming part of a longer, interregional narrative.

ONGOING IDENTITY FORMATION AND POLITICAL EXCHANGE IN *LOS DOS LAREDOS*

Like many border cities, Laredo and Nuevo Laredo experienced various forms of identity formation in relation to one another. And many of those transitions were predicated not only on local sensibilities but also national and international political realities. Shifting notions of empire and sovereignty are central to this story. Indeed, no less than seven flags have flown over and influenced the production of the international boundary line that differentiates Laredo, Texas, from Nuevo Laredo, Tamaulipas: Spain (1755–1821), France (1684–1689), Mexico (1821–1836), the Republic of Texas (1836–1845), the Republic of the Rio Grande (January 1840 to October 1840), the Confederate States of America (1861–1865), and the United States of America (1845–1861 and 1865–present). Founded in 1755 by Don Tomas Sánchez de Barrera y Garza, the Spanish territory was already developing her political identity even as American colonies were organizing their revolutionary thoughts.[18] Laredo experienced sweeping changes during her tenure as an outpost in the province of Nuevo Santander, Nueva España, but the town did not experience major sovereignty adjustments until the nineteenth century.

The first occurred when the United States annexed the state of Texas in 1846. Land ownership rights between the Nueces River (just south of San Antonio, Texas) and the Rio Grande River was a principal point of contention during the Mexican-American War (1846–1848). The military transition team in Laredo headed by Mirabeau B. Lamar, former president of the Republic of Texas (1838–1841), dealt with the contested territory dispute by holding elections. On July 3, 1847, forty voters elected a county commissioner and two justices of the peace. These public displays of political legitimacy sanctioned Laredo as a part of Texas and the United States even before the Treaty of Guadalupe Hidalgo formally took effect in 1848. Nuevo Laredo—Laredo's newly established sister city on the west bank of the Rio Grande—experienced a different governmental trajectory.[19] In September 1847, Lamar took a more bureaucratic approach; he advised the existing mayor, Don Andrés Martínez, to stay in power.[20]

That geopolitical separation produced multiple effects for *los dos Laredos*. Laredo became "the only town on the north [American] bank of the Rio Grande [in that area]."[21] Recognizing her geographic capital, the International and Great Northern rail companies arrived in Laredo in the early 1880s prompting a prodigious growth spurt that incited the city's second major transition phase.[22] One result of that lucrative economic shift was an influx of foreign-born and intranational migrants who reshaped the city's sociopolitical norms and customs. Many members of the inaugural Red Men cohort, for example, settled in Laredo after 1880. On a broader scale, the rail lines increased Laredo's visibility as a "gateway city,"[23] where international and transnational networks could flourish. Formally establishing Laredo as a port-of-entry not only laid the groundwork for new economic opportunities but also complicated existing allegiances built around struggles for political control and land rights.

As early as the 1870s, revolutionaries plotting against Porfirio Díaz thought of Laredo as a possible launching point for a military attack.[24] A bloody shootout during the local *Botas* (boots) versus *Guaraches* (Mexican sandals) election of 1886 also provides an example of how residents dealt with political differences and changing demographics publicly and violently.[25] This is not to suggest that confrontational relationships did not exist before the railroads came to the city or before the Treaty of Guadalupe Hidalgo divided the land. On the contrary, as early as the 1820s, postcolonial moments of conflict among Native Americans, Mexican citizens, and Anglo-Americans affected "conflict and accommodation" processes across the Southwest and northern Mexico.[26] The difference is that advances in transportation technology at the end of the century not only irrevocably changed economic and political dimensions of life in Laredo but also facilitated the movement and settlement of brotherhoods like the Improved Order of Red Men and analogous social groups.

In 1881, the Masons built a lodge to formally establish their presence in Laredo.[27] The Knights of Pythias, the Woodmen of the World, the Married Ladies Social Club, and the Tuesday Musical Club also changed the city's social fabric and built environment. *La sociedad mutualista "Hijos de Juarez,"* who solicited donations from "Mexican patriots residing in Laredo" to help build a park in honor of Benito Juárez in 1906,[28] and *el Club Internacional*, who organized major campaigns and conferences such as *El Primer Congreso Mexicanista* (the first Mexican Congress, 1911), influenced political networking and bi-national patriotic sensibilities.[29] As well, religious diversity in Laredo as evidenced by places of worship, Christ Church Episcopal, Presbyterian Church, Baptist, San Agustin Catholic Church, Methodist, Christian, and St. Peter's Catholic Church, among others, played a role in those processes. And the multiracial military presence at Fort McIntosh after reconstruction may have affected the way residents categorized themselves and others based on phenotypic and linguistic characteristics (i.e., Anglo Blacks, American Hispanic Blacks, or Mexican Hispanic Blacks).[30]

RESPONSES TO THE MEXICAN REVOLUTION (JANUARY–APRIL 1914)

Residents of Nuevo Laredo and Laredo experienced and reacted to Carranza's New Year's Day attack in distinct and telling ways. Nuevo Laredoans alongside Constitutionalist and Federalist soldiers, fighting under Carranza and Victoriano Huerta, respectively, experienced bloody losses and irreparable property damage. Those unforgiving realities of war— bloodshed, fires, looting, hunger, and unimaginable fear—did not give Nuevo Laredoans much choice: take up arms or seek asylum.

Laredo, relatively untouched by physical violence and protected by U.S. military forces, became a safe haven.[31] Indeed, Fort McIntosh soldiers stood or crouched down attentively at their posts, as they had done over the past year and would continue to do so leading up to the skirmishes of April 1914 (Figure 1). They spent the majority of their time watching for Mexican rebels seeking to cross into the United States—protecting the border, protecting U.S. citizens, protecting sovereignty. On a municipal level, Laredo City Council members remained silent on the subject of the battle and the Mexican Revolution generally. A week after Carranza's New Year's Day attack, they conducted a business-as-usual meeting at which they discussed the salaries of city employees, including the district commissioner, plaza gardeners, mounted police, and the market janitor.[32]

Even if city officials bureaucratically circumvented the violent realities of the Revolution, the polemical language that followed the fate of the Washington's Birthday Celebration in local newspapers offered Laredoans several opportunities to reflect on Mexico's

Figure 1. American soldiers on U.S. bank of Rio Grande, Laredo, 1914. Photo courtesy of Johnson Collection, Webb County Heritage Foundation, Laredo, Texas.

CHAPTER ELEVEN

political situation and question notions of bi-national solidarity. An article in the *Laredo Weekly Times* dated February 1, 1914, for example, informed residents that they had a choice to make. Considering the loss of human life, Venustiano Carranza had "decreed" that February 22, also the date set aside to celebrate George Washington's Birthday that year, be a day of mourning for "the late departed." The *Times* responded with the following:

> Of course it is apparent that Venustiano was not aware that there are many Mexicans in this vicinity who have been accustomed to observe February 22d [sic] as one of the greatest joyful festivals of the year—one that to them is the compound essence of the Fourth of July, Christmas and *el dieciséis de Septiembre* [Mexican Independence Day] all mixed and mingled together.[33]

In making its case for the celebration, that passage attempted to answer for Mexican citizens living in Laredo. More pressingly, it fashioned a "heterotopic"[34] vision of American heritage that also homogenized. Mulling over Mexican loyalties and cultural expectations was not unique to the *Times*.[35] The Laredo-based newspaper *La Crónica*, led by politically active Idár family, often reported on those interstitial spaces of national affiliation.[36] The difference between *La Crónica*, and the *Laredo Weekly Times*, both of which influenced public opinion during the Revolution, was their respective editorial staff's political inclinations. While the *Times* was blatantly pro-Huerta, *La Crónica*, because of its ties with Mexican political exiles who had fled Díaz's regime, was not partial to Federalist forces.

Perhaps because of the long-standing economic benefits afforded to the city by Porfirio Díaz's railway expansion, many of Laredo's power players continued to support Huerta's regime.[37] But even then, various allegiances were at play. At that point in the Revolution, Laredo had experienced an influx of Mexican refugees. Earlier waves generally supported Porfirio Díaz. Later, after Victoriano Huerta and Díaz's nephew, Felix Díaz, had violently deposed Francisco Madero as President of Mexico on February 22, 1913, émigrés could have also identified as supporters of Carranza, Alvaro Obregón, and/or Francisco "Pancho" Villa. At the same time, residents in Laredo were aware that Nuevo Laredo was in the hands of Huerta's army. Those political alliances notwithstanding, the common denominator tying Laredoans together amid shifting political loyalties was that they were all spectators, of both the Mexican Revolution and the Washington's Birthday Celebration.

But they were not the only ones watching. Journalists from as far away as New York were paying attention.[38] Also, Laredo's Red Men were well aware that the "Great Incohonees"— nationally ranked Improved Order of Red Men fraternity brothers—were assessing their nation-building performances. Indeed, a 1909 report from the national office of the Improved Order of Red Men, then based in Danvers, Massachusetts, effusively described Laredo's tradition of celebrating George Washington's Birthday.[39] Circulated across the United States and the American Empire in places like the Philippines and Panama, that newsletter effectively advertised the city of Laredo as an exemplar of frontier patriotism.[40]

Laredo's Red Men rose to the occasion. They championed the celebration in 1914, perhaps even overcompensated because of Carranza's attack. They organized events, secured financial support, and promised entertainment to sway the public. And we could imagine

Figure 2. City Hall during Washington's Birthday Celebration, circa 1914. Photo courtesy of Johnson Collection, Webb County Heritage Foundation, Laredo, Texas.

that the patriotic spectacle they produced that February mainly reflected their ideals. But that would be a mistake. It was, in many ways, a team effort. The city council, not all of who were Red Men members, for example, approved the decoration of city hall (Figure 2).[41] But it was city employees and wage laborers who actually Americanized the streets of Laredo; they physically placed banners, flags, and other patriotic memorabilia. The celebration provided countless activities in which non-Red Men members, regardless of citizenship or national allegiances, could play along.

So even if townspeople chose to follow Carranza's instruction to mourn the "late departed," they could have been distracted by a Wild West show, a carnival that featured "an Egyptian girl dancer who grips chair in her teeth,"[42] or the sight of a parade led by George and Martha Washington (Wilmer Threadgill and Miss Pauline Gilmore), John Smith and Pocahontas (Captain George Agan and Miss Josephine Staben), and Pocahontas' "maids of honor" (Misses Mary Millar, Ella Devine, Carol Simon, Marguerite Simon, and Fanny Giddens).[43] A *jamaica* and Mexican Street Fair on Martin plaza might have offered additional entertainment. According to the official program that year, those events promised to provide opportunities where "winsome senoritas [sic] take you captive. They represent the strong arm of the law—dressed as guards, policemen, jailors, and judges. You are 'pinched' by a fair senorita [sic], imprisoned by another of them, hauled before one acting as judge and fined. Here is where every hombre makes it his business to fall a victim to these fair ones."[44] If spectacle and titillating role-playing were not enough, perhaps financial gain could be persuasive. In addition to prizes for "best decorated vehicle" ($25) or winning the

CHAPTER ELEVEN

mile run race ($5),[45] food and accommodation expenses surrounding the events offered economic stimulation.

In some respects, those Red Men sponsored events did not disavow Mexican culture, history, and customs. They promoted it selectively and literally viewed it from a safe distance, politically and geographically. Moreover, the celebration allowed Laredoans to vicariously experience the Mexican Revolution safely and on their own terms. During the February 1914 celebration, for example, Laredo's Red Men screened motion pictures of the January 1, 1914, attack on Nuevo Laredo by the Constitutionalists at the Royal Theater in Laredo. According to reports, "the picture was a fine one and one could readily recognize Laredo people lined on the banks of the river or assembled about the international bridge on the American side."[46] The safe haven quality of the screening space reinforced the town's reputation as a site for tourism and diversion. During the actual battle in early January, groups traveled to Laredo from San Antonio, Corpus Christi, and other parts of Texas to witness the violence in Nuevo Laredo from the North Bank of the Rio Grande. The public screening during the Washington's Birthday Celebration that year offered residents and visitors the opportunity to experience the Revolution again and through a different medium.[47]

In both of these instances, but particularly at the Royal Theater that day, understanding the role of spectatorial practices on individual, communal, and broader political levels is key. Imagine sitting in that theater. Imagine watching yourself experience the terror (and/or the thrill) of hearing gun shots (produced offstage), of seeing wounded bodies and buildings in flames on a giant screen alongside your peers (i.e., family members, business associates, neighbors, acquaintances, and friends). The collectivizing effect of modern technology is considerable, especially when it incorporates visual effects where self-identification and minimal personal accountability go hand-in-hand.

Archival records suggest the tone of that gathering was not particularly somber.[48] The screening provided the crowd with an opportunity to reflect on the problems of a neighboring country without expectations. That is, they were not pressured to redress, voice, or even care about the grievances of Nuevo Laredoans and of Mexican citizens more broadly. They could contemplate the gravity of violence surrounded by constant reminders—banners, music, flags, and other patriotic memorabilia—that they resided in the United States of America not the Republic of Mexico.

CLANDESTINE LOYALTIES AND AFFILIATIONS

Newspaper accounts, official celebration programs, Improved Order of Red Men bulletins, municipal expenditure ledgers, personal letters, photographs, and city council minutes give us a sense of how the Washington's Birthday Celebration could serve as a sociocultural buffer, as a low-stakes response to the Mexican Revolution. Clandestine economic ventures are also relevant. Joseph Netzer, the man who has been credited with sustaining interest in the Washington Birthday's Celebration through the Mexican Revolution and the Great War, offers a compelling reference point.[49] Nezter was the most successful member of the Laredo tribe in terms of climbing the ranks of the Improved Order of Red Men. He took the position of Great Sachem of the State of Texas in 1909 thereby solidifying his status and influence locally and regionally, even beyond his one-year term.[50] Speaking solely in terms of dedication to the Improved Order of Red Men fraternity and promulgating Laredo's American identity into the 1930s, his zeal is unmatched. Understanding his patriotic fervor, however, takes a complex turn when we consider the fact that the Federal Bureau of Investigation suspected him of arms dealing during the Mexican Revolution.[51]

According to correspondence between federal officers in Laredo and Washington, D.C. in 1913, a Laredo-based agent by the name of Webster Spates conducted surveillance and attempted to prove that Netzer exported munitions to Mexican citizens. Reviewing accounting records, Spates tracked "20,000 7 millimeter cartridges, [which were] sold for $784,000." He established, [That] was the same night "that Netzer had sold the 9,000 rounds."[52] According to Bureau reports, that particular ammunition did not have a local market. Spates acquired sufficient intelligence to implicate Netzer directly, but a grand jury chose not to indict him.[53]

Whether or not Netzer's affiliation with the Improved Order of Red Men, his position as an upstanding hardware store owner, or the fact that he was president of the Laredo Board of Trade (1913)[54] helped his case is unclear. Border politics and his military past may have played a role. As well, the legal environment, which was more complicated due to cross-border trade, could have directly influenced the outcome of the case.[55] The hearing did not ruin his reputation or detract from the success of the patriotic events he sponsored. He did, in fact, initiate contact with Generals Guardiola and Quintana the next year. But it did further underscore the potential legal ramifications of aiding revolutionaries or profiting from revolutionary efforts.

In 1911, for example, *La Crónica* published the following headline: "*Se expide orden por el gobernador de Texas para que no ayuden a los revolucionarios de Mexico, y se enumeran los articulos que se conceptuan como contrabando de guerra*" (The governor of Texas issues an order listing the articles that fall within the category of war smuggling and mandating [citizens] not to provide help to Mexican Revolutionaries.)[56] Reoccurring public announcements like this one affected how and when Laredoans interacted with each other and with Nuevo Laredoans; they set the boundaries of involvement. And as the Mexican Revolution progressed, municipal actors reinforced those norms. In 1915, Laredo Mayor and Red Man, R. McComb learned that a group of Carrancista sympathizers had planned a meeting to be held at city hall. He quickly called city council members to denounce the assembly. He asserted, "The hall would be closed and no Carrancista meeting or any other kind of meeting conducted by foreign revolutionary factions would be held in this city."[57] McComb also called police to enforce his decree. A year earlier, however, Constitutionalist Army/Carrancista sympathizers organized a well-attended, open-air meeting in Laredo. That gathering, held at Luna Park in January 1914, received media attention but did not face legal repercussions.[58] Although both meetings have pro-Carranza sensibilities in common, the factor that decided their treatment was their respective physical location. Holding a meeting at city hall, the locus of government in that town (and the place where the Improved Order of Red Men staged their mock battle ever year), would have had considerable repercussions. It would have suggested that U.S. city officials, and their constituents, were sympathetic to Constitutionalist efforts in Mexico.

Establishing and maintaining the limits of engagement in print, through municipal action, and through participation in the Washington's Birthday Celebration were effective differentiating strategies during the Revolution. But transgressive behavior also played a role in that narrative. In that respect, the most prominent and controversial local figure during the Mexican Revolution was not Joseph Netzer but Amador Sánchez—a native Laredoan and Red Men member. Sánchez was Laredo's mayor during the first decade of the twentieth century (elected 1900, reelected in 1907) and later became sheriff. Previously, he had served as district clerk of Webb County for three terms.[59] Trained as a civil engineer and surveyor, he worked and profited on both sides of the border. In 1907, he and his partners were said to have "a stock ranch of 100,000 acres" in the state of Tamaulipas, Mexico.[60] His pedigree and connections made him a recognized figure in the city's group of "*gente decente*"—"literally 'decent people,' in part because this is how they saw themselves, and in part because the word *decente* represents a sense of propriety, sobriety and responsibility that they all shared."[61] This term had specific resonances in Laredo because it was a place where ethnic Mexicans were not necessarily farm laborers or ranch hands. Many owned land. Quoting a "distinguished Southerner," David Montejano explains, "in Laredo there are many influential Mexican citizens and they can't be treated like a *pelado*. The treatment given to Mexicans depends partly on the individual Mexican, who may be of high class, and partly on numbers, in Laredo there are so many you have to give them social recognition."[62]

Sánchez was not a "*pelado*." On the contrary, he was a prominent political figure and a key Red Men team member. In 1906, he organized the Improved Order of Red Men's "Indian attack" on the city. That year, when the Red Men raided City Hall, Sánchez performed without an Indian costume. But even then, he provided the highlight of that year's festivities.

> *El número más interesante, por su novedad, por su grandioso aparato y su carácter emocionante, será el asalto de los indios á Laredo, y ocupación de la ciudad. El plan fue propuesto y arreglado por el Sr. Mayor Sánchez, y aprobado por el comité organizador y por el Jefe de las Armas.* (Because of its novelty, its grandiose pomp and its thrilling nature, the most interesting act will be the attack and occupation of Laredo by the Indians. The plan was proposed and arranged by Mr. Mayor Sánchez and approved by the organizing committee and the Chief of Arms.)[63]

Sánchez conceptualized the performance so that he did not have to smear war paint on his face or don a genuine buckskin outfit to celebrate America. In playing his "role" as a Mexican-American public servant, Sánchez literally surrendered the city over to his fraternity brothers. His political persona and his patriotic aspirations seamlessly converged during the mock battle on City Hall that year. Indeed, the congratulatory tone of the aforementioned 1909 national Red Men bulletin could have been directed toward his contributions in both capacities.

Sánchez's subsequent public exploits, however, incited less favorable reactions. In 1911, using his authority as Sheriff of Webb County and the Laredo jail as a base, he unsuccessfully helped General Bernardo Reyes—Porfirio Diaz's former minister of war—take up arms to fight Francisco I. Madero for control during an early phase of the Revolution.[64] Although clearly violating neutrality laws, U.S. officials did not stop Reyes immediately when he set up camp in San Antonio or used the jail in Laredo to strategize and to store arms. It was only by the end of 1911, that a campaign against revolutionary movements on the American side of the border involving Texas Governor Colquitt, the Federal Rangers, and President Taft halted their network. Detained by federal marshals, Sánchez awaited trial in Brownsville along with other conspirators. His political connections and patriotic conduct did not garner him an immediate acquittal.[65] It took months of deliberation among the State Department, the Mexican ambassador, the Governor, congressmen, and President Taft before he received a presidential pardon. President Taft finally agreed at the end of this tenure so that the diplomatic consequences of the decision would have to be faced by Woodrow Wilson. Even then, Huerta had already taken control of the Revolution.[66] Oddly enough, these political problems did not affect Sánchez's bid for Webb County Sheriff in 1912. He won even though his name was not on the ballot. And, although politically tainted, Sánchez continued to play an active role in organizing the Washington's Birthday Celebration.

Sánchez and Netzer's indiscretions aside, fostering a collective sense of American identity among Laredoans remained the Red Men organization's main objective. Maintaining the celebration during the most violent moments of the Mexican Revolution and the most delicate phases of the Great War afforded them a powerful way to communicate their patriotic vision to border residents. But those performances also produced other benefits. The festivities not only bolstered the city's economy and its reputation as a safe tourist destination but also provided Laredoans with an opportunity to keep the violence and political instability in Nuevo Laredo at bay.

THE POWER OF PERFORMANCE

In a 1910 article on Washington Birthday's Celebration, editors at *La Crónica* commented *"Laboremos, pues, porque sea este el festival que nos sirva de anuncio para traer capital é industrias permanentes a esta región"* (Let us work to make this festival [a success] so that it attracts capital and industry permanently to this region).[67] Alongside the desire to garner long-term profit from the celebration, we should also consider that the promise of spectacle—decorated carriages, men and women in costume, parades, and moving pictures—could potentially veil the truths or realities of conflict. As *El Demócrata Fronterizo* suggested in 1911:

> *En vano buscamos en los periódicos de México algunas noticias de interés; no traen sino inverosímiles noticias de revolución, los que pueden darlas, y asuntos artísticos o literarios los demás. TODO LO ABSORVE LA REVOLUCION, Y TODO OCULTA EL MIEDO.* [We seek in vain to find newsworthy items in Mexican dailies; all they report are implausible chronicles of the revolution, those who are in a position to provide them, and the rest only offer artistic or literary notices. THE REVOLUTION ABSORBS EVERYTHING AND EVERYTHING IS HIDDEN BY FEAR.][68]

Ideas of participatory spectatorship and circumspect involvement implied in both of these public remarks remind us that the Washington's Birthday Celebration was at once a brazen and efficacious performance, particularly because it took many forms—in print, on screen, in the flesh; on local, national, and international stages—involved diverse groups of witnesses, and stimulated the city's economy.

Although it is easy to discount the George Washington's Birthday celebration as innocuous merrymaking, it shaped how Laredoans perceived and responded to the Mexican Revolution. It further intensified the importance of celebrating America and shoring up nation-state boundaries in spite of violence, economic instability, and political strife in Nuevo Laredo. And while this essay does not seek to claim that Laredoans were all equally invested in cultivating American identity, it does stress the power of performance.[69] It takes seriously the impact of collective embodied practices and their ability to temporally homogenize difference and consolidate identities. Laredoans responded to the Mexican Revolution in ways that engaged the realities of warfare. And some, like "La Rebelde" and the Idár family, left a long-lasting impression. On a citywide level, however, reveling in patriotism became the response of the majority. Not because it represented every resident's point of view but because support for the tradition in the media, in municipal spaces, and on the streets of the city absorbed those individual voices.

NOTES

I dedicate this essay to Alvaro Muñoz—a person who inspires and provokes accordingly. I must also thank Marisela R. Chávez, Gustavo Carlos Peña, and José M. Muñoz for all of their help. Also, archivists and staff members at the following locations provided invaluable assistance: The Webb County Heritage Foundation, the Laredo Public Library, Texas A&M International University Special Collections, the City of Laredo Secretary's Office, and the Red Men Museum and Library in Waco, Texas, particularly David Lintz and the board of directors of the Texas Red Men Foundation, Inc. for their financial support.

1. The battle that destroyed portions of Nuevo Laredo New Year's Day in 1914 was all but surprising. The Mexican Revolution's shifting political factions, particularly Carranza's need to establish control in northeastern Mexico against Huerta and the threat of U.S.-based incursions led by exiled Mexican power players, drew the battle to the U.S.–Mexico border. Accordingly, Nuevo Laredo's geographic position at the crossroads of rail transportation between the United States and Mexico made it an attractive wartime asset. That battle in January 1914 was not an isolated incident. Indeed, it followed a series of skirmishes and strategic destructive acts—including the burning of access roads between Monterrey and Nuevo Laredo—that occurred in the month of March 1913; it also preceded further warfare in April 1914, when Carranza's soldiers took command of Nuevo Laredo. For information on the Mexican Revolution's broader impact on the Texas/Tamaulipas, Nuevo Leon, Coahuila, Chihuahua border, see Arnoldo de Leon, ed. *War along the border: The Mexican Revolution and Tejano communities* (College Station: Texas A&M University Press, 2012); Elliot Young, *Catarino Garza's Revolution on the Texas-Mexico Border* (Durham, N. C.: Duke University Press, 2004); Benjamin H. Johnson, *Revolution in Texas: How a Forgotten Rebellion and Its Bloody Suppression Turned Mexicans into Americans* (New Haven, Conn.: Yale University Press, 2005); David Romo, *Ringside Seat to a Revolution: An Underground Cultural History of El Paso and Juárez, 1893–1923* (El Paso, Tex.: Cinco Puntos Press, 2005); José Limón, "El Primer Congreso Mexicanista de 1911: A Precursor to Contemporary Chicanismo," *Aztlan* 5, no. 1/2 (1974): 85–117; and Leonor Villegas de Magnón, *La Rebelde* (Houston, Tex.: Arte Público Press, 2004).

2. For a case study that focuses on national, transnational, and transregional ties, see Karl Jacoby, "Between North and South: The Alternative Borderlands of William H. Ellis and the African American Colony of 1895." In *Continental Crossroads: Remapping U.S.–Mexico Borderlands History* (Durham, N. C.: Duke University Press, 2004), 230.

3. Bessie Lindheim, *The Story of Laredo No. 16: Leonor Villegas de Magnón and the Mexican Revolution*, ed. Stan Green (Laredo: Texas A&M International University, 1990), 13. See also Clara Lomas, ed. *La Rebelde: Leonor Villegas de Magnón* (Houston, Tex.: Arte Público Press, 2004).

4. See, for example, the work of Américo Paredes, David Montejano, José Limón, Stan Green, Douglas Foley, Elliot Young, James Alex Garza, Benjamin H. Johnson, Cynthia Orozco, Jorge O. Gonzalez, Seb S. Wilcox, J. B. Wilkinson, and Jerry Thompson.

5. Leaflet, "WASHINGTONS' BIRTH-DAY 22 of February," 1870. Box 203, Luciano Guajardo Historical Collection, Laredo, Texas.

6. Joseph Netzer, "The Origin of Washington Birthday Celebration in Laredo, Texas," n.d. Box 203, Luciano Guajardo Historical Collection, Laredo, Texas; Letter, Joseph Netzer, n.d. Box 203, Luciano Guajardo Historical Collection, Laredo, Texas

7. As Phillip Deloria suggests of the Red Men and analogous fraternities who "played Indian" during the nineteenth century, by acting out "the rituals of governance, members gained an emotional stake in the nation's rule and a sense of American political identity." Phillip Deloria's consideration of fraternal organizations inspired by Native American cultures attends to the links among patriotism, history, and performance on a larger scale. He explicates IORM's East Coast origins, how the fraternity engaged Indian-American relations, and, most evocatively, how "they desired Indianess and not Indians." See Phillip Deloria, *Playing Indian* (New Haven, Conn.: Yale University Press, 1998), 61, 90. For additional perspectives on fraternalism in the United States, see David E. Beito, *From Mutual Aid to the Welfare State: Fraternal Societies and Social Services, 1890–1967* (Chapel Hill: University of North Carolina Press, 2000); Mark C. Carnes, *Ritual and Manhood in Victorian America* (New Haven, Conn.: Yale University Press, 1989); Mary Ann Clawson, *Constructing Brotherhood: Class, Gender, and Fraternalism* (Princeton, N. J.: Princeton University Press, 1989); and Lynn Dumenil, *Freemasonry and American Culture, 1880–1930* (Princeton, N. J.: Princeton University Press, 1984).

8. Stan Green, *A History of the Washington Birthday Celebration* (Laredo, Tex.: Border Studies, 1999), 5. For more information on the George Washington's Birthday Celebration, see Elliot Young, "Red Men, Princess Pocahontas, and George Washington: Harmonizing Race Relation in Laredo at the Turn of the Century," *Western Historical Quarterly* 29, no. 1 (1998): 48–85.

9. According U.S. Census data, Laredo's population was 14,855 in 1910 and increased to 22,710 by 1920. In 1910, the population of Webb County was 22,503 and had risen to 29,152 in 1920. The influx of spectators during the month of February not only augmented those statistics by the thousands but also created moments of consumption and purchasing that affected the city's financial outlook well into the twentieth century.

10. See, for example, S. M. Benavides, City Treasurer, General Fund "Expenses" (Feb. 1904): 99; S. M. Benavides, City Treasurer, General Fund "Expenses" (Feb. 1905): 511; S. M. Benavides, City Treasurer, General Fund "Expenses" (Feb. 1906): 529; and S. M. Benavides, City Treasurer, General Fund "Expenses" (Feb. 1907): 539. Luciano Guajardo Historical Collection, City of Laredo Expenditure Ledger, 1890–1920. Laredo Public Library, Laredo, Texas.

11. Connecting Red Men participation with political and economic participation at the turn of the twentieth century and during the Mexican Revolution was made possible by cross-listing the inaugural roster of the IORM Laredo chapter and archival documents in Laredo. See J. W. Falvella, *A Souvenir Album of Laredo the Gateway to Mexico*, 1916 (Reproduction available at the Webb County Heritage Foundation and the Laredo Public Library). At the Red Men Museum and Library in

Waco, Texas, see "Six Moons' Report, 31st Hunting Moon G.S.D. 407," *Great Council of Texas, 1898 (TRIBAL), IORM, Reservation of Texas* (Houston: J.J. Pastoriza Printing and Litho Co., 1898): 1–19. I would like to thank David Lintz, director of the Red Men library/archive in Waco, Texas, for explaining the significance of the "Great Sun of Discovery" (G.S.D.). The Red Men organization uses a particular vision of time based on Christopher Columbus's presence in the New World instead relying on the specified number of year after Christ's birth (AD). To calculate and/or understand time, as understood by members of the IORM, one must subtract 1491 from the current year. For example, AD 2010–1491= G.S.D. 519.

12. *Laredo Weekly Times*, January 4, 1914. It is important to note that this edition of the *Times* was the last for editor Louis J. Wortham.

13. *El Demócrata Fronterizo*, January 3, 1914.

14. "Celebration Will Be Held," *Laredo Weekly Times*, January 11, 1914.

15. "[?] are Meeting With Success," *Laredo Weekly Times*, January 18, 1914.

16. "Will Pull Off Sham Battle," *Laredo Weekly Times*, January 18, 1914.

17. "Celebration Plans Going Ahead: Program This Year Will be One of the Most Elaborate Yet Arranged and Will Cover Four Days," *Laredo Weekly Times*, February 1, 1914.

18. Seb S. Wilcox, "Laredo during the Texas Republic," *The Southwestern Historical Quarterly* 42, no. 2 (October 1938): 85.

19. Article V of the Treaty of Guadalupe Hidalgo, signed by Plenipotentiaries N. P. Trist, L. P. Cuevas, B. Couto, and M. Atristain at la Villa de la Virgen de Guadalupe on February 2, 1848, details the boundary line between the two Republics. Articles VIII and IX deal with citizenship rights and expectations. See "The Avalon Project: Documents in Law, History, & Diplomacy, Yale Law School" http://avalon.law.yale.edu/19th_century/guadhida.asp.

20. Seb S. Wilcox, "Laredo during the Texas Republic," 105.

21. Ibid., 84.

22. Laredo's population nearly tripled, from 3,811 to 11,319 after the railroad reached the city in 1881. See Gilberto Hinojosa, *Borderlands Town in Transition: Laredo, 1755–1870* (College Station: Texas A&M University, 1983), 229.

23. See E. H. Tarver, *The Laredo: Gateway between the United States and Mexico* (Laredo: Daily Times Press, 1902) and Stan Green, *Border Biographies*, vol. 2 illustrated (Laredo: Border Studies, 1993).

24. William Ray Lewis, "The Hayes Administration and Mexico," *The Southwestern Historical Quarterly*, 24, no. 2 (October 1920): 143. For a sense of Laredo's political climate before the turn of the century, see Carlos Cuellar and Stan Green, *The Story of Laredo no. 12: Mexican Revolutionaries in Mexico 1890–1891* (Laredo: Texas A&M International University, 1991).

25. See Jerry Don Thompson, *Laredo: A Pictorial History* (Norfolk, Va.: Donning, 1986) and Seb S. Wilcox, "The Laredo City Election and Riot of April, 1886, "*Southwestern Historical Quarterly* 45 (July 1941).

26. Although often overlooked, moments of accommodation were also prevalent. See for example, David J. Weber, "Conflicts and Accommodations: Hispanic and Anglo-American Borders in Historical Perspective, 1670–1853, " *Journal of the Southwest* 39, no. 1 (1997), 1–32; Raúl Ramos, "Finding the Balance: Béxar in Mexican/Indian Relations," *Continental Crossroads: Remapping U.S.–Mexico Borderlands History* (Durham, N. C.: Duke University Press, 2004): 35–66; Andrés Reséndez, "An Expedition and Its Many Tales," *Continental Crossroads: Remapping U.S.–Mexico Borderlands History* (Durham, N. C.: Duke University Press, 2004): 121–50.

27. "Masonic Lodge Laredo," Cabinet 5. Webb County Heritage Foundation, Laredo, Texas.

28. J. Cardenas, "El Parque Juárez: Llamamiento al Patriotismo (una Mejora Importante)," *El Demócrata Fronterizo*, February 3, 1906, 1.

29. "Celebramos el Centenario," *La Crónica*, March 5, 1910, 1; "La Celebración del Centenario," *La Crónica*, March 12, 1910, 1; "Ligera Reseña de la Expléndida Celebración del Primer Centenario de la Independencia Mexicana en Laredo, Texas," *La Crónica*, September 24, 1910, 2; N. Idár, "Primer Congreso Mexicanista, Verificado en Laredo, Texas EEUU de los Días 14 al 22 Septiembre de 1911. Discurso y Conferencias. Por la Raza y para la Raza" (Laredo, Tex., 1912); José Limón, "El Primer Congreso Mexicanista de 1911: A Precursor to Contemporary Chicanismo," 211–226; Douglas E. Foley, *From Peones to Politicos: Class and Ethnicity in a South Texas Town, 1900 to 1977* (Austin: University of Texas Press, 1977), 68; Cynthia Orozco, "The Origins of the League of United Latin American Citizens (LULAC) and the Mexican-American Civil Rights Movement in Texas with an Analysis of Women's Political Participation in a Gendered Context, 1910–1920," (PhD diss., University of California Los Angeles, 1992).

30. For an in-depth look at the presence of black squadrons in Laredo (particularly during 1870–1900), see Jorge O. Gonzalez, "The Black Experience in Laredo: 1755–1919," (Master's thesis, Laredo State University, Tex., 1986). See also L. Ward Schrantz, *Guarding the Border: The Military Memoirs of Ward Schrantz*, ed. Jeff Patrick (College Station: Texas A&M University Press, 2009) and Gerald Home, *Black and Brown: African Americans and the Mexican Revolution, 1910–1920* (New York: New York University Press, 2005).

31. "Famous Fort McIntosh Active Since 1849 Plays Large Part in Good Neighbor Policy," *Laredo—Gateway to Mexico* (1944), 4. See also Charles H. Kazan, *The Establishment of Fort McIntosh Laredo, Texas* (Laredo, Tex.: Laredo Junior College, 1936).

32. City Council Meeting, January 8, 1914, Minute Book 3 (January 4, 1894–November 11, 1918), 664. (City of Laredo, City Secretary's Office, Laredo, Tex.).

33. "Two Celebrations," *Laredo Weekly Times*, February 1, 1914.

34. We may understand that passage as a "heterotopic" moment in which "all the other real sites that can be found within a culture are simultaneously represented, contested, and inverted." Michel Foucault, "Of Other Spaces." *Diacritics* 16, no. 1 (1986), 24.

35. Earlier discussions of Mexican nationality and identity formation in Laredo offered distinct perspectives. In January 1911, for example, *El Demócrata Fronterizo*, focused not on birthright but on bureaucratic citizenship. In other words, to be considered Mexican outside of Mexico, one had to register with the Mexican consulate. See "Quienes son Mexicanos," *El Demócrata Fronterizo*, January 14, 1911, 4.

36. See, for example, "Notas del Congreso Mexicanista," *La Crónica*, September 21, 1911, 1.

37. Díaz increased the railroad system of Mexico from 400 miles in 1876 to over 15,000 in 1911, including a line from Mexico City to Laredo, Texas. Ironically, that same railway expansion helped anti-Díaz revolutionaries mobilize. Because of those advances in transportation technologies in the 1880s, Laredo had experienced the presence of anti-Díaz revolutionaries as early as 1890, General Ruiz Sandoval and General and Dr. Ignacio Martínez being the most famous. According to a report by the Consulate in Nuevo Laredo dated February 6, 1891, unknown assassins gunned down Dr. Martínez in Laredo in 1891. Carlos Cuellar and Stan Green, *The Story of Laredo no. 12: Mexican Revolutionaries in Laredo 1890–1891* (Laredo: Border Studies, 1991) 18–9.

38. "Pictorial Bulletin of Recent Noteworthy Events," *Leslie's Weekly* (March 24, 1910), 282.

39. The review reads: "Thirteen years ago in the mind of a Red Man, originated the idea of celebrating on the annual holiday, George Washington's Birthday, which is honored throughout the United

States. *The idea was not to have the usual form of a George Washington affair with patriotic speeches and the reading of the Declaration of Independence or the telling of tales such as the 'I can not tell a lie Father I did it with my little hatchet' story and the riding of the wild colt.* All of this was relegated to the background and a carnival of festivities substituted in its place. It may appear a little ridiculous to some to imagine the dignified Warrior, Statesman, and Scholar [George Washington] attending a bullfight or a roping contest, although as a young man the great general was a love of sports and dare devil accomplishments; but he would have been in his glory at the head of such a pageant as winded through the principal streets of the city [Laredo] in Snow Moon [February]. The idea was formulated in the mind of a Red Man, a member of the local tribe and he brought it up in tribal council where several minds grappled with it and after a struggle developed from that one little idea a celebration of such magnificence, and glory to the Order in such abundance that after that time from year to year it has been reenacted with improvements and additional features" (emphasis mine). See "Observance of Washington's Birthday," *Red Men's Official Journal* 9, no. 2 (G.S.D. 418, 1909).

40. Indeed, by 1905, IORM members living in the United States numbered 25,209 in New Jersey, 44,318 in Indiana, 4,880 in Texas, 747 in Arizona, and 12,864 in California. Table. *Red Men's Official Journal* 6, no. 12 (G.S.D. 415, 1906). For information about the earliest Texas-based IORM reservations, see *Records of the Great Council of the United States (1847–1867)* (Baltimore, Md.: Henry S. Huber, 1856).

41. City Council Meeting, February 2, 1914, Minute Book 3, (January 4, 1894–November 11, 1918), 668.

42. "1914 wbc notes" (Cabinet 1). Stan Green/WBCA Vertical File, Washington Birthday Celebration Historical Collection, Webb County Heritage Foundation, Laredo, Tex..

43. Ibid.

44. "Official Program: Washington Birthday Celebration, February 20 to 25, Inclusive," *Laredo Weekly Times*, February 8, 1914.

45. "1914 wbc notes" (Drawer 1). Stan Green/WBCA Vertical File, Washington Birthday Celebration Historical Collection, Webb County Heritage Foundation, Laredo, Tex..

46. "Immense Crowds Were Out," *Laredo Weekly Times*, March 1, 1914.

47. "Many Came To See Battle," *Laredo Weekly Times*, January 11, 1914.

48. "1914 wbc notes" (Drawer 1). Stan Green/WBCA Vertical File, Washington Birthday Celebration Historical Collection, Webb County Heritage Foundation, Laredo, Tex..

49. Born in Frankfurt-on-the-Main, Germany, Netzer acquired his expertise as a plumber during his travels throughout northern Europe—Germany, Austria, Serbia, and Russia—before migrating to the United States in 1879. According to Netzer's biography, he joined the U.S. Army at Baltimore, Maryland, in 1881 and quickly rose through several military ranks. And, not unlike other prominent frontiersmen, he is also often associated with the capture of Chief Geronimo. Netzer relocated to Laredo in 1889 where he joined numerous fraternal orders and opened a hardware and plumbing business. Netzer is often portrayed as an upstanding American citizen and entrepreneur. Frank W. Johnson, *A History of Texas and Texans*, vol. IV (Chicago: The American Historical Society, 1914), 1633. For a closer look at Nezter's contemporaries in Laredo, see Stan Green, *Border Biographies Illustrated*, 2nd ed. (Laredo: Border Studies, 1992), 100–102.

50. *The Laredo Weekly Times* and other English-language papers covered his lecture circuit, appearances, and encounters. "Attends Meeting: Joseph Netzer Great Sachem of State of Texas Speaks in San Antonio," *The Laredo Morning Times*, March 6, 1910. See also "Visiting Red Men Teams Were Shown Degree Work," *The Galveston Daily News* November 28, 1909. I would like to thank Sarah Reveley of San Antonio, Texas, and David Lintz of Waco, Texas, for sharing this information.

51. See Bureau Report, 25 September 1913; RDS, RG59, M274, Roll 29 812.00/9114 and Bureau Report, 1 November 1913; RDS; RG59, M274, Roll 31, 812.00/9608. For more on this case study, see James Alex Garza, "On the Edge of a Storm: Laredo and the Mexican Revolution, 1910–1917" (M.A. Thesis, Texas A&M International University, 1996), 49–50.

52. Garza, "On the Edge of a Storm," 49–50.

53. Ibid.

54. Johnson, *A History of Texas and Texans*, 1633.

55. As W. Dirk Raat reminds us, "commerce in arms was not a violation of the neutrality laws until the Arms Embargo Act of 1912. Moreover, customs regulations were often confused with neutrality statutes, with illegal embargos being instituted along the border by officers of the U.S. Army, customs officials, and immigration inspectors." W. Dirk Raat, *Revoltosos: Mexico's Rebels in the United States 1903–1923* (College Station: Texas A&M University Press, 1981), 170–71.

56. *La Crónica*, February 16, 1911, 4.

57. "Refused to Allow the Meeting," *Laredo Weekly Times*, January 8, 1915.

58. "Held Big Open-Air Meeting," *Laredo Weekly Times*, January 18, 1914.

59. Stan Green, *Border Biographies Illustrated*, 133.

60. Ibid.

61. Elliot Young, "Deconstructing 'la Raza': Identifying the 'Gente Decente' of Laredo, 1904–1911," *The Southwestern Historical Quarterly* 98, no. 2 (October 1994), 228.

62. Quoted in David Montejano, *Anglos and Mexicans in the Making of Texas, 1836–1986* (Austin: University of Texas Press, 1987), 248. See also David Montejano, "The Demise of 'Jim Crow' for Texas Mexicans, 1940–1970," *Aztlán* 16, no. 1–2 (1987), 32. For a parallel conversation about the connections between "whiteness" and property ownership in Texas, see Ariela J. Gross, "Texas Mexicans and the Politics of whiteness," *Law and History Review* 21, no. 1 (Spring 2003), 196–197. For a broader overview, see Cheryl I. Harris, "Whiteness as Property," *Harvard Law Review* 106 (1993), 1709–91.

63. "Las Fiestas del 22 de Febrero," *El Demócrata Fronterizo*, January 20, 1906, 2.

64. Charles H. Harris III and Louis R. Sadler, "The 1911 Reyes Conspiracy: The Texas Side," *The Southwestern Historical Quarterly* 83, no. 4 (April 1980), 331.

65. Ibid., 335–7.

66. Ibid., 344.

67. "El 22 de Febrero," *La Crónica*, January 29, 1910, 3. For an overview of economic conditions during that time period, see Carlos Cuellar, "The House of Armengol: Doing Business on the Rio Grande Border, 1881–1939," (M.A. Thesis, Laredo State University, 1990), 78.

68. *El Demócrata Fronterizo*, February 25, 1911, 4.

69. This essay's analytic framework draws from practice-oriented studies of nationalism and knowledge transmission, particularly the work of Benedict Anderson, *Imagined Communities: Reflections on the Origin and Spread of Nationalism* (London: Verso, 1983); Diana Taylor, *Disappearing Acts: Spectacles of Gender and Nationalism in Argentina's "Dirty War"* (Durham, N. C.: Duke University Press, 1997); and Paul Connerton, *How Societies Remember* (Cambridge, U. K.: Cambridge University Press, 1989). Its performance-oriented focus builds on studies of cultural performance as a differentiating strategy. See David M. Guss, *The Festive State: Race, Ethnicity, and Nationalism As Cultural Performance* (Berkeley: University of California Press, 2000); Kelly Askew, *Performing the Nation: Swahili Music* *and Cultural Production in Tanzania* (Chicago: University of Chicago Press, 2002); Ravina Aggarwal, *Beyond the Lines of Control: Performance and Politics on the Disputed Borders of Ladakh India* (Durham, N. C.: Duke University Press, 2004); and Fernando J. Rosenberg and Jill Lane, "Performance and Law," *e-misférica* 3.1 (June 2006).

BIBLIOGRAPHY

Aggarwal, Ravina, *Beyond Lines of Control: Performance and Politics on the Disputed Borders of Ladakh, India.* Durham, N.C.: Duke University Press, 2004.

Anderson, Benedict. *Imagined Communities: Reflections on the Origin and Spread of Nationalism.* London: Verso, 1983.

"[?] Are Meeting With Success." *Laredo Weekly Times,* January 18, 1914: 1.

Askew, Kelly. *Performing the Nation: Swahili Music and Cultural Politics in Tanzania.* Chicago: Chicago University Press, 2002.

"Attends Meeting: Joseph Netzer Great Sachem of State of Texas Speaks in San Antonio." *The Laredo Morning Times.* March 6, 1910: 2.

Cardenas, J. 1906. "El Parque Juárez: Llamamiento Al Patriotismo (una mejora importante) [The Parque Juarez: Appeal to Patriotism (a major improvement)]." *El Demócrata Fronterizo,* 3 (February 1906): 1.

"Celebramos el Centenario [Celebrating the Centennial]." *La Crónica,* March, 5 1910: 1.

"Celebration Plans Going Ahead: Program This Year Will Be One of the Most Elaborate Yet Arranged and Will Cover Four Days." *Laredo Weekly Times,* February 1, 1914: 1.

"Celebration Will Be Held." *Laredo Weekly Times,* January 11, 1914: 1.

City Council Minutes, Book 3. City Secretary's Office, Laredo, Texas.

Clawson, Mary Ann. *Constructing Brotherhood: Class, Gender, and Fraternalism.* Princeton, N.J.: Princeton University Press, 1989.

Connerton, Paul. *How Societies Remember.* Cambridge, U.K.: Cambridge University Press, 1989.

Cuellar, Carlos. "The House of Armengol: Doing Business on the Rio Grande Border, 1881–1939." Master's thesis, Laredo State University, 1990.

Cuellar, Carlos, and Stan Green. *The Story of Laredo No. 12: Mexican Revolutionaries in Mexico 1890–1891.* Laredo: Texas A&M International University, 1991.

De Leon, Arnoldo, ed. *War along the Border: The Mexican Revolution and Tejano Communities.* College Station: Texas A&M University Press, 2012.

Deloria, Phillip. *Playing Indian.* New Haven, CN: Yale University Press, 1998.

"El 22 de Febrero [February 22]." *La Crónica,* January 29, 1910: 3.

El Primer Congreso Mexicanista de 1911, Cabinet 2, Webb County Heritage Foundation, Laredo, Texas.

Faragher, John M. "Commentary." In *Rereading Frederick Jackson Turner,* by F. J. Turner. Originally published in 1920. New Haven, Conn.: Yale University Press, 1994.

Foley, Douglas E. *From Peones to Politicos: Class and Ethnicity in a South Texas Town, 1900 to 1977.* Austin: University of Texas Press, 1977.

Fort McIntosh History, Cabinet 2. Webb County Heritage Foundation, Laredo, Texas.

Foucault, Michel. "Of Other Spaces." *Diacritics,* 16, no. 1 (1986): 229–36.

Garza Gonzalez, Fernando. *Una Puerta al Pasado: La Historia de los Dos Laredos* [A Door to the Past: The History of the Two Laredos]. Nuevo Laredo, Tamaulipas, Mexico: S.N., 1998.

Garza, James Alex. "On the Edge of a Storm: Laredo and the Mexican Revolution, 1910–1917." Master's thesis, Texas A&M International University, 1996.

Gonzalez, Jorge O. "The Black Experience in Laredo: 1755–1919." Master's thesis, Laredo State University, 1986.

Green, Stan. *A History of the Washington Birthday Celebration.* Laredo, TX: Border Studies, 1995.

———. *Border Biographies Illustrated.* Vol. 2. Laredo, Tex.: Border Studies, 1993.

Gross, Ariela J. "Texas Mexicans and the Politics of Whiteness." *Law and History Review*, 21, vol. 1 (2003): 195–205.

Guss, David M. *The Festive State: Race, Ethnicity, and Nationalism As Cultural Performance*. Berkeley: University of California Press, 2000.

Harris, Charles H. III and Louis R. Sadler. "The 1911 Reyes Conspiracy: The Texas Side." *The Southwestern Historical Quarterly*, 83, vol. 4 (1980): 325–48.

Harris, Cheryl I. "Whiteness as Property." *Harvard Law Review*, 106 (1993): 1707–91.

"Held Big Open-Air Meeting." *Laredo Weekly Times*, January 18, 1914: 1.

Hijos de Juárez Sociedad Mutualista, Cabinet 3. Webb County Heritage Foundation, Laredo, Texas.

Hinojosa, Gilberto. *Borderlands Town in Transition: Laredo, 1755–1870*. College Station: Texas A&M University Press, 1983.

Hoelscher, Steven. "Making Place, Making Race: Performance of Whiteness in the Jim Crow South." *Annals of the Association of American Geographers*, 93, no. 3 (2003): 657–86.

Home, Gerald. *Black and Brown: African Americans and the Mexican Revolution, 1910–1920*. New York: New York University Press, 2005.

Idár, N. "Primer Congreso Mexicanista, verificado en Laredo, Texas EEUU de los dias 14 al 22 septiembre de 1911. Discurso y conferencias. Por la raza. [First Congress Mexicanista, verified in Laredo, Texas USA from 14 to 22 September 1911. Speeches and meetings. For the people.]" Laredo, Tex., 1912.

"Immense Crowds Were Out." *Laredo Weekly Times*, March 1, 1914: 1.

Jacobson, Matthew. *Whiteness of a Different Color: European Immigrants and the Alchemy of Race*. Cambridge, Mass.: Harvard University Press, 1998.

Jacoby, Karl. "Between North and South: The Alternative Borderlands of William H. Ellis and the African American Colony of 1895." In *Continental Crossroads: Remapping U.S.–Mexico Borderlands History*, ed. Samuel Truett and Elliott Young, pp. 209–40. Durham, N.C.: Duke University Press, 2004.

Johnson, Benjamin H. *Revolution in Texas: How a Forgotten Rebellion and Its Bloody Suppression Turned Mexicans into Americans*. New Haven, Conn.: Yale University Press, 2005.

Johnson, Frank W. *A History of Texas and Texans*. Vol. IV. Chicago: The American Historical Society, 1914.

Kazan, Charles H. *The Establishment of Fort McIntosh Laredo, Texas*. Laredo, Tex.: Laredo Junior College, 1936.

"La Celebración del Centenario [The Centennial Celebration]." *La Crónica*, March 12, 1910: 1.

"Las Fiestas del 22 de Febrero [The Celebrations of February 22]." *El Demócrata Fronterizo*. January 20, 1906: 2.

"Ligera Reseña de la Expléndida Celebración del Primer Centenario de la Independencia Mexicana en Laredo, Texas [Brief Account of the Splendid Celebration of the Centenary of Mexican Independence in Laredo, Texas]." *La Crónica*, September 24, 1910: 1.

Leonor Villegas de Magnon, Cabinet 2. Webb County Heritage Foundation, Laredo, Texas.

Lewis, William Ray. "The Hayes Administration and Mexico." *The Southwestern Historical Quarterly*, 22, no. 2 (1920): 140–53.

Limón, José. "El Primer Congreso Mexicanista de 1911: A Precursor to Contemporary Chicanismo." *Aztlan*, 5, no. 1/2 (1974): 85–117.

Lindheim, Bessie. *The Story of Laredo No. 16: Leonor Villegas de Magnon and the Mexican Revolution*, ed. Stan Green. Laredo: Texas A&M International University, 1990.

Lindsay, George W., Charles C. Conley, and Charles H. Litchman. *Official History of the Improved Order of Red Men*. Boston: The Fraternity Publishing Company, 1897.

Loren, Odin. *Border Incidents and the U.S. Consulate in Nuevo Laredo 1871–1941*. Laredo, Tex.: Border Studies, 1990.

Luciano Guajardo Historical Collection, "Washington's Birthday Celebration Association-Early Years," Box 203. Laredo Public Library, Laredo, Texas.

"Many Come To See Battle." *Laredo Weekly Times*, January 11, 1914: 1.

Mexican Revolution, Cabinet 6. Webb County Heritage Foundation, Laredo, Texas.

Montejano, David. *Anglos and Mexicans in the Making of Texas, 1836–1986.* Austin: University of Texas Press, 1987.

———. "The Demise of 'Jim Crow' for Texas Mexicans, 1940–1970." *Aztlán*, 16, no. 1/2 (1987): 27–69.

"Notas del Congreso Mexicanista [Notes of the Mexicanista Congress]." *La Crónica*, September 21, 1911: 1.

"Official Program: Washington Birthday Celebration, February 20 to 25, Inclusive." *Laredo Weekly Times*, February 8, 1914:1.

Orozco, Cynthia. "The Origins of the League of United Latin American Citizens (LULAC) and the Mexican-American Civil Rights Movement in Texas with an Analysis of Women's Political Participation in a Gendered Context, 1910–1920." PhD diss., University of California Los Angeles, 1992.

"Quienes son Mexicanos [Who are Mexicans]." *El Demócrata Fronterizo.* January 14, 1911: 4.

"Pictorial Bulletin of Recent Noteworthy Events." *Leslie's Weekly*, March 24, 1910: 12.

Ramos, Raúl. "Finding the Balance: Béxar in Mexican/Indian Relations." In *Continental Crossroads: Remapping U.S.–Mexico Borderlands History*, ed. Samuel Truett and Elliott Young, pp. 35–66. Durham, N.C.: Duke University Press, 2004.

Records of the Council of Texas, 1905–1915. The Red Men Museum and Library, Waco, Texas.

Records of the Great Council of the United States, 1905–1915. The Red Men Museum and Library, Waco, Texas.

Red Men's Official Journal, 1905–1915. The Red Men Museum and Library, Waco, Texas.

"Refused to Allow the Meeting." *Laredo Weekly Times*, January 8, 1915: 1.

Regional History Archive, Special Collection and Archive. Texas A & M International University, Laredo, Texas.

Resèndez, Andrès. "An Expedition and Its Many Tales." In *Continental Crossroads: Remapping U.S.–Mexico Borderlands History*, ed. Samuel Truett and Elliott Young, pp. 121–50. Durham, N.C.: Duke University Press, 2004.

Roediger, David. "The Pursuit of Whiteness: Property, Terror, and Expansion, 1790–1860." *Journal of the Early Republic*, 19, no. 4 (1999): 579–600.

Romo, David. *Ringside Seat to a Revolution: An Underground Cultural History of El Paso and Juárez, 1893–1923.* El Paso, Tex.: Cinco Puntos Press, 2005.

Rosenberg, Fernando J. and Jill Lane. Performance and Law. *e-misférica* 3.1 (June 2006).

Schrantz, L. Ward. *Guarding the Border: The Military Memoirs of Ward Schrantz*, ed. Jeff Patrick. College Station: Texas A&M University Press, 2009.

Seb S. Wilcox Papers. University of Texas at San Antonio Special Collections, San Antonio, Texas.

Tarver, E. H. *Laredo: The Gateway between the United States and Mexico.* Laredo, Tex.: Daily Times Print, 1889.

Taylor, Diana. *Disappearing Acts: Spectacles of Gender and Nationalism in Argentina's "Dirty War."* Durham, N.C.: Duke University Press, 1997.

Truett, Samuel. "Transnational Warrior: Emilio Kosterlitzky and the Transformation of the U.S.–Mexico Borderlands, 1873–1928." In *Continental Crossroads: Remapping U.S.–Mexico Borderlands History*, ed. Samuel Truett and Elliott Young, pp. 241–72. Durham, N.C.: Duke University Press, 2004.

"Two Celebrations." *Laredo Weekly Times*, February 1, 1914: 1.

Untitled. *La Crónica*, February 16, 1911: 4.

Untitled. *El Demócrata Fronterizo*. February 25, 1911:4.

Untitled. *El Demócrata Fronterizo*. January 3, 1914: 2.

Villegas de Magnón, Leonor. *La Rebelde*. Houston, Tex.: Arte Público Press, 2004.

"Visiting Red Men Teams Were Shown Degree Work." *The Galveston Daily News*, November 28, 1909: 3.

Washington's Birthday Celebration-Histories, Cabinet 9. Webb County Heritage Foundation, Laredo, Texas.

Webb County Civil and Criminal Court Cases, Special Collection and Archive. Texas A & M International University, Laredo, Texas.

Weber, David J. "Conflicts and Accommodations: Hispanic and Anglo-American Borders in Historical Perspective, 1670–1853." *Journal of the Southwest,* 39, no. 1 (1997): 1–32.

"Will Meet Tuesday Afternoon: Matter of Whether or Not Washington Birthday Celebration Will Occur Will Be Decided." *Laredo Weekly Times,* January 4, 1914: 1.

"Will Pull Off Sham Battle." *Laredo Weekly Times,* January 18, 1914: 1.

Wilcox, Seb S. "The Laredo City Election and Riot of April, 1886." *Southwestern Historical Quarterly,* 45 (1941): 1–23.

———. "Laredo during the Texas Republic." *The Southwestern Historical Quarterly,* 42, no. 2 (1938): 83–107.

Young, Elliot. *Catarino Garza's Revolution on the Texas-Mexico Border.* Durham, N.C.: Duke University Press, 2004.

———. "Deconstructing 'la Raza': Identifying the 'Gente Decente' of Laredo, 1904–1911." *The Southwestern Historical Quarterly,* 98, no. 2 (1994): 228.

———. "Red Men, Princess Pocahontas, and George Washington: Harmonizing Race Relation in Laredo at the Turn of the Century." *Western Historical Quarterly,* 29, no. 1 (1998): 48–85.

CHAPTER TWELVE

PANCHO VILLA'S HEAD
The Mexican Revolution in the Chicano Theatrical Imagination

Alma Martínez Carranza

And so
los oprimidos del mundo
continue to become los liberadores . . .
asi es que el gachupin y el gabacho
will be Mexicanized
but first el CHICANO must Mexicanize
himself . . .
—Luis Valdez, "Pensamiento Serpentino," 1971[1]

The "CHICANO must Mexicanize himself."[2] In this 1971 call to political mobilization, Valdez urges the Mexican diasporic population in the United States to look to Mexico's ethos, mythos, and history to forge a new American identity and spark a political movement that addresses the social injustices of their time. Seven years earlier, in 1964, while still a college student, Valdez explored this "mexicanization" in his first play, *The Shrunken Head of Pancho Villa*. Recognized as the first Chicano play to come out of the nascent 1960s Chicano Civil Rights Movement and the first to assert a "search for identity so prevalent in other Chicano plays that followed," his dark comedy exposes the sociopolitical realities of the Mexican American family in contemporary U.S. society and introduces a new genre of familial normative in American theater.[3] *The Shrunken Head of Pancho Villa* became the Chicano lens through which Mexican diaspora and mainstream theater audiences alike experienced for the first time, quotidian life in a (other) typical American family (Figure 1). Living in squalor and at the periphery of the American Dream, Valdez's Chicano family holds body and spirit together by aligning its past, present, and future with Pancho Villa and the 1910 Mexican Revolution. Valdez's surrealistic play subverts the Mexican government's version of the iconic and mythical Pancho Villa by appropriating Villa's disembodied head as a symbolic and central character. A historically complex figure, Villa was both vilified and reified by the United States and Mexico throughout his life and even more so after his death. In Valdez's imaginative and extensive use of magical realism, Villa's body may lie in Mexico, but his spirit and the spirit of the Mexican Revolution contained in his missing head are fomenting and growing in a 1950s Chicano family in San Jose, California, and in barrios across the country.

> *Sung to the tune of the Mexican Revolutionary corrido "La Cucaracha"*
> Joaquin: *(sings)* I'm gonna sing this corrido
> And I'm feeling very sad
> Cause the great Francisco Villa
> Some vato cut off his head.
> When they murder Pancho Villa
> His body they lay to rest
> But his head somebody take it
> All the way to the U.S.
> La Cockarocha, La Cockarocha
> She don' wanna caminar . . .[4]

At the opening of Act Three in *The Shrunken Head of Pancho Villa*, the character Joaquin, a rebellious young *vato* who speaks no Spanish, sings to his brother Belarmino his own Chicano version of the Mexican Revolutionary *corrido* "La Cucaracha." Belarmino, a growling, ravenous, talking head in Act I, is later revealed to be the missing head of Pancho Villa.

In Valdez's Chicano family, the presence of Mexico is felt in every aspect of the family's

Figure 1. The 1968 poster of El Teatro Campesino's first staging of *The Shrunken Head of Pancho Villa* written and directed by Luis Valdez.

lives. All speak or understand Spanish and English in varying degrees of fluency or accuracy, and all speak in Spanglish. First generation Americans like Joaquin are familiar with "La Cucaracha's" melody but can only remember key words or passages of the song's lyrics. Given the cultural and economic disenfranchisement of the Mexican diasporic population living in the United States, Joaquin's knowledge of the Mexican Revolution and his Mexican ancestry is fragmented. The appropriation and subversion of Mexican nationalist narratives such as the Mexican Revolution, Pancho Villa, and *corridos* are foundations of *The Shrunken Head of Pancho Villa* and posit Valdez's extensive dialogue with Mexico as psychologically and viscerally embedded in the lives of the Mexican diaspora in California's central valley and the southwestern United States.

THE CHICANO'S MEXICAN MEMORY

Born in the small rural town of Delano, California, located in the San Joaquin Valley, "The Salad Bowl of the World," Valdez grew up working side by side with the thousands of new and multigenerational Mexican immigrants and migrant farm workers who followed the seasonal harvests. Valdez's experience as both an American and immigrant informs his identity, his work, Chicano theater as a theatrical genre, and the performance aesthetic and political ideology of his renowned theater company, El Teatro Campesino (The Farm Workers Theatre) founded by Valdez as an organizing arm of the United Farm Workers Union in 1965.[5]

Valdez, the grandson of immigrants who fled the Mexican Revolution, turned to the narratives of Mexican identity, culture, and imagination that had been forged and sustained by generations of Mexican Americans in the United States since the 1847 Treaty of Guadalupe Hidalgo. For generations of Mexican immigrants and their U.S. born children and grandchildren, the Mexican Revolution was a collective memory inherited through a rich oral tradition. This tradition was a lifeline for the popular masses in Mexico and Mexican-originated communities in the United States. With no access to printing presses or newspapers, they preserved their unofficial histories that were otherwise erased from both U.S. and Mexican nationalist narratives.[6] So for multiple generations of Mexican Americans from the 1920s through the 1960s, the only means by which they could learn their culture and history was through informal familial history lessons, harrowing and humorous stories, popular performances, legends, jokes, riddles, songs, and *corridos*. Given the fluid and ephemeral nature of oral tradition, the line between fiction and nonfiction often became blurred. (Many Chicano families boast of at least one family member riding with Villa or Zapata.)[7] Thus, it is no surprise that the highly imaginative, sometimes mythical quality of the oral tradition would more than likely have planted the seed of the idea for Valdez's first full-length play.[8]

In "Notes on Style," the preface to *The Shrunken Head of Pancho Villa*, Valdez describes the tenets of a then nascent Chicano theater by questioning the belief that an external world exists independently of our minds and feelings. For Valdez, reality is historically situated, and it is best understood when expressed by a collective human consciousness. He proclaims an aesthetic that effectively expresses the Chicano condition by combining realist referents with surrealist imagery. In his view, such conjunction is to be found in visual expressions of popular culture (Posada) and modern art (Orozco).

> The play is not intended as a "realistic" interpretation of Chicano life. The symbolism emerging from the character of Belarmino influences the style of acting, scene design, make-up, etc. The play therefore contains realistic and surrealistic elements working together to achieve a transcendental expression of the social condition of La Raza in los Estados Unidos. The set particularly must be "real" for what it represents; but it must also contain a cartoon quality such as that found in the satirical sketches of Jose Clemente Orozco or the lithographs of Jose Guadalupe Posada. In short, it must reflect the psychological reality of the barrio.[9]

Valdez's "transcendental expression" of the Chicano experience moves his writing into the literary genre of magical realism: the term still several years away from American literature's wider use. His heightened reality and larger-than-life characterizations of poverty in America pushes the dramatic borders to such an extreme that the course of the dramatic thrust and denouement can only be explained, and its deepened meaning understood, in the realm of the fantastic.

Valdez has called his work, "a cross between Brecht and Cantinflas,"[10] linking the influences of its style directly to the renowned popular Mexican comic Cantinflas and the renowned German playwright and theoretician. By overlaying popular Mexican *carpa* with Brechtian theater, Valdez consciously subverts the strictly performative aspects of the popular Mexican itinerant tent theater genre, *carpa,* with text and staging notes that continually remind audiences that they are seeing pointed sociopolitical critiques couched in familiar Mexican visual and linguistic vernaculars that attain a new level of expressionism.[11] This innovative aesthetic and theatrical style is derived from the subjectivity of the Chicano playwrights themselves and their personal sensibility as transcultured border subjects: born and/or raised as Mexican in the United States. A bifurcated Chicano gaze looking toward Mexico with feet firmly planted in the United States becomes the mechanism that Chicano theater appropriates to dialogue with and subvert Mexican Nationalism.

Valdez locates Chicano consciousness in the figure of Pancho Villa, forging his identity from the myriad shifting stories in folklore. In the closing statement of "Notes on Style," Valdez reinforces the importance of Pancho Villa and the ideals of the Mexican Revolution in the rise of a Chicano ethos that surged from the popular masses and spoke to the immigrants who represented the ferment of a Chicano consciousness. "This is the story of a people who followed him (Pancho Villa) beyond borders, beyond death."[12]

In fact, upon his death, Villa left no personal archive unlike Carranza or Obregon[13] but rather testimonies dictated to his own personal secretary, a fact that has contributed to his mythical persona. What has defined his celebrity, and infamy, has been the popular *corridos* and legends propagated in the United States and Mexico, to whom he was a revolutionary hero, protector and gifted war strategist.[14] The following stanzas from the revolutionary *corrido* "Hoy nuestro México febrero veintitrés," (Today Our Mexico February 23) are an example of how folklore has created and kept Villa's legend alive. The *corrido* relates how Villa evaded capture by both General Pershing's 1916 U.S. Punitive Expedition from the north and Mexican President Venustiano Carranza's troops from the south. True to the oral tradition, the number of American soldiers, horses, and airplanes employed to capture Villa varies widely with the numerous versions of this popular *corrido*. The song formed part of El Teatro Campesino's musical repertoire for many years and was sung at almost every national and international performance from 1967 to 1980.

> *"Hoy nuestro México febrero veintitrés"*
> Hoy nuestro México, febrero veintitrés
> mando Wilson diez mil americanos,
> dos mil caballos, seiscientos aeroplanos,
> buscando a Villa por todo el país.

Comenzaron a volar los aeroplanos
entonces Villa un gran plan les formó
se vistió de soldado americano
y a sus tropas también las transformó.

Mas cuando vieron los gringos las maderas
con muchas barras que Villa les pintó
se bajaron con todo y aeroplanos
y Pancho Villa prisioneros los tomó.[15]

"Today our Mexico February 23"
Today our Mexico February 23
Wilson sent ten thousand Americans
two thousand horses six hundred airplanes
searching for Villa across the nation.

Airplanes began to fly
so Villa drew up a grand plan
he dressed as an American soldier
and he also transformed his troops.

So when the gringos saw the flags
with many stripes painted for them by Villa
they landed airplanes and all
and Pancho Villa took them prisoner.

There are numerous versions of this *corrido*, but what is consistent is that they all extol Villa's cunning, courage, and daring in escaping superior military forces, particularly those of the United States. Prominently missing from most of the versions is how Mexican people, fearing that the Punitive Expedition was a U.S. invasion, hid Villa at almost every point of his escape. Even at his most vulnerable and at his weakest point militarily, Villa remained a hope for the masses.[16] After Villa's assassination in 1923, the emerging postrevolutionary government continued Carranza's propaganda to vilify Villa as an illiterate bandit lacking any revolutionary ideology. The U.S. and Mexican press portrayed him as a cold-blooded murderer. As Friedrich Katz points out, "the black legend portrays him (Villa) as an evil murderer, with no redeeming qualities."[17] This darker side is recognized even in the *corrido* tradition.

Todas las gentes en Chihuahua y Ciudad Juárez
muy asustada y asombrada se quedó
de ver tanto gringo y carrancista
que Pancho Villa en los postes les colgó.

All the people of Chihuahua and Ciudad Juarez
were scared and astounded
to see so many gringos and Carranzcistas
that Pancho Villa hung for them from posts.

The Villa legend took on "gothic" qualities when in 1926 grave robbers in Chihuahua dug up his body and cut off his head. The head was never found.[18] The missing head became a working metaphor for the Mexican people: Villa and the revolutionary ideals had disappeared from view, but they lay in hiding ready and waiting for the opportune moment to rise from the dead and fulfill the promise of the Mexican Revolution.

As if in response to this sentiment, in the years following the assassinations of Villa and Zapata, the newly installed government of President Plutarco Elías Calles and eventually the Party of the Institutional Revolutionary (PRI) that ruled Mexico for seventy years, embarked on several national projects that reified the Mexican Revolution. Following the deaths of their heroes and the failure of the revolution to change their plight, state-sponsored Mexican nationalism sought to create a homogeneity of language, culture, and national identity that erased differences, facilitated political control, and unified all Mexicans under the ethnic rubric "mestizo." By centralizing and controlling a national narrative across race lines, the *indígena* could be marginalized as a race classifications, their lands appropriated, and their people relabeled as a social class thereby ensuring the country's progress and dispensing with ancient traditions and customs which proved an obstacle to modernity.[19] To institutionalize the revolution, the "Monumento a la Revolución" was reimagined, and it eventually encased the bodies of Venustiano Carranza, Francisco Madero, Plutarco Elías Calles, and Lázaro Cárdenas, as well as Villa's headless body. Divided in life by their ideological differences, these heroes were united in death to serve the political agenda of the government's nationalist project.[20]

ALIENATION VERSUS IDENTITY: THE CHICANO AMERICAN DREAM

The Shrunken Head of Pancho Villa dramatizes the severe poverty, racism, and exclusion from the American Dream that has eluded Mexican American families living on the fringes of the most powerful nation in the world. Valdez's "American" family lives in the United States, speaks English, has a son in the military, and aspires to be upwardly mobile. But at the same time, this "Mexican" American family lives in squalor, has an alcoholic father, a son who is a high school dropout, a pregnant unwed daughter, and a son who is a disembodied talking head. Breaking from conventional mainstream American playwriting of the time, Valdez's use of magical realism intentionally presents stereotypical characters of such dramatic extremes that they supersede even mainstream essentialization. From his position as auteur, Valdez constructs a new theatrical archetype of the Mexican/Chicano that forces the spectator to rethink previous reductions. In this liminal "spectacle and spectator" interstice, Valdez inverts the gaze and privileges the Chicano family as the new, albeit dysfunctional, familial American normative. This radical shift in how the United States defines "American" and cultural citizenship sets this play apart as a pivotal milestone in American theater.

Valdez's allegorical placement of Villa's head in a Chicano barrio underscores how the realms of myth, folklore, and oral tradition provide rich sources for dramatic interpretation. Villa's head metaphorically represents the Chicano and Mexican immigrant's separation from their ancestral home, culture, and history. Mexico, and the social revolutionary spirit symbolized by Villa's head, is now only a memory that lacks any potential for realization given the lack of a body. Valdez posits the head as the übermetaphor for the burgeoning Chicano Movement. The dream of a unified Chicano consciousness resides and foments in Villa's head and patiently waits for a leader to rise again from the ranks. It awaits a collective "body" of voices and peoples that will take Villa's revolutionary ideals (the head) and undertake another social revolution. The unification of the head and the body therefore represents a national Chicano Movement with the clarity of vision, unity of ideals, numbers, and power to instigate radical political change and end the hopeless cycle of poverty for both Mexicans and Chicanos in the United States. This appropriation of an alternative popular narrative is a direct contestation to the Mexican government's attempt to enforce a nationalist project.

For Chicanos, the cycle of poverty was exacerbated by the promise of the American Dream, itself a constructed econopolitical laudatory narrative of social parity, racial-ethnic homogeneity, and the possibility of limitless opportunity and abundance that ignored the darker aspects of U.S. history like African American slavery, the Native American genocide, and the Mexican-American War. The Mexican immigrant's experience in the face of this disjunctured American Dream prompted emerging young playwrights and artists to take as their central themes the examination and indictment of racism and the disenfranchisement to which his community had been subjected for decades (Figure 2). The mediation of the American Dream with Mexican nationalist modalities became the point of contention that drove the dramatic plot forward. Yet aside from its weighty themes, the play is a highly comedic and surreal send-up of the "typical" 1950s Chicano family living in barrios across the United States.

Figure 2. Taking the message to the people. Night falls on a 1974 outdoor performance by El Teatro Campesino.

In this excerpt from the play, the older son Mingo (Domingo), the antithesis of his streetwise younger brother Joaquin, has returned from the Korean War confident in his entitlement as a veteran Marine to assimilate into the American middle class only to find a gulf between his aspirations and his history as embodied in the lives of his family. In the following moment from the play, Mingo attempts to convince his mother Cruz and sister Lupe to leave their barrio home.

> Mingo: . . . I am talking about Prune Blossom Acres. America's at our doorstep. All we have to do is take one step.
> Cruz: What about Belarmino?
> Mingo: Somebody can carry him, what else? Put him in a shoebox.
> Lupe: He don't fit in a shoebox.
> Mingo: Not a real shoebox, stupid. A cardboard box. We can put holes in it so he can breathe. That ain't no problem.
> Cruz: I know Mingo but . . . its not the same. In this barrio they don' care.
> Mingo: I care!
> Cruz: And the gringos?
> Mingo: Whatta you mean, gringos?
> Cruz: Who else lives in new houses?[21]

Similar to Mexican American WWII veterans, Mingo returns home believing that his military service will finally throw open the doors of opportunity. His optimism is in stark contrast to the assumptions of Cruz and Lupe, who, given the racial-class issues of the time, reduce the new neighborhood to *gringo* (white Euro-American) and want no part of Mingo's ambitious dream. Cruz's fear that Belarmino will not survive the ridicule in the new neighborhood underscores how Chicanos in the 1960s did not yet fully aspire to upward mobility and modernity (Valdez's "Prune Blossom Acres") as these were seen as enclaves of white-European privilege and racial-economic segregation.

Mingo is determined to leave the barrio and become rich at any cost except one—he refuses to leave without his family. Reverting to another of his fundamental theses, the family as the stronghold of identity and fortitude, Valdez describes Mingo as a *vendido* (sell-out) and a crook, but, nonetheless, someone for whom family is still the walled fortress that stands between the "familiar" and the shifting ethnic-racial climate of American society beyond the barrio. In spite of this, Mingo gradually comes to realize that it is precisely these emotional and psychological ties that are holding him back.

> Mingo: . . . Americans, ma. American citizens like me and y . . . (Pause) Aw, whatta you trying to do? Get me defeated too? You wanna spend the rest of your life in this stinking barrio? . . .[22]

Eventually, Mingo finds that his family's Mexican names, dark skin, class, culture, illiteracy, and illegal status are the antithesis of the American Dream. To advance his social status, he must turn his back on the family that reinforces and perpetuates his "difference." To be *"Mexican"* has become a detriment. Similar to the Mexican government's attempted erasure of *indígena* culture and self-governance as an obstacle to modernity, Mingo's essential identity now proves an obstacle to his assimilation into modern U.S. society. Mingo's parents have become a source of shame for Mingo because they are undocumented. This significant rupture in the family is exacerbated by the fact that since 1847 multiple generations of Mexican diasporic families in the United States have served as the "underground railroad" harboring millions of undocumented immigrants crossing into the United States. To this day, almost every Chicano family has at one time or another provided temporary or long-term shelter to undocumented immigrants. This scene is one of the only moments in the play that undocumented migration is touched on and, given its brevity within the text, becomes a nonissue as this is now another character aspect of the new American family.

Through the character of Mingo, Valdez poses the question: Do immigrants need to give up their Mexican identity and assimilate into American nationalist modalities of identity to gain access to material wealth and upward mobility? The conclusion that Valdez comes to at the end of the play is "no." Becoming Chicano precludes that necessity. Chicanos do not need to subscribe to pre-established tracks of American acculturation that force them to strip all remnants of their identity.

For playwrights like Valdez, the burgeoning Chicano Movement provided an alternative path to assimilation as mantra preached by U.S. melting-pot proponents. Yet, like all nationalisms, the Chicano Movement utilized utopian tropes to unify a heterogeneous Mexican diaspora. It sought to create a unified Chicano identity that in many ways drew from the Mexican nationalist project by obscuring differences. But ultimately, divisions of class, gender, region, generations, sexual orientation, and levels of transculturation created schisms that proved insurmountable. The Chicano movement never gained the full support of Mexicans in the United States and to this day represents only the most politicized Mexican origin population.[23]

A CALL TO ACTIVISM AND A NEW CULTURAL ETHOS

The search for a new ethos of cultural citizenship did not come from U.S. national narratives taught in schools, found in books, or exhibited and preserved in museums but rather from the Mexican history of the Chicano's progeny. In the United States as in Mexico, the stories of the Mexican Revolution entered into popular mythology and folklore starting in 1923, the year of Villa's assassination, and quickly became a metaphor for resilience. For the one million poor, mostly rural, *indígena* refugees (posited here as a class rather than racial classification) who emigrated from Mexico to the southwestern United States during the Revolution, this mythology and their Mexican oral tradition provided the cultural, spiritual, and moral sustenance to overcome the deplorable working conditions they endured during and after the Depression.[24] The increasing demand for cheap manual labor in the burgeoning agribusiness sector drew large numbers of Mexican immigrants whose work grossed large profit margins for growers and kept market costs down for consumers. Two years prior to the premiere of *The Shrunken Head of Pancho Villa*, two leaders did emerge. Cesar Chavez and Dolores Huerta rallied Mexican, Mexican Americans, and Chicanos in the San Joaquin Valley, and together they carried out one of the most significant labor rights initiatives of the twentieth century: the National Farm Workers Association (later the United Farm Workers Union-UFW) founded in 1962.[25]

This racially charged political climate was in part responsible for Valdez's articulation of a new Chicano theater. A political theater practitioner, activist, and intellectual involved at multiple levels of the Chicano Movement, he was consciously aware that this new polity—the Chicano Civil Rights Movement and the political awakening of the Mexican diaspora—necessitated a new cultural framework. Once again, he turned to the Mexican and Mesoamerican roots of his parents and grandparents.

The privileging of the *indígena* in the Chicano Movement echoed to some extent the peasant revolt in Mexico that led to the Mexican Revolution. Similar to the revolutionaries demand for the large *hacendados* to relinquish their land and redistribute it to the people who worked it, the UFW and Valdez's El Teatro Campesino demanded that agribusiness reform their labor laws and practices. And, like their Mexican Revolutionary counterparts, the striking farm workers rallied behind land reforms championed by Emiliano Zapata and marched in political processions led by a standard of the *Virgen de Guadalupe*, the brown patron saint of Mexico who symbolized God's love for the *indígena* and engendered hope.

Valdez would continue to reference Mexican history, popular culture and iconography, like the *Virgen de Guadalupe* and Aztec-Mayan tropes, in almost all of his plays hereafter and, in 1974, these would be the cause of a monumental debate and irreparable fissure between Valdez and the most important Mexican and Latin American political theater practitioners of that day.

VILLA'S HEAD AND CHICANO ALLEGORY

In the opening scene of *The Shrunken Head of Pancho Villa*, Belarmino's covered head sits in the living room of a poor Chicano family living in a rural farming community in California's Central Valley. Pedro (the father) sleeps and in his dream articulates his recollection of time when he, a Mexican *indígena* and *campesino*, was lifted from the poverty of his social caste to ride with the great Villa (Figure 3). Woken out of his sleep by his son Joaquin, Pedro is jolted back into his immigrant reality: "a large, imposing two-story building sagging into total dilapidation . . . with tall cracked windows."[26] As the keeper of the spirit of the revolution and ancestral home, Pedro still carries the memory and verve of the Mexican Revolution, albeit in his dreams. Awakened, he reverts back to the broken man who, defeated by the socioeconomic condition of the immigrant, has now become the source of his family's ridicule. If Pedro, representative of the first generation of Mexican immigrants who fled the Mexican Revolution, can no longer lead a social revolution, then the mantle must pass to their children. But a problem arises now that his children have become disassociated from their parent's past. Mingo gives up his Mexican identity in exchange for the American Dream. Lupe, the younger sister, is depicted as a younger version of Cruz. The weary caretaker of all the men in the house she sees no way out other than to become pregnant and marry. In a twist that reinforces Valdez's thematic argument that the head and body must work together to create social change and break the cycle of passivity, Lupe gives birth to a headless child. Joaquin, whose name references Joaquin Murrieta the legendary California hero-bandit and Rodolfo "Corky" Gonzales's epic poem *I Am Joaquin*, is incapable of picking up the mantle

Figure 3. Luis Valdez as "Pedro" in El Teatro Campesino's 1968 production of *The Shrunken Head of Pancho Villa*.

given his inferior education, social class, and most importantly his inability to speak Spanish. This limitation extends to his inability to fully learn his Mexican history through the oral tradition, that is one of the only avenues open to him.

> Belarmino: . . . Háblame en espanish.
> Joaquin: Sorry, man, I don' speak it. No hablo español.
> Belarmino: Méndigos pochos. (*Pause.*) Mira, chavo . . . ah, you . . .
>   mexicano?, no?
> Joaquin: Nel man, I'm a Chicano.
> Belarmino: No seas pendejo.
> Joaquin: Who you calling a pendejo?!
> Belarmino: You, tu, tu Mexican! Pendejo! Mira, espérate . . . ahhh, you
>   Mexican, me Mexican . . . ahhh, this one familia Mexican,
>   eh? Mingo, no! Mingo es gringo. Comprendes?
> Joaquin: Heh, yeah, now you talking my language![27]

Another notable distinction to come out of this dialogue is that Villa, who had little education, is more educated than Joaquin because he speaks Spanish, English, and Spanglish fluently. His position is further elevated by the fact that he calls Joaquin "pocho," a disparaging word used by Mexicans to this day to describe Chicanos in the United States.[28] Unlike Chicanos, Mexicans learn their native tongue, culture, and the history in both formal and informal educational settings, while Chicanos have had to struggle to preserve their language and culture while, simultaneously, negotiating another. In the following exchange, Belarmino finally reveals his identity to Joaquin:

Joaquin:	Who are you? (*Pause.*) Who?
Belarmino:	Pos guess. You have hear . . . el Pueblo de Parral?
Joaquin:	Parral?
Belarmino:	Chihuahua!
Joaquin:	Oh, simon. Tha's the town where they kill Pancho Villa and they cut off his . . . (*Pause.*) HEAD.
Belarmino:	Exactamente.
Joaquin:	Did you ever have a horse?
Belarmino:	Siete Leguas.
Joaquin:	And a Chivi?
Belarmino:	One Dodge.
Joaquin:	1923?
Belarmino:	Simón-yes.
Joaquin:	(*Pause.*) I don' believe it. You? The head of Pancho . . .
Belarmnio:	Belarmino, please! (*Secretively.*) Muchos carefuls. I only trust you. Es one secret politico ?comprendes?[29]

Joaquin, now ardently politicized by the increasingly emboldened Belarmino, enters the stage:

Joaquin:	Chato!
Chato:	Yes, my general! (*He opens the door.*)
Joaquin:	It's about time, corporal. (*Joaquin emerges dressed in the traditional costume of the Mexican charro, complete with a pair of cartridge belts crisscrossed on his chest. Hanging from one shoulder on a strap, he carries a 30-30 carbine. On his shoulders he carries two big sacks, one on each side.*) Here you are jefita. (*He lowers the sacks.*) One hundred pounds of flour . . . and a hundred pounds of beans like I promised you.
Mingo:	Where did you get this?
Joaquin:	I'm sorry, I don't speak gavacho.[30]

In solidarity with Villa, Joaquin now tells his mother, in Spanglish, that he no longer understands *gavacho* (English). The former *vato loco* has redirected his energy and anger, like Villa, into a revolutionary cause. At this point, he has organized only one person: Chato, Lupe's boyfriend, the father of her child and one of Mingo's contracted farm workers. Moments later, Joaquin finally confronts Mingo in the name of all the farm workers that Mingo has exploited as a labor contractor:

Mingo:	Don't worry, señora. The cops are already after 'em. I bet they even end up in jail tonight. For thiefs!
Joaquin:	And you? You're the one that oughta be in jail for cheating the jefitos, the family, La Raza! You pinchi sell-out traitor!
Cruz:	Joaquin!
Mingo:	No, no señora. Let him spill the beans.

Joaquin: We rob the rich to give to the poor, like Pancho Villa! But
           you . . . [31]

Valdez resorts to a paradigmatic narrative of social banditry to show Joaquin's growing political awareness; he no longer steals tires but flour and beans to feed the poor. Joaquin becomes an outlaw and a social bandit, just like Villa; he is, indeed, a protorevolutionary for the Chicano cause. But, unlike Villa, Joaquin's exaltation at finding a righteous cause falls on deaf ears when his mother Cruz refuses the stolen goods. Through the character of Cruz, Valdez acknowledges that armed revolution is not an option in the United States. Given the U.S. historical resistance to civil uprisings and dissidence, Chicanos have neither the numbers nor a clear and unified political platform that would engender a nonviolent social upheaval that can match the ideals of the Mexican Revolution that many Mexicans today consider to be still ongoing. Villa was able to escape capture from General Pershing and the 10,000 American soldiers because he had wide popular support; in contrast, Joaquin is quickly caught by the police and sent to prison.

In Valdez's dramatic imagination, Villa is not the mythic figure of Mexico's nationalist agenda but a people's hero: a real, blood and guts, foul-talking anarchist who is as sexist and macho as he is brave and heroic. On the other hand, Valdez' beheaded Villa is clearly an allegory of the Chicano predicament with regard to political awareness. The Mexican diasporic population in the United States has the strength and the physical numbers to contest the institutionalized policies of discrimination and socio-judicial-political inequity, but in 1964, this population lacks a political identity, will, and direction; it is headless. Pancho Villa's head has followed the Mexican emigrant masses to the United States, because it is there where it is most needed. Thus, rather than reifying Villa as a passive subject, Valdez inverts the nationalistic narrative that unified all revolutionary martyrs under one rubric, and exhumes Villa as a singular political anarchistic agitator. However, in the final scenes, Joaquin does not learn Villa's lesson, no doubt to the dismay of the play's audiences. In the following exchanges, Valdez delivers a harsh criticism of Chicano political passivity and the penal system, when Joaquin, who has served prison time for the robbery, returns home "reformed":

Cruz: Joaquin, es my Joaquin!
Chato: Where he at?
Mingo: Outside in my car. I forgot he came with me. I'll go get him.
Cruz: Ay Dios! My son is outside!
Mingo: Oh, another thing. It looks like the prison term helped him a
           lot. He seems very reformed, rehabilitated. Lots of spunk. A
           clean cut American boy! Be right back. (*He exits.*)
Belarmino: Ay, Yai, Yai! Now you going to see the Revolución burst out!
           Joaquin is back![32]

Rather than questioning the penal system that incarcerates Mexican Americans at higher percentage rates than other demographics, Mingo, and later Cruz, expresses confidence that the penal system has indeed reformed Joaquin. For Mingo, this attitude is understandable given his desire to assimilate. Belarmino remains confident that Joaquin can maintain his political will despite his incarceration. On the other hand, dismissing all ideological principles, Cruz's only wish is that Joaquin's "reformation" will keep him from being a police target. Within the Mexican diaspora, Cruz's character represents the new immigrant's fear of civic engagement. Coming from a country where local and national politics are historically controlled by a powerful few and violence and corruption are the norm, the popular masses, like Cruz, prefer to vanish into Spanish speaking U.S. barrios rather than engage the government on any level. When Belarmino announces Joaquin's return Cruz exclaims, "(*Over excited*) !Viva la Revolución! (*Pause.*) I mean. Gracias a Dios, my son is back." Fearful of leaving the barrio because she is undocumented, weary of the discrimination that awaits her outside her home and, suspicious of all *gavachos*, Cruz hides her affinity to the Mexican Revolution and, in an unexpected plot twist, the fact that in actuality it was she and not Pedro that fought with Pancho Villa. In the next moment in the scene, the family sees Joaquin for the first time,

> Mingo: (*Opening the door.*) Okay, folks, here he is! (*Mingo comes in.*) Well, Jack, come in. This is where you live.
>
> Cruz: (*Standing in the doorway.*) Dios mío, my son. (*She weeps. Joaquin comes into the house. He is well dressed, BUT HE HAS NO HEAD.*)[33]

Joaquin, now "Jack," entered prison as a Chicano incarnation of Joaquin Murrieta and Pancho Villa, but rehabilitation in the California penal system has stripped him of his Mexican identity and has pacified/neutralized him by transforming him into a white Euro-American (*gavacho*). Interestingly, Valdez has given him no prescribed race and/or ethnicity. It is presumed that he is simply white Euro-American, the dominant and default normative, with all the associated privileges of the time.

In the final moment of the play, Belarmino/Villa responds to Joaquin's decapitated body and extends a caution to the audience in the following monologue,

> Well, here I sit . . . broken hearted. But thas' okay cause I still got time to wait. Sooner or later, the jefita gots to come across wis Joaquin's body. All I need is to talk sweet when she give me my beans, eh? In other words, organize her. Those people don' even believe who I am. Tha's how I wan' it. To catch 'em by surprise. So don' you worry my people, because one of these days Pancho Villa will pass among you again. Look to your mountains, your pueblos, your barrios. He will be there. Buenas noches. *Curtain.*[34]

For Villa and Valdez, the inability of Joaquin, vis-à-vis the Chicano community, to organize at this particular moment in history is only a temporary and not a permanent deterrent. Similar to Villa's eluding of The Punitive Expedition, the Chicano community will continue to hide Villa's head until the time a new leader will spring forth from the barrios.

Valdez's focus on a fomenting social revolution within the Chicano community was understandable given the severe disenfranchisement of the Chicano and Mexican American people in 1964 and, as well, Valdez's personal experience. Given these influences, Valdez's writing came from a very deep and personal place. Likening himself to Villa's head, he explains:

> In a metaphorical sense that was me back in the early 60's. That's the way I felt—that I had no legs, no arms . . . Fortunately, out of these grotesque self-portraits, my characters have attained a greater and greater degree of humanity.[35]

Being a dark-skinned *indígena*/mestizo (Valdez is of Yaqui descent) of Mexican ancestry, a U.S. citizen, and a Chicano, Valdez literally carries the scars of this multiplicity of contradictory national identities on his body. As a toddler, he tipped over a pan of boiling water and suffered second-degree burns on his back. The local hospital in San Martin, California, refused to treat him because his parents, as farm workers, did not have health insurance. Therefore, for Valdez, theater and politics came from a very personal place.[36]

THE CHICANO MEXICAN LATIN AMERICAN CONTINUUM
Valdez's politicization grew to transcend the politics of the barrio and take into account the struggles, insurgencies, and revolutions of other Latinos across the Americas. In the 1960s, while at California State University San Jose (one of only a small number of Chicanos allowed to enter at that time), he was invited to go to Cuba.[37] This trip would change Valdez and on his return frame his work and that of Chicano Theater in a broader Latin American context and as part of an important and vibrant transnational cultural-political continuum.

The two pivotal Latin American political upheavals of the twentieth century for Chicanos were the 1910 Mexican Revolution and the 1959 Cuban Revolution. Cuba was the contemporary retelling of the classic David and Goliath that ignited the imagination and political consciousness of countless students/youth around the world. In the United States, university students organized protests and free speech movements indicting the United States government for the covert CIA assassination plots of third-world socialist/communist figures (e.g., Che Guevara and Fidel Castro), military and monetary investments to defeat popular socialist uprisings and democratically elected socialist governments (as witnessed in El Salvador, Nicaragua, and Chile), economic expansionism in Latin America, and the disenfranchisement of their poorest populations. Many Chicanos did not participate in these marches and protests because although they identified with the causes, they could not identify with the mostly liberal progressive white Euro-American college and university students who were the majority demographic among the protestors. Instead, Chicanos and Chicanas organized their own communities, crafted their own agendas, and fought their own battles that played out each day in the agricultural fields, schools, job sites, and barrio streets. Inspired and emboldened by the student-led revolution in Cuba, the few Chicanos that were enrolled in college in the 1960s began to question and challenge why Mexican history, Spanish language, and popular culture were not integrated into the curriculum. As such, Chicanos were the early catalysts for their own reeducation.

Soon after premiering *The Shrunken Head of Pancho Villa* in 1964, Valdez received an invitation from the Student Committee on Travel to Cuba (SCT) to go to Cuba and experience the outcome of the Cuban social revolution. A short time after taking power in

Cuba, Castro actively sought the support of international student activists of color in an effort to build solidarity among progressive artists and intellectuals. As SCT was the first student group to travel to Cuba in open defiance of the ban and four of the SCT members were facing prosecution by the Justice Department, the U.S. government watched the group with close scrutiny.[38] In Cuba, Valdez labored side by side with Cuban farm workers in the sugar cane fields, an active witness to Cuba's social revolution. Returning to the United States, Valdez coauthored a manifesto, directed at Chicanos and the United States government that read in part:

> The Mexican in the United States has been no less a victim of American imperialism than his impoverished brothers in Latin America . . . As sons of Mexican manual laborers in California, we have traveled to Revolutionary Cuba, in defiance of the travel ban, in order to emphasize the historical and cultural unanimity of all Latin American peoples, north or south of the border.[39]

Still not self-referencing as Chicano but rather as "Mexican" and more than a year away from joining the UFW and creating El Teatro Campesino, Valdez's inclusion of Mexican Americans as victims of imperialism and postcolonialism is one of the earliest public statements of Valdez's awareness of his simultaneous identities as American, Mexican, Mexican American, and Latin American. In interviews with Valdez, he has related several anecdotes of his trip to Cuba one of which was meeting Che Guevara. The encounter that left the most lasting impression was the sugar cane workers that in appearance and labor mirrored him and his experience as a farm worker. Commenting on this reflection and the Vietnam War that was still raging in Asia at the time of his visit, Valdez recalls questioning, how we (Chicanos) could go to war with people who look like us? After visiting Cuba, his notion of Chicano nationalism became imbued with concepts of international solidarity. Thus, he could not see how people of color who share the same neocolonial and imperialist historical trajectory could take up arms against each other in a U.S.-inspired war. Given this personal identification with Mexico and now, the Cuban people and their revolution, he henceforth repositioned his identity and sociopolitical struggle as a Mexican and a Latin American as well.[40]

The kinship felt by Valdez between Chicanos and Cuba harkens back to the primordial kinship between Chicanos and Mexico that Valdez so painstakingly and fondly pens in *The Shrunken Head of Pancho Villa*. In 1965, the year of Valdez's trip to Cuba, Mexico's populous and intelligentsia continued to exhort the failure of the revolutionary ideals that would only deepen three years later with the government ordered massacre of 300 student and community protestors at Tlatelolco.[41] In Cuba, its people looked at their new revolutionary country with great hope in spite of the U.S. embargo that would create an economic chokehold for decades. And for Chicanos, the hope of radical social change for the Mexican diaspora lay with the Chicano Civil Rights Movement.

Returning to the United States, Valdez did not become a professional playwright, which would have been a strong option given the success of his first play. Instead, reverting back to the ideals of social justice and the pressing needs of the Mexican American community, he joined the United Farm Workers Union as a picket captain and soon after pulled together an acting company comprised of striking Mexican and Mexican American farm workers that he christened, El Teatro Campesino. Inspired by the Cuban Revolution, the Mexican Revolution and the essential Mexican identity passed down from generation to generation through his family, Valdez joined Cesar Chavez and Dolores Huerta and the farm workers cause. As in *The Shrunken Head of Pancho Villa*, Valdez joined Joaquin's revolutionary verve with the memory and gravitas of Villa's revolutionary master plan.

RETURN TO MEXICO

Pancho Villa, the Mexican Revolution, and Mexico itself continue to be a considerable part of Valdez's work and identity. In 2010, in a gesture Valdez called "going home," the National Theatre Company of Mexico invited him to direct his play *Zoot Suit* in Mexico City.[42] Written in 1978, *Zoot Suit* conflates two infamous events in U.S./Los Angeles history: the 1942 Sleepy Lagoon Murder Trial and the 1943 Zoot Suit Riots. Like *The Shrunken Head of Pancho Villa*, it depicts the struggle of a Chicano family, the Reyna's, living in an urban barrio. Like Joaquin, the son Henry Reyna goes to prison, yet unlike Joaquin, his conviction is overturned when the community forms a defense committee. Written fourteen years after *The Shrunken Head of Pancho Villa*, the community now "embodies" the political will. The invitation was poignant for Valdez in light of the debate his early work evoked at the 1974 "Fifth Chicano Theatre Festival First Latin American Encounter" in Mexico City, organized by the National Theatre of Aztlán (TENAZ) and the Centro Libre de Experimentación Teatral Artística (CLETA). A post-performance forum for Valdez's *La Carpa de los Rasquachi*, presided over by key Latin American political theater practitioners, critiqued Valdez because of the farm workers' veneration of the Virgen de Guadalupe and reference to Aztec/Maya indígena ancestry as essential to Chicano identity (Figure 4).[43] Valdez argued that his work represented Chicano life and political activism in the U.S., but the forum nonetheless dismissed the play as counterrevolutionary and Chicano theater overall as politically naive.[44] The festival was the first and last major encounter of Chicano and Latin American political theater groups.

Zoot Suit opened in Mexico City in April 2010 to excellent critical and popular acclaim and remains one of the most successful productions in the National Theatre Company's repertoire. In February 2011, in an unprecedented gesture by the Association of Theatre Journalists (*Agrupación de Periodistas de Teatro*), the play was awarded Best Mexican Musical of the year. This was the first non-Mexican play and first Chicano play to receive this award. Commenting on this decision, Benjamin Bernal, the president of the association responded:

> We awarded (Valdez) Best Mexican Musical because aside from the fact that he is a citizen of North American we considered him Mexican because his blood, culture and work essentially favors Mexico. We claim and recognize him as a compatriot given *Zoot Suit's* themes and the play's opening in Mexico that coincided with the legal problems of the Mexican Americans in the U.S. related to SB 1070. We considered it to be vigilant of all the issues that affect our people.[45]

In this extraordinary twist of U.S.-Mexico cultural relations, given Mexico's historically disparaging attitude toward *los que se quedaron* (those that stayed), this award acknowledges

Figure 4. Valdez (center) in E1 Teatro Campesino's 1976 production of *La Carpa de los Rasquachi* on tour in France, Italy, Belgium, Switzerland, Sweden, and the Netherlands. Note the use of iconic Mexican imagery: the farm worker as a revolutionary, the *Virgen de Guadalupe, la calavera, el diablo,* and the Mayan symbol *En Lak'ech,* "you are the other me."

Valdez and the sociopolitical issues of the Chicano population as their own. With one of six American's now identifying as Hispanic (2010 U.S. Census), this portends a growing and deepening cultural-political dialogue between the Mexican diasporic population in the United States and Mexico.[46] It also highlights Valdez and Chicano theater's continued role in weakening the geopolitical wall that is a surmountable obstacle and not a permanent deterrent to the inseverable connection between Chicanos and Mexico.[47]

NOTES

1. Luis Valdez, *Luis Valdez: Early Works* (Houston, Tex.: Arte Público Press, 1990), 172.

2. The term "Chicano" was coined in the mid-1960s to describe a Mexican or American citizen born in Mexico and/or raised as a Mexican in the United States who engaged with the sociopolitical issues of their day. "Chicano" also recognizes a symbiotic and simultaneous Mexican and American identity. The term "Mexican American" recognizes both identities as American but privileges Mexico as the distinctive ethnic characteristic. In the early Chicano Movement, this term denoted a politically conservative individual particularly after the coining of the term "Chicano." The terms "Chicano" and "Mexican American" will be used interchangeably because the play's premiere in 1964 predates the beginning of the popular use of the term.

3. Jorge Huerta, *Necessary Theatre: Six Plays About the Chicano Experience* (Houston, Tex.: Arte Público Press, 1990), 9.

4. Luis Valdez, "The Shrunken Head of Pancho Villa," *Necessary Theatre: Six Plays About the Chicano Experience,* 175.

5. For a history of the early years of Luis Valdez, El Teatro Campesino and Chicano theater, see, Jorge Huerta, *Chicano Theatre: Themes and Forms* (Arizona State University, Phoenix: Bilingual Review/Press, 1982). For an in-depth history of Cesar Chavez and the early years of the United Farm Workers Union, see Fred Ross, *Conquering Goliath* (Keene, Calif.: Taller Gráfico Press, 1989).

6. It was not until the late 1960s, when Chicanos finally began to be admitted into colleges and universities in critical numbers, that their written histories entered into official U.S. narratives. Recognizing the vast amount of unpublished Hispanic literary culture that dated back to "colonial times," Arte Público Press (University of Houston) launched the Recovering the U.S. Hispanic Heritage Project in 1992. Their mission is to "locate, preserve and disseminate Hispanic culture of the U.S. in its written form." See http://www.latinoteca.com/recovery (accessed November 12, 2011).

7. Through the oral tradition, I have learned that my great uncle, on my father's side, played the clarinet, was the town barber and once cut Pancho Villa's hair. On my mother's side, family legend tells that Villa's men killed my grandmother's father Marciel Rodriguez, an *indígena*, as my great grandmother Santitos Arispe and her five children watched on. Carlota Carranza, my great grandmother on my grandfather's side, gave birth to two illegitimate children and was summarily erased from the family tree. Francisco and María Carranza, parents of Carlota and relatives of Venustiano Carranza, raised Carlota's firstborn son, my grandfather, Francisco Carranza, or so the stories go.

8. For a history of the Hispanic oral tradition in the United States, see John H. McDowell, María Herrera-Sobek, and Rodolfo J. Cortina, "Hispanic Oral Tradition: Form and Content." In *Handbook of Hispanic Cultures in the United States: Literature and Art*, ed. Francisco Lomelí, Nicholas Kanellos, and Claudio Esteva-Fubregat (Houston, Tex.: Arte Público Press, 1993), 218–47.

9. Valdez, *Necessary Theatre: Six Plays About the Chicano Experience,* 154.

10. Max Benavidez, "Chavez and El Teatro Campesino." In *The Fight in the Fields: Cesar Chavez and the Farmworkers Movement*, ed. Susan Ferriss, Ricardo Sandoval, Diana Hembree (Orlando, Fla.: Harcourt, Brace & Company, 1977), 110.

11. For a detailed history of Mexican *carpa* and popular performance, see Socorro Merlin, *Vida y Milagros de las Carpas: La Carpa en Mexico, 1930–1950* (Mexico City: Centro Nacional de Investigación y Documentación Teatral Rodolfo Usigli, 1995).

12. Valdez, *Necessary Theatre: Six Plays About the Chicano Experience,* 155.

13. Friedrich Katz, *The Life and Times of Pancho Villa* (Stanford, Calif.: Stanford University Press, 1998), xiv.

14. At one point in history, Pancho Villa had the full support of the United States. This changed when President Wilson shifted alliances and backed President Carranza, allowing his troops to enter the United States and attack Villa from the north. Soon after, Villa raided Columbus, New Mexico. Although there has never been any proof that Villa himself was present, this was sufficient reason for President Wilson to launch the 1916 Punitive Expedition led by General John "Black Jack" Pershing and his Lieutenant George Patton.

15. In 1912, Villa's great popularity in the United States drew sixteen-year-old American pilot named Farnum Thayer Fish to Mexico and the fighting. Fish learned to fly at the Wright Brothers Aviation School in Dayton, Ohio, and flew air reconnaissance for Villa becoming the first military pilot in history and its first casualty. Fish survived. Four years later, Villa's attack on Columbus, New Mexico, would initiate the Punitive Expedition. Villa is recognized as the first to use airplanes in military air reconnaissance. Smithsonian Institution Research Information System, http://siris-archives.si.edu/ipac20/ipac.jsp?uri=full=3100001~!283044!0 (accessed April 30, 2011).

16. Katz, "The Renewed U.S. Invasion of Mexico: The Punitive Expedition," *The Life and Times of Pancho Villa* 566–82.

17. Katz, "The Early Life of Pancho Villa: The Legends," *The Life and Times of Pancho Villa,* Prologue 2.

18. Elias L. Torres, *La Cabeza de Villa y 20 Episodios Mas* (Mixcoac, Mexico: Editorial Tatos, 1938), 197–205.

19. The Mexican government "whitening" of the population with the erasure of the *indigena* as an ethnic category and its absorption into the classification of "mestizo" is discussed in Alan Knight, "Racism, Revolution, and Indigenismo: Mexico 1910–1940." In *The Idea of Race in Latin America, 1870–1940,* ed. Richard Graham (Austin: University of Texas Press, 1990), 71–113.

20. Leticia Mayer, "El Proceso de Recuperación Simbólica de Cuatro Héroes de la Revolución Mexicana de 1910 a Través de al Prensa Nacional," *Historia Mexicana* 45, no. 2 (October–December 1995), 378.

21. Valdez, *Necessary Theatre: Six Plays About the Chicano Experience,* 171.

22. Ibid.

23. Miguel Tinker Salas and María Eva Valle, "Cultura, Poder e Identidad: La Dinámica y Trayectoria de los Intelectuales Chicanos en los Estados Unidos." In *Estudios y Otras Practicas Intelectuales Latinoamericanas en Cultura y Poder,* ed. Daniel Mato (Caracas, Mexico: Faces y Clasco, 2001), 295, 296.

24. Guillermo Bonfil Batalla, *México Profundo: Reclaiming A Civilization,* trans. Phillip A. Dennis (Austin: University of Texas Press, 1996), 17.

25. The United Farm Worker's Union's 1965 "Great Delano Grape Strike" was one of the most significant Chicano political events in U.S. history. Under Cesar Chavez's and Delores Heurta's leadership, the labor and human rights abuses suffered by the *campesino* came to national attention with major victories, including the formation of the first Agricultural Labor Relations Board (ALRB) in 1975. Under California Governor George Deukmejian and President Reagan, with pressure from agribusiness, the ALRB was weakened and eventually dismantled starting in 1980 with Deukmejian's election. Acuña. *Occupied America: History of the Chicano.* (New York: Harper Collins, 1988) 369, 439.

26. Valdez, *Necessary Theatre: Six Plays About the Chicano Experience,* 153.

27. Ibid., 178.

28. "Pocho"- cha; faded, discolored; overripe; rotten; U.S.-born Mexican; lie, trick, cheat. *Williams Spanish & English Dictionary* (New York: McGraw Hill, 1988), 467.

29. Valdez, *Necessary Theatre: Six Plays About the Chicano Experience,* 179.

30. Ibid., 192.

31. Ibid., 193.

32. Ibid., 205.

33. Emphasis Valdez.

34. Valdez, *Necessary Theatre: Six Plays About the Chicano Experience,* 207.

35. David Savran, "Border Tactics: Luis Valdez Distills the Chicano Experience on Stage and Film," *American Theatre Magazine,* January 1988, 17.

36. I have collaborated with Luis Valdez as an actor since 1978. From 1999–2005 I interviewed, met, and exchanged emails with Luis formally and informally on the subject of my doctoral dissertation, the "Fifth Festival of Chicano Theatre—First Latin American Encounter." Most recently, in 2009–2010 we collaborated on the *Zoot Suit* production in Mexico City, and I again had the opportunity to interview and discuss with Luis, both formally and informally, the significance of Mexico in the Chicano experience.

37. In 1964 and through 1974, there were more Latin Americans in United States colleges and universities than Chicanos. With the enacting of Lyndon Johnson's 1964 War on Poverty Initiative, Chicanos were finally admitted in critical numbers. As such, in 1964, Valdez would have been one of only a small number of Mexican Americans attending college.

38. The Student Committee on Travel to Cuba (1963–1964) marked the emergence of a new left wing in the United States and the trip to Cuba was a groundbreaking event in the development of student radicalism in the sixties. Umezaki, Toru, "Breaking through the Cane-Curtain: The Cuban Revolution and the Emergence of New York Radicalism in 1961–1965," *The Japanese Journal of American Studies,* No. 18 (2007), 187.

39. Luis Valdez with coeditor Stan Steiner, "Introduction: 'La Plebe.'" In *An Anthology of Mexican American Literature* (New York: Vintage Books, 1972), 13–34.

40. Luis Valdez interview.

41. On orders from President Gustavo Diaz Ordaz, Minister of the Interior and former Mexican President Luis Echeverria (1970–1976) carried out the Tlatelolco massacre. The tragic event was hidden from the press, bodies were removed overnight, and all traces were erased to avoid the interruption of the 1968 Olympics that opened ten days later. In his last year as President, Echeverria ordered the headless body of Villa exhumed and moved to the "Monumento a la Revolución." A conciliatory move meant to ease the lingering tension and memory of Tlatelolco. Racial-ethnic tensions in the United States also made headlines during the Olympics when Tommie Smith and John Carlos, both African Americans, raised their fists in the "black power" salute upon receiving their gold and bronze medals. Like Valdez, Smith and Carlos both attended California State University San Jose.

42. The author initiated this international collaborative project in 2009. Funded by the Steel Leave sabbatical grant at Pomona College, the author served as U.S.-Mexico Project Coordinator for the project that also included an online bilingual study guide (http://research.pomona.edu/zootsuit) and an international symposium organized with the National Autonomous University of Mexico.

43. To view El Teatro Campesino's 2001 restaging of *La Carpa de los Rasquachis,* see Luis Valdez, El Teatro Campesino Collection (San Juan Bautista, Calif.: Hemispheric Institute Digital Video Library, 2001), http://hidvl.nyu.edu/video/000539733.html (accessed April 26, 2011).

44. Alma Martinez Carranza, *Virgin or Revolution: Luis Valdez, Augusto Boal, and the Pan American Political Theatre Impasse,* Mexico City, 1974, unpublished book manuscript and Mariano Leyva Dominguez, Grupo Mascarones Historical Archives, Mexico. "Quinto Festival de Teatros Chicanos Primer Encuentro Latinoamericano," Mexico City, 1974.

45. E-mail from Benjamin Bernal to Alma Martinez dated March 25, 2011. Translated by the author.

46. *Los Angeles Times,* http://articles.latimes.com/2011/mar/24/nation/la-na-census-hispanic-2011 0325 (accessed April 16, 2011).

47. To view El Teatro Campesino's 1999 restaging of *The Shrunken Head of Pancho Villa,* see Luis Valdez, El Teatro Campesino Collection (San Juan Bautista, Calif.: Hemispheric Institute Digital Video Library, 1999), http://hidvl.nyu.edu/video/000539599.html (accessed March 18, 2011).

BIBLIOGRAPHY

Acuña, Rodolfo F. *Occupied America: A History of Chicanos.* New York: Harper Collins, 1988.

Arte Público Press. "Recovering the U.S. Hispanic Literary Heritage." *Latinoteca.* http://www.latino teca.com/recovery (accessed November 12, 2011).

Batalla, Guillermo B. *México Profundo: Reclaiming a Civilization.* Trans. Philip A. Dennis. Austin: University of Texas Press, 1996.

Benavidez, Max. "Chavez and El Teatro Campesino." In *The Fight in the Fields: Cesar Chavez and the Farmworkers Movement*, by Susan Ferriss and Ricardo Sandoval, ed. by Diana Hembree, pp. 108–15. Florida: Harcourt, Brace & Company, 1977.

Bernal, Benjamin. "Zoot Suit 'Mejor musical mexicano.'" E-mail to author. March 25, 2011.

Ceasar, Stephen. "Hispanic Population Tops 50 Million in U.S." *Los Angeles Times*, March 24, 2011. http://articles.latimes.com/2011/mar/24/nation/la-na-census-hispanic-20110325 (accessed April 16, 2011).

Dominguez, Mariano. *Quinto Festival De Teatros Chicanos Primer Encuentro Latinoamericano*. Audio recording. Grupo Mascarones Historical Archives, Cuernavaca, Morelos, Mexico, 1974.

"Farnum T. Fish Collection." Washington, DC: National Air and Space Museum, Archives Division, 1912.

Huerta, Jorge A. *Chicano Theater: Themes and Forms*. Arizona State University: Bilingual Press, 1982.

———. *Necessary Theater: Six Plays about the Chicano Experience*. Houston: Arte Público Press, 1990.

Katz, Friedrich. *The Life and Times of Pancho Villa*. Stanford: Stanford University Press, 1998.

Knight, Alan. "Racism, Revolution, and Indigenismo: Mexico 1910–1940." In *The Idea of Race in Latin America, 1870–1940*, ed. Richard Graham, pp. 71–113. Austin: University of Texas Press, 1990.

Mayer, Leticia. "El Proceso de Recuperación Simbólica de Cuatro Héroes de la Revolución Mexicana de 1910 a Través de al Prensa Nacional." [The Symbolic Recovery Process of Four Heroes of the 1910 Mexican Revolution in the National Press.] *Historia Mexicana* 45, no. 2 (Oct.–Dec. 1995): 353–81.

McDowell, John H., María Herrera-Sobek, and Rodolfo J. Cortina. "Hispanic Oral Tradition: Form and Content." In *Handbook of Hispanic Cultures in the United States: Literature and Art*, ed. by Francisco Lomelí, Nicholas Kanellos, and Claudio Esteva-Fubregat, pp. 218–47. Houston: Arte Público Press, 1993.

Merlín, Socorro. *Vida y Milagros de las Carpas: La Carpa en Mexico, 1930–1950*. [Life and Miracles of Tent Shows: The Tent Show in Mexico, 1930–1950.] Mexico City: Centro Nacional de Investigación y Documentación Teatral Rodolfo Usigli, 1995.

Ross, Fred. *Conquering Goliath: Cesar Chavez at the Beginning*. Keene, Ca.: Taller Gráfico Press, 1989.

Tinker Salas, Miguel, and María Eva Valle. "Cultura, Poder e Identidad: La Dinámica y Trayectoria de los Intelectuales Chicanos en los Estados Unidos." [Culture, Power and Identity: The Dynamic and Trajectory of Chicano Intellectuals in the United States] In *Estudios y Otras Practicas Intelectuales Latinoamericanas en Cultura y Poder*,[Studies and Other Latin American Intellectual Practices in Culture and Power] ed. by Daniel Mato, pp. 295–305. Caracas: Faces y Clasco, 2002.

Savran, David. "Border Tactics: Luis Valdez Distills the Chicano Experience on Stage and Film." *American Theatre Magazine* (January 1988): 14–21, 56–57.

Torres, Elías L. *La Cabeza De Villa Y 20 Episodios Mas*. [Villa's Head and 20 More Episodes.] Mixcoac, Mexico: Editorial Tatos, 1938.

Umezaki, Toru. "Breaking through the Cane-Curtain: The Cuban Revolution and the Emergence of New York Radicalism in 1961–1965." *The Japanese Journal of American Studies*, 18 (2007): 187–207.

Valdez, Luis. Interview by Alma Martinez. Personal collection of the author.

———. *La Carpa de los Rasquachis*. [The Tent of the Underdogs.] Directed by Lakin Valdez. Produced by Anahuac Valdez. San Juan Bautista: El Teatro Campesino, 2001. http://hidvl.nyu.edu/video/000539733.html (accessed April 26, 2011).

———. *Luis Valdez: Early Works*. Houston: Arte Público Press, 1990.

———. "The Shrunken Head of Pancho Villa." In *Necessary Theater: Six Plays About the Chicano Experience*, ed. by Jorge A. Huerta, pp. 142–207. Houston: Arte Público Press, 1990.

———. *The Shrunken Head of Pancho Villa*. Directed by Kinan Valdez. San Juan Bautista: El Teatro Campesino, 1999. http://hidvl.nyu.edu/video/000539599.html (accessed March 18, 2011).

Valdez, Luis, and Stan Steiner. "Introduction: 'La Plebe.'" In *An Anthology of Mexican American Literature*, ed. by Luis Valdez and Stan Steiner, pp. 13–34. New York: Vintage Books, 1972.

CHAPTER THIRTEEN

AN OPEN LETTER FROM AN ARTIST TO A MEXICAN CRIME CARTEL BOSS

Guillermo Gómez-Peña

This year, Mexico celebrates both the 200th anniversary of its Independence and the 100th anniversary of its Revolution. The entire year has been proclaimed by President Felipe Calderón as "Year of the Nation."

September 15, 1810, was the day when Father Miguel Hidalgo called to take up arms against the Spanish colonial government. And the beginning of the Mexican Revolution, the first in the century, was on November 20, 1910, the day when guerilla fighters Francisco Villa and Emiliano Zapata began their first insurrectionist attack against dictator Porfirio Díaz.

President Calderón has called on Mexico to use both anniversaries "to reflect on where the country has been, where it is right now and to think about what kind of Mexico our descendants will inherit in the future." It's like a one-year-long feel-good national psychoanalysis and, the president continues, "no one should speak negatively about Mexico outside of Mexico." Because of this, not one postnational Mexican intellectual or artist living in the United States was invited to partake in the celebrations. This letter is an unsolicited contribution.

In the Zocalo of Mexico City, a large digital clock has been counting down to both, September 15 and November 20 of this year. Similar countdown clocks were located in all the capital cities of the 31 Mexican states. Paradoxically, in 2010, every day we count down, an average of 30 Mexicans are murdered by organized crime.

SEÑOR XXX,
LORD OF THE HEAVENS AND THE BEACHES,
THE HIGHWAYS, AND THE TRAILERS

I have never met you face to face and I truly hope I never do. Despite the fact you don't know me, your actions affect my daily existence in profound ways. I am one of the hundreds of thousands of postnational Mexicans whose umbilical cord to my homeland has been severed by you. I don't look forward to my increasingly less frequent visits to Mexico, because people like you have made it a terrifying place, a war zone. I have lost my country of origin to violence and fear, to the violence you helped create, and to the fear you continue to perpetrate.

I haven't had the opportunity to cry for Mexico. I haven't had the time to cry for the 30,000 "documented cases" of people killed by organized crime in the past three years; Mexicans killed by other Mexicans like you, not to mention the thousands more who have simply vanished in the Arizona desert, lost in the binational sex trade or buried in some mass grave.

It all happened so fast . . . the delusional war declared by president Calderon against your kind; your internal "cartel wars" fighting for the control of strategic territories, and the "collateral" civilian casualties. Then, there were the wholesale kidnappings and "*levantones*," your exemplary assassinations (including the now world-known beheadings and mutilations) followed by the bombings and assaults to police stations, penitentiaries, restaurants and nightclubs, and the abominable massacres of migrants and teenagers that resemble those by the Colombian and Central American Death Squads of the past.

It is happening so fast, relentlessly . . . In less than a decade, Mexico became one of the most violent countries on Earth, with monthly murder statistics sometimes higher than those of the Iraq and the Afghan wars. We are now the country with the largest number of murdered journalists and students. Violence is now our master narrative, daily headline, and cultural landscape.

Unfortunately I speak from first-hand experience. My family and friends have been touched by *your* violence. One of my closest cousins was stabbed twenty-two times by a *sicario* (hired assassin) who spent less than two months in jail for his crime. My eighty-eight year-old mother has been robbed twice at gunpoint. Other relatives and friends of mine have been kidnapped, beaten, and robbed by cops on your payroll, pseudocops, and teen gangsters. And people I knew were killed in crossfire, simply for being in the wrong place at the wrong time, meaning anywhere, anytime. And this didn't happen in Bagdad or Kandahar. It took place in Mexico City, Monterrey, Guadalajara, Tijuana, Juarez, Veracruz, Morelia, and many other cities I learned to love while traveling in my ex-country as a young man. Today, these places are all part of the international "travel alert Web sites" that contribute to the destruction of Mexico's tourism.

I haven't been able to fully grasp much less digest what exactly went wrong? And who is to blame for this madness? President Calderon for forcing us all into a war we were not prepared to win? The likes of you who carry out the violence? The politicians, military men, and policemen who protect you? The U.S. drug consumers and distributors who create the demand? The gringo mercenaries who sell you the high tech weapons? The global media that sensationalizes your cruelty and perpetrates your fear campaign? Everyone seems to play a major role in this 3-D movie that has real consequences.

I do understand the problem of inequality and poverty; the immense, ever-growing distance between poor and rich and why, when faced with a future of joblessness and despair, people are left with two equally dramatic options: to migrate north to a country that hates them or to join you and work for you, to aspire to be like you. When you have no job, access to education and decent housing for your loved ones, it seems much easier to join organized crime than to remain unemployed or underemployed, working against all odds for almost nothing. On the day of his apprehension, a young hit man told a journalist: *"Hey culeros! What's the difference between dying from starvation or dying from a bullet in your heart?"*. This is not hard to understand: It's globalization-gone-wrong; the story of a dysfunctional nation-state on the verge of losing control against the backdrop of a transnational pop culture that has swept our historical memory and humanity, tearing down even more the already ruptured social fabric and turning the youth into consumers of extreme desires and seekers of instant success.

All this has made it easier for people like you to exist.

There is also the fear generated by your exhibitionist cruelty. In the map of organized crime that now comprises more than half of Mexico's territory, the civilian population wakes up every day to fear; fear of being kidnapped or having a relative kidnapped; fear of going out and becoming a victim of random violence; fear of being robbed, raped, mutilated, . . . , disappeared. The gruesome images that document and (indirectly) perpetrate this fear appear daily in the front pages of the newspapers and comprise half of the national newscasts. The most explicit images can be found in the "narco blogs." Some of your legendary "revenge" YouTube videos became more popular than those showcasing beheadings by Al Qaeda. Your sadism is carefully staged but . . . for whom are you performing?

Your empire of violence does not stop at the border. The young gang members who work for you in Mexico are connected to other gangs on this side of the border. These gangs are comprised of postnational teen Mexicans and Salvadorans, *norteños*, *sureños* and *Mara salvatruchos*, who also kill each other while fighting for the drugs you help to smuggle and the prestige you fight to secure.

I know many Mexican parents in the United States who have lost their sons and daughters to the very same violence you have helped to instigate collaborating with crime cartels from other countries. I have attended several funerals. And when those who survive the eternal gang warfare in our U.S. Latino barrios get deported they simply rejoin your ranks back home. In this vicious circle, they will lose everything: their relatives and friends, their tattooed identity, and eventually, their lives. All that remains are some hip-hop songs and indie documentaries chronicling their death dance.

You should know that the main news that is reported here in the United States about Mexico concerns crime cartel violence. Understandably, when the Anglo Americans who have no emotional relationship to Mexico watch these news on TV, they get scared of Mexicans and Mexico. And their fear inevitably fuels the current anti-Mexican hysteria and eventually translates into irrational anti-immigration laws (such as Arizona's' infamous SB-1070 and HB-2281 laws), making it harder for all of us here in the United States to be treated as equals. In the eyes of a racist, a migrant worker, a drug smuggler, and a potential terrorist become indistinguishable.

Because you probably have several relatives and friends in the United States, I'm sure you think about these matters. But then, I wonder: What purpose does it serve you to know that you are contributing tremendously to the worsening of conditions for the U.S. Latino communities at large and to the empowerment a new xenophobic U.S. far-right?

Today as I re-write this letter, I've got more questions for you: Do you ever feel sorry and secretly cry? Do you sometimes look at yourself in the mirror and feel embarrassed or angry with yourself? Aren't you afraid for the lives of your loved ones? Do you really think that *Malverde, Judas Tadeo,* and *La Santa Muerte* (the Holy Death) are protecting you well? Are you willing to pay the huge price of putting your relatives and friends at risk for a relatively short life of unrestricted power, sex, and glamour? Do the movies, soap operas, and *corridos* that you inspire make the daily risks worthwhile? Don't you ever wonder that creating a truce with other cartels might actually be beneficial to you and to the whole country? Am I naïve for asking these questions?

For the moment all I have is my art and my words to talk back and speak up. Half of the artistic projects and writings I am currently involved in have one central theme: The culture of violence on both sides of the border. It occupies a big part of my art, and I wish it didn't. I wish I could go back to making art and writing about matters with humor and joy. Unfortunately, for the moment, my sadness and my outrage won't allow it.

I truly wish I could go back to Mexico one day and live in my old neighborhood in peace.

I am not alone.

Guillermo Gómez-Peña
Orphan of two nation-states

NOTE

I wish to thank Elaine Peña, Gretchen Coombs, Anastasia Herold, and Emma Tramposch for helping me edit the original manuscript.

AFTERWORD

REVOLUTIONARY ENCOUNTERS
OF THE TRANSNATIONAL KIND
Cross-Border Collaborations, Border Thinking,
and the Politics of Mexican Nation-State Formation

Gilbert M. Joseph

Putting academic and public historians in free-ranging conversations with literary scholars, cultural critics, performance artists, and specialists in American studies and theater studies—conversations that span national boundaries and academic generations—this eclectic and engrossing volume substantially advances our understanding of the multistranded legacies of the Mexican Revolution. It is particularly insightful in probing still-neglected processes whereby the twentieth-century's first great social revolution shaped cultural and political arenas of the United States, including the Mexican American experience in the borderlands the nations share. Moreover, at a time when "transnationality" is more often invoked as a faddish phrase than rigorously applied, *Open Borders to a Revolution* lives up to the billing of its title, powerfully demonstrating that an adequate history of the Revolution must be committed to an analysis that imbricates histories of Mexico and the United States in each other. The result is a volume that simultaneously deepens our understanding of revolutionary and postrevolutionary Mexico, sheds light on new dimensions of U.S.-Mexican relations throughout the twentieth century, and delves into the power-laden dynamics whereby cosmopolitan ideas and actors moved within and across national and international domains. While the project ambitiously aspires to contribute to a variety of discussions, its contributors are particularly committed to interrogating bounded national narratives endorsed by states on both sides of the Rio Grande/Río Bravo and the manner in which revolutionary icons and symbols were used by diverse actors to reinforce and challenge these foundational myths of state and nation formation.

The timing of this volume could not be better, given the fanfare generated by the centennial celebrations of the epic revolution of 1910. Throughout Mexico and internationally, the centennial triggered a veritable cottage industry of commemorative events, such as the Smithsonian Institution's symposium, "Creating an Archetype: The Influence of the Mexican Revolution in the United States" (September 2010), which laid the basis for the present volume. Indeed, 2010 has begun to generate a harvest of scholarly production in a field of study that was already quite robust. Long before the huge digital clocks strategically placed in the nation's major *zócalos* began their dramatic countdown to the Revolution's *centenario*—November 20, 2010—few branches of Latin American historiography had developed with such a degree of methodological sophistication and thematic richness as Mexican revolutionary studies. Certainly, no branch of Mexican historiography had more effectively utilized a regional and local approach and an array of analytic and hermeneutic techniques to probe central questions and test conventional national-level interpretations. Over the last several decades, Mexican and international historians have debated a host of "big questions" about the origins, process, outcome, and legacies of the Revolution. Did the Revolution's causation owe more to endogamous or exogenous factors? Does it make sense to regard it as a xenophobic "War of National Liberation," as John Mason Hart has termed it? To what extent did U.S. political and economic interests condition the contours of struggle and influence the Revolution's outcomes? Should the epic revolution be singled out as the culminating moment of historical struggle in Mexican history, or did its denouement more properly signal a betrayal of revolutionary ideals and the ultimate triumph of a new (not so revolutionary) state over the people? In a related, comparatively informed discussion, British historian Alan Knight asks, was the Mexican revolution "bourgeois," "nationalist," or just a "great rebellion"—that is, a nontranscendent, largely political event hijacked by the winners to shore up new or residual class interests?

And do the "high politics" of the revolution highly factionalized struggle, as critical as they were in establishing winners and losers and setting the terms for "The Revolution's" institutional consolidation, provide only a partial history of the twentieth-century's first great upheaval? Do they really map onto the messy local equations of the Mexican revolutionary process—what Knight refers to as the internal "logic of the revolution"? Significantly, representations in Mexican popular culture have come to refer to the factional struggle as "la bola," which conjures up images of a mass of intertwined humanity, or of a great boulder that rolls across the landscape, gathering force, veering in one direction, then the other, and sucking up and spitting out most everything in its path. This careening *bola* moves arbitrarily, brings death and destruction, and turns normalcy into chaos. While the whimsy of revolution is no doubt exaggerated in this popular depiction, it usefully evokes a revolution that was far from the phased and sequential affair that master narratives suggest.

In the last ten years, historians have also become increasingly preoccupied by the extent to which the Mexican Revolution was a revolution for women, both during and after the epic phase. In what ways were women's gender, class, and ethnic conditions transformed, positively and negatively, by the revolutionary process and its aftermath? To what extent did the social workers, educators, and eugenicists affiliated with the new "revolutionary state" use gender as a category in reshaping the domestic sphere and "modernizing" patriarchy?

And what blend of social reform, political coercion and incorporation, and cultural hegemony accounts for the longevity—seven decades of rule—by the Party of the Institutional Revolution (PRI)? Does the PRI's celebrated characterization as Latin America's "perfect dictatorship" (in the words of Peruvian Nobel Laureate Mario Vargas Llosa) owe mostly to the regime's capacity to promote—at least until the Tlatelolco Massacre in October 1968—an encompassing and reassuring discourse of national belonging and inclusion, amidst ISI (Import Substitution Industrialization)-fueled annual growth of 6 percent (the so-called Economic Miracle)? Or does it more properly index the Official Party's shrewd articulation of local and national institutions of patronage and clientele (the PRI's "*caciquismo revolucionario*"), which beneath a democratic facade underpinned a "soft authoritarianism" that could alternately co-opt or repress, as circumstances dictated?

Finally, is the Mexican Revolution—either as an institutional structure or a legacy of ideas, symbols, and expectations—definitively "frozen," "dead," or "over"? To what extent does the Revolution still "have legs"—a question that problematizes both the residual strength of the PRI's elaborate twentieth-century cultural project as well as the continuing relevance of popular revolutionary symbols and social memory for diverse segments of Mexican society that were shaped by that project but took issue with the authoritarianism that underwrote it? In the wake of the demise of Mexico's postrevolutionary state in a neoliberal moment of narco-induced political crisis that many also regard as distinctly *postnational*, does the revolution have any real significance? If so, what meanings can Mexican and transborder subjects recover and claim for it?

The above recounting of a succession of historical debates merely scratches the surface of the past and present vitality that distinguishes Mexican revolutionary studies.

Open Borders to a Revolution not only engages with and contributes to many of these discussions, but it also transcends them, pushing out the boundaries of cross-disciplinary inquiry and method. The book's greatest virtue, to my mind, is its marking out of two interlinked approaches or sensibilities for understanding the legacies of the Mexican Revolution and related issues of U.S.-Mexican relations: *transnational thinking* and *border thinking*. While Brazilian, Cuban, and other branches of Latin American and Caribbean studies have arrived quickly to the notion that what is called nationalism is often transnational in its character and dynamics, Mexican revolutionary studies have lagged somewhat behind. Indeed, until recently the cultural affairs of revolutionary and postrevolutionary Mexico have often been discussed, by state propagandists, critical intellectuals, and professional scholars alike in terms of a bounded nationalism celebrated for its authenticity and idiosyncrasy, and epitomized by the amorphous concept of *lo mexicano* ("the Mexican way") or its variant *mexicanidad* ("Mexican-ness"). Part official construct, part popular narrative, these concepts emerged in the 1920s as the organizing motif for a society devastated by revolutionary turmoil and in search of a unifying, modern identity. However, as a wave of recent interdisciplinary scholarship, exemplified by the present volume, effectively demonstrates, cultural-political constructs like lo mexicano or mexicanidad and their claims for *exceptionalism* must be vigorously interrogated: for starters, they were shaped, resisted, and ultimately negotiated by a multitude of state, market, and local actors and interests that *transcended* national boundaries. Moreover, they came to serve oppositional (or counterhegemonic) impulses as well as regime projects.

Yet, this volume does more than take its place on the crest of a new transnational critique of bounded renditions of Mexican history and national character. It weds transnational thinking to some of the best recent scholarship in borderlands and Mexican-American history that stresses the perspective of "border thinking." Here the editors privilege "the theoretical dimension of 'borders' as a privileged locus of enunciation [from which] to unfold a critique of pristine national signs." Not only does this approach remind us that the U.S.-Mexico borderlands were themselves a key location and protagonist in the Mexican revolution, a critical event in both nation's histories and in their common history. It also facilitates a perspective that privileges the "contact zones" and anomalous spaces of empire, thereby affording a more capacious history of U.S.-Mexican relations from the geographical and metaphorical "fringes of nationhood."

To access these interlinked approaches, a brief rehearsal of some revolutionary watersheds is in order. Generations of historians preceded by the contemporary participants themselves have emphasized the irruption of the masses onto the national stage in the decade following 1910. This paroxysm of revolution—the "Wind that Swept Mexico," as the quintessentially cosmopolitan intellectual Anita Brenner termed it—has led writers across generations, Mexicans and foreign sojourners, and scholars alike (e.g., Brenner herself, Frank Tannenbaum, José Valadés, Jesús Silva Herzog, and most recently and influentially, Alan Knight)—to stamp the epic revolution as a "genuinely popular movement." As such, according to Knight, it was "one of those relatively rare episodes in history when the mass of the people profoundly influenced events" and therefore "the precursor, the necessary precursor, of the *étatiste* 'revolution'—the 'high politics'—that followed in the 1920s and 1930s." Indeed, Mexico's epic revolution forever changed the terms by which the Mexican state would be formed. It is the revolutionary state's partial incorporation of insistent popular demands since 1920 that helps to distinguish Mexico from countries like Peru or Guatemala today. One has only to juxtapose the contrasting images of Chiaspas' neo-Zapatista rebels and Peru's Sendero Luminoso to appreciate the point. For Mexico's latter-day Zapatistas, their struggle has always been circumscribed within the framework of the revolution, the nation-state, and the revindicative constitution the Revolution bequeathed; for the Senderistas, it has been about the bankruptcy of the state and the absence of an inclusive national imaginary.

This initial notion of popular revolutionary promise—and the commitment of a new state to communitarian notions of social well-being and betterment—is what fueled the ideas, ideologies, and actions of so many of the transnational citizens depicted in the first half of this collection. Beginning with the military struggle and gathering momentum in the decades that followed, these travelers moved north and south to spread the Revolution's message or to live the political and personal ideals and fantasies they nurtured in its name. Although the Revolution rather quickly moved to the center under the winning Constitutionalist faction, displaying relatively little inclination to exercise a "world historical" role in the manner of the Soviets or, later, the Chinese and the Cubans, as this volume and other recent scholarship attests, it still had profound hemispheric and international consequences. Not only did agrarian activists affiliated with the Revolution's losing radical and populist factions fan out to other regions of Mexico, but they also created intriguing social laboratories of revolutionary reform (e.g., former Zapatista Felipe Carrillo Puerto in Yucatán); others, including internationalists like the Nicaraguan Augusto César Sandino, traveled to Central America to organize on large estates and oppose oligarchic rule. One cross-border sojourner, India's M.N. Roy, traveled to revolutionary Mexico after being exiled from the United States by President Woodrow Wilson; there he helped to found the Mexican Communist Party before moving on to Europe and Asia to work with the Third Communist International. Still other radical intellectuals, artists, and cultural workers extended Mexico's revolutionary impulse across borders: best known, of course, is Mexican muralist Diego Rivera, who pioneered expressive forms of public and plastic art that would galvanize later generations of popular and revolutionary mobilization far beyond Mexico. In this volume, Helen Delpar establishes the profound influence that Rivera and other exponents of didactic public art had on African American and U.S. left artists during the New Deal and in subsequent decades.

Although the ideology of Mexico's incipient revolutionary state (the so-called Sonoran Dynasty of Alvaro Obregón and Plutarco Elías Calles, from 1920 to 1934) was rather moderate, "the Revolution"—epitomized by its first decade of violent popular struggle, which was immediately codified in the highly nationalist Constitution of 1917 that qualified capitalist property relations—quickly riveted the attention of powerful U.S. elites. Throughout the 1920s and 1930s, Washington's posture toward Mexico alternated between threat and accommodation, which no doubt played a role in tempering the pace of reform of Mexico's new regime. At the same time, however latent before the high tide of Cardenismo, the Mexican Revolution's social, agrarian, and nationalist promise made it impossible for the United States to reflexively adhere to the economic and political assumptions and practices that had previously guided nearly a half century of unrestrained dollar and gunboat diplomacy in Mexico and Latin America. In his essay in this volume, John Britton conjures up the transnational webs and bohemian communities of nomadic U.S. intellectuals and activists, who operated with equal facility in Mexico City and New York, and who advanced formidable radical critiques of private property and American interventionism. In the process these transnational citizen diplomats penetrated (and "stretched") the highest rungs of U.S. political culture in the 1920s and early 1930s and, in a manner of speaking, constituted the Mexican origins of the New Deal. In a recent paper, historian Greg Grandin similarly underscores the international reach of the Mexican Revolution, emphasizing the hemispheric (but mostly) Latin American intelligentsia that thrust the revolution's statist notions of social property and sovereignty onto the world stage. He shows that even as bellicose U.S. business interests were applying strong pressure on President Woodrow Wilson's administration to demand the revocation of the revolutionary Constitution of 1917 and overthrow the Constitutionalist regime, President Carranza himself went on the offensive, charging Mexico's envoy to the 1919 Paris Peace Conference to "have the ideas of the new Mexican Constitution [including agrarian Article 27's notion of "social property"] incorporated as a principle of international law." In the middle decades of the twentieth century, international jurists like Chilean legal theorist Alejandro Alvarez would draw upon Mexico's revolutionary charter to formulate what they referred to as "American International Law," a corpus that featured respect for national sovereignty and state-sanctioned social and agrarian rights. Many of these social democratic principles, which challenged sacrosanct U.S. assumptions underwritten by Lockean constructions of liberalism and the Monroe Doctrine, were subsequently enshrined in the 1948 United Nations Declaration of Human Rights;

in the interim, nearly every Latin American nation had adopted a constitutional charter similar to, if not modeled on, Mexico's revolutionary constitution.

As Britton's essay suggests, the hallmark of the first section of this collection ("Travelling Borders") is its insistence on teasing out the cosmopolitan and cross-border discussions, political and cultural debates, patterns of sociability, and artistic and literary productions that issued from and helped to constitute Mexico's new revolutionary order. This ensemble of essays captures the excitement and expectations that accompany "living in revolutionary time," the personal journeys, encounters, and challenges that living (and representing) the revolution at home and abroad entails, and the disillusionment that could mark the personal realization of a "fallen utopia" (so nicely evoked in Jaime Marroquín's account of writer Katherine Ann Porter). At every turn these essays remind us of the permeability of linguistic and national borders, the plasticity and dynamism of personal identities and national signs and symbols during revolutionary times, and the contingency and open-endedness that generally characterize revolutionary processes—at least at the outset. Unfortunately, this indeterminacy is too often erased from historical accounts of revolution, especially once "The Revolution" is mythologized by the postrevolutionary state or codified in equally retrospective, just-so fashion by its most bitter critics.

The contributions by Rick López, Mary Kay Vaughan, and Theodore Cohen are particularly evocative in this regard. Here and in his recent monograph, *Crafting Mexico: Intellectuals, Artisans, and the State after the Revolution*, López eschews post facto state mythologies and teleologies, making us aware of just how contested and undefined revolutionary understandings of "Mexican-ness" were after the fighting stopped. He persuasively argues—along with Vaughan and Cohen, and other volume contributors—that, far from emanating organically from the nation's past, *mexicanidad* was "continually recreated and enacted" by a multiplicity of political, cultural, and commercial actors, many of whom intersected with, but were hardly synonymous with the revolutionary state. Indeed, in the early 1920s, the fledgling and overburdened revolutionary state was not initially in the vanguard of efforts to forge a national Mexican aesthetic, and only gradually began to enable artists and cultural entrepreneurs, who, in turn, served to enable a more muscular state cultural project beginning in the late 1920s and 1930s. López's account of Anita Brenner, the American-Mexican-Jewish woman who helped galvanize Mexico's cultural renaissance in the 1920s and effectively represented it north of the border, demonstrates that Brenner was part of "a transnational push to culturally integrate the [new revolutionary] nation around an ethnicized, or Indianized collective identity." What makes Brenner so compelling a participant in this broader effort were the personal circumstances whereby she encountered and claimed her multiple identity in the aftermath of revolution and then drew upon that experience. For Brenner, her own process of subject formation—particularly the revelation of how her Mexican Jewish ancestors had historically been forced to hide their beliefs and identities behind performances of Christianity—was analogous to the manner in which indigenous Mexicans were now able to recover and practice their own hidden traditions (the "idols behind altars"). For Brenner and other transnational intellectuals and cultural workers, the Revolution facilitated a cultural renaissance in the name of the majority of those who had fought and died for it. In Brenner's view, this renaissance turned on the principle that it was these hidden Indian traditions (along with her own Jewish ones), rather than the hegemonic veneer of Hispanic culture, that represented the authentic Mexican nation.

Vaughan and Cohen's contribution on artist/ethnographer Miguel Covarrubias and celebrated composer Carlos Chávez nicely complements López's piece in its emphasis on the intersections among art, race/ethnicity, class, and nation, on the one hand, and between nationalism and transnationalism in the creation of expansive, hybrid identities north and south, on the other. Indeed, there is an intriguing parallel between Brenner's journey into Jewish culture, in the bohemian circles that distinguished revolutionary Mexico's cultural renaissance, and Covarrubias' and Chávez's encounters with African American and other forms of African diaspora culture, largely in New York, amid the Harlem Renaissance. Although the latter have been, like Brenner, mostly associated with Mexican indigenismo in their art and music, Vaughan and Cohen capture the robustness and reach of their intellectual and cultural lives, which immersed them in various currents of European and New World modernism, as well as in the major cultural and political movements in African diasporic life. In the process, Covarrubias and Chávez gave voice to and became proto-ethnographers of the African diaspora in the Americas; in Mexico their efforts helped to revalue African elements in the nation's historical and cultural development, challenging postrevolutionary intellectuals' overweening emphasis on the role of European-indigenous *mestizaje* in the formation of national identity and culture.

All of these nomadic intellectuals' journeys were preoccupied in one way or another with new configurations of personal expression and the national popular, even as, in some genres, the Institutional Revolution's hardening myths and narratives began to foreclose such options. Thus López argues that during the 1930s and 1940s, Brenner and other foreign intellectuals and artists saw their critical contributions to the construction of an ethnicized national identity systematically erased by the nation's cultural establishment. The transnational collaborations that had marked the cultural improvisation of the freewheeling 1920s proved inconvenient for the nationalist narratives that inflected historical struggles against Gringo imperialists amid the Cardenista oil expropriation and, later, in the polarizing environment of the Cold War. Vaughan and Cohen present a somewhat more benign outcome in music and dance, one that other scholars are corroborating in new research. Having gained substantial international renown, Covarrubias and Chávez returned to live in Mexico in the late 1920s and 1930s, even as they continued to move and work in international circles. At home they became involved in the PRI's increasingly formidable and far-flung nationalist cultural project, with Chávez coming to virtually "control the production and performance of Mexican classical music" from the late 1930s until the early 1950s, and imposing his stamp on Mexican modern dance as well. While Chávez used the power of the state to sweep aside musical rivals like Julián Carrillo and Manuel Ponce, it seems clear that he continued to promote vital transnational collaborations and foreign influences in his broader effort to wed modernist music with autochthonous and black cultural traditions. The same modus operandi characterized the development of Mexican modern dance and national architecture: in these "high cultural" genres, Mexican cultural bureaucrats continued to welcome the professional and technical expertise of foreign artists, integrating them to a surprising extent into the Mexican academy and praising their contributions to the national canon.

These striking differences between folkloric and high cultural genres draw our attention to the fact that the postrevolutionary state was far from monolithic (and hardly the powerful "Leviathan" that historians formerly portrayed); nor did its cultural dependencies operate in lockstep. Such variation within the cultural state should also keep us alive to the possibilities of contingency and the power of personal encounters across national boundaries—for example, Chávez's close friendship with Aaron Copeland or the chance encounters in the 1930s and 1940s between Carlos Mérida (the head of Mexico's National School of Dance) and Celestino Gorostiza (the head of the Department of Fine Arts) with such pioneering young North American dance artists as Anna Sokolow and Waldeen Frank, each of whom would exert a powerful influence on Mexican dance in the decades that followed. Chávez and Covarrubias, Mérida and Gorostiza were all artists themselves, cosmopolitan kindred spirits of the foreign artists they enlisted into their branches of the postrevolutionary cultural establishment. In other more popular genres, such as mural painting, artisan crafts, and folkloric dance—dependencies more critical to the state's mass mediation of its cultural project—after some robust cross-border collaboration (described so well by Delpar and López here and elsewhere), cultural bureaucrats became complicit in an intense nationalist process of state simplification and aesthetic narrowing. The result was often an asphyxiating state-promoted campaign of uniformity and commodification directed at international and domestic consumers alike. By the 1950s, painters like José Luis Cuevas were complaining about a "Cortina de Nopal"—an ideological "Cactus Curtain" that coerced the content and style of their production; subsequently, cultural critics have lambasted the flags and slogans, the garishness and kitsch that came to distinguish so much of the cultural production sponsored by the PRI. Néstor García Canclini, for example, has suggested that, rather than in studies of popular culture, the appropriate location of such tacky and mercenary forms is the study of tourism and propaganda.

Several of the volume's contributions shed further light on the ideological uses of cultural productions—particularly film—by the postrevolutionary state and North American culture industries. In her complex assessment of the film "Viva Villa" (1934), Adela Pineda Franco argues that while Hollywood typically manufactured reality to suit reinforcing political and commercial interests, the final cut of "Viva Villa" accommodated the agenda of the Sonoran Dynasty to trivialize the memory of Mexico's iconic popular rebel. John Womack, Jr., the biographer of the Revolution's other great telluric hero, Emiliano Zapata, makes a similar point about Hollywood's calculations in his assessment of Elia Kazan's classic film, "Viva Zapata!" In that production, Hollywood pursued a hard-edged Cold War agenda, which was only marginally leavened by screenwriter John Steinbeck's respectful evocation of small-town rural mores (or less charitably his fascination, as Womack puts it, with the "sweet 'idiocy of rural life'"). Ultimately, Zapata and his agrarian struggle made a convenient vehicle for Hollywood to cash in at the box office with an anticommunist morality play that had many of the earmarks of a shoot 'em up western (a la "Viva Villa") in the U.S. populist tradition. In the same pithy interview, Womack suggests how strains of Cold War populism in the U.S. academy worked to reinforce the official mythologies of the PRI, generating a spate of sympathetic histories of Mexico's sturdy and enduring "revolutionary tradition," both north and south of the border prior to 1968.

Helen Delpar and Yolanda Padilla also address the manner in which art and literature advanced state political agendas. Delpar argues that the "friendly invasion" of Mexican artists, which was itself part of a larger "vogue of things Mexican" in the 1920s and 1930s, was abetted so strongly by many influential U.S. diplomats and businessmen, such as Ambassador Dwight Morrow and the Rockefellers, because they appreciated that the Revolution's nationalist bark was far worse than its bite. It was clear that the Sonoran Dynasty was moving to the right, and that, under the circumstances, a diplomacy based on Mexico's immensely popular, albeit didactic, public art was a shrewd tactic for smoothing the rough edges of binational relations. Art diplomacy was commercially profitable and it politically sanitized the selling of Mexico to the U.S. right; the fact that Calles collaborated so closely in the project reflects a level of interstate collaboration that historians have tended to elide.

Padilla's essay on the Mexican American novel of the Revolution, in addition to insightfully applying border thinking to the realm of literature—of which more presently—is particularly compelling in its analysis of how the postrevolutionary state harnessed literature to its hegemonic process of nation-state formation. Thus canonic novelists of the Revolution, such as Mariano Azuela and Martín Luis Guzmán, were—wittingly or otherwise—appropriated by the Institutional Revolution as exemplars of an authentically Mexican literary tradition. Just as the state inducted the great caudillos into a National Pantheon of Revolutionary Heroes, going so far as to enter their remains in a revolutionary mausoleum—even those, like Villa, who in life were at loggerheads with the consolidating revolutionary regime—it celebrated these writers for their own part in cementing unitary understandings of the national popular. Over the postrevolutionary decades, their work was showcased for the way it immortalized long-marginalized groups like the indigenous and mestizo *campesinado*, now held up as the proud repository of Mexican values and identity. However, as Padilla argues, these iconic novelists typically portrayed the Mexican Revolution as *la bola*, an irrepressible force fueled by the valiant peasantry's violence and rage, which were decontextualized from the local and regional grievances that make the struggle intelligible.

The contextualization of local political consciousness and identity in the U.S.-Mexico borderlands is the goal of the second half of the volume, which Padilla's essay anchors. The context is a distinctly transnational one, with cross-border dynamics suffusing all aspects of border life. Until recently, the border was often portrayed as a remote appendage of Mexico, a "cultural desert," a frontier zone of war and rebellion not easily assimilable into either the nation or the national histories emanating from the political and cultural seats of power in the central Valley of Mexico. Padilla and the contributors to the second half of the book, harnessing methods and sources from the disciplines of history, cartography, literature, and theater and performance studies, offer a radically different appreciation of the border's past, present, and future. Their contributions, informed by perspectives on the margins of two nations, inform their understandings of national projects—like those of the postrevolutionary state—which, they argue, were always embedded in transnational processes that have shaped the border region's colonial, neocolonial, and postcolonial histories, memories, and forms of consciousness. Thus, eschewing official assumptions of a geographically and politically bounded *mexicandidad*, they show how knowledge production flows from a transnational imaginary that—*mutatis mutandis*—has distinguished border subjects for centuries. Like the counterhegemonic Mexican American novel of the Revolution, Padilla and her fellow contributors emplot themes "from the vantage point of Mexican America" that have been little acknowledged in conventional Mexican—and U.S.—historical and literary narratives. These themes center on the efforts of *fronterizos*, as members of an emerging and embattled ethno-racial group, to withstand the economic exploitation, agrarian dispossession, and environmental degradation effected by states and agents of transnational capital; to debate and negotiate cultural identities; and to initiate political projects in the interstices of states that registered an impact on those states and the national narratives they produced. These essays refuse to allow *fronterizos* and Mexican Americans to be ignored or diminished by the promoters of national sovereignty who shape Mexican (or "American") historiography, even as they mark out a much more expansive, transnational imperial history that powerfully shaped the Greater Mexican nation and will continue to shape its future. In this context, contributors construct what the editors aptly term "a more versatile history of the [Mexican] Revolution," and partially redress what has thus far constituted, in Padilla's words, "the Mexican nation's unfinished business."

These essays, although steeped in local perspectives, are simultaneously attentive to the intersections among local conflicts, national projects, and international environments. In this sense, they represent the state of the art in Mexican microhistory and regional studies, a formidable specialty in Mexican historiography since the appearance of the classic studies by Luis González (*Pueblo en vilo*) and John Womack, Jr. (*Zapata and the Mexican Revolution*) more than 40 years ago. David Dorado Romo's cartographically driven study of the revolutionary transformation of El Paso's landscape is particularly exemplary in this regard. Romo uses El Paso's built environment as a valuable primary source, "rematerializing" the border as much more than a redolent metaphor, and in the process underscoring El Paso's protagonist role in catalyzing and sustaining the revolutionary process. Resonating with the evocation of bohemian communities of nomadic intellectuals in the volume's first part, Romo conjures up the rich milieu of activists, journalists, literati, diplomats, propagandists, spies, and arms runners that propelled and represented the revolution and counterrevolution during the tumultuous first decade. Romo masterfully captures the fine-grained detail that allows us to appreciate how border locations were simultaneously imperial contact zones and fault lines, where different worlds comingled and clashed. In the best tradition of *microhistoria*, he excavates the heavily saturated, memory-laden histories of sites like the Santa Fe International Bridge, investing such places with the broader import they deserve. To write the history of the Santa Fe Bridge, one must convey the graphic details of U.S. migratory vigilance and control that marked the bridge's disinfection chambers. Further reflection on the state's practices, however, inexorably raises an even more poignant and fraught international history of "pest control," turning on related discourses of race, eugenics, and state control.

The cultural studies treatment by Oswaldo Zavala of the *ciudades gemelas* of Ciudad Juárez and El Paso effectively complements Romo's microhistorical approach. Drawing on postcolonial theorists such as Walter Mignolo and Néstor García Canclini, Zavala provocatively applies understandings of "border thinking" and "alternative modernities" to inflect the protagonist subaltern roles of *fronterizos* during the epic revolution and today. Like Romo and Padilla, Zavala seeks to recapture the proactive role of the border revolution: here the emphasis is on Pancho Villa's and Pascual Orozco's capture of Juárez in 1910, which effectively toppled the Díaz dictatorship and constituted a subaltern rejection (if only a temporary one) of bourgeois leader Francisco Madero, whose ineffectual leadership portended accommodation of the *letrado* establishment, of which he was a prominent part. But Zavala does not only seek to redress history's "ungratefulness" with regard to the transnational *frontera's* pivotal participation in the Revolution: he regards Villa's capture of Ciudad Juárez as having an elective affinity—indeed as the symbolic predecessor—of present-day fronterizos' border crossing as a survival strategy. Thus, Villa represents a specter whose example haunts the border and the states that attempt to regulate it, ignoring the unfulfilled social promises of the Revolution for which he fought. In the passionate rendering of Zavala, which draws on fellow border writer Charles Bowden, undocumented migration represents a "strange new revolution," an act whereby impoverished Mexicans attempt to fashion a future. In this distinctly subaltern process against would-be hegemons on both sides of the Río Bravo, "Ciudad Juárez, the city of immigrants, of everlasting hope, the vestibule to the United States and the American dream, the natural environment for the trafficking of drugs, arms, and people, is still the location of Villa's revolution."

Zavala, an activist writer and scholar and a native of Ciudad Juárez, uses the border as a locus to critique hegemony and empathetically enunciate the possibility of subaltern alternatives in the present as well as the past. Like several other contributors, he identifies Pancho Villa as a powerful national icon whose memory has been contested by the state and its opponents. Even today, the sale of votive candles and prayer cards bearing Villa's likeness constitute something of a cottage industry on the border. A scholar of Chicano and Latin American theater, Alma Martínez shows how Villa has been a powerful touchstone for activist artists in the Chicano and farm workers' movement, such as playwright Luis Valdez. In his early work *The Shrunken Head of Pancho* Villa (1964), Valdez appropriates and surreally refashions the official stories of Mexico's Revolution, subverting hegemonic claims to them and thereby prefiguring the work of performance artists like Astrid Haddad, Guillermo Gómez-Peña, and playwright Jesusa Rodríguez, among others. As Valdez's dramatic imagination would have it, the Party of the Institutional Revolution (PRI) may have enshrined Villa's body in the Monument of the Revolution, but "the spirit of his revolutionary ideals, contained in his missing (severed) head . . . now miraculously resides in a barrio in San Jose, California"! Like Zavala, Valdez (and Martínez) invest Villa's memory and legend with a liberating potential that can inspire "America's Mexican diasporic populations to preserve their essential identity."

Still, as this volume makes clear, *fronterizos* have never been unified in their support for, or opposition to, the Mexican Revolution, in its various incarnations. As Elaine Peña's essay demonstrates, as the revolution bore down on the border city of Laredo, Laredoans did their best to keep the struggle at arm's length, hedged their bets, and profited from the gathering violence through their involvement in the illicit arms trade (a thriving industry that Romo also amply documents in El Paso). Whereas Zavala and Martínez inflect the border's properties as an antihegemonic space that resisted national narratives from Mexico City or Washington, Peña portrays Laredo's *fronterizos* as "reveling" in U.S. patriotic rituals and enacting an "American ethos."

Finally, with the defeat of the PRI in 2000—almost a decade after the Institutional Party had itself renounced Article 27 and abdicated its commitment to most of the Revolution's social promises—with the isolation of Chiapas' Zapatistas, and the subsumption of so much of the nation's energies to narco-related violence, one may be justified in wondering what's left of the Mexican revolution—whether rendered with a capital or a small "r"—despite the elaborate efforts to commemorate its centennial? Interestingly, in his open letter to a Mexican cartel boss, which concludes this volume, self-proclaimed "postnational" performance artist Guillermo Gómez-Peña makes no explicit reference to a social memory of revolution that might revivify or redeem the nation morally or politically. Rather, "[v]iolence is now our only master narrative, daily headline and cultural landscape." For Gómez-Peña, the combination of a neoliberal "globalization-gone-wrong," an inept (if not a failed) nation-state, and a noxious transnational pop culture that has stripped away historical memory and depoliticized the younger generation, rendering them more vulnerable to seduction by the cartels, seems to auger a continuing culture of violence on both sides of the border. One could perhaps imagine a more hopeful reading based on the kind of transnational collaborations and "border thinking" that this volume's contributors have documented in the past and invoked as popular strategies for addressing the troubled present.

CONTRIBUTORS

JOHN A. BRITTON is Gasque Professor of History and chair of the History Department at Francis Marion University (Florence, South Carolina), where he has taught Latin American history since 1972. He has published several books and articles on the Mexican Revolution and the responses in the United States to the Mexican Revolution including *Revolution and Ideology: Images of the Mexican Revolution in the United States* (1995). His book, *Carleton Beals: A Radical Journalist in Latin America* (1987), focused on a freelance reporter who wrote extensively about the Mexican Revolution in a career that extended from the 1920s to the 1970s. Britton has published articles in *Historia Mexicana*, *The Journal of Latin American Studies*, *The Americas*, *The Hispanic American Historical Review*, *Journalism History*, *Business History Review*, *Technology and Culture*, and *The Latin Americanist*. He has been a Contributing Editor to *The Handbook of Latin American Studies* since 1992. His current research interests include the role of international information flows and their impact on international relations, journalism, and government policies.

THEODORE COHEN is a PhD Candidate in Latin American History at the University of Maryland, College Park. His dissertation, "In Black and Brown: Intellectuals, Blackness, and Inter-Americanism in Mexico after 1910" explores how Mexican anthropologists, historians, ethnomusicologists, and local intellectuals used inter-American dialogues about race and culture to integrate blackness into postrevolutionary discussions of Mexican national identity. He has received fellowships and awards from Yale University, University of Maryland, the Conference on Latin American History, and the Gilder Lehrman Institute for American History. In the fall of 2011 he will begin a predoctoral fellowship at the Carter G. Woodson Institute for African-American and African Studies at the University of Virginia.

HELEN DELPAR received a PhD in Latin American history from Columbia University, where she studied under Lewis Hanke, and taught at the University of Alabama from 1974 until her retirement in 2006. She is the author of numerous articles and book chapters and of three monographs, all published by the University of Alabama Press: *Red Against Blue: The Liberal Party in Colombian Politics, 1863–1899* (1981), *The Enormous Vogue of Things Mexican: Cultural Relations Between the United States and Mexico, 1920–1935* (1992), *and Looking South: The Evolution of Latin Americanist Scholarship in the United States, 1850–1975* (2008).

GUILLERMO GÓMEZ-PEÑA is a performance artist/writer and the director of the art collective La Pocha Nostra. He was born in Mexico City and came to the United States in 1978. Since then he has been exploring cross-cultural issues with the use of performance, multilingual poetry, journalism, video, radio, and installation art. His performance work and eight books have contributed to the debates on cultural diversity, identity, and U.S.-Mexico relations. His art work has been presented at over seven hundred venues across the United States, Canada, Latin America, Europe, Russia, and Australia. A MacArthur Fellow and American Book Award winner, he is a regular contributor to National Public Radio, a writer for newspapers and magazines in the United States, Mexico, and Europe and a contributing editor to The Drama Review (NYU-MIT).

GILBERT M. JOSEPH is the Farnam Professor of History and International Studies at Yale University, where for eleven years he also directed the Council on Latin American and Iberian Studies. Professor Joseph's research and teaching interests focus on the history of modern Mexico and Central America, on revolutionary and social movements, and U.S.–Latin American relations. He is the author of *Revolution from Without: Yucatán, Mexico, and the United States, 1880–1924* (1982, 1988 and 1992). *Rediscovering the Past at Mexico's Periphery* (1986); and (with Allen Wells) *Summer of Discontent, Seasons of Upheaval: Elite Politics and Rural Insurgency in Yucatán, 1876–1915* (1996). He is currently completing *Mexico: The Once and Future Revolution* (with Jürgen Buchenau), and working on a new project, *Transnational Lives in the American Century*, in collaboration with cultural anthropologist Patricia Pessar, which draws upon fieldwork in Peru, Central America, and the Dominican Republic. He is also the editor of thirteen books, including (with Daniel Nugent) *Everyday Forms of State Formation: Revolution and the Negotiation of Rule in Modern Mexico* (1994, 2002); (with Catherine LeGrand and Ricardo Salvatore) *Close Encounters of Empire: Writing the Cultural History of U.S.–Latin American Relations* (1998); (with Anne Rubenstein and Eric Zolov), *Fragments of a Golden Age: The Politics of Culture in Mexico Since 1940* (2001); *Reclaiming the Political in Latin American History* (2001); (with Timothy Henderson) *The Mexico Reader: History, Culture, Politics* (2002); (with Daniela Spenser) *In from the Cold: Latin America's New Encounter with the Cold War* (2008); (with Greg Grandin) *A Century of Revolution: Insurgent and Counterinsurgent Violence during Latin America's Long Cold War* (2010); and (with Ben Fallaw and Edward Terry) *Peripheral Visions: Politics, Society, and the Challenge of Modernity in Yucatán* (2010).

RICK A. LOPEZ is Associate Professor of History at Amherst College and currently chair of the Mexican Studies Committee of the Conference of Latin American Studies. He completed his PhD at Yale University and is author of *Crafting Mexico: Intellectuals, Artisans, and the State after the Revolution* (2010), and coeditor of *Moviendo Montañas: Transformando la Geografía del Poder en el Sur de México* (2003). López has published seven articles on Mexican and Mexican-American cultural history and currently is working on a two manuscripts: "The Hidden Fascist and Jewish Roots of Mexican National Identity after the Revolution of 1910–1921" recovers the important role of fascism and Judaism in shaping postrevolutionary Mexico; and "Science, Nationalism, and Aesthetics in the Shaping of Mexico's Environmental Imagination" analyzes the development of Mexico's nationalist ecological imagination from the 1780s through the 1910s. He has been the recipient of a number of honors and awards, including the a J. Paul Getty Postdoctoral Fellowship in the History of Art and the Humanities, the James Alexander Robertson Prize for Best article on Latin America, and the New England Council of Latin American Studies' Best Dissertation Prize.

JAIME MARROQUÍN ARREDONDO is an Assistant Professor of Spanish at The George Washington University (Washington, D.C.). He obtained his PhD in Hispanic Literatures at the University of Texas at Austin, where he worked with Uruguayan poet Enrique Fierro. He is the author of *La Historia de los Prejuicios en América. La Conquista* (2007). He just finished a new book, *Describing Anahuac: the American Beginnings of Modernity (1492–1590)*, along with its Spanish version, *Los Diálogos de Cristo y la Serpiente Quetzal: México y los Inicios de la Modernidad (1492–1590)* (both forthcoming) which is about the Spanish description of American nature at the time of their conquest of La Española and Mexico.

ALMA MARTINEZ received her PhD from Stanford University in Directing and Dramatic Criticism in 2006. She holds a BA in Theatre from Whittier College, an MFA in Acting from USC, and is currently an Assistant Professor of Theatre at Pomona College in Claremont, California. Since 1978 she has collaborated with Luis Valdez as a lead actor in many of his most significant productions including *Zoot Suit* (United States, Mexico, and film version), *Corridos: Tales of Passion and Revolution* (stage and television), and *I Don't Have to Show You Any Stinkin' Badges, Mummified Deer*, among others. Martinez has published in *Paso de Gato*, Mexico's national theatre journal and is currently working on a book about the "Fifth Festival of Chicano Theatres – First Latin American Encounter," one of the most unique theatre encounters in contemporary American and Pan-American theater history. This first and last major festival organized for Chicano and Latin American political theater groups was held in Mexico City in 1974. As an actor, Martinez has performed on Broadway, Off Broadway, on United States, Mexican, and European stages, and in films, television programs, and documentaries that have garnered national and international attention, these include an Academy Award for Best Documentary Feature *(The Panama Deception)*, the George Foster Peabody Award for Excellence in Television (*Corridos: Tales of Passion & Revolution*), Runner-up Grand Jury Award for Best Documentary at the Sundance Film Festival (*Maria's Story*), the Grand Coral Award at the Havana Film Festival (*Born in East L.A.*), and a Golden Globe nomination for Best Motion Picture Comedy/Musical (*Zoot Suit*). In 2010, Martinez initiated a collaboration that brought Valdez's *Zoot Suit* to the National Theatre Company of Mexico. The play opened to wide public and critical acclaim and in 2011 the Association of Theatre Journalists voted *Zoot Suit* the "Best Mexican Musical" of the year. This is the first Chicano (non-Mexican) play ever to receive this award. Martinez served as U.S.-Mexico Project Coordinator.

MAGDALENA MIERI is currently the Director of the Program in Latino History and Culture at the National Museum of American History, Smithsonian Institution in Washington, D.C. Her role is to organize and implement a variety of programs and to develop collaborations across the museum, and at the local and national levels, to tell the rich stories of Latinos. Before her position at the Museum, she was the Museum Specialist and Director of the Latino Virtual Gallery at the Smithsonian Center for Latino Initiatives. She has been with the Smithsonian Institution since 1992. Ms. Mieri has consulted with museums in Argentina, Peru, Mexico, Uruguay and Bolivia. Before joining the Smithsonian she was Assistant Curator at the Museo de Arte Hispanoamericano in Buenos Aires, Argentina. She holds a Senior Fellow position in the Department of Anthropology, at University of Maryland, College Park, and has taught graduate level courses in the Masters of Museum Education at George Washington University and in the Certificate in Museum Scholarship at the University of Maryland. Ms. Mieri has published a number of articles on museum representation and community museums, her latest published in 2010 in *Narratives of Community: Museums and Ethnicity;* Museums Etc. Edinburg. Ms. Mieri received her BA in Museum Studies from the Argentine Institute of Museology and her MA in Anthropological Sciences from the University of Buenos Aires, Argentina.

YOLANDA PADILLA is assistant professor of English at the University of Pennsylvania. She earned her undergraduate degree from the University of California, Davis, and her PhD from the University of Chicago. Her primary area of specialization is U.S. Latina/o literature and culture, with additional interests in transnational American studies, border studies, and the study of race and gender in the Americas. She coedited (with William Orchard) *The Plays of Josefina Niggli: Recovered Landmarks of Latino Literature* (2007), which was chosen as one of twenty-four "Best of the Best Books Published by University Presses" by the American Library Association. She is currently working on a book manuscript entitled *Revolutionary Subjects: The Mexican Revolution and the Transnational Emergence of Mexican American Literature and Culture*. The book examines the role of the Mexican Revolution in shaping early twentieth-century Mexican American letters and politics. She has published essays related to this project in *Women's Studies Quarterly* and *CR: The New Centennial Review*.

ELAINE PEÑA (PhD Northwestern, 2006) is an Assistant Professor of American Studies at The George Washington University. She is the author of *Performing Piety: Working with the Virgin of Guadalupe* (2011) and editor of *Ethno-Techno: Writings on Performance, Activism, and Pedagogy* with performance artist and cultural critic Guillermo Gómez-Peña (2005). Peña has also published in various journals including *American Quarterly, e-misférica,* and *Women's History Review*.

ADELA PINEDA FRANCO is an Associate Professor of Spanish American literature in Department of Romance Studies and the Latin American Studies Program at Boston University. Her research interests focus on nineteenth- and twentieth-century Spanish American literature, culture, and film and on the relationship between politics and culture. She is the author of *Geopolíticas de la Cultura Finisecular en Buenos Aires, París y México: Las Revistas Literarias y el Modernismo* (2006) and coeditor with Leticia Brauchli of *Hacia el País del Mezcal* (2002) and, with Ignacio Sánchez, of *Alfonso Reyes y los Estudios Latinoamericanos* (2004). She was awarded a grant by the US-Mexico Fund for Culture and the Rockefeller Foundation. She is currently at work on a book project on Mexico City, its lettered culture, film, and the Mexican Revolution.

DAVID DORADO ROMO is an essayist, historian, and translator. He is the author of *Ringside Seat to a Revolution: An Underground Cultural History of El Paso and Juárez, 1893–1923*. His book received several awards in 2006 including the Texas Writer's League Violet Crown, the Western Literature Association Non-Fiction Book of the Year, the Western Writer's of America Spur Award and the Latino Literacy Now International Book Award. Romo translated *Questions and Swords* by Subcomandante Marcos in 2001 and *Soldaderas* by Elena Poniatowska in 2006. He was the executive director of the Bridge Center for Contemporary Art in El Paso and has also worked as a freelance journalist for the *Texas Monthly, Texas Observer*, and Contro-Radio in Florence, Italy. David Dorado Romo is the curator for a two-part exhibition entitled "El Paso: The Other Side of the Mexican Revolution" that will be displayed at the El Paso Museum of History and at the University of Texas at El Paso's Centennial Museum in 2011.

MARY KAY VAUGHAN specializes in the cultural, gender, and educational history of modern Mexico. Her book *Cultural Politics in Revolution: Teachers, Peasants, and Schools in Mexico, 1930–1940* received the Herbert Eugene Bolton Prize as the most outstanding book in Latin American history in 1997 and the Bryce Wood Award of the Latin American Studies Association for best book on Latin America published in English. She is also the author of *The State, Education and Social Class in Mexico, 1880–1928* (1982) and coeditor of several collections including *Women of the Mexican Countryside, 1850–1990: Creating Spaces, Shaping Transitions* (1994), *Escuela y Sociedad en el Periodo Cardenista* (1998). Her most recent publications are *The Eagle and the Virgin: Cultural Revolution and National Identity in Mexico, 1920–1940* (2006) coedited with Stephen Lewis, and *Sex in Revolution: Gender, Politics and Power in Modern Mexico* (2006) coedited with Jocelyn Olcott and Gabriela Cano. She is former editor of the *Hispanic American Historical Review* and current president of the Conference on Latin American History. She has received fellowships from the John Simon Guggenheim Foundation, the National Endowment for the Humanities, the Council for the International Exchange of Scholars (Fulbright), and the Social Science Research Council and grants from the MacArthur Foundation, the Fulbright Hays Program, and the Illinois Humanities Council. She has been visiting professor at the Benemerita Universidad Autonoma de Puebla and the Departamento de Investigaciones Educativas in Mexico City. She is currently completing the life history of painter Jose Zuniga, a biographical approach to understanding the Mexico City youth rebellion of the 1960s.

OSWALDO ZAVALA (Ciudad Juárez, 1975) is an Assistant Professor of Latin American literature at the College of Staten Island, City University of New York (CUNY), specializing in contemporary Mexican narrative. He obtained a dual doctorate in Hispanic literature from the University of Texas at Austin and in comparative literature from the University of Paris III, Sorbonne Nouvelle. His work has appeared in academic journals and books in México, the U.S. and Europe. He coedited with José Ramón Ruisánchez *Materias Dispuestas: Juan Villoro ante la Crítica* (2012). He is currently writing a book on Chilean author Roberto Bolaño.

INDEX

art and artists
  art diplomacy, 247
  authentically American sources of inspiration, 43
  conflicts between generations of Mexican
    artists, 72
  Covarrubias promotion of, 74
  cultural diplomacy and exhibits, 41, 46, 50–51,
    57, 58
  cultural relations with France, 68–69, 82
  culture of violence as theme for, 238
  enthusiasm for Mexican art, 54, 57
  exhibitions and opportunities to view art, 41–42,
    45–48, 50–51, 56–57, 59–60n24
  ideal goal for art, 42
  invasion of U.S. by Mexican art, 41–42, 58
  MoMA exhibit and appreciation for Mexican
    art, 51
  political neutralization of Mexican art, x–xi
  positive reception of Mexican art, x
  renaissance after Revolution, 42, 44, 51, 57–58
  Revolutionary ideas, influence of on, 44, 45,
    57–58, 243
  rural areas, study art in, 51
  subjects chosen by American painters in Mexico,
    51–52
  subjects chosen by Mexican artists, 57, 58
  U.S., expansion of artistic community in, 43, 58
  utopian view of Mexicanness and direction of,
    ix–x
  See also folk art, Mexican (applied art); murals
    and muralism
Art Center exhibit, 45, 59–60n24
Ashton, Dore, 57
Association of Foreign Oil Producers, 8–10
Aston, Charles, 73
Ayala, Daniel, 76
Azcárraga Milmo, Emilio, 46, 56
Aztec ballet (*Los Cuatro Soles*) (Chávez), 69, 75
Aztec Eagle award, 129
Aztec Hotel, 43
Azuela, Mariano, 104–5n20, 135, 136, 139, 157,
  170n11, 247

Baker, Josephine, 73
Bali, 73–74
Balmori, Santos, 82
Baltimore, Maryland, xii
bandits and banditry, 95–96, 101, 104–5n20,
  107n48
Baqueiro Foster, Gerónimo, 76, 77, 80, 81

Baray, Pablo, 158–59, 170–71nn23–24
barbaric and civilized people, distinctions between,
  viii, 134–36
Barbarous Mexico (Turner), 158
Barnsdall House, 43
Barreda, Octavio, 69
La batalla de Ciudad Juárez (Berumen and Siller),
  176, 177–80, 184, 186–87n10
Bathers (Acapulco) (Durieux), 52
Batouala (Maran), 73
The Battle of Carrizal, 166
Beals, Carleton
  ambiance and environment of Mexico City, 19
  arrest of, 20–21
  Bolshevik propaganda role of, 16
  Brenner, relationship with, 125
  Communist organizers and sympathizers in
    Mexico City, 16–17
  Connecticut, settlement in, 20
  materialism, capitalism, and Western culture,
    discomfort among intellectuals about, 111
  property rights and land reform commentary,
    11–15, 20, 21–22, 23, 25–26
  public diplomacy and techniques of hospitality, 16
  revolutionary sympathizer role, 8, 17–19, 20–21,
    25–26, 111
Beery, Wallace, 93–95, *93*, 99, 104n8, 106n32
Being and Time (Heidegger), 112–13
Benjamin, Walter, 91–92
Benton, Thomas Hart, 52–53
Berumen, Miguel Ángel, 176, 177–80, 184, 185,
  186–87n10
Biddle, Francis, 47, 51
Biddle, George, 51, 53, 54, 55, *55*
Billy the Kid (Copland), 78
Biskind, Peter, xii
Blues (Chávez), 75
The Blues (Handy), 70
blues music, Covarrubias illustrations of, 70
Boal, Pierre, 23
Boas, Franz, 73
la bola, 240, 247
Bolshevik influence, 16, 17
Bontemps, Arna, 81
border, United States–Mexico
  agrarian land reform policies, 143–46, 222
  authentic Mexicans and, 135, 137
  contact zones and fault lines, 168–69, 242, 248
  contempt of central Mexico for northern
    frontier, 134–35, 136, 137

Lamar, Mirabeau B., 194–95

Lange, Dorothea, 77

Laredo, Texas

  arms trafficking operations, xii, 200, 202, 208n55, 249–50

  Díaz, support for, 197

  fraternal and social organizations in, 195

  growth of population and economic opportunities, 195, 205n22

  intellectual and cultural life in, 133–34

  IORM headquarters, xii

  IORM members, settlement of, 195

  labor activism and social justice for laborers, 146

  Mexican nationality and identity in, 197, 206n35

  Nuevo Laredo, relationship with, 191–92, 194–95, 205n19

  Nuevo Laredo battle, strategic location for following, 191

  opinions about Revolution in, 191–92, 196, 197, 249–50

  patriotism in, 197–98

  population statistics, 204n9, 205n22

  railroads and the strategic location of, 195, 205n22

  railroad system expansion by Díaz, 197, 206n37

  religious diversity in, 195

  strategic location for role in Revolution, 195

  U.S. patriotic rituals, celebration of, 250

  Washington's Birthday celebration, 191, 192–94, 196–203, *198*, 204n9, 206–7n39

  Washington's Birthday celebration as sociocultural buffer to Revolution, 199–203

Lea, Tom, Sr., 159

The League of Mexican Women (La Liga Femenil Mexicanista), 192

The Life of General Villa, 166

La Liga Femenil Mexicanista (The League of Mexican Women), 192

The Lights of the Battle (*Las luces de la batalla*) exhibit, 185, 189n66

Limón, José, 82

Lippmann, Walter, 14–15, 25

lithographs, 41, 46–47

Littlefield, Catherine, 76

El Llano en Llamas (Rulfo), 143–44

Llorente, Enrique, 171n28

Locke, Alain, 70, 72, 73, 74, 76

logical reason and science, 113, 115–20

London, Jack, 9

Los Angeles Museum of Art, 47

Las luces de la batalla (*The Lights of the Battle*) exhibit, 185, 189n66

Luna-Lawn, Juanita, 158

Luz y Sombra (E. Gamiochipi), 157

Mabarak, Carlos Jiménez, 81–82

Madero, Francisco I.

  assassination of, 9, 188n51

  Ciudad Juárez battle, xi, 175, 178–79, 186n3, 249

  Ciudad Juárez battle and fidelity to Revolution, 180–83

  coup d'état against, 188n51

  El Paso, connection to, 155

  headquarters of, 162–63, 177–78

  Jewish heritage, accusations of, 127

  rise to power and election of, 9, 175–76, 182–83, 186n8, 188n47

  Viva Villa! portrayal of, 96, 97

Madero, Gustavo, 178

Magic in Medicine (Alston), 54

Magnolia Petroleum Building, 43

Making a Fresco (Rivera), 47

Man and Machines (G. Greenwood), 52

Man at the Crossroads (Rivera), 47, 48

Maran, René, 73

María Concepción (Porter), x, 111, 112, 113–15, 119–20

Maris, Mona, 95, 106n32

Market, Oaxaca (Cook), 51

Martínez, Don Andrés, 195

Mason, Charlotte, 84n22

Maugard, Adolfo Best, 42, 69

Mayan influence on art and architecture, 43, 54

McConnell, Burt, 24

McDonald, James D., 10

McKelway, Alexander, 10

Mella, Julio Antonio, 20

Memorias de mi Viaje (*Recollections of my Trip*) (B. Torres), 158

Mencken, H. L., 72

Mérida, Carlos, 69, 246

Metropolitan Museum of Art exhibits, 45–46, 56–57

Mexican Americans

  American Dream and assimilation of, 218–21, 222–27

  Chicano, concept and characteristics of, 230n2

  Chicano Civil Rights Movement, 213, 222, 225

  Chicano histories and narratives, 215, 231n6

  concept and characteristics of, 230n2